Childhood Social Development

Essential Readings in Developmental Psychology

Series Editors: Darwin Muir and Alan Slater
Queen's University, Kingston, Ontario, and the *University of Exeter*

In this brand new series of nine books, Darwin Muir and Alan Slater, together with a team of expert editors, bring together selections of readings illustrating important methodological, empirical and theoretical issues in the area of developmental psychology. Volumes in the series and their editors are listed below:

Infant Development	Darwin Muir and Alan Slater
Childhood Social Development	Wendy Craig
Childhood Cognitive Development	Kang Lee
Adolescent Development	Gerald Adams
The Psychology of Aging	William Gekoski
The Nature/Nurture Issue	Steven Ceci and Wendy Williams
Educational Attainment	Charles Desforges
Language Development	Elizabeth Bates and Michael Tomasello
Developmental Disorders	Darwin Muir, Alan Slater, Wendy Williams and Steven Ceci

Each of the books is introduced by the volume editor with a rationale behind the chosen papers. Each reading is then introduced and contextualized within the individual subject debate as well as within the wider context of developmental psychology. A selection of further reading is also assigned, making each volume an ideal teaching resource for both classroom and individual study settings.

Childhood Social Development
The Essential Readings

Edited by Wendy Craig

BLACKWELL
Publishers

First published 2000

2 4 6 8 10 9 7 5 3 1

Blackwell Publishers Inc.
350 Main Street
Malden, Massachusetts 02148
USA

Blackwell Publishers Ltd
108 Cowley Road
Oxford OX4 1JF
UK

Library of Congress Cataloging-in-Publication Data has been applied for.

ISBN 0-631-21740-1 (hbk.)
ISBN 0-631-21741-X (pbk.)

British Library Cataloguing-in-Publication Data

A CIP catalogue record for this book is available from the British Library.

Typeset in $10\frac{1}{2}$ on 13 pt Photina
by Best-set Typesetter Ltd., Hong Kong
Printed in Great Britain by MPG Books Ltd, Bodmin, Cornwall

This book is printed on acid-free paper

Contents

Preface

Human beings are social animals, and the primary focus of this reader is to examine social and emotional development in children. Our daily lives are embedded in thousands of interactions with others. When we interact with others, not only is our own development influenced, but we also influence the development of others. Furthermore, how successfully we interact with others and others interact with us is related to both positive and negative outcomes in cognitive, social, and emotional functioning. Research in social development has exploded over the last few decades. As a consequence, there has been significant advancement in our understanding of the bidirectional influences of socialization, and the importance for successful adaptation of relationships with parents, peers, and significant others. Numerous theoretical and empirical papers have been published to describe and explain how children's social interactions and relationships develop, how they are maintained and transformed over time and across settings, and how they determine healthy and unhealthy development. As a result, new theories have been proposed, new methodologies have been invented, and new understandings of children's development have been achieved.

Childhood Social Development is designed to introduce students to this exciting and growing field. It is intended for readers who are newcomers to the field of social development research and are interested in reading current and original articles by developmental theorists and researchers on various aspects of social development. This book also is designed as a supplementary text for undergraduate and graduate courses in developmental psychology and social development.

The selection of articles is based on several criteria. (1) The articles should represent the *current state* of research into social development: thus, 11 of the 13 articles have been published in the 1990s. (2) The articles should be *representative* of current theoretical and methodological approaches in social development, as well as illustrating elegant empirical research. (3) The articles should be *accessible*, in the sense of being understandable to students with limited backgrounds in psychology. (4) Finally, because this book is one of a series, we have tried to avoid repeating the same article in different readers.

I would like to thank Alan Slater and Darwin Muir for their editorial work, patience, and encouragement. I also thank four anonymous reviewers for their constructive comments and suggestions. Finally, I am grateful for the assistance of editors from Blackwell Publishers.

Wendy Craig

Acknowledgments

Ainsworth, M. D. S. "Infant–mother attachment," *American Psychologist* 34, 1979. Copyright © 1979 by the American Psychological Association. Reprinted with permission.

Bagwell, C. L., Newcomb, A. F., & Bukowski, W. M. "Preadolescent friendship and peer rejection as predictors of adult adjustment," *Child Development* 69, 1998. © Society for Research in Child Development, Inc., University of Michigan.

Coie, J. D., & Jacobs, M. R. "The role of social context in the prevention of conduct disorder," *Development and Psychopathology* 5, 1993 (Cambridge University Press).

Craig, W. M., & Pepler, D. J. "Observations of bullying and victimization in the schoolyard," *Canadian Journal of School Psychology* 2, 1997. Courtesy of Canadian Association of School Psychologists.

Crick, N. R. "Engagement in gender normative versus nonnormative forms of aggression: Links to social-psychological adjustment," *Developmental Psychology* 33, 1997. Copyright © 1997 by the American Psychological Association. Reprinted with permission.

Hartup, W. W. "The company they keep: Friendships and their developmental significance," *Child Development* 67, 1996. © Society for Research in Child Development, Inc., University of Michigan.

Ladd, G. W., Kochenderfer, B. J., & Coleman, C. C. "Friendship quality as a predictor of young children's early school adjustment," *Child Development* 67, 1996. © Society for Research in Child Development, Inc., University of Michigan.

Maccoby, E. E. "Gender and relationships," *American Psychologist* 45, 1990. Copyright © 1990 by the American Psychological Association. Reprinted with permission.

Mahoney, J. L., & Cairns, R. B. "Do extracurricular activities protect against early school dropout?" *Developmental Psychology* 33, 1997. Copyright © 1997 by the American Psychological Association. Reprinted with permission.

Marsh, H. W., Craven, R., & Debus, R. "Structure, stability and development of young children's self concepts: A multicohort multioccasion study," *Child Development* 69, 1998. © Society for Research in Child Development, Inc., University of Michigan.

Patterson, G. R., DeBaryshe, B., & Ramsey, E. "A developmental perspective on antisocial behaviour," *American Psychologist* 44, 1989. Copyright © 1989 by the American Psychological Association. Reprinted with permission.

Pettit, G. S., Bates, J. E., & Dodge, K. A. "Supportive parenting, ecological context, and children's adjustment: A seven-year longitudinal study," *Child Development* 68, 1997. © Society for Research in Child Development, Inc., University of Michigan.

Smetana, J. G., Killen, M., & Turiel, E. "Children's reasoning about interpersonal and moral conflicts," *Child Development* 62, 1991. © Society for Research in Child Development, Inc., University of Michigan.

Introduction
What is Social Development?

Wendy Craig

Social development is concerned with the development of social interactions: how they originate, how they change over the lifespan, and how they contribute to individual development. A social interaction is defined as acts that one individual contributes to the direction and control of another individual's (or group of individuals') actions. By definition, social interaction requires two or more participants. The nature of the interactions is influenced by the broader social network and individual characteristics of those involved in the interaction (interactants). While human beings have thousands of social interactions on a daily basis, and social development focuses on these interactions, ironically social development also is concerned with the process of individuation (the ways the individuals come to recognize their distinctiveness from others). The focus of social development is to both describe and explain the systematic changes in infants', children's, adolescents', and adults' social interactions, as well as the significance of these social interactions to the process of individuation.

Damon (1983) argues that there are two functions of social development: socialization and individuation. Socialization is the process whereby individuals learn to establish and maintain relationships with others, become accepted members of society, regulate their own behavior in accordance with society's codes and standards, and get along with others. Socialization occurs in a bidirectional manner: that is, social behavior is not just a consequence or an end product of interacting. The child is not a passive recipient of socialization. Children are elicitors and processors of life experiences. They participate in determining the nature of social relationships, bringing their own personalities and characteristics to their interactions. The interaction is bidirectional in the sense that it changes both the child and those with whom the child interacts. Thus, socialization is a complex interaction between the child and others in their social network. A central focus of research is the examination of how the bidirectionality of social interactions operates and why differential influences are observed in infancy, childhood, and adulthood.

The process of socialization and bidirectional influence begins early and continues throughout the lifespan. For example, a baby seeks close proximity and emotional contact with the parent, and the mother responds in such ways as to encourage the contact (see chapter 1). Children learn to act cooperatively and with appropriate social skills in order to form friendships at school (see chapters 3, 4, and 6). In adolescence, individuals interact with peers to help each other develop a sense of self, their own moral conduct, and their career identity (see chapters 9, 10, and 11). These are some of the social interaction processes that shape an individual's functioning in life.

The second function that Damon mentions is individuation, or differentiation: the process of defining oneself as unique and distinct from others. This function involves an understanding of individual characteristics, such as sex roles, morality, and definition of self, and reconciling these characteristics with the requisites of interpersonal relationships. Individuals need to define themselves and find a social network that will support, appreciate, and recognize the unique characteristics, needs, and nature of the individual. The third part in this volume has readings on self, gender, and moral development that are representative of this individuation function.

Both functions, socialization and individuation, are critical for personal adaptation. Through learning to interact with others and developing a sense of identity, a person maintains satisfying relationships with others and society at large. Failure to integrate these two functions may lead to interpersonal conflicts, social isolation, or the development of aggressive behavior, as well as problematic cognitive and emotional development. These processes are distinct, but also need to be integrative.

From a developmental perspective, as individuals learn more about others, they also learn more about themselves, and vice versa. Social interactions provide feedback about the other person, as well as about the nature of the self. Information is accrued about how to get along with others, about the course of relating to others, about what others are like, and about what the self is like. In the course of normal development, these processes go hand in hand, supporting each other's growth; they begin in infancy and continue throughout the lifespan.

In addition to providing some understanding of the functions of socialization, the readings in this book are concerned with three main issues in the field of social development: (1) how social interactions and relationships are initially established; (2) how they are maintained over time and across settings; and (3) how they become modified and transformed. With respect to the first issue, we are concerned with the processes involved in the formation of social relationships, as well as the structure and development of different types of social relationship over time, such as parent–child (Ainsworth, chapter 1), child–peer (Hartup, chapter 3), and friendships (Bagwell, Newcomb, & Bukowski, chapter 4). Chapter 1 focuses on the mother–infant attachment and in doing so identifies the primary social relationship in development and the importance of this relationship. The early social development of infants is marked by a strong emotional bond between the mother and her infant (and sometimes other attachment figures such as fathers, siblings, and mother substitutes). As presented in Ainsworth's paper, this process lays the foundation for all other social relationships.

At each stage in development new relationships are formed, which differ qualitatively (e.g. becoming more complex and differentiated) from previous relationships. For example, an infant's attachment to a parent is soon expanded to include the extended family, peer relationships, and society at large. The papers in chapters 3 and 4 highlight the importance of other social relationships, namely peers and friendships. In addition, a successful relationship in one context will contribute to successful relationships in other contexts (e.g. secure parent attachment and positive peer relationships). That is to say, there is continuity in social development.

The second and third issues mentioned above are concerned with continuities, discontinuities, and transformations in social relationships. The questions addressed include: how are social interactions and relationships *maintained* over time and across settings, and how are interactions and relationships *modified* and transformed? Robert Hinde (1976) argued that social acts take place in social relationships and social interactions occur within relationships. In essence, he suggested that it is important to understand the context of social interaction, as well as the nature and purpose of that relationship. This area of research is concerned with the processes involved in forming relationships and highlights the relevance of the moment-to-moment social exchanges in relationships that influence the course of the relationship. For example, how do social interactions maintain the relationship? Do they initiate a new relationship, or do they end a relationship?

Pettit, Bates, and Dodge (chapter 2) demonstrate that parent–child interactions characterized by support and interest are related to adaptation in other relationships and contexts (the school). Craig and Pepler (chapter 5) present a view on negative interactions with peers (bullying). Crick (chapter 11) highlights a type of aggression that is more likely to characterize aggressive interactions in girls than boys. Finally, Patterson, DeBaryshe, and Ramsey (chapter 12) show that the continuity of negative interactions with parents contributes to poor peer relationships and the development of aggressive behavior. These readings provide examples of the notion that specific sequences of events in the context of a relationship can endure over time and have a broader significance to the relationships of the participants. As well, the significance of these interactions varies from relationship to relationship and is largely determined by the purposes and goals of that relationship. In essence, these areas of research consider the development and transformation of all relationships over time.

It is clear from this brief introduction that the three issues discussed above are interrelated. For example, the processes implicated in the origin of social interactions and relationships are related to the processes involved in their maintenance and modification. Nonetheless, it is rare than a single investigation focuses simultaneously on all three of these issues. In summary, psychologists are interested in social development for both theoretical and practical reasons.

Outline of this Book

This book is divided into four parts. Within each part there is a developmental progression of the articles. For example, in part I, on social relationships, the articles discuss the importance of the parent–infant attachment, the role of supportive parenting in childhood, and the significance and importance of the peer group in childhood and adolescence. This part identifies significant social relationships, and the nature of social development at different developmental periods are identified. Part II covers social processes that occur within specific contexts, such as the family and school. Part III presents articles that discuss the development relationship between social interactions and the individuation process in areas such as gender identity, self-identity, and moral identity. Part IV considers the relationships between early social development and later adaptive or maladaptive functioning. In this part, particular emphasis is placed on how the implications from research on social development influence practical problems, and how the research findings can be applied to educational practice, prevention, social policy, and societal issues (Coie & Jacobs, chapter 13).

Social development is a lifelong process, but this book primarily describes social development in infancy, childhood, and adolescence. The rationale for this restriction includes recognition of the significance of these periods in development and the course of social development in these periods. Although there is only a small sample of papers on current issues in the field of social development, they are intended to represent significant theoretical contributions and scientific and methodological advances in the field.

Through these readings, it should become evident that human social development is complex. To present a complete picture, along with the social influence of the interactants, one must consider as well the social, cultural, and historical context of an individual's life.

References

Damon, W. (1983). *Social and personality development*. New York: W. W. Norton.
Hinde, R. (1976). On describing relationships. *Journal of Child Psychology and Psychiatry*, 17, 1–19.

Part I

Social Relationships

Introduction to Part I

Socialization of children, adolescents, and adults is a reciprocal process whereby each person influences the others' development. This section considers the importance of different socialization agents, beginning with the family and then discussing the role of the peer group. It is important to consider whether children's peer relationships develop independently from their parent–child relationships, or if they are linked. Many theorists argue that there is a relationship between children's early family experiences and their ability to form and maintain friendships with peers. From experiences within the family, children develop an understanding of themselves, others, and interpersonal relationships, as well as learning specific behaviors. The articles in this section consider facets of parent–child relationships and friendships that may contribute to healthy social, cognitive, and emotional development.

ONE

Attachments

Introduction

Bowlby proposed that infants have the instinctual ability to emit communicative signals to which adults are biologically predisposed to respond. From an evolutionary perspective, these signals are both valuable and adaptive: to survive, the infant must maintain proximity to a caregiver; given that infants initially lack the locomotor or muscular abilities to approach their caregivers, they must motivate caregivers to maintain contact with them. Thus, infants emit signals that are physiologically and psychologically arousing, and reinforce the caregiver for approaching (Lamb, Ketterlinus, & Fracasso, 1992). Because these signals serve to keep the infant consistently close to the caregiver, Bowlby (1969) termed them "attachment behaviors." He further theorized that attachment behaviors are part of a larger developmental process, comprising four phases: (1) indiscriminate social responsiveness; (2) discriminating sociability; (3) maintenance of proximity to a discriminated figure; and (4) goal-corrected partnerships.

1   *Indiscriminate social responsiveness* is typically observed in infants one to two months of age. During this phase, infants develop a repertoire of attachment signals and begin to relate their production of signals to the approach of caregivers. As their interactions with caregivers become more frequent, consistent, and patterned, infants begin to recognize their caregivers and associate them with the relief of distress, fulfillment of needs, and provision of pleasurable social stimulation (Lamb et al., 1992). Infants associate varying types and qualities of experience with particular caregivers, and demonstrate preferences for the people from whom they receive most attention.

2   The emergence of specific infant caregiver preferences marks the onset of the *discriminating sociability* phase of attachment, which

characterizes infants from two to around seven months of age. Typically, infants will show preferences for those caregivers who are most frequently associated with comfort, security, and pleasurable face-to-face play. As the infant selectively seeks the attention of particular people, their patterns of interaction with them are maintained or intensified. This interaction is critical to the infant's social development, as it is through experiences with preferred caregivers that infants acquire an understanding of three fundamental principles of adaptive social behavior: reciprocity, effectance, and trust (Bowlby, 1969). The acquisition of these principles represents a significant developmental milestone in the attachment process, as it is children's understanding of these principles that forms the basis of their internalized conceptual models of social interaction – "internal working models." These internal working models act as referent frameworks in children's interpretation and negotiation of novel social situations.

The principles of reciprocity, effectance, and trust embody two concepts or models: those of self, and of others. Children's self-models reflect their sense of self-worth and the degree to which they expect others will respond to them positively; other-models reflect the degree to which others are expected to be available and supportive (Griffin & Bartholomew, 1994). Internal working models reflect the degree to which children are confident in social interactions, and the extent to which they can construct coherent, predictable representations of themselves and others in the world.

3   As children become aware of the tenets of positive social interaction, their growing social skills are complemented by rapid, commensurate development in their physical, cognitive, and language abilities. Consequently, they are able actively and intentionally to seek out and *maintain proximity to their preferred caregivers* (Lamb et al., 1992). It is when children are able to assume some degree of autonomy and responsibility in their interactions with particular caregivers that they are considered to have moved into the third phase of attachment. This phase is characteristic of children in the approximate age range seven months through two years, and is distinguished by the crystallization of the attachment relationship through the child's purposeful maintenance of proximity to the attachment figure. At this stage, the child's attachment is often manifested in wariness of strangers and distress at separation from the attachment figure (Bowlby, 1969).

4   In the final stage of attachment, *the goal corrected partnerships*, children's relationships with their attachment figures change to reflect their growing autonomy. At this time (from around three years), children have acquired linguistic, motor, and cognitive skills that allow them to communicate in a relatively sophisticated manner, undertake planful activities, and engage in perspective-taking. The role of the attachment figure necessarily shifts in focus from meeting the child's basic survival needs to the role of socialization agent, who responds to the child's developing needs for guidance in learning socially competent behavior (Lamb et al., 1992). Through continued nurturance, the cultivation of emotional and social awareness, and the provision of an effective behavioral model, the attachment figure acts to set developmentally appropriate limits for the child and teach social norms and values.

As children begin to assert their independence, conflicts may arise, and the child and attachment figure must work together to negotiate mutually acceptable compromises. The processes and outcomes associated with these child/attachment-figure negotiations constitute important influences on the further development of children's internal working models of social relationships, including their conceptualization of appropriate social problem-solving skills (Bowlby, 1969). With development, children rely less upon attachment figures and more upon their internal working models to navigate social situations, and attachment behaviors typically diminish in their frequency. As the child reaches adulthood, attachment behaviors are likely to be most activated during times of stress, when the support of the attachment figure is required (Bowlby, 1980).

The central outcome of the attachment process is the development of an internal working model of social interaction that serves (throughout the lifespan) to organize an individual's behavior in unfamiliar situations, based upon past attachment experiences and the expectations that the individual has derived from these experiences. Although such models may be modified in accordance with new experiences, an individual's internal working model becomes increasingly stable over time (Erickson, Korfmacher, & Egeland, 1992). Attachment theory highlights the significance of the parent–child bond and how this relationship lays the foundation for the quality and nature of other social relationships. The article by Ainsworth describes the different types of attachment classification, their correlates, and typical infant responses of each attachment type.

References

Bowlby, J. (1969). *Attachment and loss: Vol. I. Attachment.* London: Hogarth.
Bowlby, J. (1980). *Attachment and loss: Vol. III. Loss.* New York: Basic Books.
Erickson, M., Korfmacher, J., & Egeland, B. (1992). Attachments past and present: Implications for therapeutic intervention with mother–infant dyads. *Development and Psychopathology, 4,* 495–507.
Griffin, D., & Bartholomew, K. (1994). Models of the self and other: Fundamental dimensions underlying measures of adult attachment. *Journal of Personality and Social Psychology, 67*(3), 430–45.
Lamb, M., Ketterlinus, R., & Fracasso, M. (1992). Parent–child relationships. In M. Bornstein and M. Lamb (eds), *Developmental psychology: An advanced textbook* (3rd edn) (pp. 465–518). Hillsdale, NJ: Lawrence Erlbaum.

Infant–Mother Attachment

Mary D. Salter Ainsworth

Bowlby's (1969) ethological–evolutionary attachment theory implies that it is an essential part of the ground plan of the human species – as well as that of many other species – for an infant to become attached to a mother figure. This figure need not be the natural mother but can be anyone who plays the role of principal caregiver. This ground plan is fulfilled, except under extraordinary circumstances when the baby experiences too little interaction with any one caregiver to support the formation of an attachment. The literature on maternal deprivation describes some of these circumstances, but it cannot be reviewed here, except to note that research has not yet specified an acceptable minimum amount of interaction required for attachment formation.

However, there have been substantial recent advances in the areas of individual differences in the way attachment behavior becomes organized, differential experiences associated with the various attachment patterns, and the value of such patterns in forecasting subsequent development. These advances have been much aided by a standardized laboratory situation that was devised to supplement a naturalistic, longitudinal investigation of the development of infant–mother attachment in the first year of life. This *strange situations*, as we entitled it, has proved to be an excellent basis for the assessment of such attachment in one-year-olds (Ainsworth, Blehar, Waters, & Wall, 1978).

The assessment procedure consists of classification according to the pattern of behavior shown in the strange situation, particularly in the episodes of reunion after separation. Eight patterns were identified, but I shall deal here only with the three main groups into which they fell – Groups A, B, and C. To summarize, Group B babies use their mothers as a secure base from which to explore in the preseparation episodes; their attachment behavior is greatly intensified by the separation episodes so that exploration diminishes and distress is likely; and in the reunion episodes they seek contact with, proximity to, or at least interaction with their mothers. Group C babies tend to show some signs of anxiety even in the preseparation episodes; they are intensely distressed by separation; and in the reunion episodes they are ambivalent with the mother, seeking close contact with her and yet resisting contact or interaction. Group A babies, in sharp contrast, rarely cry in the separation episodes and, in the reunion episodes, avoid the mother, either mingling proximity-seeking and avoidant behaviors or ignoring her altogether.

Comparison of Strange-Situation Behavior and Behavior Elsewhere

Groups A, B, and C in our longitudinal sample were compared in regard to their behavior at home during the first year. Stayton and Ainsworth (1973) had identified a security–anxiety dimension in a factor analysis of fourth-quarter infant behavior. Group B infants were identified as securely attached because they significantly more often displayed behaviors characteristic of the secure pole of this dimension, whereas both of the other groups were identified as anxious because their behaviors were characteristic of the anxious pole. A second dimension was clearly related to close bodily contact, and this was important in distinguishing Group A babies from those in the other two groups, in that Group A babies behaved less positively to being held and yet more negatively to being put down. The groups were also distinguished by two behaviors not included in the factor analysis – cooperativeness and anger. Group B babies were more cooperative and less angry than either A or C babies; Group A babies were even more angry than those in Group C. Clearly, something went awry in the physical-contact interaction Group A babies had with their mothers, and as I explain below, I believe it is this that makes them especially prone to anger.

Ainsworth et al. (1978) reviewed findings of other investigators who had compared A–B–C groups of one-year-olds in terms of their behavior elsewhere. Their findings regarding socioemotional behavior support the summary just cited, and in addition three investigations using cognitive measures found an advantage in favor of the securely attached.

Comparison of Infant Strange-Situation Behavior with Maternal Home Behavior

Mothers of the securely attached (Group B) babies were, throughout the first year, more sensitively responsive to infant signals than were the mothers of the two anxiously attached groups, in terms of a variety of measures spanning all of the most common contexts for mother–infant interaction (Ainsworth et al., 1978). Such responsiveness, I suggest, enables an infant to form expectations, primitive at first, that moderate his or her responses to events, both internal and environmental. Gradually, such an infant constructs an inner representation – or "working model" (Bowlby, 1969) – of his or her mother as generally accessible and responsive to him or her. Therein lies his or her security. In contrast, babies whose mothers have disregarded their signals, or have responded to them belatedly or in a grossly inappropriate fashion, have no basis for believing the mother to be accessible and responsive; consequently they are anxious, not knowing what to expect of her.

In regard to interaction in close bodily contact, the most striking finding is that the mothers of avoidant (Group A) babies all evinced a deep-seated aversion to it, whereas none of the other mothers did. In addition they were more rejecting, more often angry, and yet more restricted in the expression of affect than were Group B or C mothers. Main (e.g., in press) and Ainsworth et al. (1978) have presented a theoretical account of the dynamics of interaction of avoidant babies and their rejecting mothers. This emphasizes the acute approach–avoidance conflict experienced by these infants when their attachment behavior is activated at high intensity – a conflict stemming from painful rebuff consequent upon seeking close bodily contact. Avoidance is viewed as a defensive maneuver, lessening the anxiety and anger experienced in the conflict situation and enabling the baby nevertheless to remain within a tolerable range of proximity to the mother.

Findings and interpretations such as these raise the issue of direction of effects. To what extent is the pattern of attachment of a baby attributable to the mother's behavior throughout the first year, and to what extent is it attributable to built-in differences in potential and temperament? I have considered this problem elsewhere (Ainsworth, 1979) and have concluded that in our sample of normal babies there is a strong case to be made for differences in attachment quality being attributable to maternal behavior. Two studies, however (Connell 1976; Waters, Vaughn, & Egeland, in press), have suggested that Group C babies may as newborns be constitutionally "difficult." Particularly if the mother's personality or life situation makes it hard for her to be sensitively responsive to infant cues, such a baby seems indeed likely to form an attachment relationship of anxious quality.

Contexts of Mother–Infant Interaction

Of the various contexts in which mother–infant interaction commonly takes place, the face-to-face situation has been the focus of most recent research. By many (e.g., Walters & Parke, 1965), interaction mediated by distance receptors and behaviors has been judged especially important in the establishment of human relationships. Microanalytic studies, based on frame-by-frame analysis of film records, show clearly that maternal sensitivity to infant behavioral cues is essential for successful pacing of face-to-face interaction (e.g., Brazelton, Koslowski, & Main, 1974; Stern, 1974). Telling evidence of the role of vision, both in the infant's development of attachment to the mother and in the mother's responsiveness to the infant, comes from Fraiberg's (1977) longitudinal study of blind infants.

So persuasive have been the studies of interaction involving distance receptors that interaction involving close bodily contact has been largely ignored. The evolutionary perspective of attachment theory attributes focal importance to bodily contact. Other primate species rely on the maintenance of close mother–infant contact as crucial for infant survival. Societies of hunter–gatherers, living much as the earliest humans did, are conspicuous for very much more mother–infant contact than are western societies (e.g., Konner, 1976). Blurton Jones (1972) presented evidence suggesting that humans evolved as a species in which infants are carried by the mother and are fed at frequent intervals, rather than as a species in which infants are left for long periods, are cached in a safe place, and are fed but infrequently. Bowlby (1969) pointed out that when attachment behavior is intensely activated it is close bodily contact that is specifically required. Indeed, Bell and Ainsworth (1972) found that even with the white, middle-class mothers of their sample, the most frequent and the most effective response to an infant's crying throughout the first year was to pick up the baby. A recent analysis of our longitudinal findings (Blehar, Ainsworth, & Main, 1979) suggests that mother–infant interaction relevant to close bodily contact is at least as important a context of interaction as face-to-face is, perhaps especially in the first few months of life. Within the limits represented by our sample, however, we found that it was *how* the mother holds her baby rather than *how much* she holds him or her that affects the way in which attachment develops.

In recent years the feeding situation has been neglected as a context for mother–infant interaction, except insofar as it is viewed as a setting for purely social, face-to-face interaction. Earlier, mother's gratification or frustration of infant interest to both psychoanalytically oriented and social-learning research, on the assumption that a mother's gratification or frustration of infant instinctual drives, or her role as a secondary reinforcer, determined the nature of the baby's tie to her. Such research yielded no evidence that methods of feeding significantly affected the course of infant development, although these negative findings seem almost certainly to reflect methodological deficiencies (Caldwell, 1964). In contrast, we have found that sensitive maternal responsiveness to infant signals relevant to feeding is closely related to the security or anxiety of attachment that eventually develops (Ainsworth & Bell, 1969). Indeed, this analysis seemed to redefine the meaning of "demand" feeding – letting infant behavioral cues determine not only when feeding is begun but also when it is terminated, how the pacing of feeding proceeds, and how new foods are introduced.

Our findings do not permit us to attribute overriding importance to any one context of mother–infant interaction. Whether the context is feeding, close bodily contact, face-to-face interaction, or indeed the situation defined by the infant's crying, mother–infant interaction provides the baby with opportunity to build up expectations of the mother and, eventually, a working model of her as more or less accessible and responsive. Indeed, our findings suggest that a mother who is sensitively responsive to signals in one context tends also to be responsive to signals in other contexts.

Practical Implications for Intervention

What I have so far summarized about research findings pertaining both to contexts of interaction and to qualitative differences in infant–mother attachment has implications for parenting education, for intervention by professionals to help a mother to achieve better interaction with her baby, and for the practices of substitute caregivers. I cannot go into detail here – and indeed such detail would need to be based on much fuller reports of the relevant research than I am able to include here. Among the intervention programs with which I am familiar, some parent–child development centers have reported success in the application of our research findings in improving and sustaining the rate of development of very young children through improving the quality of mother–infant interaction (e.g., Andrews, Blumenthal, Bache, & Wiener, 1975). Furthermore, the expert clinical interventions of Fraiberg and her associates with families at risk have focused on increasing maternal responsiveness to infant behavioral cues (e.g., Shapiro, Fraiberg, & Adelson, 1976). It may be that such intervention, although obviously expensive, provides the most effective mode of helping dyads in which the difficulty stems from deep-seated difficulties in the mother's personality, such as the aversion to bodily contact characteristic of our Group A mothers.

Using the Mother as a Secure Base from Which to Explore

Attachment theory conceives of the behavioral system serving attachment as only one of several important systems, each with its own activators, terminators, predictable outcomes, and functions. During the prolonged period of human infancy, when the protective function of attachment is especially important, its interplay with exploratory behavior is noteworthy. The function of exploration is learning about the environment – which is particularly important in a species possessing much potential for adaptation to a wide range of environments. Attachment and exploration support each other. When attachment behavior is intensely activated, a baby tends to seek proximity contact rather than exploring; when attachment behavior is at low intensity a baby is free to respond to the pull of novelty. The presence of an attachment figure, particularly one who is believed to be accessible and responsive, leaves the baby open to stimulation that may activate exploration.

Nevertheless, it is often believed that somehow attachment may interfere with the development of independence. Our studies provide no support for such a belief. For example, Blehar et al. (1979) found that babies who respond positively to close bodily contact with their mothers also tend to respond positively to being put down again and to move off into independent exploratory play. Fostering the growth of secure attachment facilitates rather than hampers the growth of healthy self-reliance (Bowlby, 1973).

Response to Separation from Attachment Figures

Schaffer (1971) suggested that the crucial criterion for whether a baby has become attached to a specific figure is that he or she does not consider this figure interchangeable with any other figure. Thus, for an infant to protest the mother's departure or continued absence is a dependable criterion for attachment (Schaffer & Callender, 1959). This does not imply that protest is an invariable response to separation from an attachment figure under all circumstances; the context of the separation influences the likelihood and intensity of protest. Thus there is ample evidence, which cannot be cited here, that protest is unlikely to occur, at least initially, in the case of voluntary separations, when the infant willingly leaves the mother in order to explore elsewhere. Protest is less likely to occur if the baby is left with another attachment figure than if he or she is left with an unfamiliar person or alone. Being left in an unfamiliar environment is more distressing than comparable separations in the familiar environment of the home – in which many infants are able to build up expectations that reassure them of mother's accessibility and responsiveness even though she may be absent. Changes attributable to developmental processes affect separation protest in complex ways. Further research will undoubtedly be able to account for these shifts in terms of progressive cognitive achievements.

Major separations of days, months, or even years must be distinguished from the very brief separations, lasting only minutes, that have been studied most intensively both in the laboratory and at home.

Securely attached infants may be able to tolerate very brief separations with equanimity, yet they are likely to be distressed in major separations, especially when cared for by unfamiliar persons in unfamiliar environments. Even so, Robertson and Robertson (1971) showed that sensitive substitute parenting can do much to mute separation distress and avert the more serious consequences of major separations.

Despite a steady increase in our understanding of the complexities of response to and effects of separation from attachment figures in infancy and early childhood, it is difficult to suggest clear-cut guidelines for parents and others responsible for infant and child care. So much depends on the circumstances under which separation taken place, on the degree to which the separation environment can substitute satisfactorily for home and parents, on the child's stage of development and previous experience, and on the nature of his or her relationship with attachment figures. No wonder that the issue of the separations implicit in day care is controversial. Further research is clearly needed. Meanwhile, it would seem wise for parents – if they have a choice – to move cautiously rather than plunging into substitute-care arrangements with a blithe assumption that all is bound to go well.

Other Attachment Figures

Many have interpreted Bowlby's attachment theory as claiming that an infant can become attached to only one person – the mother. This is a mistaken interpretation. There are, however, three implications of attachment theory relevant to the issue of "multiple" attachments. First, as reported by Ainsworth (1967) and Schaffer and Emerson (1964), infants are highly selective in their choices of attachment figures from among the various persons familiar to them. No infant has been observed to have many attachment figures. Second, not all social relationships may be identified as attachments. Harlow (1971) distinguished between the infant–mother and peer–peer affectional systems, although under certain circumstances peers may become attachment figures in the absence of anyone more appropriate (see, e.g., Freud, & Dann, 1951; Harlow, 1963). Third, the fact that a baby may have several attachment figures does not imply that they are all equally important. Bowlby (1969) suggested that they are not – that there is a principal attachment figure, usually the principal caregiver, and one or more secondary figures. Thus a hierarchy is implied. A baby may both enjoy and derive security from all of his or her attachment figures but, under certain circumstances (e.g., illness, fatigue, stress), is likely to show a clear preference among them.

In recent years there has been a surge of interest in the father as an attachment figure. Relatively lacking is research into attachments to caregivers other than parents. Do babies become attached to their regular baby-sitters or to caregivers in day-care centers? Studies by Fleener (1973), Farran and Ramey (1977), and Ricciuti (1974) have suggested that they may but that the preference is nevertheless for the mother figure. Fox (1977) compared the mother and the *metapelet* as providers of security to kibbutz-reared infants in a strange situation, but surely much more research is needed into the behavior of infants and young children toward caregivers as attachment figures in the substitute-care environment.

Consequences of Attachment

A number of investigators, including Main (1973, and, with Londerville, 1979), Matas, Arend, and Sroufe (1978), and Waters, Wittman, and Sroufe (in press), having assessed the quality of one-year-olds' attachment, have followed the children through to ascertain whether this assessment bears a significant relationship to later be-havioral measures in the second, third, or even sixth year of life. We (Ainsworth et al., 1978) have reviewed these investigations in some detail; only a brief summary can be given here.

In comparison with anxiously attached infants, those who are securely attached as one-year-olds are later more cooperative with and affectively more positive as well as less aggressive and/or avoidant toward their mothers and other less familiar adults. Later on, they emerge as more competent and more sympathetic in interaction with peers. In free-play situations they have longer bouts of exploration and display more intense exploratory interest, and in problem-solving situations they are more enthusiastic, more persistent, and better able to elicit and accept their mothers' help. They are more curious, more self-directed, more ego-resilient – and they usually tend to achieve better scores on both developmental tests and measures of language develop-ment. Some studies also reported differences between the two groups of anxious attached infants, with the avoidant ones (Group A) continuing to be more aggressive, noncompliant, and avoidant, and the ambivalent ones (Group C) emerging as more easily frustrated, less persistent, and generally less competent.

Conclusion

It is clear that the nature of an infant's attachment to his or her mother as a one-year-old is related both to earlier interaction with the mother and to various aspects of later development. The implication is that the way in which the infant organizes his or her behavior toward the mother affects the way in which he or she organizes behavior toward other aspects of the environment, both animate and inanimate. This organization provides a core of continuity in development despite changes that come with developmental acquisitions, both cognitive and socioemotional.

This is not to insist that the organizational attachment is fixed in the first year of life and is insensitive to marked changes in maternal behavior or to relevant life events occurring later on. Nor is it implied that attachments to figures other than the mother are unimportant as supplementing or compensating for anxieties in infant–mother attachment – although too little is yet known about how various attachments relate together to influence the way in which infants organize their perception of and approach to the world. Despite the need for further research, however, the yield of findings to date provides relevant leads for policies education in parenting, and intervention procedures intended to further the welfare of infants and young children.

References

Ainsworth, M. D. S. *Infancy in Uganda: Infant care the growth of love.* Baltimore, Md.: Johns Hopkins University Press, 1967.

Ainsworth, M. D. S. Attachment as related to mother–infant interaction. In J. S. Rosenblatt, R. A. Hinde, C. Beer, & M. Busnel (Eds.), *Advances in the study of behavior* (Vol. 9). New York: Academic Press, 1979.

Ainsworth, M. D. S., & Bell, S. M. Some contemporary patterns of mother–infant interaction in the feeding situation. In A. Ambrose (Ed.), *Stimulation in early infancy.* London: Academic Press, 1969.

Ainsworth, M. D. S., Blehar, M. C., Waters, E., & Wall, S. *Patterns of attachment: A psychological study of the strange situation.* Hillsdale, NJ: Erlbaum, 1978.

Andrews, S. R., Blumenthal, J. B., Bache, W. L., & Wiener, G. Fourth year report: New Orleans Parent–Child Development center. Unpublished document, March 1975. (Available from Susan R. Andrew, 6917 Glenn Street, Metairie, Louisiana 70003.)

Bell, S. M., & Ainsworth, M. D. S. Infant crying and maternal responsiveness. *Child Development,* 1972, *43,* 1171–1190.

Blehar, M. C., Ainsworth, M. D. S., & Main, M. Mother–infant interaction relevant to close bodily contact. Monograph in preparation, 1979.

Blurton Jones, N. G. Comparative aspects of mother–child contact. In N. G. Blurton Jones (Ed.), *Ethological studies of child behaviour.* London: Cambridge University Press, 1972.

Bowlby, J. *Attachment and loss: Vol. 1. Attachment.* New York: Basic Books, 1969.

Bowlby, J. *Attachment and loss: Vol. 2. Separation: Anxiety and anger.* New York: Basic Books, 1973.

Brazelton, T. B., Koslowski, B., & Main, M. The origins of reciprocity: The early mother-infant interaction. In M. Lewis & L. A. Rosenblum (Eds.), *The effect of the infant on its caregiver.* New York: Wiley, 1974.

Caldwell, B. M. The effects of infant care. In M. L. Hoffamn & L. W. Hoffman (Eds.), *Review of child development research* (Vol. 1). New York: Russell Sage Foundation, 1964.

Connell, D. B. Individual differences in attachment: An investigation into stability, implications, and relationships to the structure of early language development. Unpublished doctoral dissertation, Syracuse University, 1976.

Farran, D. C., & Ramey, C. T. Infant day care and attachment behavior toward mother and teachers. *Child Development,* 1977, *48,* 1112–1116.

Fleener, D. E. Experimental production of infant–maternal attachment behaviors. *Proceedings of the 81st Annual Convention of the American Psychological Association,* 1973, *8,* 57–58. (Summary)

Fox, N. Attachment of kibbutz infants to mother. *Child Development,* 1977, *48,* 1228–1239.

Fraiberg, S. *Insights from the blind.* New York: Basic Books, 1977.

Freud, A., & Dann, S. An experiment in group upbringing. *Psychoanalytic Study of the Child,* 1951, *6,* 127–168.

Harlow, H. F. The maternal affectional system. In B. M. Foss (Ed.), *Determinants of infant behaviour* (Vol. 2). New York: Wiley, 1963.

Harlow, H. F. *Learning to love.* San Francisco: Albion, 1971.

Konner, M. J. Maternal care, infant behavior, and development among the !Kung. In R. B. Lee & I. DeVore (Eds.), *Kalahari hunter–gatherers.* Cambridge, MA: Harvard University Press, 1976.

Main, M. Exploration, play, level of cognitive functioning as related to child–mother attachment. Unpublished doctoral dissertation, Johns Hopkins University, 1973.

Main, M. Avoidance in the service of proximity. In K. Immelmann, G. Barlow, M. Main, & L. Petrinovich (Eds.), *Behavioral development: The Bielefeld Interdisciplinary Project.* New York: Cambridge University Press, in press.

Main, M., & Londerville, S. B. Compliance and aggression in toddlerhood: Precursors and correlates. Paper in preparation, 1979.

Matas, L., Arend, R. A., & Sroufe, L. A. Continuity of adaptation in the second year: The relationship between quality of attachment and later competence. *Child Development,* 1978, *49,* 547–556.

Ricciuti, H. N. Fear and the development of social attachments in the first year of life. In M. Lewis & L. A. Rosenblum (Eds.), *The origins of fear.* New York: Wiley, 1974.

Robertson, J., & Robertson, J. Young children in brief separation: A fresh look. *Psychoanalytic Study of the Child,* 1971, *26,* 264–315.

Schaffer, H. R. *The growth of sociability.* London: Penguin Books, 1971.

Schaffer, H. R., & Callender, W. M. Psychological effects of hospitalization in infancy. *Pediatrics,* 1959, *25,* 528–539.

Schaffer, H. R., & Emerson, P. E. The development of social attachments in infancy. *Monographs of the Society for Research in Child Development,* 1964, *3,* (Serial No. 94).

Shapiro, V., Fraiberg, S., & Adelson, E., Infant–parent psychotherapy on behalf of a child in a critical nutritional state. *Psychoanalytic Study of the Child,* 1976, *31,* 461–491.

Stayton, D. J., & Ainsworth, M. D. S. Individual differences in infant responses to brief, everyday separations as related to other infant and maternal behaviors. *Developmental Psychology,* 1973, *9,* 226–235.

Stern, D. N. Mother and infant at play: The dyadic interaction involving facial, vocal, and gaze behaviors. In M. Lewis & L. A. Rosenblum (Eds.), *The effect of the infant on its caregiver.* New York: Wiley, 1974.

Walters, R. H., & Parke, R. D. The role of the distance receptors in the development of social responsiveness. In L. P. Lipsitt & C. C. Spiker (Eds.), *Advances in child development and behavior.* New York: Academic Press, 1965.

Water, E., Vaughn, B. E., & Egeland, B. R. Individual differences in infant–mother attachment relationships at age one: Antecedents in neonatal behavior in an urban economically disadvantaged sample. *Child Development,* in press.

Waters, E., Wittman, J., & Sroufe, L. A. Attachment, positive affect, and competence in the peer group: Two studies in construct validation. *Child Development,* in press.

TWO

Parenting

Introduction

Parenting is a bidirectional process whereby parents socialize children and children socialize parents. Individuals receive little or no formal education about how to be effective parents. Most individuals learn how to parent through their own experiences either as a parent or as a child with their own parents. Researchers interested in social development have investigated the question of what aspects of parenting promote competent social development in their children.

This study, by Pettit, Bates, and Dodge, highlights several important issues. First, supportive parenting of children in kindergarten (typically five years old) is characterized by proactive teaching, calm discussion in disciplinary encounters, warmth, and general interest in a child's activities and friends. These factors contribute to the children's behavioral, social, and academic adjustment at the end of grade 6 (around 11 years of age). Second, for children who may be exposed to a number of family stressors, such as single parenting and low socio-economic status, supportive parenting decreases their chances of having negative outcomes. Third, although supportive parenting was related to positive outcomes for both boys and girls, the effect was stronger for girls. Finally, different cultures tended to demonstrate varying amounts of supportive parenting. Consequently, recognizing and understanding cultural differences in parenting is an important issue.

This study has several methodological strengths that represent important aspects for designing studies. The study is conducted longitudinally, over a seven-year period. There is a multi-informant approach: that is, constructs are based on interviews, parent reports, observations of interactions, teacher reports, and school records. This approach strengthens the reliability and validity of the results. In summary, this well-designed study highlights the importance of supportive parents in contributing to healthy development in social as well as academic domains.

Supportive Parenting, Ecological Context, and Children's Adjustment: A Seven-Year Longitudinal Study

Gregory S. Pettit, John E. Bates, and Kenneth A. Dodge

Introduction

The search for those aspects of parenting that may play formative roles in children's social development has long occupied the attention of socialization researchers. A wide range of stylistic dimensions and specific parenting practices thought to promote child adaptation in the dominant culture of the United States have been examined over the years (Darling & Steinberg, 1993). Baumrind's conceptualization of parenting style probably is best known in this regard (e.g., Baumrind, 1967) and has been pivotal in showing that effective parenting is constituted of multiple elements that are melded together to form distinct styles. Authoritative parents, for example, tend to be warm and accepting, democratic in decision making, and firm in establishing behavioral guidelines. Research based on Baumrind's framework has produced a large and impressive body of findings linking authoritative parenting with positive adjustment outcomes in children and adolescents (e.g., see Baumrind, 1989; Darling & Steinberg, 1993).

The authoritative style represents a constellation of developmentally appropriate and supportive parenting attributes. There has been considerable research interest in the separate constituents of the authoritative style, as well as in other kinds of "supportive" parenting practices that may be empirically distinct from the constituents of the authoritative style. Among the presumably supportive aspects of parenting that have been investigated are positive affect (Biringen & Robinson, 1991), child-centeredness (Gest, Neeman, Hubbard, Masten, & Tellegen, 1993), proactive teaching (Holden, 1985), positive reinforcement (Patterson, Reid, & Dishion, 1992), inductive discipline (Hart, DeWolf, Wozniak, & Burts, 1992), and the provision of appropriate play experiences, especially in the context of managing children's peer contacts (Ladd, Profilet, & Hart, 1992). Some investigators have collapsed across these or related parenting behaviors to create broadly construed dimensions of parental positivity (e.g., Conger et al., 1992; Gest et al., 1993; Gottman, Katz, & Hooven, 1996; McCord, 1996). The assumption in such studies appears to be that overall positive and supportive parenting (henceforth denoted as SP) should have generic benefits across a range of child-developmental outcomes.

Models of parenting effectiveness also have been articulated in which differing aspects of SP are expected to be associated with differing types of child outcome (e.g., Patterson et al., 1992; Pettit & Mize, 1993). Two recent studies are illustrative in this regard. Grolnick and Slowiaczek (1994) examined the predictive relations between three types of parents' involvement in their children's schooling and different types of academic outcomes. The parenting domains were found to be generally independent of one another and somewhat differentially related to the school outcomes. Patterson et al. (1992), in their study of antisocial behavior in high-risk boys, also identified three distinct aspects of positive and supportive parenting. There was little empirical overlap among constructs, and each correlated only modestly with other aspects of parenting (monitoring and discipline). As with Grolnick and Slowiaczek, some pattern distinctiveness was found in the prediction of child behavior. Thus, there is some evidence that aspects or domains of SP are relatively independent and are associated with child outcomes in a differentiated manner.

In the current study, we sought to expand the study of SP by addressing two major questions. The first question is whether measures of SP predict child outcomes once the effects of harsh parenting (HP) have been controlled. This is an important question because of the possibility that SP may be a marker for the absence of HP and therefore may account for little unique variance in child outcomes. Another way of thinking about this issue is in terms of main effects: Are the most poorly adjusted children reared in families where there is both an absence of

SP and a presence of HP (two significant main effects), or is the presence of HP sufficient to produce these outcomes (one significant main effect)? The evidence is mixed. Pettit and Bates (1989) found that the absence of proactive involvement better predicted concurrent mother-rated behavior problems than the presence of negative control and conflict. Pettit, Bates, and Dodge (1993) reported a similar, but weaker, pattern of findings in a separate community sample. Patterson et al. (1992), on the other hand, not only found weaker associations between measures of positive parenting and child outcomes (problem behavior, social skills, and mood) than between measures of ineffective discipline and monitoring and child outcomes, but once the discipline and monitoring measures were controlled in a regression analysis, the impact of the positive parenting measures became negligible. Patterson et al. (1992) suggest that the predictive significance of positive and supportive aspects of parenting may be more pronounced in younger and comparatively more normative samples of children.

For the most part, studies examining the relative impact of SP and HP on children's adjustment use cross-sectional (Patterson et al., 1992; Russell & Russell, 1996) or short-term longitudinal (Pettit et al., 1993) designs. In the current study, we examined the predictive significance of SP over a seven-year time period. Parenting measures were obtained the summer prior to kindergarten. An effort was made to obtain operationally "clean" indexes of supportive parenting by insuring that a low score indicated the absence of SP rather than the presence of HP. Similarly, HP was assessed in a manner that insured that low scores reflected absence of HP rather than presence of SP. Adjustment outcomes were assessed in kindergarten and again in grade 6. The design thus afforded an opportunity to examine the extent to which SP, independently of HP, forecasted cross-time changes in patterns of adjustment from early childhood to early adolescence. The child-developmental outcomes selected for study were externalizing behavior problems, social skills in peer relations, and academic performance. These outcome domains were of interest because they encompass three broad and important aspects of children's adjustment during the early and middle childhood years (Cowan, Cowan, Schulz, & Heming, 1994).

Four types of parenting behavior that might be construed as positive and supportive were examined. These consist of parents' observed warmth, use of inductive discipline techniques, interest and involvement in their children's peer contacts, and proactive teaching of social skills. Each of these types of SP has been linked with individual differences in children's behavioral and academic adjustment (e.g., Cowan et al., 1994; Denham, Renwick, & Holt, 1991; Mize & Pettit, 1997; Russell & Russell, 1996). We had no specific a priori hypotheses regarding which type of SP might be most strongly associated with which type of child adjustment. Based on past research, however, it seemed reasonable to expect that warmth and inductive discipline might be associated with lower levels of behavior problems, because of evidence linking these parenting qualities to the development of conscience (Kochanska, 1993) and the learning of noncombative conflict resolution skills (Pettit, Dodge, & Brown, 1988). We also thought that proactive teaching of social skills and interest and involvement in the child's social life might be associated with social skills in peer relations because of evidence suggesting that these parenting qualities promote the child's development of prosocial and affiliative expectations regarding relationships and enhance the child's social-cognitive and behavioral repertoire (Mize & Pettit, 1997; Pettit & Mize, 1993). However, because behavior problems, social skills, and academic performance tend to be highly intercorrelated (Parker & Asher, 1987), and because each type of parenting has been found to be associated with more than one type of outcome (e.g., Patterson et al., 1992; Pettit & Bates, 1989), we were less interested in which parenting measure might predict which outcome, and more interested in whether the parenting measures – individually and as an aggregate – accounted for significant variance in each of the child outcomes.

We also assessed parents' use of harsh, physical punishment in disciplinary encounters. Inclusion of this measure allowed for an examination of the relative overlap of supportive parenting versus harsh and punitive parenting in the prediction of child adjustment. Implicit in the decision to use four measures of SP but only one of HP is our belief that SP is more multidimensional than HP. As noted by Parke (1992), there are many ways in which parents may positively and constructively engage their children, and parents may pick and choose from the array of possibilities. For example, some parents may be prone to display affection openly but do little in the way of proactive teaching of social skills (Mize & Pettit, 1997). Although it is possible that there could be similar domain-specific variations in harsh, restrictive parenting, this seemed unlikely to us. There is, in fact, evidence that measures of parental negativity cohere empirically to a greater degree than measures of parental positivity (Patterson et al., 1992), suggesting that aspects of HP go hand in hand to a greater extent than do aspects of SP.

The second major question addressed in this study was whether SP might moderate the impact of family adversity on child outcomes. We defined family adversity in terms of major social address variables (Bronfenbrenner & Crouter, 1983) that are associated with increased risk for maladjustment: low socioeconomic status (SES), being raised in a single-parent household, and family stress. Child maladjustment and ineffective parenting are more common in families experiencing each type of adversity (Hetherington & Martin, 1986). For example, Conger et al. (1992) found that family economic distress (i.e., low income, unstable employment, and indebtedness) was associated with lower levels of positive adjustment and higher levels of behavioral problems among adolescent males, and these predictive associations were found to be mediated by ineffective parenting practices. Similarly, Bank, Forgatch, Patterson, and Fetrow (1993) found that single parenthood was associated with less effective parenting (e.g., inconsistent discipline), which in turn was associated with boys' social maladjustment. These findings led us to ask whether the presence of SP might offset the risks associated with family adversity. Positive and supportive aspects of parenting have been shown to moderate the effects of other kinds of risk factors, such as peer rejection (Patterson, Cohn, & Kao, 1989) and harsh parenting (Deater-Deckard & Dodge, in press), and there are suggestions in the resiliency literature that SP-relevant attributes (such as positivity, consistency, and child-centeredness) serve as protective factors in high-stress families (Masten et al., 1988). We therefore examined the extent to which SP served as a moderator or buffer for low SES, single parenthood, and family stress. SP would constitute a moderator if the negative consequences associated with these family risks varied as a function of different levels of SP.

A final issue considered in the current study was whether the modeled processes (SP and HP as additive main effects, SP as a moderator of family adversity) differed as a function of ethnicity and child sex. Although some have argued for developmental universalism with respect to socialization processes in different ethnic groups (Rowe, Vazsonyi, & Flannery, 1994), others have reported evidence of ethnic differences in the links between parenting measures and children's adjustment (Deater-Deckard & Dodge, in press). These differences largely have been restricted to parents' use of harsh discipline and authoritarian decision-making practices (Deater-Deckard, Dodge, Bates, & Pettit, 1996; Lamborn, Dornbush, & Steinberg, 1996). It is not clear whether such differences also would be seen in relations between SP and child outcomes. To examine this issue, correlational analyses were conducted separately for European American children and African American children, and ethnicity was used as a moderator variable in regression analyses.

Child sex also was examined as a potential moderator of the relations between SP, adversity, and child outcomes. Sex differences frequently have been reported both in parents' socialization strategies and in the associations among children's adjustment and parents' use of those strategies (Maccoby & Martin, 1983). Moreover, there is some evidence that risk and protective factors interact in different ways for boys and girls. For example, Masten et al. (1988) found that parenting quality interacted with family stress in the prediction of girls' (but not boys') disruptive behavior. Therefore, as with ethnicity, correlational analyses were conducted separately for boys and girls, and child sex was considered as a possible moderator variable in regression analyses.

Parenting patterns in this study were assessed during an extensive home interview session conducted in the summer prior to the children's entry into kindergarten. Subsequent assessments were made of the children's behavior problems, peer competence, and academic performance in kindergarten and grade 6. The study thus provided an opportunity for documenting the distinctive roles that early SP might play in facilitating children's later adjustment to kindergarten and, still later, to grade 6.

Method

Sample and overview

This study was conducted as part of the Child Development Project, a multisite longitudinal study of the early family and social experience precursors of children's social and behavioral adjustment (Dodge, Pettit, & Bates, 1994; Pettit, Clawson, Bates, & Dodge, 1996). Participating families were recruited into one of two cohorts (those with children entering kindergarten in 1987 and 1988) at each of three sites: Knoxville and Nashville, TN, and Bloomington, IN. Most families (85%)

were recruited during the spring at kindergarten preregistration, with the remaining families being contacted during on-site registration at the beginning of the school year. Research assistants randomly approached parents and asked them if they would be interested in participating in a longitudinal study of child development. Of those so contacted, approximately 75% agreed to participate. The sample was diverse with respect to child sex (52% boys), ethnicity (80% European American, 18% African American, 2% other ethnic groups), and family composition (26% resided with single mothers at the time of recruitment). The Hollingshead (1979) Four Factor Index of Social Status, computed from demographic information provided by the parents, indicated a predominantly middle-class sample, with an average family score on the index of 40.4 ($SD = 14.0$). However, a range of social statuses was represented, with 9%, 17%, 25%, 33%, and 16% of the families being classified into the five possible classes (from lowest to highest), according to Hollingshead's recommendation.

Comparable proportions of boys and girls were in European American and African American families. However, single parents were disproportionately represented in African American families: 50% of participating African American families were single parent, whereas only 18% of participating European American families were single parent, χ^2 (1, $N = 574$) = 56.8, $p < .001$. The Hollingshead SES score also was lower among African American families ($M = 27.0$) compared to European American families ($M = 47.2$), $F(1, 558) = 111.5, p < .001$.

A total of 585 families completed the first assessment prior to kindergarten, when the children were five years old. Follow-up assessments of the children were conducted in kindergarten and every grade thereafter through grade 6 (approximately age 11 years). Participant attrition averaged 3.3% per year. Attrited participants were not different from ongoing participants in initial child adjustment or family background characteristics (see Deater-Deckard et al., 1996). Adjustment outcome data were collected on approximately 80% of the participating children. These children generally were representative of the original sample with respect to child sex, ethnicity, SES, and single-parent status. For the sake of consistency in the temporal ordering of variables, cross-time changes in the latter two categories (SES and single-parent households) were not considered in this report.

Procedure

Parents were interviewed in their homes during the summer preceding their children's entry into kindergarten. Two researchers visited the home, where one interviewed the mother and father (if he was available), and the other interviewed the child. While one parent was being interviewed, the other parent filled out a set of questionnaires. The 90-minute audio-recorded interview with each parent was conducted by a trained interviewer and included both open-ended and structured questions about each of three early childhood eras (the first 12 months, 12+ months until one year ago, and the past year; only the latter two periods are considered here). Questions concerned the child's developmental and child-care history, family stressors, parenting behavior, and current child behavior. Interviewer training consisted of a four-week training period of reading a procedure manual, observing other interviews, and conducting interviews with a supervisor present. Interviewers were trained to a reliability of .80 or higher (percent agreement across all items, using the supervisor's scores as the criterion) prior to conducting any real interviews. Reliability of actual scores was assessed through independent ratings of 56 randomly selected families (9.6% of total) made by a second coder who sat in with the interviewer and scored the developmental history in real time. Because a third of the participant families lacked a father interview, all derived variables are based on the mother interview only.

During the home visit, both the parent and child interviewers had opportunities to observe the child and mother during interaction with each other (upon greeting, during transitions, and at the end). Each interviewer independently completed a post-visit inventory to summarize their impressions of mother–child interactions. The inventory included items from the HOME Scale (Caldwell & Bradley, 1984).

During the spring of the kindergarten academic year, the children's classroom teachers completed the Teacher Rating Form (Achenbach & Edelbrock, 1986) and the Teacher Checklist of Peer Relations (Coie & Dodge, 1988). The same instruments were used in the grade 6 assessment. Also at this time, research staff requested permission to view the child's academic records to record grades and achievement test scores.

Measures

Supportive parenting. Four parenting measures conceptualized as supportive were generated from the interview, the parent questionnaires, and the post-interview ratings. The first measure indexes mothers' reported involvement in their children's social contacts with peers. Parents were asked during the interview to describe their children's exposure to peers in each of the two developmental periods. Interviewers asked the parent to identify the situations (e.g., neighborhood children, preschool, family gatherings) in which the child interacted with other children, whether the child had been around any children that the parent considered to be aggressive, whether the child had any close friends that she or he talked about, and whether the child had been involved in any conflictual interactions with peers. On the basis of the parents' descriptions, the interviewer rated the "parent's awareness of and concern about the child's social experience and willingness to use such considerations to structure the child's experiences." The interviewer impressions were summarized on an extensively anchored five-point rating scale, in which a "1" indicated that the parent was unaware or uninterested in most of the child's peer experiences, and a "5" indicated a very high level of parental interest and involvement. The ratings across the two eras were averaged to yield an overall positive involvement score ($\alpha = .92$ across the two eras; correlation between independent raters $= .32$).

A second indicator of supportive parenting was derived from the Conflict Tactics Scale (Straus, 1987). The Conflict Tactics Scale (CTS) is a set of ratings completed by the parent to describe behaviors used by family members in the course of disagreements and other situations that may give rise to conflict. Scale scores for each of 14 behaviors (ranging from calm discussion to violence) range from 1 (never) to 6 (more than once a month). Two behaviors were of interest here, each of which was concerned with mothers' responses to the child: "tried to discuss an issue calmly," and "did discuss an issue calmly." Ratings of the frequency of these two behaviors were obtained for each of two developmental periods (this past year and prior to this past year). A four-item composite ($\alpha = .86$) was formed to index mothers' use of calm discussion in disciplinary encounters with their children.

A third indicator of supportive parenting came from an orally administered questionnaire (the Concerns and Constraints Questionnaire) in which parents were presented with five hypothetical situations in which a child misbehaved in his or her interactions with peers (e.g., a child refuses to relinquish a toy after a reasonable length of time). Parents were asked to describe ways in which the child might have been prevented from acting this way in the first place. Parents' responses were scored as "do nothing (unpreventable)" (1), "after-the-fact punishment" (2), "after-the-fact guidance and reasoning" (3), "before-the-fact, preventive but general" (4), and "before-the-fact, preventive and situation and method specific" (5). Parents who used either of the latter two categories received a score of "1"; parents using any other category received a score of "0." Scores were summed across the five stories ($\alpha = .70$) to create a measure of proactive teaching. Reliability assessments were available only for a subset of families ($n = 24$) for this instrument. The correlation between independent raters for the number of times (zero to five) that the mother suggested a proactive strategy was .56.

The final measure of supportive parenting was based on observed mother warmth to the child. After the home visit, each of the two home visitors completed a 47-item Post-Visit Inventory. The home visitor assessed the warmth of the mother's behavior toward the child by noting the occurrence (occurred = 1, did not occur = 0) of each of four behavioral events: "mother speaks to child with a positive tone," "mother expresses a positive attitude when speaking of the child," "mother initiates positive physical contact with the child," and "mother accepts positive physical contact from the child." A few items could not be completed owing to insufficient information (e.g., if the child did not initiate any positive physical contact it was not possible to rate mothers' acceptance of that contact). These and all other missing data were recoded as "0" (i.e., did not occur). The two visitors' agreement on the sum of the ratings was substantial ($r = .58$), so the eight items (four from each of the two visitors) were averaged to create a score for observed mother warmth to the child ($\alpha = .61$).

Harsh parenting. A measure of restrictive discipline also was derived as an index of harsh parenting. During the interview, the mother was asked to respond in an open-ended fashion to each of several questions for each era: "Who usually disciplined your child?" "How?" "Was your child ever physically punished?" "How often?" For each era, the interviewer provided a rating for the parent's use of restrictive discipline, based on the parent's answers. The rating ranged from "nonrestrictive,

Table 1   Correlations among parenting measures and kindergarten and grade 6 child adjustment

		Supportive parenting			
Child adjustment	Harsh discipline	Warmth	Involvement	Calm discussion	Proactive teaching
Externalizing problems:					
Kindergarten	.07	−.08	−.05	−.13**	−.14**
Grade 6	.17**	−.14**	−.11*	−.17**	−.13**
Social skillfulness:					
Kindergarten	−.13**	.09	.10*	.13**	.11*
Grade 6	−.17**	.09	.05	.11*	.09
Academic performance:					
Kindergarten	−.18**	.13**	.19**	.10	.17**
Grade 6	−.20**	.14**	.25**	.27**	.11*
Mean	2.39	.86	3.25	4.29	.45
SD	.84	.22	1.05	1.23	.33

Ns = 524–573 for kindergarten adjustment; 423–439 for grade 6 adjustment.
*p < .05; **p < .01.

mostly positive guidance" (1) to "severe, strict, often physical" (5). To insure that the rating indexed the extent to which harsh, restrictive discipline was present, rather than the degree to which positive guidance was absent, the rating was rescaled such that low scores (1, 2, and 3) were combined. The resulting scale indexed harsh, restrictive discipline on an absent-to-present continuum. Ratings across the two eras were averaged to yield a score for harsh, restrictive discipline (α = .61, inter-rater r = .80). Means and standard deviations of all parenting variables are shown in table 1.

Family adversity. Family adversity was indexed by single parenthood, socioeconomic status, and family stress. SES was computed on the basis of mothers' and fathers' occupation and years of education (Hollingshead, 1979). As recommended by Hollingshead, when fathers (or adult male partners) did not reside in the home, the mothers' scores were double-weighted.

    Family life stress was assessed during the interview. The interviewer asked the mother to recall each era, aiding memory with a standard list of ten major stressors (e.g., death, family moves, legal problems). Following these questions, the interviewer completed five point ratings of (1) the extent of stressful, challenging events faced by the child and the family (ranging from "minimal challenge" to "severe frequent challenges") (interrater $r = .79$), and (2) the parent's expression of distress regarding these challenges (ranging from "very little distress" to "high distress") (interrater $r = .65$). The two ratings from the two eras were averaged ($M = 2.71$, $SD = .86$) to yield a score for family life stress ($\alpha = .81$).

School adjustment. During the spring of each school year, the child's teacher completed the 112 item Child Behavior Checklist – Teacher Report Form (TRF; Achenbach & Edelbrock, 1986). The TRF includes a series of ratings about school performance and a standard checklist of child behavior problems. Sample behavior problem items include "gets in many fights" and "disobedient at school." For each item, teachers note whether the statement is not true for the child (0), somewhat or sometimes true (1), or very true or often true (2). The *externalizing problems* summary score was used in the current study to index children's behavior problems in kindergarten and grade 6. This score consists of 35 items for both girls and boys.

Children's social skills in peer relations were assessed with the Teacher Checklist of Peer Relations (Coie & Dodge, 1988). This checklist contains a set of items that assess teacher judgments of children's social skillfulness on five-point scales (ranging from "very poor" to "very good") and includes items such as "understands others' feelings" and "is aware of the effects of his/her behavior on other children." The seven items comprising this scale were averaged to create a measure of *social skills in peer relations* ($\alpha = .95$ and .89 for kindergarten and grade 6, respectively).

Data on *academic performance* were drawn from teacher ratings (kindergarten) and archival school records (grade 6). The kindergarten measure was derived from the TRF and was based on teacher ratings on five-point scales of "how much the child is learning" and "how hard the child is working," compared to typical students (ranging from "much less" to "much more"), plus the average rating of the child's performance in the academic disciplines of reading, writing, and math (0 = failing, 1 = below average, 2 = average, and 3 = above average). The ratings of "learning," "working," and overall academic performance were standardized and summed ($\alpha = .89$).

The grade 6 academic performance data were collected during the spring of that year, and are based on records compiled for the most recently completed year of school (i.e., grade 5). Staff members examined each child's file and noted the grades earned in six subject areas (reading, math, language arts, spelling, social studies, and science). Conventional grade conversions were used (i.e., $A = 4$, $B = 3$, $C = 2$, $D = 1$). A composite grade-point average (GPA) was calculated for each child by averaging the grades received across all subjects ($\alpha = .93$). If grades were missing for some subject areas, the GPA is based on the number of subject areas in which grades were assigned.

Staff members also inspected the school files for achievement test scores. Because different types of tests were used, the percentile rankings for three common scales (reading, language, math) were noted. A composite achievement test score was then computed by averaging the three summary scores ($\alpha = .90$). Because the composite GPA and achievement test scores were highly correlated, $r(405) = .69$, the two scores were standardized and summed to form a single measure of academic performance. Equivalent academic data were not available for kindergarten.

Results

Interrelations among parenting, family adversity, and child adjustment

Parenting measures.   Correlations computed among the four SP measures revealed a very modest pattern of association, $rs(555–578) = .03$ to .22, indicating that mothers who were high on one aspect of SP were not especially likely to be high on the others. The correlations between the SP measures and harsh discipline were similarly modest, ranging from −.02 to −.20.

Family adversity measures.   As one would expect, SES, family stress, and single-parent status were correlated significantly ($p < .01$). Lower SES was associated with higher family stress, $r(561) = −.25$. Single-parent families experienced more stress, $r(567) = .30$, and were more likely to have been classified in the lower two Hollingshead social status classes (47%), compared to intact families (14%).

Children's school adjustment. In kindergarten, higher levels of externalizing problems were associated with lower ratings of social skillfulness, $r(570) = -.49$, and academic performance, $r(539) = -.27$; the latter two measures were significantly, positively correlated, $r(544) = .69$. Similar patterns of covariation among adjustment measures were found in grade 6: Higher levels of externalizing problems were associated with lower ratings of social skillfulness, $r(442) = -.63$, and poorer academic performance, $r(418) = -.34$. Social skillfulness was associated with better academic performance, $r(420) = -.46$.

Moderately high stabilities across years (and across raters) also were found. Correlations between kindergarten and grade 6 adjustment measures were .38 for externalizing problems, .37 for social skillfulness, and .52 for academic performance.

Relations between parenting and children's school adjustment

Correlations among the parenting measures and the school adjustment variables are presented in table 1. There are several points worth noting about these correlations. First, the overall pattern is consistent with expectation, albeit modest in magnitude: High levels of SP and low levels of HP predict better adjustment in both kindergarten and grade 6. The predictive patterns are comparatively stronger for externalizing problems and academic performance, particularly in grade 6. Second, with the exception of social skillfulness in grade 6, each outcome is predicted both by HP and by one or more SP measures. At the bivariate level, involvement is less consistently predictive of outcomes (only two of six correlations are significant at $p < .01$), whereas proactive teaching and calm discussion (as well as HP) are more consistently predictive of outcomes (five of six correlations are significant).

Child sex and ethnic differences. Separate correlations were computed for boys and girls and for European American and African American children. These correlations are not tabled, owing to space considerations, but are available from the first author. Although the overall patterns of correlations were similar to what was found for the full sample, there were two notable divergences in the predictive relations involving warmth and harsh discipline. Harsh discipline was associated with lower levels of kindergarten social skillfulness among girls,

$r(274) = -.21$, $p < .01$, than among boys, $r(292) = -.05$, *ns* (difference via z test significant at .05). Warmth, however, was associated with better grade 6 academic performance among girls, $r(220) = .26$, $p < .01$, than among boys, $r(208) = .02$, *ns*, and this difference was significant ($p < .05$). In addition, proactive teaching predicted lower levels of externalizing problems for boys, $r(290) = -.21$, but not for girls, $r(274) = -.06$.

In terms of ethnic differences, warmth correlated more consistently with grade 6 school adjustment among African American children than among European American children, whereas the opposite pattern was seen for harsh discipline. For African American children, warmth was associated with fewer externalizing problems, $r(68) = -.23$, and higher levels of social skillfulness, $r(68) = .17$ (*ps* < .05). The corresponding correlations for European American children were $-.02$ and .01 (*ns*). For European American children, harsh discipline was associated with poorer academic performance, $r(361) = -.24$, $p < .01$. The corresponding correlation for African American children was .11 (*ns*), and the difference in correlations was significant ($p < .01$).

Regression analyses: Evidence for additive effects of supportive parenting and harsh parenting?   Two sets of analyses were conducted for each type of child adjustment variable. We first examined whether measures of SP and HP additively and incrementally predicted children's adjustment in kindergarten. Child sex and ethnicity were entered on the first step. HP was entered on the second step. Measures of SP were entered (simultaneously) on the third step. Interactions among child sex/ethnicity and each of the parenting variables were entered at the fourth step. Interaction terms (multiplicative product of child sex/ethnicity and the parenting measure) were entered one at a time, as recommended by Cohen and Cohen (1993).

The analyses for kindergarten adjustment outcomes are summarized in table 2. Externalizing problems were predicted by low levels of calm discussion and proactive teaching, social skillfulness was predicted by high levels of calm discussion and low levels of harsh discipline, and academic performance was predicted by high levels of warmth and involvement and low levels of harsh discipline. The overall amount of variance accounted for in outcome was quite modest, ranging from 2% to 3%.

Table 2 Summary of regression analyses for relations between parenting measures and child adjustment in kindergarten

				Supportive parenting		
Child adjustment	*Harsh discipline*	*Warmth*	*Involvement*	*Calm discussion*	*Proactive teaching*	ΔR^2
Externalizing problems	.04	−.05	.01	−.12**	−.12**	.03**
Social skillfulness	−.10*	.04	.03	.09*	.08	.02*
Academic performance	−.13**	.09*	.10*	.03	.06	.03**

Standard partial betas after controlling for child sex and ethnicity. ΔR^2 refers to change in R^2 for supportive parenting after controlling for child sex, ethnicity, and harsh discipline.
*p < .05; **p < .01.

Two significant interactions with child sex were found, and these mirrored the bivariate correlations. Child sex interacted with proactive teaching in the prediction of externalizing problems, $R^2 = .01, p < .05$. As noted earlier, mothers' proactive teaching was negatively associated with boys' externalizing but unrelated to girls' externalizing. Child sex interacted with harsh discipline in the prediction of social skillfulness, $R^2 = .01, p < .05$. Again, as noted before, mothers' harsh discipline was negatively correlated with girls' social skillfulness but unrelated to boys' social skillfulness. No other interaction effects were significant.

In the next set of analyses, we examined the prediction of grade 6 adjustment from the parenting measures. Of particular interest was whether the SP measures, independent of HP, forecasted change in adjustment for kindergarten to grade 6. A series of regression analyses was again computed, with kindergarten adjustment entered as the first step, child sex and ethnicity entered as the second step, the parenting measures (SP and HP) entered simultaneously as the third step, and interaction terms (calculated as before) entered in the final step. The results of these analyses are summarized in table 3.

After controlling for kindergarten adjustment, child sex and ethnicity, and HP, the SP measures accounted for little variance in grade 6 externalizing problems or social skillfulness. There was a significant interaction between ethnicity and warmth for externalizing problems, $R^2 = .01, p < .02$. To evaluate this interaction, we computed separate

Table 3 Summary of regression analyses for relations between parenting measures and child adjustment in grade 6

		Supportive parenting				
Child adjustment	Harsh discipline	Warmth	Involvement	Calm discussion	Proactive teaching	ΔR^2
Externalizing problems	.11*	−.06	.02	−.02	−.06	.01
Social skillfulness	−.09*	.04	−.06	.01	.06	.01
Academic performance	−.05	.01	.09*	.13**	−.01	.03**

Standard partial betas after controlling for child sex, ethnicity, and kindergarten adjustment. ΔR^2 refers to change in R^2 for supportive parenting after controlling for child sex, ethnicity, kindergarten adjustment, and harsh discipline.
*$p < .05$; **$p < .01$.

partial correlations for the European American subsample and the African American subsample. The correlations were between warmth and grade 6 externalizing, controlling for kindergarten externalizing. Warmth was associated with a decrease in externalizing problems for African American children, partial $r(68) = -.22$, but not for European American children, partial $r(351) = -.02$.

Grade 6 academic performance was significantly related to the earlier parenting measures. An increase in level of academic performance from kindergarten to grade 6 was associated with higher levels of prekindergarten involvement and use of calm discussion. There were no significant interactions for grade 6 academic performance.

Does supportive parenting moderate or buffer the effects of family adversity?

In these analyses, we sought to determine the extent to which the presence of SP might offset the risks associated with low SES, single parenthood, and family stress. Correlational analyses revealed that, as expected, low SES, high family stress, and single parenthood were associated with poorer adjustment in both kindergarten and grade 6 (see table 4). The correlational patterns were similar for boys and girls and for European American and African American children, with the exception that SES was negatively correlated with kindergarten externalizing for European

Table 4   Correlations among family adversity measures and child adjustment in kindergarten and grade 6

Child adjustment	Family adversity measures		
	SES	Family stress	Single parenthood
Externalizing problems:			
Kindergarten	−.23	.14	.16
Grade 6	−.33 (−.24)	.17 (.12)	.22 (.16)
Social skillfulness:			
Kindergarten	.28	−.16	−.20
Grade 6	.24 (.13)	−.15 (−.10*)	−.25 (−.17)
Academic performance:			
Kindergarten	.35	−.18	−.21
Grade 6	.52 (.34)	−.22 (−.14)	−.28 (−.17)

All tabled correlations significant at p < .01, except *p < .05. Single parenthood is coded as 0 = intact family, 1 = single parent. Numbers in parentheses are partial correlations, controlling for kindergarten adjustment. Ns = 536–574 for kindergarten adjustment; 425–444 for grade 6 adjustment.

American children, $r(453) = -.27$, $p < .01$, but was unrelated to kindergarten externalizing problems among African American children, $r(96) = -.01$ (difference in correlations significant at $p < .05$).

Table 4 also shows partial correlations between the family adversity measures and the grade 6 outcomes, controlling for kindergarten adjustment. In each instance, the presence of family adversity was associated with significantly poorer grade 6 adjustment.

We next examined links between family adversity and measures of parenting. SES was associated with higher levels of warmth, $r(562) = .20$, involvement, $r(567) = .37$, and calm discussion, $r(554) = .23$, and lower levels of harsh discipline, $r(571) = -.18$ (all $ps < .01$). High family stress was associated with less involvement, $r(572) = -.14$, and calm discussion, $r(551) = -.12$, and more harsh discipline, $r(572) = .17$ (all $ps < .01$). Single parenthood was associated with lower levels of warmth, $r(574) = -.16$, involvement, $r(574) = -.12$, and calm discussion, $r(558) = -.18$ (all $ps < .01$). The correlational patterns were highly similar for boys and girls. Two correlations varied as a function of ethnicity. SES was associated with greater levels of involvement among European

Americans, $r(459) = .37$, $p < .01$, but not among African Americans, $r(93) = .05$, and single parenthood was associated with less warmth among African Americans, $r(94) = -.32$, $p < .05$, but not among European Americans, $r(468) = -.06$ (differences between correlations significant at $p < .05$).

The main analyses were concerned with the interaction of SP and family adversity in the prediction of changes in adjustment from kindergarten to grade 6. A global SP score was used in these analyses because of the general prediction that the presence of (relatively) high levels of SP would offset some of the risks associated with family adversity, and because cumulative protective factors appear to more consistently moderate the impact of risk than individual factors considered separately (McCord, 1996). The global SP measure was created by standardizing and summing the individual SP measures (warmth, involvement, calm discussion, proactive teaching). However, because the individual SP measures do not form a unitary construct – the average r between measures was only .14 – it also was of interest to examine which SP measures might be responsible for any obtained effects. Therefore, follow-up analyses were conducted when the interaction between global SP and family adversity was significant. Because collapsing across low-correlated measures may mask significant relations between individual measures and outcomes, we also note any instances where individual SP measures showed effects that were different from that shown by the global SP measure.

A series of regressions was computed for each grade 6 adjustment measure. In each analysis, variables were entered in the following order: child sex and ethnicity (as a set), kindergarten adjustment, family adversity (either SES, family stress, or single-parent status) and global SP (as a set), the interaction of family adversity and global SP, and higher-order interactions between family adversity, global SP, and child sex. (It was not possible to examine higher-order interactions involving ethnicity because of very small cell sizes.) To minimize redundancy with findings discussed earlier, only the results of steps involving interaction terms will be described.

Externalizing behavior problems in grade 6 were predicted by the interaction of SES and global SP, $R^2 = .02$, $p < .001$, even after controlling for child sex and ethnicity, kindergarten adjustment, and the main effects of SES and SP. No higher-order interactions involving child sex were significant. To interpret the interaction effect, we created a dichotomous SES risk score (the lowest two Hollingshead classes versus the upper three classes) and a dichotomous SP score (splitting the sample at the median on global SP) and computed an analysis of covariance in which global SP (low versus high) and SES risk (low versus high) were factors, and kindergarten externalizing was the covariate. This interaction was significant, $F(1, 405) = 4.18, p < .05$. Inspection of the adjusted means indicated that, given the presence of SES risk, grade 6 externalizing scores were higher when global SP was low ($M = 13.9, n = 74$) than when global SP was high ($M = 8.4, n = 26$). When SES risk was absent, externalizing scores were similar for low and high SP groups ($Ms = 5.4$ and 5.0, $ns = 136$ and 174, respectively). These findings are consistent with the premise that the presence of high amounts of SP buffers the effect of SES on later behavioral adjustment.

Examination of individual SP measures showed that three measures (warmth, calm discussion, and proactive teaching) interacted significantly with SES in the prediction of grade 6 externalizing problems. Inspection of means revealed patterns similar to that described above for the global measure.

Externalizing problems in grade 6 also were predicted by the interaction of single-parent status and global SP, $R^2 = .01, p < .05$. Inspection of the means (adjusted for kindergarten adjustment) showed that the grade 6 externalizing scores of children in single-parent families were considerably higher when SP was low ($M = 13.6, n = 65$) than when SP was high ($M = 7.2, n = 38$). In contrast, the grade 6 externalizing scores of children in intact families were similar for low and high groups ($Ms = 6.1$ and 5.2, $ns = 147$ and 166, respectively). Examination of individual SP measures showed that only one measure – warmth – interacted significantly with single-parent status in the prediction of grade 6 externalizing, with mean scores following the same general pattern as the global SP measure.

The interaction of global SP and family stress was not significant for externalizing problems. However, the individual SP measure of proactive teaching did interact significantly with stress in the prediction of grade 6 externalizing, $R^2 = .01, p < .05$. This effect was examined further by dichotomizing proactive teaching (median split) and computing a partial correlation (controlling for kindergarten adjustment) between stress and grade 6 externalizing for the low and high groups. Stress correlated somewhat more strongly with externalizing in the low proactive teaching group, $r(228) = .17$, than in the high proactive teaching group, $r(193) = .11$.

There were no higher-order interactions involving marital status, SP, and child sex for grade 6 externalizing problems. Also, there were no significant interactions between SP and family stress (including higher-order interactions) for children's externalizing problems.

Social skillfulness in grade 6 was predicted by a three-way interaction among single-parent status, global SP, and child sex, $R^2 = .01$, $p = .05$. Inspection of adjusted means revealed a pattern suggesting that high levels of SP buffered the effects of single-parent status more strongly for boys than for girls. The social skillfulness scores of boys from single-parent, high-SP families ($M = 3.1$, $n = 14$) did not differ significantly (at $p < .05$ via one-way ANOVA) from that of boys in high- or low-SP intact families ($Ms = 3.4$ and 3.6, $ns = 72$ and 89, respectively). As might be expected, boys in low-SP single-parent families had the lowest grade 6 social skillfulness scores ($M = 2.8$, $n = 30$). However, the social skillfulness scores of girls from single-parent, high-SP families ($M = 3.2$) were significantly lower than those of girls in high- or low-SP intact families ($Ms = 4.0$ and 4.0, $ns = 79$ and 75, respectively). Girls in the low-SP intact family group had intermediate scores ($M = 3.5$, $n = 35$). Taken together, these results suggest that high levels of SP offset the risks associated with single-parent status for boys (boys in this group did not differ from boys from intact families) but not for girls (girls in this group had lower social skillfulness scores than girls from intact families).

Examination of individual SP measures indicated that only involvement significantly interacted with single-parent status and child sex, $R^2 = .02$, $p < .01$. Inspection of means revealed a pattern similar to that found with the global SP score. One individual SP measure also demonstrated an effect that was not mirrored in the global SP analysis: Warmth interacted with SES in the prediction of grade 6 social skillfulness, $R^2 = .01$, $p < .05$. To further examine this interaction, we split the sample at the median and computed the partial correlation (controlling for kindergarten social skillfulness) between SES and grade 6 social skillfulness. The resulting partial correlation between SES and social skillfulness in the low-warmth group was .16; the partial correlation in the high-warmth group was .07. No other effects were significant for social skillfulness. Academic performance in grade 6 was not predicted by the interaction of SP with any family adversity measure.

Discussion

Our overarching goal in this study was to clarify the role of supportive parenting in the socialization process. The measures of SP that were used – proactive teaching, calm discussion in disciplinary encounters, warmth, and interest and involvement in the child's peer activities – were derived from assessments conducted before children entered kindergarten and were found to predict children's behavioral, social, and academic adjustment in both kindergarten and grade 6. Each kindergarten adjustment outcome was associated with multiple SP measures, even after the effects of harsh discipline had been controlled. Multiple SP measures also predicted changes in children's academic performance from kindergarten to grade 6, again after controlling for HP. These predictive relations were of a modest magnitude, but they do suggest that early positive and supportive parenting qualities may play a distinct role in promoting children's school adjustment.

SP also was found to buffer some of the developmental risks associated with early family adversity. SP was most strongly related to child adjustment in grade 6 for those children who had been reared in single-parent and/or low-SES families in their early years. This suggests that SP may serve as a protective factor against the risks associated with certain types of family adversity.

Evidence of differentiated predictions?

Some researchers have collapsed across various indicators of SP, creating summary scores that reflect overall positivity (e.g., Gest et al., 1993; Masten et al., 1988; Patterson et al., 1989). Other researchers have created separate indicators of SP (Grolnick & Slowiaczek, 1994; Patterson et al., 1992). Implied in the first approach is the idea that "all good things go together" and that parents who are relatively supportive in one domain are likely to be supportive in others. Implied in the second approach is the idea that parents may be high in some aspects of SP but not high in others. In the current study, the SP measures were for the most part unrelated to one another, even though each was related to one or more child outcomes. Why might the domains of SP as we have assessed them be independent? Perhaps, as Parke (1992) has described, the variety of possible beneficial socialization practices available to parents is analogous to a "cafeteria model," in which parents pick and choose in variously sized portions. The ingredients may to some extent be interchangeable, in terms of their effects, with no one ingredient being any more important than the others, so long as at least one of the key ingredients is present.

The SP constructs selected for study were those that were considered to have special significance for promoting children's successful adaptation during the school-age years. In no sense, however, would we argue that we have assessed the full array of possible SP variables. Although we think it interesting that some of the SP measures were more highly related to some types of child outcome than to others, we are hesitant to make too much out of the individual predictor-outcome associations because they were not specified a priori and they were not explicitly theory-driven. Still, the obtained relations seem sensible and generally are consistent with prior literature, and we briefly discuss them here to provide an interpretative framework.

Children's externalizing problems (i.e., their absence) and social skillfulness with peers in kindergarten were best predicted by calm discussion and proactive teaching. Parents who rely on calm discussion and other inductive approaches in disciplinary encounters (or who report that they do so) may inculcate in their children a sense of respect for contrasting perspectives and a belief that disputes can be resolved through nonaversive means (Hart et al., 1992). Proactive teaching has been shown to forecast both current and future adjustment (Pettit & Bates, 1989; Pettit et al., 1993). In the current study, parents who endorsed a preventive, situation-specific approach to teaching their children social skills had children with fewer behavior problems. Insofar as mothers' endorsement of the preventive approach actually reflected their tutoring and instruction in how to avoid and resolve conflicts with peers, these children should be expected to show better behavioral adjustment.

Children's academic performance in kindergarten was predicted by a combination of warmth and involvement, and children's academic performance in grade 6 was predicted by a combination of calm discussion and involvement. Warmth may have special significance for children's developing school capabilities because it provides a foundation on which children develop positive views of themselves and their competence (Patterson et al., 1989). As noted above, calm discussion may promote the development of effective conflict resolution behaviors, which may lead to better classroom deportment and, correspondingly, more attention to, and interest in, school-relevant activities.

The finding that mothers' involvement and interest in the child's social contacts and activities predicted kindergarten and grade 6 academic performance must be interpreted with caution, owing to the modest level of interrater reliability obtained for the involvement measure. Subsequent discussions with interviewers indicated that they sometimes had difficulty in deciding on an appropriate rating, in part because they were required not only to make a judgment about a mother's awareness and concern about her child's peer activities, but also about the mother's tendency to react to such concerns by "structuring" the child's experience. As Mize, Pettit, and Brown (1995) have argued, mothers may have a variety of different reasons for becoming involved in their children's peer activities (e.g., concerns about their children's social skills and maturity; a belief that social skills are important and teachable). The fact that the rating of maternal involvement in the present study did not take account of parents' apparent motives may have contributed to differences in raters' judgments about mothers' levels of interest and involvement. With these limitations in mind, we tentatively speculate that mothers' general involvement and interest in their children's social lives in early childhood sets the stage for later academic success because a mother who is highly involved has more opportunities for incidental teaching of both socially and academically relevant content, and because a mother who is highly involved is more likely to carefully monitor and supervise her child's academic progress.

Although these findings are consistent in showing that measures of SP account for variance in child outcomes not attributable to HP, the findings cannot be used to contrast the relative importance of supportiveness versus harshness in predicting outcomes (as in Pettit & Bates, 1989, and Russell & Russell, 1996), because harsh parenting was underspecified in this study relative to supportiveness. That is, only one aspect of harshness was assessed (harsh, restrictive discipline), and only two rating items contributed to its measurement. However, it should be noted that an ample literature suggests that restrictive, power-assertive disciplinary practices represent the *sine qua non* of harsh parenting, and in the present study restrictive discipline was significantly correlated with two of the three adjustment outcomes in kindergarten, and all three adjustment outcomes in grade 6. Although the present study by no means provides an exhaustive test of the supportive versus harsh parenting issue, it did allow for a reasonably fair appraisal of the additive, incremental predictiveness of SP. Findings of incremental prediction do not, of course, rule out the possibility of an interaction between SP and HP in the prediction of child outcomes. As Baumrind (1967) and others have so amply demonstrated, the functional significance of a parenting behavior can hinge on how it is combined with other parenting behaviors. There is, in fact, evidence that harsh discipline is associated with negative outcomes for children in low-warmth families but not for children in high-warmth families (Deater-Deckard & Dodge, in press).

Does supportive parenting buffer children from the negative impact of family adversity?

In the resilience literature (e.g., Gest et al., 1993; Masten et al., 1988), when one kind of experience or event moderates the negative impact of risk or adversity, that experience is described as a buffer or protective factor. Our second major objective in the present study was to test the hypothesis that SP would moderate relations between family adversity and child adjustment. This hypothesis received support in that the presence of high levels of overall SP was associated with significantly improved adjustment from kindergarten to grade 6 for children experiencing early family adversity. These effects were seen for both externalizing problems and social skillfulness, although the latter was qualified by child sex (discussed below). Thus, our findings are consistent with a parent-effectiveness buffering hypothesis, which postulates that the adverse effects of family risk should be diminished when SP is present (Gest et al., 1993; Patterson et al., 1989). In effect, this may mean that the diminishment in parenting effectiveness often seen in families experiencing adversity and hardship (e.g., Conger et al., 1992) has not occurred in high-SP families, owing perhaps to favorable parenting attributes (e.g., resourcefulness), child attributes (e.g., nondemanding temperament), or external social supports. It is not clear whether the presence of SP serves to directly counter the risks associated with SES and single-parent status or whether the presence of SP is a marker for a generally salutary family environment.

Differences in predictive patterns as a function of child sex and ethnicity

In this study, we also were interested in whether there were differences in parenting-outcome linkages for boys and girls, and for African American and European American children. Although the overall patterns of findings were similar across these groups, there were some notable differences as well. We do not wish to make too much of these differences because we did not generate specific sex- or ethnicity-based hypotheses. However, the differences do seem sensible and fit with some emerging literature. Warmth, in particular, emerged as a variable showing particular sensitivity to child sex and ethnicity. That is, warmth predicted better adjustment (higher academic performance) for girls than for boys, and better adjustment (lower externalizing scores and higher social skillfulness scores) for African American children than for European American children. It may be that mothers' positive engagement (warmth) is especially important for girls' developing competencies, a hypothesis that has received some support in the domain of peer relations (Mize & Pettit, 1997). It also may be the case that warmth occupies a more central position in African American socialization than in European American socialization (whereas the opposite may be true for harsh discipline; see Deater-Deckard & Dodge, in press), perhaps because of differences in how the display of warmth (and harsh discipline) is interpreted by children and parents.

There also were indications of a sex difference in the protective functions of SP. For girls, the presence of high amounts of SP did not offset the negative impact of single-parent status on later social skillfulness, whereas for boys high amounts of SP did offset the risk associated with single-parent status. It may be that girls' developing social competence is especially sensitive to variations in their mothers' marital status, even to the extent that mothers' SP cannot help the girls overcome the disadvantage.

Sex and ethnic differences also were found in the links between parenting and family adversity. For example, in European American families, lower SES was associated with less maternal involvement. In African American families, SES and involvement were unrelated. On the other hand, in African American families, single-parent status was associated with less warmth, but warmth and single-parent status were unrelated in European American families. Although these relations may reflect differing social ecologies (e.g., that single-parent European American mothers are less socioeconomically disadvantaged than single-parent African American mothers, or that lower-SES African American mothers, compared to lower-SES European American mothers, have more extended and supportive family networks), in the absence of theory – and corroborating data – it is premature to assign a great amount of developmental significance to these findings.

Limitations

There are several limitations to this study that merit consideration. Our parenting assessments were based on information gleaned during a single home visit. Three of the four SP measures, as well as the HP measure, were derived from interviewers' ratings or parents' ratings on questionnaires. We do, however, have evidence that our SP and HP measures converge in meaningful ways with observational indexes of parenting positivity and negativity taken on a subset of the participants (see Pettit et al., 1996). Still, a wider range of parenting measures, utilizing more varied assessment techniques (as in Patterson et al., 1992), clearly is desirable and would strengthen confidence in the meaning of SP-relevant constructs.

Some of the parenting scores used in the present investigation necessitated a rescaling so as insure that the scale score was expressed on a continuum of supportiveness (or harshness). This had the desirable effect of allowing for a cleaner comparison of measures of SP and HP, but it had the undesirable effect of reducing the range of scores. This reduction in range of scores may have attenuated the correlations among these measures and child adjustment outcomes. It is a common practice in research on parenting to create scores that represent positive and supportive aspects of parenting on the high end, and negative aspects of parenting on the low end. For example, Dumka and Roosa (1993) constructed a measure to represent "positive mother–child relationship" in which acceptance and rejection (reverse scored) were combined. Such approaches are problematic when the research goal is to contrast parenting dimensions or to seek to clarify the processes by which parenting attributes exert an impact on child outcomes (Darling & Steinberg, 1993). Given the centrality of positive and supportive parenting to many current formulations of effective socialization (e.g.,

Rothbaum & Weisz, 1994), it is important for researchers to be clear in specifying the constituents of their constructs and labeling the constructs in a manner that is consistent with their measurement.

The current study also is limited in the range of outcomes considered. It would have been desirable to have assessed a wider array of child adaptations, both positive and negative. For instance, it may be that certain attributes of supportive parenting play important roles in children's development of empathy, prosocial behavior, and emotional competence. On the negative side, the absence of supportive parenting also may be related to the development of internalizing problems, such as anxiety and depression.

It is apparent that the effect sizes associated with supportive parenting are uniformly modest in magnitude, especially with respect to the prediction of grade 6 outcomes. The significant interaction effects (i.e., those involving child sex/ethnicity in interaction with SP) account for as little as 1% of the variance in grade 6 outcomes. Are such effects important? It has been noted that interaction effects in correlational field research are difficult to detect, and that effect sizes as small as those reported here may have practical and theoretical significance (McClelland & Judd, 1993). Our multivariate tests were fairly conservative in that we controlled for prior adjustment and child sex and ethnicity and extended our predictions over a seven-year period. Nonetheless, in the absence of replication, and given the fact that no specific a priori predictions were made regarding the differing SP measures, it is most appropriate to interpret these findings in a cautious and tentative manner.

This same caution extends to the more complex interaction effects involving child sex and ethnicity. Higher-order effects were not common here, but the small cell sizes for some analyses likely made the detection of such effects difficult. We were limited especially in our examination of ethnic differences in SP as a moderator of adversity, because of uneven ethnic distributions in single-parent and low-SES families. Larger samples and perhaps some oversampling in selected groups would be necessary to adequately address the issue of ethnic similarities and differences in the moderating impact of SP.

It will be important in future research to assess supportive parenting both cross-sectionally and longitudinally. In the absence of longitudinal data on parenting, it is impossible to know whether the link between parenting at a single time and adjustment at a later time is due to concurrent parenting practices or something unique and formative in early parenting. Pettit and Bates (1989), for example, found that early (assessed at six and 13 months) and later (assessed at four years) forms of positive involvement were incrementally predictive of pre-schoolers' behavioral adjustment. And, even though the longitudinal design affords certain advantages with respect to disentangling parent and child effects, one cannot conclude from correlational data that variations in parenting contribute causally to children's adjustment. It remains an open possibility that children's emerging competencies "pull" more positive behaviors from parents. It also is possible that shared genetic propensities to engage in constructive and supportive behavior account for the link between SP and adaptive child outcomes.

In summary, this study joins with other recent studies (e.g., Cowan et al., 1994) in providing evidence that supportive parenting qualities assessed in early childhood forecast children's successful adaptation across the elementary school years. These results suggest that SP is linked with child outcomes both directly (i.e., as additive main effects) and indirectly (by moderating the effects of adversity).

References

Achenbach, T. M., & Edelbrock, C. S. (1986). *Manual for the Teacher's Report Form and Teacher Version of the Child Behavior Profile*. Burlington: University of Vermont.

Bank, L., Forgatch, M. S., Patterson, G. R., & Fetrow, R. A. (1993). Parenting practices of single mothers: Mediators of negative contextual factors. *Journal of Marriage and the Family, 55*, 371–384.

Baumrind, D. (1967). Child care practices anteceding three patterns of preschool behavior. *Genetic Psychology Monographs, 75*, 43–88.

Baumrind, D. (1989). Rearing competent children. In W. Damon (Ed.), *Child development today and tomorrow* (pp. 349–378). San Francisco: Jossey-Bass.

Biringen, Z., & Robinson, J. (1991). Emotional availability in mother–child interactions: A reconceptualization for research. *American Journal of Orthopsychiatry, 61*, 258–271.

Bronfenbrenner, U., & Crouter, A. C. (1983). The evolution of environmental models in developmental research. In W. Kessen (Ed.), P. H. Mussen (Series Ed.), *Handbook of child psychology: Vol. 1. History, theory, and methods* (pp. 357–414). New York: Wiley.

Caldwell, B., & Bradley, R. (1984). *HOME Observation for Measurement of the Environment.* Little Rock, AR: Center for Child Development and Education.

Cohen, J., & Cohen, P. (1993). *Applied multiple regression/correlation analysis for the behavioral sciences* (2d ed.). Hillsdale, NJ: Erlbaum.

Coie, J. D., & Dodge, K. A. (1988). Multiple sources of data on social behavior and social status in the school: A cross-age comparison. *Child Development, 59,* 815–829.

Conger, R. D., Conger, K. J., Elder, G. H., Lorenz, F. O., Simons, R. L., & Whitbeck, L. B. (1992). A family process model of economic hardship and adjustment in early adolescent boys. *Child Development, 62,* 525–541.

Cowan, P. A., Cowan, C. P., Schulz, M., & Heming, G. (1994). Prebirth to preschool factors in children's adaptation to kindergarten. In R. D. Parke & S. G. Kellam (Eds.), *Exploring family relationships with other social contexts* (pp. 75–114). Hillsdale, NJ: Erlbaum.

Darling, N., & Steinberg, L. (1993). Parenting style as context: An integrative model. *Psychological Bulletin, 113,* 487–496.

Deater-Deckard, K., & Dodge, K. A. (in press). Externalizing behavior problems and discipline revisited: Nonlinear effects and variations by culture, context, and gender. *Psychological Inquiry.*

Deater-Deckard, K., Dodge, K. A., Bates, J. E., & Pettit, G. S. (1996). Physical discipline among African American and European American mothers: Links to children's externalizing behaviors. *Developmental Psychology, 32,* 1065–1072.

Denham, S. A., Renwick, S. M., & Holt, R. W. (1991). Working and playing together: Prediction of preschool social-emotional competence from mother–child interaction. *Child Development, 62,* 242–249.

Dodge, K. A., Pettit, G. S., & Bates, J. E. (1994). Socialization mediators of the relation between socioeconomic status and child conduct problems. *Child Development, 65,* 649–665.

Dumka, L. E., & Roosa, M. W. (1993). Factors mediating problem drinking and mothers' personal adjustment. *Journal of Family Psychology, 7,* 333–343.

Gest, S. D., Neeman, J., Hubbard, J. J., Masten, A. S., & Tellegen, A. (1993). Parenting quality, adversity, and conduct problems in adolescence: Testing process-oriented models of resilience. *Development and Psychopathology, 5,* 663–682.

Gottman, J. M., Katz, L. F., & Hooven, C. (1996). Parental meta-emotion philosophy and the emotional life of families: Theoretical models and preliminary data. *Journal of Family Psychology, 10,* 243–268.

Grolnick, W. S., & Slowiaczek, M. L. (1994). Parents' involvement in children's schooling: A multidimensional conceptualization and motivational model. *Child Development, 65,* 237–252.

Hart, C. H., DeWolf, M., Wozniak, P., & Burts, D. C. (1992). Maternal and paternal disciplinary styles: Relations with preschoolers' playground behavioral orientations and peer status. *Child Development, 63,* 879–892.

Hetherington, E. M., & Martin, B. (1986). Family factors and psychopathology in children. In H. Quay & J. Werry (Eds.), *Psychopathological disorders of childhood* (3d ed., pp. 332–390). New York: Wiley.

Holden, G. W. (1985). How parents create a social environment via proactive behavior. In T. Garling & J. Valsinger (Eds.), *Children within environments* (pp. 193–215). New York: Plenum.

Hollingshead, A. A. (1979). Four Factor Index of Social Status. Unpublished manuscript, Yale University, New Haven, CT.

Kochanska, G. (1993). Toward a synthesis of parental socialization and child temperament in early development of conscience. *Child Development, 64,* 325–347.

Ladd, G. W., Profilet, S., & Hart, C. (1992). Parents' management of children's peer relations: Facilitating and supervising children's activities in the peer culture. In R. D. Parke & G. W. Ladd (Eds.), *Family–peer relationships: Modes of linkage* (pp. 215–253). Hillsdale, NJ: Erlbaum.

Lamborn, S. D., Dornbush, S. M., & Steinberg, L. (1996). Ethnicity and community context as moderators of the relations between family decision making and adolescent adjustment. *Child Development, 67,* 283–301.

Maccoby, E. E., & Martin, J. A. (1983). Socialization in the context of the family: Parent–child interaction. In E. M. Hetherington (Ed.), P. H. Mussen (Series Ed.), *Handbook of child psychology: Vol. 4. Socialization, personality, and social development* (pp. 1–101). New York: Wiley.

Masten, A. S., Garmezy, N., Tellegen, A., Pellegrini, D. S., Larkin, K., & Larsen, A. (1988). Competence and stress in school children: The moderating effects of individual and family qualities. *Journal of Child Psychology and Psychiatry, 29,* 745–764.

McClelland, G. H., & Judd, C. M. (1993). Statistical difficulties of detecting interactions and moderator effects. *Psychological Bulletin, 114,* 376–390.

McCord, J. (1996). Family as a crucible for violence: Comment on Gorman-Smith et al. (1996). *Journal of Family Psychology, 10,* 147–152.

Mize, J., & Pettit, G. S. (1997). Mothers' social coaching, mother–child relationship style, and children's peer competence: Is the medium the message? *Child Development, 68,* 291–311.

Mize, J., Pettit, G. S., & Brown, E. G. (1995). Mothers' supervision of their children's peer play: Relations with beliefs, perception, and knowledge. *Developmental Psychology, 31,* 311–321.

Parke, R. D. (1992). Epilogue: Remaining issues and future trends in the study of family–peer relationships. In R. D. Parke & G. W. Ladd (Eds.), *Family–peer relationships: Modes of linkage* (pp. 425–438). Hillsdale, NJ: Erlbaum.

Parker, J. G., & Asher, S. R. (1987). Peer relations and later personal adjustment: Are low-accepted children at risk? *Psychological Bulletin, 102,* 357–389.

Patterson, C. J., Cohn, D. A., & Kao, B. T. (1989). Maternal warmth as a protective factor against risks associated with peer rejection among children. *Development and Psychopathology, 1,* 21–38.

Patterson, G. R., Reid, J. B., & Dishion, T. J. (1992). *Antisocial boys.* Eugene, OR: Castalia.

Pettit, G. S., & Bates, J. E. (1989). Family interaction patterns and children's behavior problems from infancy to 4 years. *Developmental Psychology, 25,* 413–420.

Pettit, G. S., Bates, J. E., & Dodge, K. A. (1993). Family interaction patterns and children's conduct problems at home and school: A longitudinal perspective. *School Psychology Review, 22,* 403–420.

Pettit, G. S., Clawson, M., Bates, J. E., & Dodge, K. A. (1996). Stability and change in peer-rejected status: The role of child behavior, parenting, and family ecology. *Merrill-Palmer Quarterly, 42,* 267–294.

Pettit, G. S., Dodge, K. A., & Brown, M. (1988). Early family experience, social problem solving patterns, and children's social competence. *Child Development, 59,* 815–829.

Pettit, G. S., & Mize, J. (1993). Substance and style: Understanding the ways in which parents teach children about social relationships. In S. Duck (Ed.), *Understanding relationship processes: Vol. 2. Learning about relationships* (pp. 118–151). Newbury Park, CA: Sage.

Rothbaum, F., & Weisz, J. R. (1994). Parental caregiving and child externalizing behavior in nonclinical samples: A metaanalysis. *Psychological Bulletin, 116,* 55–74.

Rowe, D. C., Vazsonyi, A. T., & Flannery, D. J. (1994). No more than skin deep: Ethnic and racial similarity in developmental process. *Psychological Review, 101,* 396–413.

Russell, A., & Russell, G. (1996). Positive parenting and boys' and girls' misbehavior during a home observation. *International Journal of Behavioral Development, 19,* 291–307.

Straus, M. A. (1987). Measuring physical and emotional abuse of children with the Conflict Tactics Scale. Unpublished manuscript, Family Research Laboratory, University of New Hampshire, Durham.

THREE

Friendships

Introduction

Friendships are reciprocal, voluntary relationships based on affection. They are essential to the acquisition of skills and competencies in a child's social, emotional, and cognitive development. Children who experience difficulties with their peers are at risk for long-term negative consequences, such as dropping out of school and engaging in antisocial behavior (Parker & Asher, 1987).

Friendships vary across the developmental periods with respect to the definition of a friend, the behaviors that occur within friendships, the quality of friendships, and the number of friends. Children's conceptions of friendship change from being concrete to becoming more abstract with age. These age-related changes are reflected in children's behavior with their friends. With age, there is an increased stability in children's friendships, more reciprocal altruism, and more intimate personal knowledge. Finally, with increasing age, children move from primarily dyadic friendships to belonging to a peer network and peer cliques.

Hartup's article addresses three developmental issues regarding friendships: the significance of having friends; who the friends are; and the quality of friendships. He highlights the significance of having friends: children who have friendships are more socially competent than children who do not. However, it also is important to consider who the friends are. Despite the old saying that "opposites attract," the reality is that we tend to make friends with individuals who are similar to ourselves. This attraction to others who are similar can be both positive and negative. For example, if a child hangs around with prosocial children who have well-developed social skills, their peer group can provide positive role models. For a minority of children, however, their peer group may be comprised of children who have similar behavior problems. Aggressive children seek out and associate with children who will accept them and who are like themselves, in terms of behavior, values, and goals (Hymel, Wagner & Butler, 1990). Within this social group, they have little opportunity for positive peer interactions, and these are presumed to play an important role in the development of cognitive and social skills. Rather, the peer groups of aggressive children provide a rich source of positive reinforcement for antisocial behaviour. Thus, who your friends are can play an important role in development.

A final issue addressed in Hartup's article relates to the quality of friendships. Some friendships are secure and plain-sailing, while others are filled with disagreement and contention. Children and adolescents who perceive that their friendships are supportive are more likely to be popular, socially competent higher achievers, and exhibit fewer behavior problems than those with less supportive friendships (Cauce, 1986).

References

Cauce, A. M. (1986). Social networks and social competence: Exploring the effects of early adolescent friendships. *American Journal of Community Psychology, 8*, 607–28.

Hymel, S., Wagner, E., & Butler, L. J. (1990). Reputational bias: View from the peer group. In S. R. Asher & J. D. Coie (eds), *Peer rejection childhood*. New York: Cambridge University Press.

Parker, J. G., & Asher, S. R. (1987). Peer relationships and later personal adjustment: Are low accepted children at risk? *Psychological Bulletin, 102*, 357–89.

The Company They Keep: Friendships and Their Developmental Significance

Willard W. Hartup

On February 16, 1995, in the small Minnesota town of Delano, a 14-year-old boy and his best friend ambushed and killed his mother as she returned home. The circumstances surrounding this event were described in the next edition of the *Minneapolis Star Tribune* (February 18, 1995): The boy had "several learning disabilities – including attention deficit disorder." He had been "difficult" for a long time and, within the last year, had gotten in trouble with a step-brother by wrecking a car and carrying a gun to a movie theater. The mother was described as having a wonderful relationship with her daughter but having "difficulties" with her son. The family dwelling contained guns.

Against these child, family, and ecological conditions is a significant social history: The boy was ". . . a lonely and unliked kid who was the frequent victim of schoolmates' taunts, jeers, and assaults. He had trouble with school work and trouble with other kids. . . . He was often teased on the bus and at school because of his appearance and abilities. . . . He got teased bad. Every day, he got teased. He'd get pushed around. But he couldn't really help himself. He was kind of skinny. . . . He didn't really have that many friends."

The boy actually had two good friends: One appears to have had things relatively well put together. But with this friend, the subject ". . . passed [a] gun safety course for hunting; they took the class together." The second friend (with whom the murder was committed) was a troublesome child. These two boys described themselves as the "best of friends," and spent much time together. The boys have admitted to planning the ambush (one saying they had planned it for weeks, the other for a few hours). They were armed and waiting when the mother arrived home from work. One conclusion seems relatively certain: this murder was an unlikely event until these two antisocial friends reached consensus about doing it.

An important message emerges from this incident: Child characteristics, intersecting with family relationships and social setting, cycle through peer relations in two ways to affect developmental outcome: (*a*) through acceptance and rejection by other children in the aggregate; and (*b*) through dyadic relationships, especially with friends. Considerable evidence now tells us that "being liked" by other children (an aggregate condition) supports good developmental outcome; conversely, "being disliked" (another aggregate condition) is a risk factor (Parker & Asher, 1987). But the evidence concerning friendships and their developmental significance is weak – mainly because these relationships have not been studied extensively enough or with sufficient differentiation.

On the too-rare occasions in which friendships are taken into account developmentally – either in diagnosis or research – children are differentiated merely according to whether or not they have friends. This emphasis on having friends is based on two assumptions: First, making and keeping friends requires good reality-testing and social skills; "having friends" is thus a proxy for "being socially skilled." Second, friendships are believed to be developmental wellsprings in the sense that children must suspend egoism, embrace egalitarian attitudes, and deal with conflict effectively in order to maintain them (Sullivan, 1953). On two counts, then, having friends is thought to bode well for the future.

Striking differences exist, however, among these relationships – both from child to child and companion to companion. First, enormous variation occurs in who the child's friends are: Some companions are outgoing and rarely get into trouble; others are antisocial; still others are good children but socially clumsy. These choices would seem rather obviously to contribute to socialization – not only by affecting reputations (as the adage admonishes) but through what transpires between the children. Knowing that a teenager has friends tells us one thing, but the identity of his or her friends tells us something else.

Second, friendships differ from one another qualitatively, that is, in their *content* or normative foundations (e.g., whether or not the two children engage in antisocial behavior), their *constructiveness* (e.g., whether conflict resolution commonly involves negotiation or whether it involves power assertion), their *closeness* (e.g., whether or not the children spend much time together and engage in many different activities), their *symmetry* (e.g., whether social power is vested more or less equally or more or less unequally in the two children), and their *affective substrates* (e.g., whether the relationship is supportive and secure or whether it is nonsupportive and conflict ridden). Qualitative differences in these relationships may have developmental implications in the same way that qualitative variations in adult – child relationships do (Ainsworth, Blehar, Waters, & Wall, 1978).

This essay begins, then, with the argument that one cannot describe friendships and their developmental significance without distinguishing between *having friends, the identity of the child's friends* (e.g., personality characteristics of the child's friends), and *friendship quality*. In the sections that follow, these relationship dimensions are examined separately and in turn. Three conclusions emerge: First, having friends is a normatively significant condition during childhood and adolescence. Second, friendships carry both developmental advantages and disadvantages so that a romanticized view of these relationships distorts them and what they may contribute to developmental outcome. Third, the identity of the child's friends and friendship quality may be more closely tied to individual differences than merely whether or not the child has friends.

Having Friends

Measurement issues

Children's friends can be identified in four main ways: (*a*) by asking the children, their mothers, or their teachers to name the child's friends and determining whether these choices are reciprocated; (*b*) by asking children to assess their liking for one another; (*c*) by observing the extent to which children seek and maintain proximity with one another; and (*d*) by measuring reciprocities and cóordinations in their social interaction. Concordances among various indicators turn out to be substantial, but method variance is also considerable; the "insiders" (the children themselves) do not always agree with the "outsiders" (teachers) or the observational record (Hartup, 1992; Howes, 1989).

Some variation among measures derives from the fact that social attraction is difficult for outsiders to know about. Method variance also derives from special difficulties connected with self-reports: First, children without friends almost always can name "friends" when asked to do so (Furman, in press). Second, friendship frequently seems to investigators to be a dichotomous condition (friend vs. nonfriend), whereas variation is more continuous (best friend/good friend/occasional friend/not friend). Third, whether these categories form a Guttman scale has not been determined, although researchers sometimes assume that they do (see Doyle, Markiewicz, & Hardy, 1994). Fourth, the status of so-called unilateral or unreciprocated friendship choice is unclear. Sometimes, when children's choices are not reciprocated, social interaction differs from when friendship choices are mutual; in other respects, the social exchange does not. Unilateral friends, for example, use tactics during disagreements with one another that are different from the ones used by mutual friends but similar to those used by nonfriends (e.g., standing firm). Simultaneously, conflict *outcomes* among unilateral friends (e.g., whether interaction continues) are more similar to those characterizing mutual friends than those characterizing nonfriends (Hartup, Laursen, Stewart, & Eastenson, 1988).

Developmental significance

The developmental significance of having friends (apart from the identity of the child's friends or the quality of these relationships) has been examined in three main ways: (*a*) comparing the social interaction that occurs between friends and between nonfriends; (*b*) comparing children who have friends with those who don't; and (*c*) examining the extent to which having friends moderates behavioral outcomes across certain normative transitions.

Behavior with friends and nonfriends. Behaviors differentiating friends from nonfriends have been specified in more than 80 studies (Newcomb & Bagwell, 1995); four are cited here. In the first of these (Newcomb & Brady, 1982), school-aged children were asked to explore a "creativity box" with either a friend or a classmate who was not a friend. More extensive exploration was observed among the children with their friends; conversation was more vigorous and mutually oriented; the emotional exchange was more positive. Most important, when tested individually, the children who explored the box with a friend remembered more about it afterward.

Second, Azmitia and Montgomery (1993) examined problem solving among 11-year-olds (mainly their dialogues) working on "isolation of variables" problems either with friends or acquaintances (the children were required to deduce which pizza ingredients caused certain characters in a series of stories to get sick and die). Friends spontaneously justified their suggestions more frequently than acquaintances, elaborated on their partners' proposals, engaged in a greater percentage of conflicts during their conversations, and more often checked results. Most important, the children working with friends did better than children working with nonfriends – on the most difficult versions of the task only. Clearly, "a friend in need is a friend indeed." The children's conversations were related to their problem solving through engagement in transactive conflicts. That is, task performance was facilitated to a greater extent between friends than between nonfriends by free airing of the children's differences in a cooperative, task-oriented context.

Third, we recently examined conversations between friends and nonfriends (ten-year-olds) in an inner-city magnet school while the children wrote stories collaboratively on a computer (Hartup, Daiute, Zajac, & Sholl, 1995). Stories dealt with the rain forest – subject matter that the children had studied during a six-week science project. Baseline story writing was measured with the children writing alone; control subjects *always* wrote alone. Results indicate that friends did not talk more during collaboration than nonfriends but, nevertheless, (a) engaged in more mutually oriented and less individualistic utterances; (b) agreed with one another more often (but did not disagree more readily); (c) repeated their own and the other's assertions more often; (d) posed alternatives and provided elaborations more frequently; (e) spent twice as much time as nonfriends talking about writing content, the vocabulary being used, and writing mechanics; and (f) spent less time engaged in "off-task" talk. Principal component analyses confirm that the structure of friends' talk was strongly focused on the task (i.e., the text) and was assertively collaborative – reminiscent of the dialogs used by experts and novices as discovered in other social problem-solving studies (Rogoff, 1990). Our stories themselves show that, overall, the ones collaboratively written by friends were better than the ones written by nonfriends, a difference that seems to rest on better use of Standard English rather than the narrative elements included in the text. Results suggest, overall, that the affordances of "being friends" differ from the affordances of "being acquaintances" in social problem solving (Hartup, in press).

Fourth, we examined conflict and competition among school-aged children playing a board game when they had been taught different rules (Hartup, French, Laursen, Johnston, & Ogawa, 1993). Disagreements occurred more frequently between friends than between nonfriends and lasted longer. Conflict resolution, however, differed by friendship and sex: (a) boys used assertions *without rationales* more frequently than girls – but only when friends were observed; (b) girls, on the other hand, used assertions *with rationales* more frequently than boys but, again, only with friends. Sex differences in conflict talk, widely cited in the literature (see Maccoby, 1990), thus seem to be relationship manifestations rather than manifestations of individual children.

Based on these and the other available data sets, a recent meta-analysis identified significant friend versus nonfriend effects across four broad-band categories (Newcomb & Bagwell, 1995): *positive engagement* (i.e., talk, smiling, and laughter); *conflict management* (i.e., disengagement and negotiation vs. power assertion); *task activity* (i.e., being oriented to the task as opposed to being off task); and *relationship properties* (i.e., equality in the exchange as well as mutuality and affirmation). Behaviorally speaking, friendships clearly are "communal relationships" (Clark & Mills, 1979). Reciprocity constitutes their deep structure.

Existing data suggest that four cognitive and motivational conditions afford these distinctive interactions: (a) friends know one another better than nonfriends and are thus able to communicate with one another more efficiently and effectively (Ladd & Emerson, 1984); (b) friends and nonfriends have different expectations of one another, especially concerning assistance and support (Bigelow, 1977); (c) an affective climate more favorable to exploration and problem solving exists between friends than between nonfriends – namely, a "climate of agreement" (Gottman, 1983); and (d) friends more readily than nonfriends seek ways of resolving disagreements that support continued interaction between them (Hartup & Laursen, 1992).

Unfortunately, the developmental significance of these differences is not known. Only fragmentary information tells us about short-term consequences in problem solving and behavioral regulation. Recalled events (Newcomb & Brady, 1982), deductive reasoning (Azmitia &

Montgomery, 1993), conflict rates (Hartup et al., 1988), creative writing (Hartup et al., 1995), and social/moral judgments (Nelson & Aboud, 1985) are better supported by transactions with friends than by transactions with nonfriends. But only a small number of investigations exists in each case – sometimes only one. The bottom line: Process-outcome studies are badly needed to tell us whether friends engage in better scaffolding than nonfriends, or whether it only seems like they do. Once process/outcome connections are established, we can then – and only then – conclude that friendships have normative significance (i.e., that children employ their friends adaptively on a daily basis as cognitive and social resources).

Having friends versus not having friends. Does having friends contribute to developmental differentiation (i.e., contribute to individual differences)? For the answer to this question to be affirmative, children who have friends must differ from those who do not.

Cross-sectional comparisons show that, first, children who have friends are more socially competent and less troubled than children who do not; they are more sociable, cooperative, altruistic, self-confident, and less lonely (Hartup, 1993; Newcomb & Bagwell, in press). Second, troubled children (e.g., clinic-referred children) are more likely to be friendless than nonreferred control cases (Rutter & Garmezy, 1983). Friendlessness is not always assessed in the same manner in these studies, but the results are consistent: Not one data set suggests that children with friends are worse off than children who do not have them.

Although friended/friendless comparisons are consistent across data sets, the results are difficult to interpret. First, having friends in these studies usually means having good supportive friends; thus having friends is confounded with friendship quality. Second, causal direction is impossible to establish: Friendship experience may contribute to self-esteem, for example, but self-confident children may make friends more readily than less confident children.

Longitudinal studies can be more convincing concerning developmental significance. Unfortunately, few exist. Short-term studies suggest that certain benefits accrue across school transitions: First, attitudes toward school are better among kindergartners (five-year-olds) who have friends at the beginning and who maintain them than those who don't. Making new friends also predicts gains in school performance over the kindergarten year (Ladd, 1990). Second, with data collected from ten-year-olds across a one-year interval, friendship experience enhanced self-esteem (Bukowski, Hoza, & Newcomb, 1991). Third, psychosocial disturbances have been reported less frequently when school changes occur in the company of good friends than when they don't (Berndt & Hawkins, 1991; Simmons, Burgeson, & Reef, 1988). Having friends thus seems to contribute specifically to affective outcomes across normative school transitions.

One long-term investigation (Bagwell, Newcomb, & Bukowski, 1994) raises questions, however, about "having friends" as a developmental predictor: Eleven-year-old children were identified as either friended or friendless on two separate occasions; subjects were re-evaluated at 23 years of age. Having friends and sociometric status (i.e., social acceptance) *together* predicted school success, aspirations, trouble with the law, and several other outcomes. Unique contributions to adult adjustment, however, were verified only for sociometric status. And even then, when stability in the childhood adjustment measures was taken into account, neither sociometric status nor friendship predicted adult outcomes.

Comment

Overall, the developmental significance of having friends is far from clear. Social interaction between friends differs from social interaction between nonfriends, but this does not tell us much more than that these relationships are unique social entities. Correlational studies are difficult to interpret because the effects of having friends are difficult to disentangle from the effects of friendship quality. Short-term longitudinal studies suggest that having friends supports adaptation during normative transitions, but more substantial evidence is needed concerning these effects. Child differences may interact with friendship experience in relation to developmental outcome rather than being main effects. Having friends, for example, may differentiate mainly among children who are vulnerable in some way prior to the transition. Stress associated with developmental transitions is known to accentuate differences among vulnerable children to a greater extent than among nonvulnerable ones (Caspi & Moffitt, 1991). Similarly, developmental interventions often have greater effects on vulnerable than on nonvulnerable individuals (see Crockenberg, 1981).

The Identity of the Child's Friends

We turn now to the identity of the child's friends. Several questions can be asked: With whom does the child become friends? Can the identity of a child's friends be forecast from what we know about the child? What is the developmental significance of the company a child keeps?

Who are children's friends?

Consider, first, that children make friends on the basis of common interests and common activities. Common ground is a *sine qua non* in friendship relations throughout childhood and adolescence, suggesting that friends ought to be similar to one another in abilities and outlook. Folklore sometimes suggests that "opposites attract," but this notion has not found general support in the empirical literature. The weight of the evidence suggests that, instead, "Beast knows beast; birds of a feather flock together" (Aristotle, *Rhetoric*, Book 11).

Similarities between friends, however, vary from attribute to attribute, in most cases according to *reputational salience* (i.e., according to the importance of an attribute in determining the child's social reputation). Considerable evidence supports this "reputational salience hypothesis": Behavior ratings obtained more than 60 years ago by Robert Challman (1932) showed that social cooperation (an attribute with considerable reputational salience) was more concordant among friends than nonfriends; intelligence (an attribute without reputational salience among young children) was not. Among boys, physical activity (reputationally salient among males) was more similar among friends than nonfriends. Among girls, attractiveness of personality and social network size (both more reputationally salient among females than among males) were more similar among friends than nonfriends.

More recent data also suggest that behavioral concordances among school-aged children and their friends are greater than among children and nonfriends (Haselager, Hartup, Van Lieshout, & Riksen-Walraven, 1995). Peer ratings were obtained in a large number of fifth-grade classrooms centering on three constructs: prosocial behavior, antisocial behavior, and social withdrawal (shyness). First, friends were more similar to one another than nonfriends within each construct cluster (i.e., mean difference scores were significantly smaller). Second, correlations between friends were greater for antisocial behavior (i.e., fighting, disruption, and bullying) than for prosocial behavior (i.e., cooperation, offering help to others) or social withdrawal (i.e., shyness, dependency, and being victimized). These differences may reflect differences among these three attributes in reputational salience: Fighting, for example, is more consistently related to reputation than either cooperation or shyness (Coie, Dodge, & Kupersmidt, 1990). Our results also show important sex differences: (*a*) Friends were more similar to one another among girls than among boys in both prosocial and antisocial behavior (see also Cairns & Cairns, 1994); and (*b*) friends were more similar among boys than among girls in shyness. These gender variations are consistent with the reputational salience hypothesis, too: Being kind to others and being mean to them have greater implications for girls' social reputations than boys', whereas shyness/withdrawal has more to do with boys reputations than girls' (Stevenson-Hinde & Hinde, 1986).

Concordance data from other studies are consistent with the reputational salience notion: Among adolescents, friends are most similar to one another in two general areas: (*a*) school-related attitudes, aspirations, and achievement (Epstein, 1983; Kandel, 1978b); and (*b*) normative activities such as smoking, drinking, drug use, antisocial behavior, and dating (Dishion, Andrews, & Crosby, 1995; Epstein, 1983; Kandel, 1978b; Tolson & Urberg, 1993). Sexual activity among adolescents is also consistent with the reputational salience hypothesis. Among girls (both African-American and white) in the United States, friends have been found to be similar in sexual behavior and attitudes, even when age and antisocial attitudes are taken into account. Among boys, however, sexual activity (especially engaging in sexual intercourse) was not concordant (Billy, Rodgers, & Udry, 1984). The authors argue that sexual activity is more closely related to social reputation among adolescent girls than it is among boys, thus accounting for the gender differences in the results.

Still other investigators, employing the social network as a unit of analysis, have discovered that members of friendship networks are concordant on such salient dimensions as sports, academic activities, and drug use (Brown, 1989). Antisocial behavior also distinguishes social networks from one another beginning in middle childhood (Cairns, Cairns, Neckerman, Gest, & Garieppy, 1988).

Friendship concordances: Sources and developmental implications

Similarities between friends are one thing, but where do they come from and where do they lead? Developmental implications cannot be specified without understanding that these similarities derive from three sources: (a) *sociodemographic conditions* that bring children into proximity with one another; (b) *social selection* through which children construct relationships with children who are similar to themselves rather than different; and (c) *mutual socialization* through which children become similar to their friends by interacting with them.

Sociodemographic conditions.   Demographic conditions determine the neighborhoods in which children live, the schools in which they enroll, and the classes they attend. Concordances among children and their friends in socioeconomic status, ethnicity, and chronological age thus derive in considerable measure from social forces that constrain the "peer pool" and the child's access to it. One should not underestimate, however, the extent to which some of these concordances derive from the children's own choices. Among children attending schools that are mixed-age, mixed-race, and mixed socioeconomically, friends are still more similar to one another in these attributes than nonfriends are (Goldman, 1981; McCandless & Hoyt, 1961).

Selection.   Some similarities among friends derive from the well-known tendency among human beings (not alone among the various species) for choosing close associates who resemble themselves. Recent studies confirm that the similarity-attraction hypothesis applies to children: Among elementary school children who began an experimental session as strangers, differential attraction was evident in some groups (40%). Within them, more social contact occurred between preferred than between nonpreferred partners, and correlations were higher between preferred than nonpreferred partners in sociability and the cognitive maturity of their play (Rubin, Lynch, Coplan, Rose-Krasnor, & Booth, 1994).

But friendship selection is embedded in assortative processes occurring in larger social networks. Dishion and his colleagues (Dishion, Patterson, & Griesler, 1994) believe that these network concordances emerge through a process called "shopping" in which children and adolescents construct relationships that maximize interpersonal payoffs. Children are not believed to choose friends who are similar to themselves on a rational basis so much as on an experiential one. Accordingly, relationships become established when they "feel right." Similar individuals cleave to one another more readily than dissimilar individuals because they are more likely to find common ground in both their activities and their conversations. Antisocial children are thus most likely to make friends with other antisocial children and, in so doing, their common characteristics merge to create a "dyadic antisocial trait." Similarly, soccer players or musicians make friends, merge themselves dyadically, and set the stage for becoming even more similar to one another.

Selection thus acts simultaneously to determine the identity of the child's friends through two interlocking processes: (*a*) similarity and attraction occurring within dyads; and (*b*) assortative network formation occurring within groups. These processes undoubtedly combine differently from child to child in affecting developmental outcome: Cooperative, friendly, nonaggressive children can choose friends resembling themselves from a wide array of choices; antisocial children can also choose their friends on the basis of similarity and attraction – but frequently from a more restricted range of social alternatives.

Mutual socialization. What behavioral outcomes stem from mutual socialization? The weight of the evidence suggests, first, that children and their friends who ascribe to conventional norms move further over time in the direction of normative behavior (Ball, 1981; Epstein, 1983; Kandel & Andrews, 1986). But does antisocial behavior increase over time among children in antisocial networks? Does troublesome behavior escalate among children – especially into criminal activity – through membership in these networks? Answers to these questions have been surprisingly difficult to provide, especially since children perceive their friends as exerting more pressure toward desirable than toward undesirable conduct (Brown, Clasen, & Eicher, 1986). Nevertheless, increases in undesirable behavior through antisocial friends among children who are themselves at risk for antisocial behavior is now relatively well documented (Ball, 1981; Berndt & Keefe, 1992; Dishion, 1990; Dishion et al., 1994). Conversely, "desisting" is forecast as strongly by a turning away from antisocial friends as by any other variable (Mulvey & Aber, 1988).

What occurs on a day-to-day basis between aggressive children and their friends? Jocks and their friends? "Brains" and their friends? One guesses that children model normative behaviors *for* their friends and simultaneously receive reinforcement *from* them. Antisocial children, for example, are known to engage in large amounts of talk with their friends – talk that is deviant even when the children are being video-taped in the laboratory (Dishion et al., 1994, 1995). Ordinary children talk a lot with their friends, too, but the content is not generally as deviant (Newcomb & Bagwell, 1995). Antisocial children use coercion with one another (Dishion et al., 1995); ordinary children, on the other hand, are freewheeling with their criticisms and persuasion but are less likely to be coercive (Berndt & Keefe, 1992; Hartup et al., 1993). Finally, one guesses that friends support one another in seeking environments that support their commonly held worldviews, although not much is known about this.

Other results show that selection *combines* with socialization to effect similarity between friends. Kandel (1978a) studied changes over the course of a year in drug use, educational aspirations, and delinquency in early adolescence, discovering that similarity stemmed from both sources in approximately equal amounts. Relative effects, however, vary according to the norms and the children involved (see Hartup, 1993).

Comment

Children and their friends are similar to one another, especially in attributes with reputational salience. One must acknowledge that effect sizes are modest and that friends are not carbon copies of one another. One must also acknowledge that the reputational salience hypothesis has never been subjected to direct test and it needs to be. Nevertheless, the identity of the child's friends is a significant consideration in predicting developmental outcome. Friends may be generally intimate, caring, and supportive, thus fostering good developmental prognosis. At the same time, the activities in which they support one another (the relationship *content*) may be extremely deviant, suggesting an altogether different prognosis.

Friendship Quality

Conceptual and measurement issues

Qualitative assessment of child and adolescent friendships currently involves two main strategies: (*a*) *dimensional analysis* through which one determines whether certain elements are present or absent in the social interaction between friends (e.g., companionship, intimacy, conflict, or power asymmetries); and (*b*) *typological or categorical analysis* through which one identifies patterns in social interaction believed to be critical to social development and adaptation (Furman, in press).

Dimensional assessment. Most current dimensional assessments are based on "provisions" or "features" that children mention when talking about these relationships (Berndt & Perry, 1986; Bukowski, Hoza, & Boivin, 1994; Furman & Adler, 1982; Furman & Buhrmester, 1985; Parker & Asher, 1993); most instruments tap five or six domains. Domain scores, however, are correlated with one another (Berndt & Perry, 1986; Parker & Asher, 1993), and most factor analyses yield two-factor solutions. Both Berndt (in press) and Furman (in press) argue that "positive" and "negative" dimensions adequately describe most dimensional assessments, although some data sets suggest that more elaborate solutions are warranted (e.g., Ladd, Kochenderfer, & Coleman, in press).

Typological assessment. Typological assessment is evolving slowly since the functional significance of friendships remains uncertain. Can one, for example, regard friendships as attachments? Probably not. No one has demonstrated that "the secure base phenomenon," so common among children and their caregivers, constitutes the functional core of children's friendships. Friends have been shown to be secure bases in one or two instances (Ipsa, 1981; Schwartz, 1972), but one is not overwhelmed with the evidence that children and their friends are bound to one another as attachment objects. Children describe their relationships with friends differently from their relationships with their caregivers – as *more* companionable, intimate, and egalitarian and, simultaneously, as *less* affectionate and reliable (Furman & Buhrmester, 1985). For these reasons, some writers describe friendships as affiliative relationships rather than attachments (Weiss, 1986). The challenge, then, is to describe what good-quality affiliative relationships are.

One new classification system has been devised on the basis of family systems theory (Shulman, 1993). Well-functioning friendships are considered to be balanced between closeness and intimacy, on the one hand, and individuality, on the other. The family systems model suggests three friendship types: *interdependent* ones, with cooperation and autonomy balanced; *disengaged* ones, in which friends are disconnected in spite of their efforts to maintain proximity with one another; and *consensus-sensitive* or *enmeshed* relationships, in which agreement and cohesion are maximized. Empirical data are based largely on children's interactions in a cooperative task adapted from family systems research (Reiss, 1981) and document the existence of interdependent and disengaged relationships – a promising beginning. Once again, however, caution should be exercised: Friendship networks may not revolve around the same equilibrative axes as families do.

Developmental Significance

Cross-sectional studies. Among the various qualitative dimensions, *support* (positivity) and *contention* (negativity) have been examined most extensively in relation to child outcomes. Support is positively correlated with school involvement and achievement (Berndt & Hawkins, 1991; Cauce, 1986) and negatively correlated with school-based problems (Kurdek & Sinclair, 1988); positively correlated with popularity and good social reputations (Cauce, 1986); positively correlated with self-esteem (Mannarino, 1978; McGuire & Weisz, 1982; Perry, 1987) and psychosocial adjustment (Buhrmester, 1990) as well as negatively correlated with identity problems (Papini, Farmer, Clark, Micke, & Barnett, 1990) and depression – especially among girls (Compas, Slavin, Wagner, & Cannatta, 1986). Results are thus consistent but, once again, impossible to interpret. We cannot tell whether supportive relationships contribute to the competence of the individual child or vice versa.

Longitudinal studies. Longitudinal studies dealing with friendship quality (positive vs. negative) emphasize school attitudes, involvement, and achievement. Studying children across the transition from elementary to junior high school [typically aged 12 to 13], Berndt (1989) measured the size of the friendship network, friendship stability, and

self-reported friendship quality (positivity) as well as popularity, attitudes toward school, and achievement. First, network size was
negatively related to friendship support as reported by the children, suggesting that children recognize what researchers have been slow to
learn, namely, that friendships are not all alike. Second, several nonsignificant results are illuminating: Neither number of friends nor
friendship stability contributed to changes in school adjustment – either
across the school transition or across the first year in the new school.
School adjustment was relatively stable across the transition and was
related to friendship stability cross-sectionally but not with earlier
adjustment factored out. Third, the self-rated supportiveness of the
child's friends, assessed shortly after entrance to the new school, predicted increasing popularity and increasingly positive attitudes toward
classmates over the next year, suggesting that positive qualities in one's
friendship relations support a widening social world in new school
environments.

Other investigations focus on friendship qualities as predictors of
school adaptation within the school year. Among five-year-olds enrolled
in kindergarten (Ladd et al., in press), for example, those having
friendships characterized by "aid" and "validation" improved in school
attitudes over the year with initial attitudes toward school factored
out. Perceived conflict in friendships, on the other hand, predicted
increasing forms of school maladjustment, especially among boys,
including school loneliness and avoidance as well as school liking and
engagement.

One other investigation (Berndt & Keefe, 1992) focused on both positive and negative friendship qualities and their correlations across time
with school adjustment and self-esteem among adolescents. Students
with supportive, intimate friendships became increasingly involved with
school, while those who considered their friendships to be conflict-
ridden and rivalrous became increasingly disruptive and troublesome.
Friendship quality was not correlated with changes in self-esteem, possibly because self-esteem was relatively stable from the beginning to
the end of the year. Additional analyses (Berndt, in press) suggest that
developmental prediction is better for the negative dimensions in these
relationships than the positive ones.

Other investigators have examined the interactions between stress
and social support as related to behavioral outcome. With elementary
school children, increases in peer support over several years predict both

increasingly better adaptation and better grade point averages (Dubow, Tisak, Causey, Hryshko, & Reid, 1991). Other results, however, suggest that support from school personnel was associated with decreases in distress across a two-year period but not support from friends (controlling for initial adjustment). Regression models showed that, actually, school grades predicted changes in friends' support rather than the reverse (DuBois, Felner, Brand, Adan, & Evans, 1992). Among adolescents, however, results are more complex: Windle (1992) reported that, among girls, friend support is positively correlated with alcohol use but negatively correlated with depression (with initial adjustment levels factored out). Among boys, friendship support is associated with outcome depending on stress levels: When stress is high, friend support encourages both alcohol use and depression; when stress is low or moderate, both alcohol use and depression are associated with having *nonsupportive* friends.

The dissonances encountered in these results would be reduced considerably were the identity of the children's friends to be known. Children and adolescents with behavior difficulties frequently have friends who themselves are troublesome (Dishion et al., 1995). These friends may provide one another with emotional support, but the interactions that occur between them may not be the same as those occurring between nontroubled children and their friends. Knowing who the child's friends are might account for the empirical anomalies.

Other difficulties in accounting for these results derive from the fact that the referents used in measuring social support in these studies (except in Berndt's work) consisted of friendship networks (the child's "friends") rather than a "best friend." And still other complications arise from the use of one child's assessments of relationship qualities (the subject's) when the evidence suggests that discrepancies between partners may correlate more strongly with adjustment difficulties than the perceptions of either partner alone (East, 1991). Nevertheless, these studies provide tantalizing tidbits suggesting that friendship quality bears a causal relation to developmental outcome.

Comment

What kinds of research are needed to better understand the developmental implications of friendship quality? One can argue that we are not urgently in need of cross-time studies narrowly focused on friendships and their vicissitudes. Rather, we need comprehensive studies in which interaction effects rather than main effects are emphasized and that encompass a wide range of variables as they cycle through time: (*a*) measures of the child, including temperament and other relevant early characteristics; (*b*) measures of early relationships, especially their affective and cognitive qualities; (*c*) measures of early success in encounters with relevant institutions, especially the schools; (*d*) status and reputation among other children (sociometric status); *and* (*e*) friendship measures that simultaneously include whether a child has friends, who the child's friends are, and what these relationships are like.

Coming close to this model are recent studies conducted by the Oregon Social Learning Center (e.g., Dishion et al., 1994; Patterson, Reid, & Dishion, 1992). Child characteristics and family relations in early childhood have not been examined extensively by these investigators, but their work establishes linkages between coerciveness and monitoring within parent–child and sibling relationships, on the one hand, and troublesomeness and antisocial behavior among school-aged boys on the other. These studies also establish that poor parental discipline and monitoring predict peer rejection and academic failures, and that these conditions, in turn, predict increasing involvement with antisocial friends. Among children with these early histories, the immediate connection to serious conduct difficulties in adolescence now seems to be friendship with another deviant child. Exactly these conditions existed in the social history of that Minnesota teenager who, together with his best friend, killed his mother early in 1995.

Conclusion

Friendships in childhood and adolescence would seem to be developmentally significant – both normatively and differentially. When children have friends, they use them as cognitive and social resources on an everyday basis. Normative transitions and the stress carried with them seem to be better negotiated when children have friends than when they don't, especially when children are at risk. Differential significance, however, seems to derive mainly from the identity of the child's friends and the quality of the relationships between them. Supportive relationships between socially skilled individuals appear to be developmental advantages, whereas coercive and conflict-ridden relationships are developmental disadvantages, especially among antisocial children.

Nevertheless, friendship and its developmental significance may vary from child to child. New studies show that child characteristics interact with early relationships and environmental conditions, cycling in turn through relations with other children to determine behavioral outcome (Hartup & Van Lieshout, 1995). The work cited in this essay strongly suggests that friendship assessments deserve greater attention in studying these developmental pathways than they are currently given. These assessments, however, need to be comprehensive. Along with knowing whether or not children have friends, we must know who their friends are and the quality of their relationships with them.

References

Ainsworth, M. D. S., Blehar, M. C., Waters, E., & Wall, S. (1978). *Patterns of attachment: A psychological study of the Strange Situation.* Hillsdale, NJ: Erlbaum.

Azmitia, M., & Montgomery, R. (1993). Friendship, transactive dialogues, and the development of scientific reasoning. *Social Development, 2,* 202–221.

Bagwell, C., Newcomb, A. F., & Bukowski, W. M. (1994). Early adolescent friendship as a predictor of adult adjustment: A twelve-year follow-up investigation. Unpublished manuscript, University of Richmond.

Ball, S. J. (1981). *Beachside comprehensive.* Cambridge: Cambridge University Press.

Berndt, T. J. (1989). Obtaining support from friends during childhood and adolescence. In D. Belle (Ed.), *Children's social networks and social supports* (pp. 308–331). New York: Wiley.

Berndt, T. J. (in press). Exploring the effects of friendship quality on social development. In W. M. Bukowski, A. F. Newcomb, & W. W. Hartup (Eds.), *The company they keep: Friendships in childhood and adolescence.* Cambridge: Cambridge University Press.

Berndt, T. J., & Hawkins, J. A. (1991). Effects of friendship on adolescents' adjustment to junior high school. Unpublished manuscript, Purdue University.

Berndt, T. J., & Keefe, K. (1992). Friends' influence on adolescents' perceptions of themselves in school. In D. H. Schunk & J. L. Meece (Eds.), *Students' perceptions in the classroom* (pp. 51–73). Hillsdale, NJ: Erlbaum.

Berndt, T. J., & Perry, T. B. (1986). Children's perceptions of friendship as supportive relationships. *Developmental Psychology, 22,* 640–648.

Bigelow, B. J. (1977). Children's friendship expectations: A cognitive developmental study. *Child Development, 48,* 246–253.

Billy, J. O. G., Rodgers, J. L., & Udry, J. R. (1984). Adolescent sexual behavior and friendship choice. *Social Forces, 62,* 653–678.

Brown, B. B. (1989). The role of peer groups in adolescents' adjustment to secondary school. In T. J. Berndt & G. W. Ladd (Eds.), *Peer relationships in child development* (pp. 188–215). New York: Wiley.

Brown, B. B., Clasen, D. R., & Eicher, S. A. (1986). Perceptions of peer pressure, peer conformity dispositions, and self-reported behavior among adolescents. *Developmental Psychology, 22,* 521–530.

Buhrmester, D. (1990). Intimacy of friendship, interpersonal competence, and adjustment during preadolescence and adolescence. *Child Development, 61,* 1101–1111.

Bukowski, W. M., Hoza, B., & Boivin, M. (1994). Measuring friendship quality during pre- and early adolescence: The development and psychometric properties of the Friendship Qualities Scale. *Journal of Personal and Social Relationships, 11,* 471–484.

Bukowski, W. M., Hoza, B., & Newcomb, A. F. (1991). Friendship, popularity, and the "self" during early adolescence. Unpublished manuscript, Concordia University (Montreal).

Cairns, R. B., & Cairns, B. D. (1994). *Lifelines and risks.* Cambridge: Cambridge University Press.

Cairns, R. B., Cairns, B. D., Neckerman, H. J., Gest, S., & Garieppy, J.-L. (1988). Peer networks and aggressive behavior: Peer support or peer rejection? *Developmental Psychology, 24,* 815–823.

Caspi, A., & Moffitt, T. E. (1991). Individual differences are accentuated during periods of social change: The sample case of girls at puberty. *Journal of Personality and Social Psychology, 61,* 157–168.

Cauce, A. M. (1986). Social networks and social competence: Exploring the effects of early adolescent friendships. *American Journal of Community Psychology, 14,* 607–628.

Challman, R. C. (1932). Factors influencing friendships among preschool children. *Child Development, 3,* 146–158.

Clark, M. S., & Mills, J. (1979). Interpersonal attraction in exchange and communal relationships. *Journal of Personality and Social Psychology, 37,* 12–24.

Coie, J. D., Dodge, K. A., & Kupersmidt, J. B. (1990). Peer group behavior and social status. In S. R. Asher & J. D. Coie (Eds.), *Peer rejection in childhood* (pp. 17–59). Cambridge: Cambridge University Press.

Compas, B. E., Slavin, L. A., Wagner, B. A., & Cannatta, K. (1986). Relationship of life events and social support with psychological dysfunction among adolescents. *Journal of Youth and Adolescence, 15,* 205–221.

Crockenberg, S. B. (1981). Infant irritability, mother responsiveness, and social support influences on the security of mother–infant attachment. *Child Development, 52,* 857–865.

Dishion, T. J. (1990). The peer context of troublesome child and adolescent behavior. In P. Leone (Ed.), *Understanding troubled and troublesome youth.* Newbury Park, CA: Sage.

Dishion, T. J., Andrews, D. W., & Crosby, L. (1995). Anti-social boys and their friends in early adolescence: Relationship characteristics, quality, and interactional process. *Child Development, 66,* 139–151.

Dishion, T. J., Patterson, G. R., & Griesler, P. C. (1994). Peer adaptations in the development of antisocial behavior: A confluence model. In L. R. Huesmann (Ed.), *Current perspectives on aggressive behavior* (pp. 61–95). New York: Plenum.

Doyle, A. B., Markiewicz, D., & Hardy, C. (1994). Mothers' and children's friendships: Intergenerational associations. *Journal of Social and Personal Relationships, 11,* 363–377.

DuBois, D. L., Felner, R. D., Brand, S., Adan, A. M., & Evans, E. G. (1992). A prospective study of life stress, social support, and adaptation in early adolescence. *Child Development, 63,* 542–557.

Dubow, E. F., Tisak, J., Causey, D., Hryshko, A., & Reid, G. (1991). A two-year longitudinal study of stressful life events, social support, and social problem-solving skills: Contributions to children's behavioral and academic adjustment. *Child Development, 62,* 583–599.

East, P. L. (1991). The parent–child relationships of withdrawn, aggressive, and sociable children: Child and parent perspectives. *Merrill-Palmer Quarterly, 37,* 425–444.

Epstein, J. L. (1983). Examining theories of adolescent friendship. In J. L. Epstein & N. L. Karweit (Eds.), *Friends in school* (pp. 39–61). San Diego: Academic Press.

Furman, W. (in press). The measurement of friendship perceptions: Conceptual and methodological issues. In W. M. Bukowski, A. F. Newcomb, & W. W. Hartup (Eds.), *The company they keep: Friendships in childhood and adolescence.* Cambridge: Cambridge University Press.

Furman, W., & Adler, T. (1982). The Friendship Questionnaire. Unpublished manuscript, University of Denver.

Furman, W., & Buhrmester, D. (1985). Children's perceptions of the personal relationships in their social networks. *Developmental Psychology, 21,* 1016–1022.

Goldman, J. A. (1981). The social interaction of preschool children in same-age versus mixed-age groupings. *Child Development, 52,* 644–650.

Gottman, J. M. (1983). How children become friends. *Monographs of the Society for Research in Child Development, 48*(3, Serial No. 201).

Hartup, W. W. (1992). Friendships and their developmental significance. In H. McGurk (Ed.), *Childhood social development* (pp. 175–205). Hove, UK: Erlbaum.

Hartup, W. W. (1993). Adolescents and their friends. In B. Laursen (Ed.), *Close friendships in adolescence* (pp. 3–22). San Francisco: Jossey-Bass.

Hartup, W. W. (in press). Cooperation, close relationships, and cognitive development. In W. M. Bukowski, A. F. Newcomb, & W. W. Hartup (Eds.), *The company they keep: Friendships in childhood and adolescence.* Cambridge: Cambridge University Press.

Hartup, W. W., Daiute, C., Zajac, R., & Sholl, W. (1995). Collaboration in creative writing by friends and nonfriends. Unpublished manuscript, University of Minnesota.

Hartup, W. W., French, D. C., Laursen, B., Johnston, K. M., & Ogawa, J. (1993). Conflict and friendship relations in middle childhood: Behavior in a closed-field situation. *Child Development, 64*, 445–454.

Hartup, W. W., & Laursen, B. (1992). Conflict and context in peer relations. In C. H. Hart (Ed.), *Children on playgrounds: Research perspectives and applications* (pp. 44–84). Albany: State University of New York Press.

Hartup, W. W., Laursen, B., Stewart, M. I., & Eastenson, A. (1988). Conflict and the friendship relations of young children. *Child Development, 59*, 1590–1600.

Hartup, W. W., & Van Lieshout, C. F. M. (1995). Personality development in social context. In J. T. Spence (Ed.), *Annual Review of Psychology, 46*, 655–687.

Haselager, G. J. T., Hartup, W. W., Van Lieshout, C. F. M., & Riksen-Walraven, M. (1995). Friendship similarity in middle childhood as a function of sex and sociometric status. Unpublished manuscript, University of Nijmegen.

Howes, C. (1989). Peer interaction of young children. *Monographs of the Society for Research in Child Development, 53*(Serial No. 217).

Ipsa, J. (1981). Peer support among Soviet day care toddlers. *International Journal of Behavioral Development, 4*, 255–269.

Kandel, D. B. (1978a). Homophily, selection, and socialization in adolescent friendships. *American Journal of Sociology, 84*, 427–436.

Kandel, D. B. (1978b). Similarity in real-life adolescent pairs. *Journal of Personality and Social Psychology, 36*, 306–312.

Kandel, D. B., & Andrews, K. (1986). Processes of adolescent socialization by parents and peers. *International Journal of the Addictions, 22*, 319–342.

Kurdek, L. A., & Sinclair, R. J. (1988). Adjustment of young adolescents in two-parent nuclear, stepfather, and mother-custody families. *Journal of Consulting and Clinical Psychology, 56*, 91–96.

Ladd, G. W. (1990). Having friends, keeping friends, making friends, and being liked by peers in the classroom: Predictors of children's early school adjustment? *Child Development, 61*, 1081–1100.

Ladd, G. W., & Emerson, E. S. (1984). Shared knowledge in children's friendships. *Developmental Psychology, 20*, 932–940.

Ladd, G. W., Kochenderfer, B. J., & Coleman, C. C. (in press). Friendship quality as a predictor of young children's early school adjustment. *Child Development*.

Maccoby, E. E. (1990). Gender and relationships: A developmental account. *American Psychologist, 45*, 513–520.

Mannarino, A. P. (1978). Friendship patterns and self-concept development in preadolescent males. *Journal of Genetic Psychology, 133*, 105–110.

McCandless, B. R., & Hoyt, J. M. (1961). Sex, ethnicity and play preferences of preschool children. *Journal of Abnormal and Social Psychology, 62*, 683–685.

McGuire, K. D., & Weisz, J. R. (1982). Social cognition and behavior correlates of preadolescent chumship. *Child Development, 53*, 1478–1484.

Mulvey, E. P., & Aber, M. S. (1988). Growing out of delinquency: Development and desistance. In R. Jenkins, & W. Brown (Eds.), *The abandonment of delinquent behavior: Promoting the turn-around.* New York: Praeger.

Nelson, J., & Aboud, F. E. (1985). The resolution of social conflict between friends. *Child Development, 56*, 1009–1017.

Newcomb, A. F., & Bagwell, C. (1995). Children's friendship relations: A meta-analytic review. *Psychological Bulletin, 177*, 306–347.

Newcomb, A. F., & Bagwell, C. (in press). The developmental significance of children's friendship relations. In W. M. Bukowski, A. F. Newcomb, & W. W. Hartup (Eds.), *The company they keep: Friendship in childhood and adolescence.* Cambridge: Cambridge University Press.

Newcomb, A. F., & Brady, J. E. (1982). Mutuality in boys' friendship relations. *Child Development, 53*, 392–395.

Papini, D. R., Farmer, F. F., Clark, S. M., Micke, J. C., & Barnett, J. K. (1990). Early adolescent age and gender differences in patterns of emotional self-disclosure to parents and friends. *Adolescence, 25*, 959–976.

Parker, J. G., & Asher, S. R. (1987). Peer relations and later personal adjustment: Are low-accepted children at risk? *Psychological Bulletin, 102*, 357–389.

Parker, J. G., & Asher, S. R. (1993). Friendship and friendship quality in middle childhood: Links with peer group acceptance and feelings of loneliness and social dissatisfaction. *Developmental Psychology, 29*, 611–621.

Patterson, G. R., Reid, J. B., & Dishion, T. J. (1992). *Antisocial boys.* Eugene, OR: Castalia.

Perry, T. B. (1987). *The relation of adolescent self-perceptions to their social relationships.* Unpublished doctoral dissertation, University of Oklahoma.

Reiss, D. (1981). *The family's construction of reality.* Cambridge, MA: Harvard University Press.

Rogoff, B. (1990). *Apprenticeship in thinking.* New York: Oxford University Press.

Rubin, K. H., Lynch, D., Coplan, R., Rose-Krasnor, L., & Booth, C. L. (1994). "Birds of a feather . . .": Behavioral concordances and preferential personal attraction in children. *Child Development, 65*, 1778–1785.

Rutter, M., & Garmezy, N. (1983). Developmental psychopathology. In E. M. Hetherington (Ed.), P. H. Mussen (Series Ed.), *Handbook of child psychology: Vol. 4. Socialization, personality, and social development* (pp. 775–911). New York: Wiley.

Schwartz, J. C. (1972). Effects of peer familiarity on the behavior of preschoolers in a novel situation. *Journal of Personality and Social Psychology, 24,* 276–284.

Shulman, S. (1993). Close friendships in early and middle adolescence: Typology and friendship reasoning. In B. Laursen (Ed.), *Close friendships in adolescence* (pp. 55–72). San Francisco: Jossey-Bass.

Simmons, R. G., Burgeson, R., & Reef, M. J. (1988). Cumulative change at entry to adolescence. In M. Gunnar & W. A. Collins (Eds.), *Minnesota symposia on child psychology* (Vol. 21, pp. 123–150). Hillsdale, NJ: Erlbaum.

Stevenson-Hinde, J., & Hinde, R. A. (1986). Changes in associations between characteristics and interaction. In R. Plomin & J. Dunn (Eds.), *The study of temperament: Changes, continuities and challenges* (pp. 115–129). Hillsdale, NJ: Erlbaum.

Sullivan, H. S. (1953). *The interpersonal theory of psychiatry.* New York: Norton.

Tolson, J. M., & Urberg, K. A. (1993). Similarity between adolescent best friends. *Journal of Adolescent Research, 8,* 274–288.

Weiss, R. S. (1986). Continuities and transformations in social relationships from childhood to adulthood. In W. W. Hartup & Z. Rubin (Eds.), *Relationships and development* (pp. 95–110). Hillsdale, NJ: Erlbaum.

Windle, M. (1992). A longitudinal study of stress buffering for adolescent problem behaviors. *Developmental Psychology, 28,* 522–530.

FOUR

Peer Relations

Introduction

Although there has been an increase in the literature on the development and significance of peer relationships, there are still many unanswered questions. Understanding the link between peer relationships and developmental outcomes is of considerable interest to developmental and clinical psychologists. Most research in this area describes children's friendships, but little research has been done on the effects of friendships on children's lives. There is some evidence to suggest that there are short-term positive effects of friendship in young children (Ladd, Kochenderfer, & Coleman, 1996) and in adolescents (Berndt, 1996).

This prospective study by Bagwell, Newcomb, and Bukowski considers the relative importance of friendship, and peer rejection, for positive adult outcomes. There are several unique aspects to this study: (1) it presents a longitudinal design that tests a model linking friendships and developmental outcomes; (2) several outcomes are considered, including school/career adjustment, social participation, perceived competence, mental health difficulties, and law-violating behaviors; (3) it examines the unique predictive importance of having reciprocated friendships, as well as peer rejection. The findings indicate that both friendship and rejection are important predictors of distinct types of outcome.

References

Berndt, T. J. (1996). Exploring the effects of friendship quality on social development. In W. M. Bukowski, A. F. Newcomb, & W. W. Hartup (eds), *The company they keep: Friendships in childhood and adolescence* (pp. 346–65). New York: Cambridge University Press.

Ladd, G. W., Kochenderfer, B. J., & Coleman, C. C. (1996). Friendship quality as a predictor of young children's early school adjustment. *Child Development, 67*, 1103–18.

Preadolescent Friendship and Peer Rejection as Predictors of Adult Adjustment

Catherine L. Bagwell, Andrew F. Newcomb, and William M. Bukowski

Introduction

In exploring friendship's developmental significance, researchers have become sensitive to the potentially different provisions afforded by general peer and friendship relations. Central to this investigation is the recognition that acceptance and rejection are unilateral concepts that summarize the feelings of the peer group about one child. In contrast, friendship is a mutual relationship between two children in which reciprocal liking is quintessential. Although friendship and peer acceptance are indeed related, a child may have a close friendship but not occupy a prominent position in the peer group. Likewise, children rejected by the peer group often have a mutual friend (Bukowski & Hoza, 1989; Parker & Asher, 1993).

The extent to which childhood peer and friendship relations have unique and/or redundant associations with adult outcome warrants careful investigation. A familiar list of studies establishes the connections between poor peer relations and later maladjustment (e.g., Cowen, Pederson, Babigian, Izzo, & Trost, 1973; Roff, Sells, & Golden, 1972), and reviews of this literature reveal three general outcomes related to peer rejection and other indicators of poor peer relations. The strongest associations between peer difficulties and adjustment are found in the prediction of early school withdrawal and delinquency or criminality, and peer difficulties have also been associated with a myriad of mental health problems (Kupersmidt, Coie, & Dodge, 1990; Parker & Asher, 1987).

These prospective and retrospective studies support the logical assumption that the stronger affective tie of friendship would also be important for adaptive adjustment. Inasmuch as these two types of social relationships are distinct, however, friendship may foster competencies that no other relationship, including nominal peer relations, can afford. Theoretical writings, most notably the seminal work of Sullivan (1953), suggest that establishing a close friendship is a significant developmental task for preadolescents. Sullivan proposes that certain social relationships are best suited for meeting specific interpersonal needs that arise at different stages in development. In middle childhood, the need for acceptance is met by participation in the general peer group, whereas the transition to preadolescence is characterized by the emerging need for interpersonal intimacy. The intimacy need is fulfilled within a chumship as friends are sensitive to one another's needs and seek mutual satisfaction.

Theoretically, the relation between positive friendship experience and adjustment should be most apparent in preadolescence (Sullivan, 1953). Short-term longitudinal studies conducted with young children (Ladd, 1990; Ladd, Kochenderfer, & Coleman, 1996) and with adolescents (Berndt, 1996; Berndt & Keefe, 1995; Vernberg, 1990) indicate linkages between friendship and adjustment. These studies are critical steps in the quest to document empirically the developmental significance of friendships, yet there is no empirical evidence of the association of friendship in preadolescence and later adjustment.

The underlying question of how friendship experience affects social and emotional development assumes that the impact of friends on a child's life is more than momentary. Buhrmester (1996) distinguishes between the immediate impact of friendships on children's daily lives and their long-term formative impact on development. The long-term influence occurs as friendship provisions such as increased interpersonal competence or validation of self-worth spill over into other contexts, including later relationships or competence in the workplace. Although not without limitations (Berndt, 1996), longer-term longitudinal and follow-up studies provide an important methodology for examining the formative impact of preadolescent friendships on development.

In support of this endeavor, the present follow-up study examined the unique and redundant contributions of preadolescent peer rejection and friendship to adult outcome. The simultaneous consideration of these social relations is important because their effects may be related. Although we hypothesized that friendship and peer rejection would both be predictive of adult outcome, we also expected that different global domains of adjustment would be primarily associated with one or the other preadolescent peer experience. We had four specific hypotheses about the relative importance of friendship and peer rejection for predicting global aspects of adult adjustment in the domains of overall life status adjustment, perceived general self-worth, severity of psychopathological symptoms, and functioning in adult relationships (i.e., competence in romantic and friendship relations and friendship quality).

The first hypothesis is that the measure of overall life status adjustment would be more associated with peer rejection than with having a friend in preadolescence. There are three general groupings of specific measures that comprise the overall life status adjustment scale, and each of these is expected to be more closely linked to early peer rejection than to friendship. The first grouping consists of school/career adjustment and includes the measures of school performance, job performance, and aspiration level. Theoretical models include the assertion that peer rejection is at least a marker for childhood adjustment problems (Coie, 1990). Peer rejection is assessed within the school context; thus, it is expected to be a marker of maladjustment in the interrelated contexts of school and career. The second grouping of life status measures assesses social participation (i.e., social life, activity involvement, family interaction). Furman and Robbins (1985) propose that one unique developmental function of peer acceptance is providing a sense of inclusion, and this belongingness should be reflected in participating in organizations and having a satisfying social life. Finally, the grouping of life status measures that includes trouble with the law and mental health difficulties indexes maladjustment. Evidence for the links between peer rejection and these aspects of disorder are more empirically than theoretically based. Nevertheless, substantial evidence suggests that peer rejection is associated with delinquency and mental health problems, particularly externalizing symptomatology (Kupersmidt et al., 1990; Parker & Asher, 1987).

The second hypothesis is that perceived general self-worth in adulthood is uniquely related to having or not having a mutual friendship in

preadolescence. This hypothesis is firmly grounded in theoretical conceptualizations of the importance of friendship in preadolescence.
Sullivan (1953) contends that preadolescent chumships have long-term
implications for an individual's feelings of competence and self-worth.
Indeed, consensual validation of self-worth is a hallmark of the collaborative relationship that exists between two friends. The sense of self-
worth that comes from the social reciprocities of friendship is expected
to be important at all stages of life and to promote successful coping,
especially in dealing with developmental transitions such as school
transitions and puberty (Hartup, 1996).

The third hypothesis about the relative importance of friendship
and peer rejection in the prediction of psychopathological symptoms
is largely based on empirical as opposed to theoretical evidence. Given
the well-established link between peer rejection and later psychopathology (see Kupersmidt et al., 1990; Parker & Asher, 1987;
Parker, Rubin, Price, & DeRosier, 1995, for reviews), we hypothesized
that the severity of psychopathological symptoms in adulthood
would best be predicted by preadolescent peer rejection. The limited
theoretical evidence for the association of friendship and mental
health difficulties derives from Sullivan's (1953) assertion that failing to
form a close friendship in preadolescence may lead to feelings of
loneliness. Based on this idea, it is hypothesized that the lack of a
supportive and intimate friendship in preadolescence may be more
related to internalizing distress such as loneliness and depression than
is peer rejection.

Our final hypothesis is that the presence or absence of a preadolescent friendship is a better predictor of functioning in adult friend and
romantic relationships than is peer rejection. This hypothesis stems from
two related theoretical ideas about the importance of friendship. First,
a critical function of friendships in preadolescence is to promote skills
and competencies that serve as the building blocks for future relationships (Hartup & Sancilio, 1986). For example, success in managing
interpersonal intimacy in preadolescent friendships has implications
for the development of later romantic relationships (Sullivan, 1953).
Second, some continuity in individuals' experience of interpersonal
relationships over time is expected, and children who lack the necessary
skills to successfully form a mutual friendship in preadolescence are
likely to have similar difficulties in forming high-quality friendships
later in life.

Method

Participants

Sixty young adults (mean age = 23.2 years) who had taken part in a
short-term longitudinal study begun when they were in fifth grade [aged
ten] participated in the current follow-up investigation. The participants
were originally recruited from all fifth-grade classes of five elementary
schools located in a suburban Midwestern community. The original
sample consisted of 334 participants (175 males and 159 females) who
represented over 90% of the fifth-grade students in the five elementary
schools (mean age = 10.3 years).

The follow-up investigation included 15 males and 15 females (all
Caucasian) in each of two groups – those who had a stable, mutual
best friend in fifth grade and those who did not have a mutual friend
in fifth grade ($N = 60$). At both fifth-grade assessments, children nominated their three best friends. Members of the *friended* group chose the
same first best friend at both assessments, and this friendship choice
was reciprocal, that is, the named first best friend nominated the participant as his or her first best friend at both time periods. The *chumless*
group consisted of participants who did not receive a reciprocal nomination by any of their three friendship choices at either fifth-grade
assessment. These stringent criteria for the two groups are important
for testing theoretical assertions about the developmental significance
of friendship.

Recruitment procedure and attrition

Approximately one third of the original sample met our inclusion criteria for either the friended ($N = 58$) or chumless ($N = 55$) group. Potential
participants in the follow-up study were relocated based on high school
alumni data, local and national telephone books and city directories, and
information from classmates. Our objective was to include 15 males and
15 females in each of the chumless and friended groups, and participant
recruitment continued until this goal was met. In the process of locating
these 60 participants, one chumless male refused to participate, and
three chumless males agreed to participate but failed to return their completed questionnaires even after multiple follow-up contacts. Thus, 19

males in the chumless group were actually contacted. To examine whether there were systematic differences in participant recruitment, one-way analyses of variance were used to compare the 60 participants and the 53 nonparticipants in the friended and chumless groups. No significant differences were found on any of the preadolescent measures of peer rejection, social reputation, or perceived competence.

Preadolescent assessment

The preadolescent data collections considered in the present analysis include two assessments in the spring of the participants' fifth-grade year, and a sixth-grade assessment that occurred approximately 12 months after the first data collection when the students had moved to a consolidated middle school (see Bukowski & Newcomb, 1984; Newcomb & Bukowski, 1983, 1984). The fifth-grade data collections were separated by a one-month interval, and all 334 students completed both of these assessments. The fifth-grade data collections were selected as the primary assessments for the present follow-up study because the fifth-grade children had generally associated with the same peers for at least several years and were expected to have formed well-established friendships and because the fifth-grade data were more complete than the sixth-grade data. One set of new information that was collected in sixth grade but not in fifth grade (i.e., a measure of self-competence) is included in the present follow-up study as well.

During the two fifth-grade assessments, students completed a sociometric questionnaire on which they nominated three same-sex grademates as their best friends and three with whom they would least like to play. Children were assigned rejection scores based on the number of times they were nominated by same-sex peers as a least-preferred playmate, and these raw scores were standardized by school and gender. The rejection score used in the present analyses was the average of the participant's standardized score for least-liked playmate nominations at the two fifth-grade assessments.

In addition, the students were asked to choose classmates for 14 roles in a hypothetical class play. These roles were submitted to a factor analysis, and four factors consistently emerged (see Newcomb & Bukowski, 1983). The roles were thus combined to create the composite reputation scores of class competence (e.g., class president, tries to help), social prominence (e.g., liked by everyone, team captain), aggression (e.g., mean cruel boss, picks on smaller kids), and immaturity (e.g., afraid and acts like a little kid, acts sad). These composite scores represented the average standardized number of nominations received for each individual role in the particular composite reputation. The reliabilities of these four composite reputations were acceptable (all αs > .60). In the present analyses, the reputation scores are the average of the two fifth-grade scores. Finally, at the sixth-grade data collection, all but two participants also completed the Perceived Competence Scale for Children (Harter, 1982), which measures children's perceptions of their competence in four domains – cognitive, social, physical, and general self-worth.

Adult assessment

The measures used in the current follow-up investigation (described below) were presented in a questionnaire booklet that required approximately one hour to complete. The questionnaire booklets were either mailed to participants or given to them in person, and the participants completed the instruments at their convenience. With minor exceptions (see Ns in table 1), participants correctly completed all sections of the booklet. Upon return of the assessment booklet, participants were given $25.00 in compensation for their time and were administered a short interview on the quality of their preadolescent friendship. These ten-minute interviews were conducted either in person when the questionnaire booklet was retrieved or over the phone. Participants were also asked to indicate the name, address, and phone number of their present same-sex best friend, and in instances where this information was released, the friend was contacted and asked to complete a two-part assessment about the target participant. Those friends who completed questionnaire booklets were paid $10.00.

Life status. A slightly modified version of the Status Questionnaire developed by Morison and Masten (1991) was used to obtain biographical information about the participants since middle school. Two judges independently rated each questionnaire on the primary scale of overall adjustment and the eight specific domains of functioning: school performance, job performance, family interaction, aspiration level, social life, activity involvement, trouble with the law, and mental health

Table 1 Correlations between friendship status, peer rejection, gender, and the dependent measures

Measure	F	R	G	Measure	F	R	G
Social reputation:				Adult perceived competence:			
Class competence	.36	−.36	.13	General self-worth[a]	.37	−.20	−.07
Social prominence	.50	−.26	.18	Job competence[a]	.19	−.06	.07
Aggression	−.39	.67	−.12	Intellectual competence[a]	.19	−.15	.20
Immaturity	−.39	.78	−.13	Social skills[a]	.19	−.10	−.09
Preadolescent competence:				Parent relationships[a]	.22	−.24	−.07
General self-worth[b]	.11	−.06	.17	Friendships[a]	.17	−.30	−.01
Cognitive competence[b]	.03	.01	−.11	Morality[a]	.25	−.04	−.31
Social competence[b]	.21	−.13	.12	Romantic relationships[a]	.29	−.13	−.14
Physical competence[b]	.20	−.05	.32	Athletic competence[a]	.32	−.40	.39
Friendship quality:				Adult psychopathological:			
Overall quality[b]	.42	−.32	.18	Global Severity Index	−.27	.27	−.14
Conflict[d]	−.30	.02	−.39	Somatization	−.19	.30	−.16
Enjoyment[d]	.34	.03	.04	Obsessive-compulsive	−.12	−.04	−.11
Help[d]	.35	.11	−.04	Interpersonal sensitivity	−.24	.24	−.13
Disclosure[d]	.37	−.01	−.46	Depression	−.38	.25	−.06
Support[d]	.30	.29	−.34	Anxiety	−.11	.16	−.16
Sensitivity[d]	.36	.22	−.20	Hostility	−.23	.18	−.05
Satisfaction[d]	.26	.03	.06	Phobic anxiety	−.18	.26	−.21
Loyalty[d]	.38	.19	.11	Paranoid ideation	−.29	.24	−.10
Affection[d]	.50	.07	.08	Psychoticism	−.22	.30	−.12
Reconciliation[d]	.14	.15	.21	Adult relationship status:			
Adult life status:				Friendship competence	.17	−.17	−.11
Overall adjustment	.38	−.53	.08	Romantic competence	.23	−.10	−.02
School performance	.27	−.49	.09	Friendship quality[e]	.13	.03	−.31
Job performance[d]	.15	−.25	.09	Best friend report of adult			
Family interaction	.31	−.18	−.08	relationship status:			
Aspiration level	.22	−.50	.01	Friendship competence[e]	.25	.08	.12
Social life	.25	−.30	−.19	Friendship quality[e]	.14	−.01	−.07
Activity involvement	−.01	−.28	−.04	Independent variables:			
Trouble with the law	.33	−.26	−.05	Rejection	−.45		−.17
Mental health difficulties	.13	.07	−.08				

All ns not equal to 60 are as follows: [a]*n = 59,* [b]*n = 58,* [c]*n = 57,* [d]*n = 48, and* [e]*n = 36. For relationships with n ≥ 57, correlations greater than ±.25 are significant at p < .05, correlations greater than ±.32 are significant at p < .01, and correlations greater than ±.41 are significant at p < .001. For relationships with n = 48, correlations greater than ±.27 are significant at p < .05, correlations greater than ±.36 are significant at p < .01, and correlations greater than ±.44 are significant at p < .001. None of the correlations with n = 36 is significant. F = friendship status (coded 0 = chumless and 1 = friended), R = peer rejection, G = gender (coded 0 = female and 1 = male).*

difficulties. Raters used a five-point Likert scale (1 = well below average to 5 = well above average) on all except the mental health difficulties measure, which was evaluated on a three-point scale. For all nine sub-scales, higher scores represent better adjustment. Judgments were made comparatively based on the entire sample for seven of the nine scales. The trouble with the law and mental health difficulties scales were not rated comparatively; instead, an absolute scale was used. Consistent with the interrater reliability reported by Morison and Masten (1991), correlations between the two judges ranged from .84 to .96.

Perceived competence.   A modified version of the Perceived Competence Scale for College Students (Harter, 1990) was used to assess the participants' perceptions of their general self-worth and competence in eight specific domains: job competence, intellectual competence, social skills, parent relationships, friendships, morality, romantic relationships, and athletic competence. The three subscales of appearance, humor, and creativity were excluded from the present analyses because any relation between these dimensions and friendship status or peer rejection in preadolescence was not expected to be psychologically meaningful. Four items indexed each specific domain, and the primary general self-worth scale included six items. All subscales were found to evidence acceptable internal consistency (α ranged from .59 to .93).

Psychopathological symptoms.   The participants' reports of psychopathological symptoms were assessed with the Brief Symptom Inventory (BSI), a 53-item self-report inventory designed to reflect patterns of psychological symptoms (Derogatis, 1992). Participants indicated on a five-point scale (0 = not at all to 4 = extremely) the degree to which they had experienced distress from each symptom during the past week. The Global Severity Index (GSI) as well as the nine specific symptom dimensions of somatization, obsessive-compulsive, interpersonal sensitivity, depression, anxiety, hostility, phobic anxiety, paranoid ideation, and psychoticism are included in the present analyses. The GSI represents the participant's overall degree of symptomatology and is the average score on all 53 items. Scores on the specific symptom dimensions represent the participant's average score on the items in each domain.

Relationship competence and friendship quality.   The Interpersonal Competence Questionnaire (ICQ; Buhrmester, Furman, Wittenberg, & Reis, 1988) assessed the participants' perceptions of their competence in five domains of both friendship and romantic relationships. Intercorrelations between the five competence domains were high for both romantic relationships, $r(58) = .26$ to .79, and friendships, $r(58) = .35$

to .71; thus, all 40 items were collapsed into one score for competence in friendships (α = .95) and one score for competence in romantic relationships (α = 0.96). The quality of the participants' relationship with their current best friend was assessed with an adapted version of the McGill Friendship Questionnaire (Mendelson & Aboud, 1996). Because of the high correlations between subscales, $r(58)$ = .45 to . 78, the mean of all items was used as an index of friendship quality (α = .97).

When participants released the name of their current best friend, those friends were asked to complete a two-part questionnaire about their relationship with the target participant.[1] For the first part of the questionnaire, the friends responded to the ICQ statements indicating the degree of competence the target participant displayed in his or her relationship with the friend. The best friends of target participants also completed the friendship quality measure, responding to the statements about the target participant. For both of these questionnaires, correlations between individual subscales were high, $r(22)$ = .30 to .69 on ICQ, and $r(22)$ = .29 to .79 on friendship quality measure, and the items were collapsed into one measure for friendship competence (α = .94) and one measure for friendship quality (α = .97).

Retrospective report of preadolescent friendship quality. After completion of the questionnaire booklet, participants were administered a brief interview about their best friend in fifth grade. When participants could not remember the name of their best friend or indicated someone other than who they nominated in fifth grade, they were given the name of the person nominated as their best friend at the first fifth-grade data collection.[2] Although participants were allowed to discuss the friendship they freely recalled, only information about their relationship with the peer they nominated as a best friend in fifth grade was of interest in the current analyses. Three open-ended questions (i.e., describe your relationship with your best friend; describe what you did together; were there any negative features of your relationship?) were designed to index the participants' memories of their friendship and the quality of their relationship.

Independent judges rated the overall quality of the relationship on a 1 (lowest quality) to 5 (highest quality) scale based on responses to these open-ended questions. For example, a rating of 3 indicated an average quality relationship where there were no special positive or negative aspects of the friendship. Highest quality friendships (i.e., a rating of 5) were those that were especially intense and intimate, whereas lowest quality friendships (i.e., a rating of 1) contained many negative features, such as a lack of reciprocity or frequent and intense conflict. Interrater agreement for this rating scale was satisfactory ($r = .89$).

The participants also rated their fifth-grade friendship on ten seven-point scales (1 = not at all to 7 = very much) that indexed specific positive and negative friendship features: conflict, enjoyment, help, disclosure, support, sensitivity, satisfaction, loyalty, affection, and reconciliation. The participants' score on each of the ten specific indices of friendship quality was simply their rating on the seven-point scale. These dimensions of relationship quality are consistent with those assessed in previous measures of friendship quality (Bukowski, Hoza, & Boivin, 1994; Parker & Asher, 1993).

Results

First, we examined the characteristics of friended and chumless children in preadolescence and the association between friendship status and peer rejection as concurrent predictors of preadolescent adjustment. In these regression analyses, criterion variables included the children's social reputations in fifth grade, their perceived competence in sixth grade, and their adult retrospective report of friendship quality in fifth grade. We next concentrated on our primary question of the relative importance of mutual friendship and peer rejection as predictors of adult adjustment. In addressing this question, measures of life status, perceived competence, psychopathological symptoms, and adult relationship competence and friendship quality were regressed on preadolescent friendship status and peer rejection.

Gender was entered on the first step in each regression. However, gender was associated with aspects of preadolescent and adult adjustment in only a few instances. When gender was significant, this variable was maintained in the final models. In all other cases, the analyses were executed again with gender excluded to obtain the best-fitting model. Our two primary predictors of friendship status and peer rejection were expected to be at least somewhat related. As such, we examined the potential problem of multicollinearity with the Variance Inflation Factor (VIF). Following the recommendations of Neter, Wasserman, and Kutner (1990), none of the VIF values exceeded 10, and none of the mean VIF values for the predictor variables in any regression analysis were considerably larger than 1. Thus, multicollinearity did not appear to hinder our interpretation of unique effects of the predictor variables.

The outcome measures of life status and perceived competence in adulthood had comparable preadolescent measures. The pairing of preadolescent and adult measures was based on logical equivalency in domains of functioning. For example, the perceived competence measure used in adulthood was modeled after the preadolescent measure of perceived competence. The primary difference was the greater number of specific competence dimensions in the adult measure. As such, the preadolescent self-competence scores were expected to provide important control variables in assessing changes in competence from preadolescence to adulthood. The preadolescent competence domain that was most equivalent to each adult domain was used as a control variable.

The social reputation measures were expected to provide adequate preadolescent indicators to control for the stability of aspects of life status into adulthood. Specifically, the preadolescent reputation of class competence was used as a control variable in the analyses of adult job performance and aspiration level. Likewise, social prominence in preadolescence was comparable to social life and activity involvement in adulthood. The preadolescent aggression reputation was expected to be most related to trouble with the law and mental health difficulties in adulthood. In addition, immaturity was also used as a control variable for adult mental health difficulties because of its association with social withdrawal. The single preadolescent role of being smart was used as a control variable for school performance. Finally, overall life status adjustment and family interaction did not have comparable preadolescent measures to use as control variables.

For each adult criterion variable, the comparable preadolescent measure was entered on the first step of the hierarchical multiple regression (or second if gender was significant), and friendship status and peer rejection were entered next. To the extent that there was significant consistency in functioning over time, these analyses provided a rigorous examination of the relation between preadolescent social relationships and changes in functioning from preadolescence to adulthood. Consequently, any significant predictors of changes in adjustment are especially noteworthy (Berndt & Keefe, 1995).

Preadolescent friendship status and peer rejection as predictors of concurrent adjustment

Social reputations. Table 1 shows that friendship status and peer rejection in fifth grade were both powerful indicators of concurrent measures of social reputations. As shown in table 2, however, the multivariate regressions indicated that friendship status was a unique predictor of social prominence, and preadolescents with friends had more prominent reputations than their chumless peers. Furthermore, peer rejection predicted a unique portion of the variance in social reputations for aggression and immaturity. Almost half of the variance in the immaturity reputation was explained by peer rejection. Preadolescents with higher rejection scores were perceived by peers as more immature and aggressive than those with lower levels of peer rejection. In contrast, neither friendship status nor peer rejection was uniquely associated with competence in classroom activities.

Table 2 Summary of regression analyses of friendship status and peer rejection on fifth-grade social reputations and sixth-grade perceived competence

Measure	R^2	β_G	sr^2_G	β_F	sr^2_F	β_R	sr^2_R
Social reputation:							
Class competence	.18**	...	...	.25	.05	−.24	.05
Social prominence	.25***	...	...	.48	.19***	−.04	.00
Aggression	.46***	...	...	−.11	.01	.62	.31***
Immaturity	.62***	...	...	−.05	.00	.76	.46***
Perceived competence:							
General self-worth	.01	...	...	.10	.01	−.02	.00
Cognitive competence	.00	...	...	.05	.00	.03	.00
Social competence	.05	...	...	.18	.03	−.05	.00
Physical competence	.16*	.35	.12**	.25	.05	.13	.01

Significance tests for β and sr^2 are identical, and notations of significance are placed only on sr^2; sr^2 = squared semipartial correlation; G = gender (coded 0 = female and 1 = male), F = friendship status (coded 0 = chumless and 1 = friended), R = peer rejection.
*p < .05; **p < .01; ***p < .001.

Perceived competence.   Although fifth-grade adjustment as assessed by social reputations was highly related to competence in peer relations, perceived self-competence in sixth grade had no association with having friends or being rejected by peers one year earlier (see table 1). This lack of connection between self-competence and social relationships held for all four domains of cognitive, social, physical, and general self-worth. As indicated in table 2, gender was significantly related to physical competence, and boys viewed themselves as more competent in this domain than did girls.

Friendship quality.   Young adults' retrospective report of the quality of their relationship with their best friend in fifth grade yielded consistent associations with preadolescent friendship status. Friendship status was significantly correlated with all dimensions of quality except satisfaction and reconciliation (see table 1). Young adults who had a friend in preadolescence reported greater overall quality as well as greater enjoyment, help and assistance, intimate disclosure, emotional support, sensitivity, loyalty, and mutual affection in their preadolescent friendships than did those young adults who had been chumless. Furthermore, the friendships of friended preadolescents were remembered as less conflict-ridden than were the relationships between chumless preadolescents and the peer they nominated as a best friend.

Peer rejection accounted for a significant portion of the variance in the overall quality of preadolescents' best friendship, and lower levels of peer rejection were associated with higher-quality relationships (see table 1). Nevertheless, peer rejection was correlated with young adults' retrospective report of only one specific domain of the quality of their best friendship in fifth grade – higher levels of peer rejection were associated with greater support in friendships. Finally, gender was associated with retrospective reports of three domains of friendship quality – conflict, disclosure, and emotional support. As shown in table 1, females reported greater emotional support, self-disclosure, and conflict in their preadolescent best friendships than did males.

The regression of ratings of the overall quality of friendships from retrospective report on friendship and peer rejection indicated that only friendship status was uniquely related to friendship quality. Adults who had a friend in fifth grade recalled higher-quality friendships than adults who were chumless in fifth grade ($\beta = .35$, $sr^2 = .10$, $p < .05$).

Suppression effects hindered the interpretation of the multivariate regressions predicting the specific dimensions of friendship quality. The relations among the domains of friendship quality, peer rejection, and friendship status revealed an overall tendency for children with friends to be low on social rejection, although both having friends and being rejected in preadolescence were positively associated with young adults' retrospective report of specific dimensions of the quality of their fifth-grade best friendship. As such, interpretation of these effects should be limited to the zero-order correlations described above.

Preadolescent friendship status and peer rejection as predictors of adult adjustment

Life status. The primary scale of overall adjustment was especially useful in the current follow-up assessment because it was based on bio-graphical information that spanned the entire 12-year period from the fifth-grade assessments to the follow-up assessment. As shown in table 1, friendship status was correlated with overall adjustment, and friended preadolescents were better adjusted in adulthood than were chumless preadolescents. Furthermore, higher levels of preadolescent peer rejec-tion were uniquely associated with poorer overall life status adjustment (see table 3). The presence/absence of a mutual friend, however, did not explain a unique portion of the variance in overall adjustment when considered in the multivariate regression with peer rejection.

Turning to the eight specific domains of life status adjustment, friend-ship status was correlated with school functioning, family interactions, and difficulties with authority figures and the law (see table 1). In all cases, the effect was in the expected direction – friended preadolescents experienced better adjustment in school and in family relationships, and they had less trouble with authorities than did their chumless peers. Higher levels of preadolescent peer rejection were also associated with poorer school competence and greater trouble with authorities. Fur-thermore, as shown in table 1, being rejected by peers in preadolescence was associated with lower aspiration levels, participation in fewer orga-nizations and activities with others, and a less active social life across adolescence and early adulthood.

The associations between the two aspects of preadolescent peer rela-tions and adult adjustment were further clarified by examining their unique association with each specific domain of adult functioning in

Table 3 Summary of regression analyses of friendship status and peer rejection on life status adjustment

Adult measure	Fifth-grade trait controlled	R^2	β_T	sr^2_T	β_F	sr^2_F	β_R	sr^2_R
Overall adjustment	None	.30***	...	...	.18	.02	−.45	.16***
School performance	Smart	.28***	.21	.04	.02	.00	−.41	.13**
Job performance	Competence	.13*	−.29	.07	.11	.01	−.30	.07*
Family interaction	None	.10	...	...	.29	.07*	−.05	.00
Aspiration level	Competence	.31***	.28	.06	−.08	.00	−.43	.14**
Social life	Prominence	.11	.12	.01	.09	.00	−.23	.04
Activity involvement	Prominence	.10	−.02	.00	−.16	.02	−.36	.10*
Trouble with the law	Aggression	.12	−.03	.00	.26	.05	−.13	.01
Mental health difficulties	Aggression and immaturity	.06	.01 −.27	.00 .02	.19	.03	.36	.03

Significance tests for β and sr^2 are identical, and notations of significance are placed only on sr^2; sr^2 = squared semipartial correlation, T = fifth-grade trait, F = friendship status (coded 0 = chumless and 1 = friended), R = peer rejection.
*p < .05; **p < .01; ***p < .001.

the multivariate regressions presented in table 3. In these regressions, comparable measures of preadolescent adjustment were first entered into the equation, followed by friendship status and peer rejection. The combination of these three variables accounted for a significant portion of the variance in the specific domains of school performance, job performance, and aspiration level. Examination of the unique associations of friendship status and peer rejection with these outcome variables indicated that school adjustment, which was correlated with both friendship status and peer rejection, was uniquely associated only with peer rejection. In addition, peer rejection was uniquely associated with aspiration level and job performance in the multivariate regressions.

Perceived competence. The most apparent finding in the prediction of young adults' perceptions of competence was the stability in their self-assessments of competence from sixth grade to adulthood. Table 4 reveals that sixth-grade perceptions of competence predicted levels of adult general self-worth and competence in social skills, friendships, and romantic relationships as well as job, intellectual, and athletic competence. Despite this stability, friendship was a significant unique predictor of general self-worth in adulthood, even when entered in

Table 4 Summary of regression analyses of friendship status and peer rejection on perceived competence in adulthood

Adult measure	Sixth-grade competence measure controlled	R^2	β_G	sr^2_G	β_T	sr^2_T	β_F	sr^2_F	β_R	sr^2_R
General self-worth	General	.24**	. . .	. . .	.34	.11**	.31	.08*	−.01	.00
Job competence	Cognitive	.12	. . .	. . .	.28	.08*	.21	.04	.01	.00
Intellectual competence	Cognitive	.20**	. . .	. . .	.41	.17**	.11	.01	−.09	.01
Social skills	Social	.14*	. . .	. . .	.34	.11*	.10	.01	.00	.00
Parent relationships	Social	.06	. . .	. . .	−.03	.00	.12	.01	−.16	.02
Friendships	Social	.20**	. . .	. . .	.31	.09*	.01	.00	−.27	.06
Morality	Social	.19*	−.30	.08*	−.16	.03	.28	.06*	.00	.00
Romantic relationships	Social	.18*	. . .	. . .	.33	.11*	.21	.03	.03	.00
Athletic competence	Physical	.46***	. . .	. . .	.55	.29***	.04	.00	−.35	.10**

Significance tests for β and sr^2 are identical, and notations of significance are placed only on sr^2; sr^2 = squared semi-partial correlation, G = gender (coded 0 = female and 1 = male), T = fifth-grade trait, F = friendship status (coded 0 = chumless and 1 = friended), R = peer rejection.
*p < .05; **p < .01; ***p < .001.

combination with peer rejection and after controlling for the stability of perceptions of general competence in preadolescence. As expected, friended preadolescents viewed themselves more positively in adulthood than did preadolescents who were chumless.

At the level of specific competence dimensions, young adults' perceptions of competence in moral behavior, romantic relationships, and athletics were also related to friendship status in fifth grade (see table 1). Young adults who had friends in preadolescence viewed themselves as more competent in these domains than did those who had been friendless in fifth grade. Nevertheless, these findings were clarified by the multivariate regressions presented in table 4. For the morality subscale, the significant effect of friendship was maintained even after controlling for preadolescent competence. The significant gender effect accounted for nearly 10% of the variance in moral competence as women viewed themselves as more competent in their standards of moral behavior than did men. Competence in romantic relationships, however, was not uniquely related to preadolescent friendship status when the level of preadolescent social competence was controlled.

Athletic competence was correlated not only with preadolescent friendship status but also with peer rejection, and when entered into the regression simultaneously, a unique portion of variance was explained only by peer rejection. Higher levels of preadolescent peer rejection were associated with less athletic competence in young adulthood, even when preadolescent athletic competence was controlled. Greater rejection by peers was also negatively correlated with competence in adulthood friendship relations (see table 1), but once preadolescent social competence was controlled, this relation was no longer significant.

Psychopathological symptoms. A clinically elevated level of symptomatology was defined as a *T* score of 70 or greater on a subscale of the BSI. Approximately 12% of the participants evidenced clinically significant elevation on the overall severity of psychopathological symptoms (i.e., the GSI). On the nine specific symptom dimensions, the level of clinically elevated symptomatology in the current sample ranged from 3% to 17%. These levels are consistent with the general population.

Friendship status in preadolescence was related to the overall severity of psychopathological symptoms in adulthood, as well as to specific symptoms of depression and paranoid ideation (see table 1). In both the global and two specific domains, friended preadolescents evidenced less symptomatology in young adulthood than did preadolescents who were chumless. The index of global symptom severity was also related to preadolescent peer rejection, and higher levels of peer rejection were related to greater psychological maladjustment in young adulthood. Nevertheless, when both friendship and rejection were included as predictors, neither accounted for a unique portion of the variance in global severity of psychopathological symptoms (see table 5).

In contrast, the unique relation between friendship status and depressive symptomatology was maintained even when peer rejection was also included as a predictor of these symptoms. As shown in table 1, the symptom dimensions of somatization, phobic anxiety, and psychoticism were correlated only with preadolescent peer rejection. Preadolescents who encountered greater peer rejection experienced more distress in these domains of psychopathology in adulthood than did their less-rejected peers. These associations were not significant, however, when both friendship status and peer rejection were included as predictors (see table 5).

Table 5 Summary of regression analyses of friendship status and peer rejection on adult psychopathological symptoms

Symptom dimension	R^2	β_F	sr^2_F	β_R	sr^2_R
Global Severity Index	.10*	−.19	.03	.18	.03
Somatization	.09	−.07	.00	.27	.06
Obsessive-compulsive	.02	−.17	.02	−.11	.01
Interpersonal sensitivity	.08	−.16	.02	.16	.02
Depression	.15**	−.33	.09*	.10	.01
Anxiety	.03	−.05	.00	.13	.01
Hostility	.06	−.19	.03	.09	.01
Phobic anxiety	.07	−.08	.00	.22	.04
Paranoid ideation	.10*	−.23	.04	.13	.01
Psychoticism	.10*	−.11	.01	.26	.05

Significance tests for β and sr^2 are identical, and notations of significance are placed only on sr^2; sr^2 = squared semipartial correlation, F = friendship status, R = peer rejection.
$^*p < .05$; $^{**}p < .01$; $^{***}p < .001$.

Relationship competence and friendship quality.   Our measures of young adults' competence in romantic relationships and friendships yielded no association between current functioning and preadolescent friendship status or peer rejection. Furthermore, the quality of participants' current best friendship was not related to preadolescent measures of peer competence. The lack of findings for friendship competence and quality was apparent both in the young adults' self-report and in the report of the young adults' current best friend. The only significant finding in these analyses indicated that females reported a higher-quality relationship with their current best friend than did males in young adulthood.

Discussion

Despite theoretical assertions that preadolescent friendships play an important if not essential role in social and emotional development (Hartup, 1996; Sullivan, 1953), the empirical investigation of these hypotheses via long-term prospective study has been absent. In the current study, the relative significance of friendship and peer rejection for positive adult adjustment is examined in the domains of life status, perceived competence, and psychopathological symptoms. All three of these adjustment domains were significantly associated with peer relations in preadolescence; yet, the most important conclusion from the present findings is that peer acceptance/rejection and participation in mutual friendships are not redundant predictors of adult adjustment. Instead, different components of peer relationships are associated with different aspects of adult functioning.

On the global measure of life status, both having a mutual friend in fifth grade and low levels of peer rejection predict successful adult adjustment. As hypothesized, however, only peer rejection is uniquely associated with variations in overall life status adjustment. Within specific life status domains, the most telling findings indicate that even when levels of competence in preadolescence are controlled, greater rejection by peers in fifth grade is associated with lower school performance, vocational competence, aspiration level, and less participation in social activities. Mutual friendship in fifth grade is also associated with aspects of positive life status adjustment, but when considered with peer rejection, friendship status has unique predictive implications only for positive relations with family members.

These findings about specific domains of life status adjustment are generally consistent with theoretical speculations and prior research. The links between peer rejection and school adjustment are congruent with previous findings that academic difficulties and school dropout are related to poor peer acceptance (Coie, Lochman, Terry, & Hyman, 1992; Ollendick, Weist, Borden, & Greene, 1992). In short-term longitudinal studies with younger children, having high-quality friendships and maintaining friendships were related to successful school transitions (Ladd, 1990; Ladd et al., 1996). Although the present findings suggest that friendship is not unrelated to school success, children's experience of rejection by classmates has greater long-term implications for their success and involvement in educational endeavors.

The association between preadolescent friendship and successful family interaction is not surprising, and suggests some continuity in close relationships over time. Given research establishing links between early parent–child attachment and successful friendships in childhood and preadolescence (Elicker, Englund, & Sroufe, 1992; Park & Waters,

1989), the current findings may reflect an ongoing positive adjustment in family relationships that existed before preadolescent peer experiences. Regardless of the direction of the effect, the close affective tie of preadolescent mutual friendships appears to be associated with other close relationships, namely, family relationships.

A surprising finding from the life status measure indicates that friendship and peer rejection together predict trouble with the law across adolescence and adulthood, yet neither uniquely predicts maladjustment in this domain. Empirical examination of the association between peer rejection and delinquent behavior reveals that peer rejection is highly related to antisocial outcomes (Coie et al., 1992). Nevertheless, the absence of a mutual friendship in preadolescence also appears to have implications for externalizing difficulties across adolescence and young adulthood. This relation deserves greater empirical attention, especially as the friendships of antisocial boys are characterized by low satisfaction and reinforcement for talk about antisocial behavior (Dishion, Andrews, & Crosby, 1995).

The finding that general self-worth is uniquely predicted by friendship status even when levels of preadolescent self-competence was controlled supports one of Sullivan's (1953) primary views about the importance of preadolescent friendships, that is, friendships provide opportunities for validation of self-worth and a unique context for exploration and development of personal strengths. Sixth-grade measures of perceived competence were not related to friendship status or peer rejection one year earlier, but the association between having a friend in preadolescence and high levels of general self-worth in adulthood is moderately strong. Perhaps these findings demonstrate the formative impact of friendships on children's social and emotional development (see Buhrmester, 1996). In particular, the aspects of preadolescent friendships that are most important for promoting self-worth and self-competence may have a more long-term, as opposed to immediate, impact on a child's well-being.

Although both higher levels of peer rejection and being chumless in preadolescence predict greater distress from psychopathological symptoms in adulthood, neither aspect of preadolescent peer relations is uniquely associated with levels of clinical symptomatology. The lack of a unique relation between peer rejection and psychopathological symptoms is somewhat surprising given the significant body of research asserting this association (see Kupersmidt et al., 1990; Parker & Asher,

1987; Parker et al., 1995). The present findings do not contradict previous research, yet they indicate that having a friend in preadolescence may be just as important for later psychological health as is being accepted by the general peer group. In light of these findings, the link between friendship and mental health adjustment deserves greater attention, and further prospective as well as case-control study examining the particular associations between having friends, friendship quality, and psychological adjustment is warranted.

Turning to the more specific symptom dimensions, the most important finding was that the presence of depressive symptomatology in adulthood is uniquely associated with being chumless in preadolescence. Friendships are generally supportive relationships that promote self-esteem and provide a setting for intimate disclosure, emotional support, and mutual understanding (Newcomb & Bagwell, 1995). The lack of experience with these supportive features of a close friendship may contribute to depressive symptoms. Furthermore, friends may provide an important buffer against stress, and this protective component may help ward off depressive feelings associated with stressful life situations (Parker et al., 1995). The present findings extend other concurrent and short-term longitudinal associations between friendship and depression (e.g., Vernberg, 1990), and indicate that the failure to form a close friendship in preadolescence has important implications for the presence of depressive symptoms in adulthood.

Overall, our findings for life status adjustment, perceived competence, and psychopathological symptoms reinforce the associations between preadolescent peer relations and global measures of adult adjustment. Although not overwhelming, the findings indicate that there are indeed specific areas of functioning that are associated with success in certain types of preadolescent peer relationships. Nevertheless, we hypothesized that measures of competence in adult friendship and romantic relationships as well as the quality of the participants' current best friendship would be predicted by preadolescent friendship experience. No associations between peer rejection or friendship status were found for these measures. Furthermore, reports by the participants' current best friends on the quality of their relationship and the participants' level of social competence in their friendship did not vary as a function of preadolescent peer experience.

These latter findings should be interpreted with caution due to the small sample size in these analyses and the possibility of systematic attrition. Fifteen of the participants were unwilling to release the name of their best friend, and for another nine participants, we were unable to receive completed questionnaires from their best friends. Also, the absence of interscale discrimination in our measures of relationship competence and friendship quality reduced our prospects of finding true differences. Given these limitations of the present study, our initial hypotheses should not be abandoned without further empirical investigation, especially because of the theoretical rationale supporting these associations.

The measurement of friendship quality is one relatively recent advance in the study of children's friendship and is based on the assumption that friendships vary in the degree to which positive and negative attributes exist (Berndt, 1996; Hartup, 1996; Parker & Asher, 1993). Our initial preadolescent assessment did not include a measure of friendship quality. Nevertheless, based on a retrospective report of the quality of the participants' fifth-grade best friendship, it appears that, as expected, friended children had a higher overall quality relationship than chumless children. Although a retrospective report is not without limitations, these results suggest that conclusions about the importance of having a friend may be somewhat confounded with friendship quality. As in most examinations of children with and without friends, having friends appears to mean having supportive friendships of high quality (Hartup, 1996).

The current findings need to be placed in a conceptual framework. Although we find a relation between preadolescent friendship, rejection, and adult adjustment, we have not necessarily established a causal link between preadolescent peer relations and adult outcome. Nevertheless, a causal model where poor adult adjustment is directly caused by failures in preadolescent peer relations is one possible explanation. A second view suggests that lacking friends and being rejected by the peer group in preadolescence are only markers for behavioral and adjustment difficulties but have no implications for maladjustment in adulthood. In this incidental model, poor peer relationships are merely an epiphenomenon of the underlying disturbance that causes both poor peer relationships and poor adult outcomes (Parker & Asher, 1987).

A potentially more useful model claims the middle ground between the causal and incidental models. In this model, children's experience with peers moderates the relation between risk variables and maladjustment. Positive experiences with peers and friends provide some degree of resiliency for a child who is at risk for poor outcomes due to earlier socialization experiences, genetic vulnerabilities, or ecological factors. Conversely, the additional stress of rejection by peers and failing to establish a mutual friendship can interact synergistically with the existing difficulties of the vulnerable child and thus exacerbate the potential for negative outcomes (Kupersmidt et al., 1990).

Clearly, the design of the current study prohibits the evaluation of the causal model. The study is correlational in nature, and no matter how convincing the results, the conclusion that poor preadolescent peer and friendship relations cause poor adult outcome cannot be made. We are thus left with the possibility that poor peer relations are only a marker for underlying difficulties that will produce maladaptive outcomes, or that they moderate the emergence of these difficulties into more extreme adjustment problems. Despite the uncertainty about the particular model that accurately describes the implications of preadolescent peer experience for later adjustment, our findings highlight the nonredundant nature of friendship and rejection by the general peer group and suggest that both aspects of peer relations have important implications for adaptive development.

Notes

1   We were unable to collect completed questionnaire booklets from 24 of the participants' current best friends. Fifteen participants (one friended male, two friended females, seven chumless males, and five chumless females) did not release the name of their best friend. The current best friends of five participants (one friended male, two friended females, one chumless male, and one chumless female) did not return the questionnaire booklet even after two booklets were sent and multiple phone calls were made. We were unable to contact the best friends of four participants (one friended male, two friended females, and one chumless male) because the participants did not have their friends' correct addresses or phone numbers.

2   Ten participants (three friended females, five chumless females, and two chumless males) did not remember their fifth-grade best friend well enough to complete the ratings on the retrospective report of friendship quality. These ten participants were excluded from analyses involving the specific dimensions of friendship quality but not from analyses of the overall friendship quality ratings.

References

Berndt, T. J. (1996). Exploring the effects of friendship quality on social development. In W. M. Bukowski, A. F. Newcomb, & W. W. Hartup (Eds.), *The company they keep: Friendships in childhood and adolescence* (pp. 346–365). New York: Cambridge University Press.

Berndt, T., & Keefe, K. (1995). Friends' influence on adolescents' adjustment to school. *Child Development, 66,* 1312–1329.

Buhrmester, D. (1996). Need fulfillment, interpersonal competence, and the developmental contexts of early adolescent friendship. In. W. M. Bukowski, A. F. Newcomb, & W. W. Hartup (Eds.), *The company they keep: Friendships in childhood and adolescence* (pp. 158–185). New York: Cambridge University Press.

Buhrmester, D., Furman, W., Wittenberg, M. T., & Reis, H. T. (1988). Five domains of interpersonal competence in peer relationships. *Journal of Personality and Social Psychology, 55,* 991–1008.

Bukowski, W. M., & Hoza, B. (1989). Popularity and friendship: Issues in theory, measurement, and outcome. In T. Berndt & G. Ladd (Eds.), *Peer relationships in child development* (pp. 15–45). New York: Wiley.

Bukowski, W. M., Hoza, B., & Boivin, M. (1994). Measuring friendship quality during pre- and early adolescence: The development and psychometric properties of the Friendship Qualities Scale. *Journal of Social and Personal Relationships, 11,* 471–485.

Bukowski, W. M., & Newcomb, A. F. (1984). The stability and determinants of sociometric status and friendship choice: A longitudinal perspective. *Developmental Psychology, 20,* 941–552.

Coie, J. D. (1990). Toward a theory of peer rejection. In S. R. Asher & J. D. Coie (Eds.), *Peer rejection in childhood* (pp. 365–401). New York: Cambridge University Press.

Coie, J. D., Lochman, J. E., Terry, R., & Hyman, C. (1992). Predicting early adolescent disorder from childhood aggression and peer rejection. *Journal of Consulting and Clinical Psychology, 60,* 783–792.

Cowen, E. L., Pederson, A., Babigian, H., Izzo, L. D., & Trost, M. A. (1973). Long-term follow-up of early detected vulnerable children. *Journal of Consulting and Clinical Psychology, 41,* 438–446.

Derogatis, L. R. (1992). *The Brief Symptom Inventory (BSI): Administration, scoring and procedures manual – II.* Minneapolis: National Computer Systems, Inc.

Dishion, T. J., Andrews, D. W., & Crosby, L. (1995). Antisocial boys and their friends in early adolescence: Relationship characteristics, quality, and interactional process. *Child Development, 66,* 139–151.

Elicker, J., Englund, M., & Sroufe, L. A. (1992). Predicting peer competence and peer relationships in childhood from early parent–child relationships. In

R. D. Parke & G. W. Ladd (Eds.), *Family peer relationships: Models of linkage* (pp. 77–106). Hillsdale, NJ: Erlbaum.

Furman, W., & Robbins, P. (1985). What's the point? Issues in the selection of treatment objectives. In B. H. Schneider, K. H. Rubin, & J. E. Ledingham (Eds.), *Children's peer relations: Issues in assessment and intervention* (pp. 41–54). New York: Springer-Verlag.

Harter, S. (1982). The Perceived Competence Scale for Children. *Child Development, 53,* 87–97.

Harter, S. (1990). The Perceived Competence Scale for College Students. Unpublished manuscript, University of Denver.

Hartup, W. W. (1996). The company they keep: Friendships and their developmental significance. *Child Development, 67,* 1–13.

Hartup, W. W., & Sancilio, M. F. (1986). Children's friendships. In E. Schopler & G. B. Mesibov (Eds.), *Social behavior in autism* (pp. 61–79). New York: Plenum.

Kupersmidt, J. B., Coie, J. D., & Dodge, K. A. (1990). The role of poor peer relationships in the development of disorder. In S. R. Asher & J. D. Coie (Eds.), *Peer rejection in childhood* (pp. 274–305). New York: Cambridge University Press.

Ladd, G. W. (1990). Having friends, keeping friends, making friends, and being liked by peers in the classroom: Predictors of children's early school adjustment? *Child Development, 61,* 1081–1090.

Ladd, G. W., Kochenderfer, B. J., & Coleman, C. C. (1996). Friendship quality as a predictor of young children's early school adjustment. *Child Development, 67,* 1103–1118.

Mendelson, M. J., & Aboud, F. E. (1996, August). *Measuring friendship quality in late adolescents and young adults.* Poster presented at the annual meeting of the American Psychological Association, Toronto.

Morison, P., & Masten, A. S. (1991). Peer reputation in middle childhood as a predictor of adaptation in adolescence: A seven-year follow-up. *Child Development, 62,* 991–1007.

Neter, J., Wasserman, W., & Kutner, M. H. (1990). *Applied linear statistical models: Regression, analysis of variance, and experimental designs* (3d ed.). Boston: Irwin.

Newcomb, A. F., & Bagwell, C. L. (1995). Children's friendship relations: A meta-analytic review. *Psychological Bulletin, 117,* 306–347.

Newcomb, A. F., & Bukowski, W. M. (1983). Social impact and social preference as determinants of children's peer group status. *Developmental Psychology, 19,* 856–867.

Newcomb, A. F., & Bukowski, W. M. (1984). A longitudinal study of the utility of social preference and social impact sociometric classification schemes. *Child Development, 55,* 1434–1447.

Ollendick, T. H., Weist, M. D., Borden, M. G., & Greene, R. W. (1992). Sociometric status and academic, behavioral, and psychological adjustment: A five-year longitudinal study. *Journal of Consulting and Clinical Psychology, 60,* 80–87.

Park, K. A., & Waters, E. (1989). Security of attachment and preschool friendships. *Child Development, 60,* 1076–1081.

Parker, J. G., & Asher, S. R. (1987). Peer relations and later personal adjustment: Are low accepted children "at risk"? *Psychological Bulletin, 102,* 357–389.

Parker, J. G., & Asher, S. R. (1993). Friendship and friendship quality in middle childhood: Links with peer group acceptance and feelings of loneliness and social dissatisfaction. *Developmental Psychology, 29,* 611–621.

Parker, J. G., Rubin, K. H., Price, J., & DeRosier, M. E. (1995). Peer relationships, child development, and adjustment: A developmental psychopathology perspective. In D. Cicchetti & D. Cohen (Eds.), *Developmental psychopathology: Vol. 2. Risk, disorder, and adaptation* (pp. 96–161). New York: Wiley.

Roff, M., Sells, S. B., & Golden, M. M. (1972). *Social adjustment and personality development in children.* Minneapolis: University of Minnesota.

Sullivan, H. S. (1953). *The interpersonal theory of psychiatry.* New York: Norton.

Vernberg, E. M. (1990). Psychological adjustment and experiences with peers during early adolescence: Reciprocal, incidental, or unidirectional relationships? *Journal of Abnormal Child Psychology, 18,* 187–198.

The School Context

Introduction to Part II

In a typical school year, students spend more than one third of their waking hours in school or in school-related activities. Thus, children spend a significant part of their lives at school. In most Western countries virtually all children and adolescents up to age 17 are enrolled in school. In addition to teaching children and adolescents to read and write, and other academic skills, schools help children develop fundamental aspects of their personality, such as socializing with peers and developing identity, autonomy, and their own sense of morality. The articles in this section are designed to highlight the significance of the role that the school context plays in the development of competencies and in the socialization of children and adolescents.

FIVE

Bullying and Victimization

Introduction

Recently in North America, there have been several incidents where children who are bullied frequently or isolated from the mainstream peer groups have brought guns to school and shot teachers and students. These students have been regularly victimized or picked on by their peer group. Approximately 10 percent of students are frightened at school through most of the school day. Some of these students avoid lunch, recess, and playtime out of fear that they will be humiliated or picked on by bullies. These are students who are targeted over and over again by individuals who are stronger or bigger than themselves. The consequences of being a victim or a bully are significant. Children who are regularly victimized suffer from anxiety, low self-esteem, depression, and academic problems. Some victims, sadly, attempt suicide out of desperation and in extreme cases may even act out violently, as in the recent shootings. Bullies are at risk for conduct disorder and delinquency in adolescence and for serious criminal and antisocial behavior in adulthood. They, too, often drop out of school and in adulthood may have difficulty holding a job and sustaining healthy intimate relationships.

Bullying is not a new problem at school. Only recently, however, have researchers recognized the long-term negative effects of being involved in bullying. This article is the first study that conducted naturalistic observations of bullying at school. It provides descriptive information on the frequency of bullying, the content of bullying, the role of the peers in bullying, and intervening in bullying. In addition, the study used remote microphones and hidden video cameras to observe the students interacting at lunch and recess. This methodology is new and provides a rich source of data and greater understanding of the problem of bullying.

Observations of Bullying and Victimization in the School Yard

Wendy M. Craig and Debra J. Pepler

Bullying is a form of social interaction in which a more dominant individual (the bully) exhibits aggressive behavior intended to cause distress to a less dominant individual (the victim) (Smith & Thompson, 1991). Research in Norway, Canada, Britain, and Ireland reveals that bullying is a frequent and normative behavior in schools (Ekblab & Olweus, 1986; Olweus, 1987; Perry, Kusel, & Perry, 1988; Pepler, Craig, Ziegler, & Charach, 1994; Whitney & Smith, 1993). In a nationwide survey conducted in Norway, 9% of students reported being bullied twice a term or more frequently while 7% reported bullying others in the same time frame. Fewer children reported being bullied (3%) and bullying others on a weekly basis (2%) than twice a term. In Canada, 19% of students reported being bullied more than twice a term, while 8% reported being bullied at least once a week. Similarly, 15% of children reported bullying others more than twice a term, while 9% of children reported bullying others on a weekly basis (Charach, Pepler, & Ziegler, 1995). This rate in Canada is nearly four times as high as the rates from Norway (Olweus, 1991), but comparable to those from Ireland (O'Moore, 1991). To date, however, there are no published studies using systematic observation to assess bullying (Farrington, 1993). The unique contribution of the present study is the examination of bullying from naturalistic observations of children on the school playground.

The theoretical foundations for the present research derive from an integration of individual difference, social-interactional, and ecological perspectives. The individual difference or personality perspective relates involvement in bullying to characteristics such as the temperament, gender, and behavioral tendencies of bullies and victims. The seminal work of Olweus in Norway derives from this perspective. He identified bullies as having an antisocial personality combined with physical strength and victims as having an anxious personality pattern combined with physical weakness (Olweus, 1991). Although the individual difference perspective has provided a strong foundation for understanding bullying, it contributes a static (i.e., attributes bullying to individual characteristics) rather than a dynamic (e.g., understanding the importance of the social context and the role of others) understanding of bullying. We have, therefore, also incorporated a social-interactional perspective to understand bullying as a dynamic phenomenon which unfolds within a social context. The social-interactional model was proposed to explain the development of antisocial behavior within the family context (Patterson, DeBaryshe, & Ramsey, 1989; Patterson, Reid, & Dishion, 1992; Reid & Patterson, 1989). Based on naturalistic observations, Patterson and his colleagues described the coercive process by which children develop a negative and hostile interaction style when their parents or siblings react irritably and ineffectively to aggressive behaviors. This perspective identifies the bidirectional influence of aggressive children and their parents in the development of aggressive behavior. Children are thought to transfer the aggressive interaction patterns learned in the home to the school context (Patterson et al., 1989). A similar analysis of the bidirectional effects of bullies' and victims' behaviors might clarify bullying interactions.

As recommended for studies concerning other aspects of aggression (e.g., Cairns & Cairns, 1991; Coie & Jacobs, 1993), a broad relational or ecological perspective must be imposed on the study of bullying. Hence, the theoretical perspective of bullying must extend beyond a juxtaposition of individual and social interactional frameworks. In other words, the interactions of bullies and victims cannot be fully explained by merely the convergence of two personality patterns, but must be considered within a complex of interactional influences, such as the peer group and the school social system.

Students report that the playground is the most likely location for bullying (Whitney & Smith, 1993; Olweus, 1991; Pepler et al., 1994). The combined influences of the peer group and the adult supervisors likely affect bullying interactions on the school playground. Huesmann and Eron (1984) identified three contextual processes that increase the likelihood of aggression: observing aggression, receiving aggression, and reinforcement for aggression. Peers likely play a role in all three of these processes. They may serve as instigators of bullying, models for aggression and/or may join in a bullying episode. The peer group may reinforce interactions by serving as an audience for the theater of bullying. On the other hand, peers and adults can intervene to stop bullying and decrease its likelihood. For example, 75% of teachers report that they always intervene in bullying episodes on the playground (Charach et al., 1995); however, in contrast, children report that adults intervene in only a small proportion of bullying episodes (Pepler, Craig, Ziegler, & Charach, 1993). Naturalistic observations of bullying may clarify this discrepancy between teacher and student reports.

To date, the vast majority of studies on bullying and victimization have employed questionnaire or interview methodologies. These methods provide assessments of the prevalence of bullying problems, characteristics of the bully and/or victim, characteristics of bullying episodes, and peer attitudes. Questionnaires and interview methods are limited, however, by their inability to identify the complex, multilevel processes underlying bully–victim interactions and by the children's ability to accurately report on the phenomenon of bullying. Naturalistic observations of children's aggression have several advantages over laboratory studies (e.g., Caprara, Passerini, Pastorelli, Renzi, & Zeli, 1986; Pepler & Craig, 1995). First, behaviors can be recorded within the context in which they occur; hence, external validity is high. Secondly, bullying interactions can be studied in-vivo with the opportunity to observe not only the bullies and victims, but also the behaviors of others involved (i.e., peers, teachers). Finally, the remote audiovisual technology employed in the present research provides an opportunity to observe spontaneous incidents of bullying not normally witnessed by adults (Pepler & Craig, 1995). Because the remote technology in the present study obtains both audio and visual aspects, it will be possible to examine both direct and indirect aggression.

The present study has several objectives. The main objective is to describe the frequency, duration, and type of bullying. A second objective is to describe the individual factors of gender, age, race, and aggressive reputation of bullies and victims. A third objective is to describe the social interactions of the bully/victim dyad, while the final objective is to describe the social ecology of peer involvement and intervention by both peers and adults during bullying episodes.

Method

The present research is an extension of an ongoing research program examining the peer relations of aggressive and socially competent children (i.e., children socially skilled in their interactions) (Pepler, Craig, & Roberts, 1995). As part of this research, a sample of 41 aggressive and 41 socially competent children (matched for age, gender, and ethnicity) were videotaped on the playgrounds of two elementary schools during both the winter and spring semesters during unstructured play (at recess and lunch.). At each point in time, the videotaping took place over a three-week period. The schools were in middle-class neighborhoods, had approximately 300 students in grades 1 through 6 [aged six to twelve], and the students attending them represented a variety of ethnic groups.

Participants

The sample for the present study included all children targeted in the original study who were observed in a bullying episode during 48 hours of playground observations. In the original study, classroom teachers nominated aggressive and socially competent children. Group assignment was validated by comparing aggressive and socially competent children on both teacher and peer ratings. On the Child Behavior Checklist Teacher Report Form (Achenbach & Edelbrock, 1986) mean teacher ratings of aggressive children's externalizing problems were in the clinical range ($M = 66.2$) and were significantly higher than those for the socially competent children ($M = 43.2$ $F(1,37) = 214.7, p < .0001$). On the Revised Class Play Peer Nomination Form (Masten, Morrison, & Pellegrini, 1985) peers rated aggressive children ($M = 5.09$) as being significantly more aggressive than the socially competent children ($M = -1.28$, $F(1,37) = 35.4, p < .0001$).

Eighty-two percent of the original aggressive children and 76% of the original socially competent children were involved in bullying, either as a bully or a victim. Thus, from the original study, there were 34 teacher-nominated aggressive children (25 boys, 9 girls) and 31 teacher-nominated socially competent children (23 boys, 8 girls). The mean age of participants was 9.9 years (*s.d.* = 1.1 years). The children were from low- to middle-income families and varied with respect to ethnicity (43% Caucasian, 25% African descent, and 32% mixed or other ethnicity). The distribution of bullies, victims, and bully/victims (children who both bullied and were bullied) by gender is provided in table 1. Bullies and victims were defined as children who participated in that role in at least two observed episodes. Bully/victims were children who were observed being bullies in at least two episodes and being victimized in at least two episodes. Two episodes were chosen as the criteria for group composition to reflect the repeated nature of bullying. The mean number of episodes children were involved in was 3.6, *s.d.* = 1.4, range: 11 episodes.

Children were filmed randomly at lunch or recess for approximately equal time sampling periods. Children in the study had an average of 53 minutes of observation time (*s.d.* = 12.0, range: 36–82 minutes).

To observe children's interactions, the video camera was set up in a classroom overlooking the playground. During filming, each target child wore a small remote microphone and pocket-sized transmitter. The remote microphone picked up not only the target's speech, but also that of others around him/her. All children who wore the microphones were aware that they were being filmed. They were instructed to play as they normally would during lunch and recess.

Observers identified bullying episodes, coded contextual factors, and marked the location of bullying episodes on a detailed site plan of the school property. Inter-reliabilities for the identification of episodes, the contextual variables, and the playground locations were calculated

Table 1   Distributions and proportions of bullies, victims, and bully/victims by gender

	Bullies		*Victims*		*Bully/victims*	
	Males	Females	Males	Females	Males	Females
Aggressive	3	3	4	2	18	4
	(4.6%)	(4.6%)	(6.1%)	(3.1%)	(27.7%)	(6.1%)
Nonaggressive	0	6	2	0	20	3
	(1.5%)	(9.2%)	(3.1%)	(0%)	(30.8%)	(4.6%)

through percent of agreement. Bullying episodes were identified by two female observers with 90% interrater reliability. An agreement was considered positive when both raters identified a bullying episode and concurred to a duration within five seconds at the beginning and the end of an identified episode. One male and two female observers coded the contextual variables. An agreement was counted if observers identified the same contextual variables for an episode. Three variables with a percent agreement less than 75 were discarded (height of the bully, weight of the bully, weight of the victim). The percent agreement for the remaining contextual variables ranged from 87% to 100%. Interrater reliability was based on 33% of the episodes that were independently rated for all three observers.

Following each episode, observers also completed a Global Rating Measure adapted from Observer Impression Sheet developed by the Oregon Social Learning Center. The measure comprised 23 questions rated on a five-point scale, as well as 19 bipolar adjectives rated on a seven-point scale. The questions assessed level of covertness of the episode, perceived attitude of the bully and the victim, presence of adults and their role, the role of the peer group, and reactivity to the camera. The overall agreement for the Global Rating Measure was 87%, ranging from 76% to 100%. (For more information on the Global Rating Measure, please contact the first author.)

Results

The results are divided into four sections: nature of bullying, individual characteristics of bullies and victims, social interactional factors, and social ecology. School and seasonal effects were assessed and where there were significant differences, they are reported. Otherwise the analyses are collapsed over these variables.

There were 314 bullying episodes observed during 48 hours of playground observations of aggressive and nonaggressive children. This amounts to 6.5 episodes of bullying per hour. Two percent of bullying interactions were uncodeable. The audio recording indicated that bullying was occurring (e.g., "Give me the skipping rope or I'll kill you"), but the children were not visible on the film (e.g., behind a school building). Each bullying episode was timed from onset to termination while the majority of bullying episodes were short-lived and there was substantial variability in duration. The mean duration of bullying episodes was 38 seconds (*s.d.* = 66.6 seconds), with a range from 2 to 466 seconds.

Taking into account the amount of time spent filming at each school (by using proportional variables), chi-square analyses indicated a significant association between school and season in the number of bullying episodes per hour χ^2 (2,314) = 28.90, $p < .001$). From the winter to the spring, the rate of bullying increased at School 1, whereas it decreased at School 2. There were no other school or seasonal differences; thus the remaining results are presented collapsing over these variables.

We were concerned that reactivity to the camera and microphones might affect the frequency of observed bullying. As a validity measure, for each episode, observers rated the reactivity to the camera for bully(ies), victim(s), and peers on a five-point scale ranging from frequently playing to the camera to not attending to the camera. After combining the categories of overt and extremely overt, bullies, victims, and adults were judged as reacting to the camera in 2.7%, 2.2%, and .4% of the episodes, respectively. Thus, children's overall behavior on the playgrounds during bullying episodes was relatively unaffected by the microphones and filming.

Verbal aggression was observed in 50% of the episodes, while physical aggression was observed in 29%. Both physical and verbal aggression were observed in 21% of the episodes. Observers noted the use of objects in physically aggressive bullying (e.g., knives, skipping ropes, sticks, and balls) with bullies using an object as a weapon to attack or threaten a victim in 4% of the episodes. There was only one episode in which a victim was observed to have a weapon.

The majority of the episodes (80%) comprised direct bullying, 18% comprised indirect bullying, and 2% comprised both direct and indirect bullying. Gossiping, coded as a unique form of indirect bullying, was observed in 7% of the episodes. Bullying with sexist content was not observed in any episode. Episodes were also coded for racial content (i.e., if the bully exaggerated or made fun of a stereotype of the victim's race). Bullying involving racial content occurred during 4% of the episodes.

We were interested in whether the nature of bullying varied as a function of the duration of the episode. Thus, episodes were categorized into three levels of duration: episodes of short duration (less than 12 seconds), medium duration episodes (between 12 and 39 seconds), and long episodes (greater than 40 seconds). There was a significant relationship between duration and type of aggression (χ^2 (2,314) = 5.81, $p < .05$). The episodes of short duration were relatively equally distributed between verbal aggression (22% of episodes) and physical aggression (17% of episodes). The medium and long episodes were more likely to be verbal (21% of the medium episodes and 21% of the long episodes) than physical (12% of the medium episodes and 7% of the long episodes). Similarly, there was a significant relationship between the duration of an episode and the type of bullying (χ^2 (2,314) = 8.96, $p < .01$). Episodes of short duration had more direct bullying (33%) compared to medium (25%) and long episodes (24%). Of the short-duration episodes, 90% involved direct bullying. Four percent of the episodes of short duration had indirect bullying compared to 9% of the medium episodes and 6% of the long episodes.

There was also a significant relationship between the type of aggression and the type of bullying (χ^2 (2,314) = 7.50, $p < .001$). Children were more likely to use direct rather then indirect bullying, regardless of whether they were being physically or verbally aggressive. In 44% of the episodes, there was direct verbal bullying (e.g., calling someone names) and in 19% of the episodes there was indirect verbal bullying (e.g., spreading a nasty rumor). Thirty-one percent of the episodes involved direct physical bullying (e.g., hitting), while 3% of the episodes comprised indirect physical bullying (e.g., shutting someone out of a group). The remaining 3% of the episodes involved both types of aggression.

Individual characteristics of bullies and victims

Number and gender of bullies, victims, and bully/victims.   The individual factors were also examined by classifying children as bullies, victims, and bully/victims if they were observed in more than two episodes. Twenty percent of children were observed bullying others, 12.1% of children were observed being victimized, and 67.9% of the sample bullied and were victimized.

In 90% of the episodes, there was only one bully, in 9% of the episodes there were two bullies, and in fewer than 1% of the episodes there were three bullies. Ninety-two percent of the episodes involved only one victim, 6% of the episodes involved two victims, and fewer than 2% of the episodes involved three or more victims.

The representation of boys' and girls' involvement in bullying was examined by considering the rate of bullying per hour by gender. Seventy-two percent of the filming was conducted with a boy wearing the microphone and 28% with a girl wearing the microphone. To control for the discrepancy in the hours spent filming boys and girls, proportional variables were constructed to indicate rates of bullying per hour. A z-test of proportions indicated a significant difference in the proportional frequencies of boys and girls observed bullying, $z = 4.12$, $p < .001$. Boys were involved in bullying at a rate of 5.2 episodes per hour while girls bullied at a rate of 2.7 episodes per hour.

Grade level.   Children were divided into two grade levels: primary level (ages six to eight) or junior level (ages nine to eleven). In 2% of the episodes, the grade level of either the bully or the victim was uncodeable. A chi-square analysis indicated no grade level differences in the classification of children as bullies, victims or bully/victims.

Aggressive reputation.   There was relatively equivalent participation by the aggressive and socially competent children in bullying and victimization. Aggressive children bullied others at a rate of 2.54 episodes per hour, while socially competent children bullied others at a rate of 2.02 episodes per hour. Aggressive children were victimized by others at a rate of 2.08 episodes per hour, while socially competent children were victimized at a rate of 2.08 episodes per hour.

Social-interactional factors

The social-interactional context of bullying interactions was assessed for the gender, grade, and race composition of the dyads and for the affective behavioral tone.

Bully/victim dyad.   Z-tests for proportions assessed differences in the gender of victims targeted by boy and girl bullies. Boy bullies were more likely to target same-sex victims than girl bullies ($z = 6.31$, $p < .001$). In 86% of the episodes involving boy bullies, boys were the victims. In 48% of the episodes involving girl bullies, girls were the victims. Conversely, boys were less likely than girls to bully a victim of the opposite sex ($z = -6.57$, $p < .001$). In 11% of the episodes involving boy bullies, the victims were girls. In 49% of the episodes involving girl bullies, the victims were boys. There was no significant difference between boys and girls in the number of episodes in which the victims were both boys and girls.

In 67% of the episodes, bullies victimized children in the same-age grouping (35% of the episodes involved primary students and 32% of the episodes involved junior students). Bullies from a junior grade victimized primary children in 5% of the episodes. In 2% of the episodes primary children were aggressive to junior children. Bullies did not discriminate their victims based on racial characteristics. In 59% of the episodes, the bully and the victim were of the same race and in 41% of the episodes the bully and the victim were of different races.

Global ratings of children's behavior in bullying interactions. For each episode, bullies and victims were coded on a seven-point scale for a number of bipolar affective and behavioral attributes (e.g., noncompliant–compliant, cold–warm, hostile–calm). The means and standard deviations by group are reported in table 2. A MANOVA comparing bullies and victims indicated that bullies were rated as being more

Table 2 Mean proportions and standard deviations of global ratings for bullies and victims

	Bullies		Victims		F-Values
	M	SD	M	SD	
Non-compliant–Compliant	2.1	1.0	4.0	2.0	258.2*
Cold–Warm	2.9	1.5	4.4	1.7	207.9*
Hostile–Calm	3.3	1.7	4.4	1.8	91.5*
Insensitive–Sensitive	2.2	1.2	4.3	1.6	368.9*
Dull–Spirited	5.1	1.3	4.7	1.6	13.8*
Depressed–Happy	4.9	1.1	4.5	1.6	17.6*
Physically Aggressive**	2.9	1.8	4.8	2.2	220.2*
Verbally Aggressive**	2.2	1.3	4.2	2.3	208.7*
Loud–Quiet	2.7	1.4	3.9	1.9	103.5*
Provocative	2.0	1.1	4.4	2.5	260.8*
Resistant–Resigned	2.4	1.1	4.0	2.4	218.6*
Sarcastic–Soothing	2.4	1.2	4.1	1.7	503.8*
Dominant–Passive	2.2	1.1	4.8	1.7	405.4*
Leader–Follower	2.4	1.3	4.8	1.7	344.2*

*Significant at p < .001.
**Higher scores indicate more aggression.

provocative, hostile, insensitive, active, physically and verbally aggressive, sarcastic, and dominant than victims. In addition, bullies were rated as being happier, colder, louder, and more of a leader than victims ($F(3,304) = 995.21, p < .001$).

A z-test of proportions indicated that bullies were significantly more hostile than victims ($z = 14.82, p < .001$). Bullies were rated as being hostile to the victim in 85% of the episodes, whereas victims were rated as hostile to the bully in 41% of the episodes. Bullies were coded as enjoying the interaction in significantly more episodes than victims ($z = 15.49, p < .001$) (77% and 13%, for bullies and victims, respectively). In 79% of the episodes, victims were coded as being tormented, indicating the severity of the majority of episodes. Bullies and victims were coded as being fearful prior to the bullying in 1% and 11% of the episodes, respectively.

Social ecology

The ecology of bullying was described according to the location and covertness of the episodes, and the nature of peer and adult involvement.

Location and covertness of bullying. Sixty-eight percent of the bullying episodes were observed within 120 feet of the school building, 19% were within 120 and 240 feet of the school building, and 13% were further than 240 feet from the school building. The playgrounds were approximately 200 by 360 feet. There were no associations between the type of aggression or the type of bullying displayed in the bullying episode and the location of bullying. In addition, there was no relationship between the duration of an episode and the location of the episode. Finally, there was no relation between the frequency of teacher intervention and the location of bullying.

Observers rated the extent to which each bullying episode was hidden from peers or adults on a five-point scale (ranging from extremely covert to extremely overt). Ratings of 4 or 5 on the scale were deemed to be overt. Significantly more episodes were rated as overt (84%) than covert (16%) ($z = -15.5, p < .001$).

Peers were involved in some capacity during 85% of the bullying episodes observed on the school playground. Four levels of involvement were coded: active participation in the episode, observing the interaction, involvement in an activity with the bully or victim, and intervening in the interaction. In 30% of the episodes, peers actively participated in the bullying episode as an aggressor, and in 23% of the episodes peers just witnessed the bullying interaction. Peers were involved in a joint game with the bully or victim during 61% of the episodes. Peers intervened in 12% of the bullying episodes. Peers intervened significantly less often in a socially appropriate manner (3.5%) than in a socially inappropriate manner (7.4%) ($z = 2.48$, $p < .05$). Peers were observed to be present in 85% of episodes and they intervened in 13% of the episodes in which they were present. These percentages do not total to a hundred since peers could be involved in more than one role during an episode.

There was substantial variability in the number of peers involved in bullying episodes. This variability is not reflected in the above percentages because they indicate at least one peer but several peers may have participated in the identified manner. For example, in two thirds of the episodes in which peers were actively involved there was only one peer; whereas, in 2% of the episodes there were six. In 58% of the onlooking episodes there was only one peer; however, in 2% of the episodes there were six peers. The number of peers participating in a joint game with the bully ranged from one (35% of the episodes) to eighteen (1% of the episodes). These results suggest that are large number of children are in close proximity and participate in bullying episodes.

There was a significant association between the gender and the nature of peer involvement ($\chi^2(4, 301) = 11.4$, $p < .001$). In 55% of the episodes where peers were actively involved, the peers were boys, in 37% they were girls, and in 8% of the episodes they were both genders. For peers in joint activity, 55% of the episodes involved boys, 23% of the episodes involved girls, and in 22% of the episodes there were both boys and girls. Boys were onlookers to bullying more than girls (62% versus 23% of the episodes, respectively). In 15% of the episodes, the onlookers were both genders. Finally, the majority of peers who intervened were boys. In 84% of the episodes with a socially appropriate peer intervention, the intervener was a boy. Similarly, in 65% of the episodes with an inappropriate peer intervention, the intervener was a boy. Due to the small number of episodes in which peers intervened, it was not possible to test for gender differences in the frequency of peer intervention in bullying.

Global ratings of peer participation. Peers were coded as being significantly more respectful to bullies than victims ($z = -2.73$, $p < .05$). Peers were coded as being respectful to the bully in 74% of the episodes and to the victim in 23% of the episodes. Peers also were coded as being significantly more friendly to bullies than victims ($z = 6.43$, $p < .001$). The peers were coded as being friendly to the bully in 57% of the episodes, whereas they were friendly to the victim in 31% of the episodes. The peer group was coded as taking pleasure in the bullying in 30% of the episodes, as neutral in 46% of the episodes, and as uncomfortable in 24% of the episodes. In 81% of the episodes, the peers were coded as reinforcing the bullying episode.

School staff intervention in bullying episodes.   School staff were found to have intervened in 4% of the observed bullying episodes. Staff were visible within the camera frame during an additional 13% of episodes; hence they intervened in approximately 25% of the episodes in which they were proximal. A z-test of proportions indicated that peers intervened more frequently than adults ($z = 3.96$, $p < .01$) (in 13% versus 4% of episodes, respectively). However, adults were almost twice as likely to intervene in bullying episodes when present (23% versus 13%). On the Global Rating Scale, observers judged that school staff were unaware of bullying in about 80% of the episodes.

Discussion

The present study incorporates an observational methodology to examine bullying and victimization. The validity of observational technology is evident by the correspondence with the students' self reports. Bullying was observed frequently and the number of children involved in the present playground observations corresponds closely to self-report data on bullying. In a previous analysis of these observations, we calculated that based on the school populations 26–33% of students in the schools were observed bullying others more than once on the school playground (Craig, 1993). According to self-report data, 24% of students indicated they had bullied once or twice in the last school term (Charach et al., 1995). Both the observational and questionnaire studies raise concerns about the frequency with which children bully others during unstructured play periods at school.

Bullying was surprisingly normative on the school playground with children identified by teachers as nonaggressive being just as likely to bully as those identified as aggressive. Given the wide range of children observed bullying, it appears that children who bully on the playground do not simply represent the most deviant children in the school. This problem behavior is significant involving both boys and girls and both older and younger children in elementary school. Although some of the episodes we observed involved mild forms of teasing or "roughing up," the vast majority of episodes were rated as tormenting the victims. Hence, the observations in the present study raise serious concerns for the psychological and physical well-being of children at school.

To understand bullying and victimization, we need to integrate the theoretical perspectives of individuals, social-interactional, and eco-logical systems. The problem of bullying is too complex to be solely explained by individual personality traits. While some children may have developed a behavior style consistent with a bully or victim, the social interactions and the social ecology of the school playground likely shape the expression of bullying. The lack of differences on individual characteristics such as grade and aggressive reputation suggests that there may be subtypes of bullies and victims (Stephenson & Smith, 1987). In future research, these subtypes may be distinguished by the frequency, severity, pervasiveness of involvement in bullying episodes (Loeber, 1990; Stephenson & Smith, 1989). Children who are consis-tently observed in bullying episodes may be chronic bullies, victims, or bully/victims. For example, in the case of bullies, their aggressive be-havior on the playground may reflect a stable antisocial personality pattern (Olweus, 1991). In contrast, children who engage in bullying less consistently may be individuals whose aggressive behaviors are more situationally determined.

A second inference of the widespread involvement of individuals in bullying is that the interactions of bullies and victims cannot be fully explained by the convergence of two personality patterns, but must be considered within an ecological framework of interactional influence, such as the peer group and the school social system. In keeping with the recommendations of Cairns and Cairns (1991) and Coie and Jacobs (1993), these observations highlight the social context of bullying. The results of this study indicate that bullying is an interpersonal activity which arises most within the context of at least one other person (i.e., the peer group) and that the peer group likely plays a major role in providing the reinforcements and contingencies for these behavior problems.

Research on aggression has recently begun to examine the dyadic contextual influences on aggression. Dodge, Coie, Pettit, and Price (1990) observed different types of dyads and found that the type of partner determined the quality of play. For example, they found that when two highly aggressive boys interacted, angry reactive aggression occurred. Given that males were present more often than females as peer participants, one of the factors that may be influencing the instigation of bullying is the presence of males. Boys are more attracted to aggressive interactions than girls (Serbin et al., 1993) and may find bullying episodes more stimulating and arousing than female peers. Boys may also use bullying as a display of dominance which, by definition, is most effectively communicated with an audience (Campbell, 1993). Consequently, male bullies may receive more reinforcement and encouragement from their peers for their bullying behavior.

Boys may have bullied more than girls because they are more likely than females to engage in rough-and-tumble play (Smith & Boulton, 1990). Aggressive behavior, such as bullying, is more likely to occur when children are engaged in active rough-and-tumble play than when they engage in parallel or cooperative play (Dodge et al., 1990). Rough-and-tumble play may escalate into aggression due to the misinterpretation of another's action (Smith & Boulton, 1990). Since males engage more frequently in rough-and-tumble play than girls, the social context for boys may elicit or provoke bullying and aggression.

Finally, female bullying may be qualitatively different than male bullying. Girls may be more likely to bully when peers are not present. For girls, bullying may be a one-on-one relational experience rather than a group experience. This result parallels the research on girls' play patterns and friendships. Girls are more likely than boys to spend time with one peer, whereas boys are more likely to spend time in a group (Pepler et al., 1994). Thus, female bullying may be more difficult to detect (Rivers & Smith, 1994). Peer processes such as the level of activity prior to the bullying episode, the affective quality of the group's atmosphere, and the type of group activity are important foci for future research.

Olweus (1991) identified social contagion as a potential peer mechanism which may serve to initiate, maintain and exacerbate bullying on the school playground. The two processes involved in the social contagion effect are reinforcement and modeling. In the majority of episodes in the present study, peers were found as reinforcing the bully. The reinforcement provided by peer attention and involvement may serve to maintain the power of the bully over the victim, as well as the dominance of the bully within the peer group. The dimensions of the peer group context may influence the way that the group responds to bullying among its members. DeRosier et al. (1994) suggest that social contagion may occur because the aggressive acts toward a victim are a safe focus of the group's negative feelings. If there is conflict within the group prior to the bullying episode, a cohesive bullying effort may serve to dissipate the group's negative feeling.

In addition, peers may model the negative behaviors of the bully toward the victim. The global ratings indicated that the peer group was less respectful and friendly to the victim than the bully. The peer group may be modeling the bullies' behaviors. The differential attention to bullies by the peer group may further reinforce them for their power assertion, as well as confirm for victims that they are deserving of the attack. In this way, the victim becomes scape-goated by the group. The peer group's disrespect for victims suggests that empathy from the peer group needs to be developed for victims.

Peers were involved in the vast majority of bullying episodes either as co-conspirators or as witnesses to the abuse; however, they intervened to stop bullying almost three times more often than adults. When intervention was examined as a function of time present, peers were less likely than adults to intervene. One explanation for the lack of intervention by peers may be that they are afraid of reprisals from bullies. Laboratory research indicates that when a peer group sides with the victim, the level of post-aggression conflict rises (DeRosier et al., 1994). Hence siding with the victim in a playground confrontation may escalate bullying. For boys and girls, there may be different aspects of the group context that influence the onset of bullying and the way it is responded to. DeRoiser et al. (1994) found that the dyadic interaction quality (e.g., cohesion) determined whether the group responded to aggression, but other group qualities (i.e., the level of the group's conflict, the playful competitiveness prior to the episode) determined the nature of the response. Future research should examine the level of activity prior to the bullying episode, the affective quality of the group's atmosphere, and the type of group activity.

Similar social-interactional processes likely operate at the school level to maintain bullying interactions. Adults intervened in relatively few episodes and were judged to be unaware of the vast majority of episodes. A lack of consequences for aggressive behavior provides prime opportunities to acquire aggressive patterns (Huesmann & Eron, 1984). Bullying generally occurred without adult witnesses. The average duration of bullying incidents was relatively brief (38 seconds). While we were able to observe these brief exchanges with the remote audiovisual technology, it is unlikely that teachers would detect such transitory bullying episodes on a large school playground. Indirect forms of bullying may be particularly difficult to detect, as they comprise an aggressor who manipulates others to attack the victim, or makes use of the social structure in order to harm the victim, without being personally involved in the attack (Lagerspetz, Bjorkqvist, & Peltonen, 1988).

An additional problem for the supervising adults is that bullying is difficult to distinguish from other forms of social interaction such as rough-and-tumble play and playful teasing (Pellegrini, 1988). Teachers may witness mild bullying behaviors, but not intervene because they perceive these as normative, nonaggressive, and not stressful for the victim. Teachers may intervene consistently in episodes with angry and hostile affect which they can clearly identify as bullying. As a result, the teachers may perceive they are intervening regularly to stop bullying when in fact our observations indicate that they are inconsistent and infrequent in their attempts to control bullying. Thus, the prevalence of bullying may be related to infrequent and inconsistent adult intervention and monitoring of students' activities on the playground. Research on antisocial behavior within families indicates that poor parental supervision of children's activities contributes to the development of aggressive behaviors (Patterson, 1982). The combination of the brevity of bullying, the difficulty of recognizing bullying, and inconsistent intervention contributes to the prevalence of bullying.

The results of the present study lead to specific suggestions for clinicians and educators in their efforts to reduce violence at their schools. Interventions need to be systemic in nature focusing on not only the individual bullies and victims, but also on the child's other social systems, such as the peers, the school, and the classroom (American Psychological Association, 1993). Intervening at the school level may include the development of an anti-violence policy and ensuring equity among students (e.g., between genders, among cultural groups). To complement the social policy changes in the school environment, an increase in supervision of the halls and playground and more structured activities and organized games on the playground are necessary. Intervention efforts aimed at teachers merit the following: regular school conference days on bullying and victimization are important to increase teachers' awareness and understanding of the problems; increased resources, such as a specific curriculum and strategies to facilitate their classroom discussions and interventions in bullying problems; development of an anti-bullying curriculum which would contain suggestions of topics to be discussed during class time, role playing, and activities.

The results suggest that peers play a central role in bullying episodes. Consequently, it is important to engage peers in an effort to decrease bullying on the playground. Programs such as peer mentoring and conflict management may serve to promote an attitude which disapproves of violence toward others and encourage peer intervention to stop aggressive interactions. Within an anti-bullying program, students must develop an awareness of the problem, a willingness to report bullying, and a sense of security in the knowledge that protection and support are available from teachers, administrators, and other peers. Finally, individual work with the bullies (i.e., anger management, social skills) and victims (i.e., self-esteem enhancement, assertiveness skills training) remain essential.

The present study extends our understanding of bullying with observations of naturally occurring episodes on the school playground. It is important, however, to consider these results in the context of the limitations of the study. This study evolved from an ongoing project on the peer relations of aggressive and nonaggressive children; therefore, caution must be taken in generalizing the results since the sample may not be representative. A second limitation of the present study was that the severity of bullying was not coded. Without a severity rating, we are unable to determine whether the aggressive children were primarily responsible for the extreme bullying and the nonaggressive children were instigating mild forms of peer abuse. Still further, the results of the present study stem from a rather limited sample of children drawn from two elementary schools. Thus, before generalizing the results, replication of the current findings is important. Finally, the study did not examine the effects of the school ethos on bullying. Factors such as the development of an anti-bullying policy have a significant impact on reducing bullying (Olweus, 1991).

Nevertheless, the observational methodology employed in the present study has proven to be an unobtrusive and effective strategy for studying bullying by providing a perspective into dimensions of children's interactions which are normally unavailable to adults. Bullying occurs frequently on elementary school playgrounds and is a complex phenomenon which must be considered from an integration of individual difference, social-interactional, and ecological perspectives. These observational data provide a foundation upon which we can start to build a theory of bullying and victimization which could prove invaluable for clinicians and educators.

References

Achenbach, T. M., & Edelbrock, C. (1986). *Manual for the teacher's report form and version of the child behavior profile.* USA: Queen City Printers.

American Psychological Association (1993). *Commission on violence and youth. (Report, Vol. I).* Washington, DC.

Cairns, R. B., & Cairns, B. D. (1991). Social cognition and social networks: A developmental perspective. In D. J. Pepler & K. H. Rubin (Eds.), *The development and treatment of childhood aggression* (pp. 249–278). Hillsdale, NJ: Erlbaum.

Campbell, A. (1993). *Men, women, and aggression.* New York: Basic Books.

Caprara, G. V., Passerini, S., Pastorelli, R. P., Renzi, P., & Zeli, A. (1986). Instigating and measuring interpersonal aggression and hostility: A methodological contribution. *Aggressive Behavior, 12,* 237–247.

Charach, A., Pepler, D. J., & Ziegler, S. (1995). Bullying at school: A Canadian perspective. *Education Canada, 35,* 12–18.

Cohen, J. (1960). A coefficient of agreement for nominal scales. *Educational and Psychological Measurement, 220,* 37–46.

Coi, J. D., & Jacobs, M. R. (1993). The role of social context in the prevention of conduct disorder. *Development and Psychopathology, 5,* 263–275.

Craig, W. M. (1993). Naturalistic observations of bullies and victims on the playground. Unpublished doctoral dissertation, York University, Toronto.

DeRosier, M., Cillessen, A., Coie, J. D., & Dodge, K. A. (1994). Group context and children's aggressive behavior. *Child Development, 65,* 1069–1079.

Dodge, K. A., Coie, J. D., Pettit, G. S., & Price, J. M. (1990). Peer status and aggression in boys' groups: Developmental and contextual analyses. *Child Development, 61,* 1289–1309.

Ekblab, S., & Olweus, D. (1986). Applicability of Olweus' Aggression Inventory in a sample of Chinese primary school children. *Aggressive Behavior, 12,* 315–324.

Farrington, D. P. (1993). Understanding and preventing bullying. In M. Tonry & N. Morris (Eds.), *Crime and Justice,* Vol. 17 (pp. 381–458). Chicago: University of Chicago Press.

Huesmann, L. R., & Eron, L. D. (1984). Cognitive processes and the persistence of aggressive behavior. *Aggressive Behavior, 10,* 243–251.

Lagerspetz, K., Bjorkqvist, K., & Peltonen, T. (1988). Is indirect aggression typical of females? Gender differences in aggressiveness in 11- to 12-year-old children. *Aggressive Behavior, 14,* 403–414.

Loeber, R. (1990). Development and risk factors of juvenile antisocial behavior and delinquency. *Clinical Psychology Review, 10,* 1–41.

Masten, A. S., Morrison, P., & Pellegrini, D. S. (1985). A revised class play method of peer assessment. *Development Psychology, 21,* 523–533.

Olweus, D. (1987). School-yard bullying – grounds for intervention. *School Safety, 6,* 4–11.

Olweus, D. (1991). Bully/victim problems among school children: Some basic facts and effects of a school based intervention program. In D. Pepler & K. Rubin (Eds.), *The development and treatment of childhood aggression* (pp. 411–438). Hillsdale, NJ: Erlbaum.

O'Moore, A. (1991). What do teachers need to know? In M. Elliott (Ed.), *Bullying: A practical guide to coping for schools* (pp. 56–69). Harlow: Longman.

Patterson, G. R. (1982). *Coercive family process: A social learning approach,* Vol. 3. Eugene, OR: Castalia Publishing Co.

Patterson, G. R., DeBaryshe, B. D., & Ramsey, E. (1989). A developmental perspective on antisocial behaviour. *American Psychologist, 44,* 329–335.

Patterson, G. R., Reid, J. B., & Dishion, T. J. (1992). *Antisocial boys.* Eugene, OR: Castalia.

Pellegrini, A. D. (1988). Elementary school children's rough and tumble play and social competence. *Developmental Psychology, 24,* 802–806.

Pepler, D. J., & Craig, W. M. (1995). A peek behind the fence: Naturalistic observations of aggressive children with remote audio-visual recording. *Developmental Psychology, 31,* 548–553.

Pepler, D. J., Craig, W. M., & Roberts, W. R. (1995). Aggression in the peer group: Assessing the negative socialization process. In J. McCord (Ed.), *Coercion and punishment in long-term perspectives* (pp. 213–228). New York: Cambridge University Press.

Pepler, D. J., Craig, W. M., Ziegler, S., & Charach, A. (1993). A school-based antibullying intervention: Preliminary evaluation. In D. Tattum (Ed.), *Understanding and managing bullying* (pp. 76–91). London: Heinemann Books.

Pepler, D., Craig, W. M., Ziegler, S., & Charach, A. (1994). Bullying: A community problem. *Canadian Journal of Community Mental Health*, *13*, 95–110.

Perry, D., Kusel, S., & Perry, L. (1988). Victims of peer aggression. *Developmental Psychology*, *24*, 807–814.

Reid, J. B., & Patterson, G. R. (1989). The development of antisocial behaviour patterns in childhood and adolescence. *European Journal of Personality*, *3*, 107–120.

Rivers, I., & Smith, P. K. (1994). Types of bullying behaviour and their correlates. *Aggressive Behavior*, *20*(5), 359–368.

Serbin, L. A., Marchessault, K., McAffer, V., Peters, P., & Schwartzman, A. E. (1993). Patterns of social behavior on the playground in 9–11 year old girls and boys: Relation to teacher perceptions and to peer ratings of aggression, withdrawal, and likeability. In C. Hart (Ed.), *Children on the playground* (pp. 162–183). NY: SUNY Press.

Smith, P. K., & Boulton, M. (1990). Rough and tumble play, aggression and dominance: Perception and behaviors in children's encounters. *Human Development*, *33*, 271–282.

Smith, P. K., & Thompson, D. (1991). *Practical approaches to bullying*. London, UK: David Fulton Publishers.

Stephenson, P., & Smith, D. (1987). Anatomy of a playground bully. *Education*, *170*, 11–15.

Stephenson, P., & Smith, D. (1989). Bullying in two English comprehensive schools. In E. Roland & E. Munthe (Eds.), *Bullying: An international perspective*. London, UK: David Fulton Publishers.

Weinrott, M. R., Reid, J. B., & Bauske, B. W. (1981). Supplementing naturalistic observations with observer impressions. *Behavioral Assessment*, *3*, 151–159.

Whitney, I., & Smith, P. K. (1993). A survey of the nature and extent of bullying in junior/middle and secondary schools. *Educational Research*, *35*, 3–25.

SIX

Friendship and School Adjustment

Introduction

Friendship plays a significant role in the lives of children. The word "friend" appears in most children's vocabularies by age four, and friendships also can be identified in infants and toddlers, although cognitive and linguistic aspects of these early relationships are not always obvious. Hartup and Sancilio (1986) argue that friendships provide children with (1) contexts for skill learning and development, (2) emotional and cognitive support, and (3) models for developing future relationships. An emerging area is concerned with the contributions of children's classroom peer relationships to their adjustment to school. When children enter school, they are expected to master a "readiness curriculum" that provides them with prereading and pre-mathematical skills. Many of these lessons are conducted in small groups and activity centers where children need to interact with peers. In this way, peers are influential collaborators in the classroom and may influence and aid each other's learning and development. There is growing evidence to suggest that the relationships children form with peers in the classroom will affect their adjustment at school (e.g., Parker & Asher, 1987).

Within classrooms, it is possible to identify children's individual friends as well as the group of peers that they associate with. Friendship is defined as a reciprocal emotional or affiliative bond between a child and another classmate, and implies a voluntary, mutual, relationship. The following article examines kindergarten children's understanding of friendship, their ability to report on their friendships, and the impact of these friendships on healthy school functioning. The significance of this article is that it highlights the important role that peers play in children's lives as early as five years of age.

References

Hartup, W. W., & Sancilio, M. F. (1986). Children's friendships. In E. Schopler & G. B. Mesibov (eds), *Social behavior in autism* (pp. 61–80). New York: Plenum.

Parker, J. G., & Asher, S. R. (1987). Peer relationships and later personal adjustment: Are low accepted children at risk? *Psychological Bulletin, 102*, 357–89.

Friendship Quality as a Predictor of Young Children's Early School Adjustment

Gary W. Ladd, Becky J. Kochenderfer, and Cynthia C. Coleman

A prominent but understudied premise in the peer relations literature is that friendship affects children's development and adjustment (Berndt & Ladd, 1989). This premise is based on the perspective that, beyond the contributions of other socializers (e.g., parents, teachers), friends make substantial and possibly unique contributions to children's development. Hartup and Sancilio (1986), for example, contend that friendships provide children with (1) a context for skill learning and development, (2) emotional and cognitive resources, and (3) models for later relationships.

Recently, investigators have elaborated upon this perspective by distinguishing conceptually among differing aspects of friendship. Bukowski and Hoza (1989), for example, propose a model in which they identify three different aspects or indicators of friendship: (1) presence or absence of friendship (i.e., whether a child is a participant in a mutually reciprocated friendship with a peer or not); (2) number of friendships (i.e., extensivity of the child's friendship network); and (3) quality of friendship (e.g., features of the dyadic relationship, such as the level of support, companionship, or conflict it provides for the child).

Thus far, investigators who have examined the linkage between friendship and adjustment have tended to employ measures that correspond to the first and second indicators in Bukowski and Hoza's model (i.e., participation in friendship and number of friends). However, in recent reviews and theoretical papers, friendship quality has received increasing attention as a potential contributor to children's adjustment. More specifically, it has been proposed that the relational or dynamic features of friendships (e.g., companionship, support, conflict) create various psychological benefits and costs for children that, in turn, affect their development and adjustment (see Asher & Parker, 1989; Berndt, 1989; Berndt & Perry, 1986; Buhrmester & Furman, 1987; Bukowski & Hoza, 1989; Furman & Buhrmester, 1985; Parker & Asher, 1993; Sharabany, Gershoni, & Hofman, 1981). These social "provisions," as Weiss (1974) termed them, may be present to varying degrees in children's friendships, depending on the nature of the relationship (e.g., stability) and the characteristics of the partners (e.g., gender).

Research on friendship quality is at an early stage; investigators' initial efforts have been focused on construct specification and measurement (i.e., identifying and reliably measuring important friendship features). A review of existing measures (see Ladd & Kochenderfer, in press) shows that investigators have targeted a number of relational processes or provisions as indicators of friendship quality. Included among the features investigators have attempted to measure with grade school children and adolescents are play, prosocial behavior, intimacy, loyalty, attachment, and conflict (Berndt & Perry, 1986); reliable alliance, enhancement of worth, instrumental help, companionship, affection, intimacy (Furman & Buhrmester, 1985); companionship, security, conflict, help, and closeness (Bukowski, Boivin, & Hoza, 1991); validation and caring, help, companionship and recreation, intimate exchange, conflict and betrayal, conflict resolution (Parker & Asher, 1993). As Ladd and Kochenderfer (in press) have noted, some of these features may best be viewed as relationship *processes* (i.e., observable forms of interaction or exchange, such as conflict, help, or guidance) whereas others more likely represent relationship *provisions* (i.e., the putative benefits that children derive from their participation in friendship, such as perceived support, self-worth, or security). Moreover, these features have, for the most part, been assessed from the child's (i.e., the participant's) perspective, yielding data on *perceived* friendship processes or provisions.

Less is known about the relation between specific friendship processes and children's development and adjustment, although findings from recent studies have begun to shed light on this linkage. Bukowski and Hoza (1990) have shown that, during the preadolescent years, specific friendship provisions such as security and closeness forecast later affective outcomes such as loneliness. Similarly, in an investigation conducted with third-through fifth-grade children, Parker and Asher (1993) found that six different facets of children's friendships correlated with their feelings of loneliness in school. Children who reported higher levels of loneliness viewed their friendships as not only more conflictual but also less validating, companionate, helpful, and intimate.

There is also evidence to suggest that the processes that transpire within children's friendships influence important *relationship* outcomes, such as children's appraisals of their friendships (i.e., perceived satisfaction) and their desire to sustain these relationships over time (i.e., friendship stability). Linkages between perceived friendship processes and friendship satisfaction were first explored by Parker and Asher (1993) with samples of grade-school-age children. These investigators found that satisfaction was positively correlated with rewarding friendship processes (i.e., perceived validation and caring, companionship and recreation, help and guidance, intimate exchange), and negatively correlated with aversive features of friendship (i.e., perceived conflict and betrayal). Evidence gathered with older samples also points to a link between perceived friendship processes and the stability of children's friendships. Based on interviews conducted with both fourth and eighth graders, Berndt, Hawkins, and Hoyle (1986) found that friends who reported higher levels of intimate exchange were more likely to remain friends over the course of a school year.

An important limitation of past research is that, with a few notable exceptions (e.g., Gottman, 1983; Howes, 1983; Park & Waters, 1989), little effort has been devoted to mapping the features of young children's friendships, especially from the child's perspective. Thus far, research on friendship features has been conducted primarily with samples of older children (e.g., eight- to twelve-year-olds) and adolescents; we know almost nothing about how young children perceive the quality of their friendships. Moreover, little or nothing is known about how specific friendship processes may impact various relationship outcomes (e.g., friendship satisfaction, stability) or child adjustment outcomes in important socialization contexts such as school. Therefore, the purpose of the present study was to gather data on young children's perceptions of specific friendship processes and determine whether individual differences in these perceptions were associated with specific *relationship* outcomes (i.e., friendship satisfaction and stability) and *child adjustment* outcomes in the school context (i.e., children's success in adjusting to kindergarten).

To address these aims, independent friendship dyads (i.e., all dyads were unique or contained different pairs of friends) were identified within kindergarten classrooms, and one member of each dyad completed a friendship quality interview. Evidence of reciprocation and stability in children's friendship choices was used to ensure that the selected dyads were in fact important and enduring friendships.[1] Specifically, friendships were defined as pairs of children who mutually nominated each other as best friends (i.e., reciprocation) and who remained friends over a two-month period prior to the friendship quality interview (i.e., stability).

To assess children's friendship perceptions, we developed a friendship quality interview that was appropriate for young children. This interview was patterned after instruments developed for older children and adolescents (e.g., Berndt & Perry, 1986; Bukowski et al., 1991; Furman & Buhrmester, 1985; Parker & Asher, 1993) and included items that were designed to tap six friendship processes: companionship, validation, aid, self-disclosure, conflict, and exclusivity. These six processes were measured because they were hypothesized to be important features of young children's friendships and, therefore, significant predictors of the friendship (e.g., satisfaction, stability) and school adjustment outcomes targeted in this investigation.

Measures of companionship (i.e., engaging in common activities with a friend) and validation (i.e., receiving positive feedback or support from a friend) were included because these processes, in one form or another, appear to be integral elements of friendship at all ages (see Asher & Parker, 1989; Furman & Bierman, 1983; Gottman, 1983). Aid (i.e., receiving assistance from a friend in the face of emotional or instrumental problems) was assessed because it represents a concrete form of support young children value and are capable of offering their friends (Asher & Parker, 1989; Furman & Bierman, 1983). We also included measures of self-disclosure (i.e., discussing secrets or negative affect with a friend) and conflict (i.e., engaging in arguing, bossy, rejecting, or other contentious behaviors with a friend) because these processes have been shown to be important determinants of friendship formation and maintenance in young children (Gottman, 1983; Hartup, Laursen, Stewart, & Eastenson, 1988; Parker & Gottman, 1989; Vespo & Caplan, 1988). For exploratory purposes, we also included a measure of exclusivity (i.e., perceived selectivity of friends' liking and association). Exclusivity has been identified as a potentially important aspect of friendship in older children (especially girls; see Grotpeter, 1994; Thorne, 1986) but has not been examined with young children.

These six processes were hypothesized to be determinants of the two relationship outcomes examined in this investigation, namely, friendship satisfaction and stability. Although the effects of specific friendship processes have not been well researched with young children, a number of writers have argued that processes such as validation, companionship, aid, and self-disclosure have relationship-enhancing effects on friendship and that processes such as conflict may have disruptive or detrimental effects on friendship (e.g., Asher & Parker, 1989; Parker & Gottman, 1989). Less well considered are the potential effects of exclusivity on friendship satisfaction and stability. However, friends who value each other more highly and seek out each other's company more consistently may develop relationships that are not only more intense and engaged but also more satisfying and stable.

The relationship processes that occur in friendships may also affect children's adjustment in important socialization contexts such as school (see Ladd & Kochenderfer, in press). From better-quality friendships, that is, those that offer children higher levels of validation, companionship, aid, or exclusivity, children may derive both emotional and instrumental provisions that enable them to cope successfully with the demands of school (see Howes, 1988; Ladd, 1990; Ladd & Kochenderfer, in press). For example, friends who are more validating or exclusive may enhance children's feelings of self-worth; friends who offer higher levels of companionship and aid may increase children's feelings of security and competence in the classroom. Conversely, classroom friendships that are characterized by higher levels of conflict may undermine these same provisions and, thereby, reduce or eliminate the resources that children need to succeed in school.

Unfortunately, the present state of theory in this literature does not allow us to make more specific predictions about the potential effects of friendship processes on children's school adjustment (for an analysis of this literature, see Ladd & Kochenderfer, in press). However, a key aim of this investigation was to gather evidence that would clarify further these linkages – that is, elucidate the relation between specific friendship processes and differing school adjustment outcomes. Toward this end, several aspects of children's school adjustment were assessed in this investigation. These included measures of children's school affect (i.e., perceived affect in school; loneliness), perceptions (i.e., perceived peer support, school liking), involvement (i.e., desire to avoid school, teacher-rated classroom engagement), and performance (i.e., academic readiness and achievement).

Method
Subject Selection and Sample

All of the children who participated in this study were selected because they were found to have a reciprocated and stable best friendship in their kindergarten classroom. To identify participants, children with informed parental consent participated in sociometric interviews that were administered in 11 kindergarten classrooms (permission rates exceeded 80% in all classrooms) on two occasions separated by a two-month interval: late fall (October) and early winter (January). During each interview occasion, children were shown pictures of classmates and asked to (a) nominate up to five "best" friends (e.g., point to their best friend, then their next best friend, and so on; M number of nominations given = 4.12; SD = .87) and (b) rank the nominees according to how much they considered each to be a "best" friend (see Parker & Asher, 1993).

Stable best friendship dyads were then identified in each classroom by selecting pairs of children who had mutually nominated each other as "best" friends on *both* interview occasions. Only those children for whom a reciprocated stable friendship could be identified were eligible to be included in the sample (49% of the children who participated in the sociometric interviews). The friendship pairs that met these criteria were further screened to ensure that all of the children who participated in the study were members of "independent" dyads. That is, a child identified as a subject's friend could not be designated as a friend for any other subject in the sample, and only one member of each dyad could serve as a subject (i.e., be interviewed). This criterion was employed to prevent subjects from reporting about the same friendship (i.e., interviewing both members of a dyad) and to eliminate the possibility that more than one child could be interviewed about the same friend.

The resulting sample consisted of 82 kindergarten children (40 boys and 42 girls), most of whom were members of low- to middle-SES families (*M* occupation scores for primary wage earners on the Featherman and Stevens [1982] MSEI2 scale was 29.65; SD = 24.53; a score of 30 on this scale is assigned to occupations such as postal clerks, plumbers, and machine operators). The average age of the children was 5.61 years, and the ethnic/racial composition of the sample was 14.6% African American, 78% Caucasian, 2.4% Hispanic, 4.9% other.

Measures

Friendship features

Several versions of the Friendship Features Interview for Young Children (FFIYC) were pilot tested on samples of preschool and kindergarten children, and findings from these administrations were used to develop items that were appropriate for young children in length, content, and wording. The version of the FFIYC that was used in this investigation contained a total of 30 items (questions), each of which was keyed to one of eight constructs, including (*a*) the six friendship processes (i.e., companionship, validation, aid, self-disclosure, conflict, and exclusivity), (*b*) friendship satisfaction, and (*c*) friend's impact on child's affective experience at school (i.e., perceived affect in school). Children were asked to respond to each question on the scale by answering "no" (scored as 0), "sometimes" (scored as 1) or "yes" (scored as 2).

Friendship processes.   To tap each of the conceptually distinct friendship processes, six sets of items were written, each of which contained three to four semantically similar items (questions). (Note: the actual scales used in this study were empirically derived and are described in the "Results" section.) The companionship scale consisted of four items that were designed to tap children's perceptions of how much their friend included them in school-related activities (e.g., "Does [friend's name] do things with you during activity time?"). Four items were included on the validation scale to index children's perceptions of the extent of positive feedback or support they received from their friend (e.g., "Does [friend's name] tell you that you are good at things you do in class?"). Aid was assessed with four items that were intended to measure children's perceptions of the degree of assistance their friend provides with emotional or instrumental problems (e.g., "If some kids at school were teasing you, would [friend's name] tell them to stop?"). Self-disclosure was measured with three items that were intended to tap differences in the extent to which children shared private information (e.g., secrets) or feelings (i.e., negative affect) with their friend (e.g., "Do you and [friend's name] talk about things that make you sad?"). Conflict was assessed by asking children to respond to four items that indexed the extent to which they (or their friend) engaged in angry, bossy, rejecting, or other contentions behaviors (e.g., "Some friends make fun of each other. Does [friend's name] ever make fun of you?"). Four items were used to measure exclusivity, or the extent to which children perceived their friendship as mutually selective in both liking and association (e.g., "Does [friend's name] mostly do things with *you* at school?").

Friendship satisfaction.   Children's satisfaction with their friendship was measured with four items that were included in the friendship features interview. Each of these items was phrased so that children were asked to make an evaluation of their friendship, that is, to indicate how satisfied they felt with the relationship (e.g., "Is [friend's name] a good friend to you?" "How glad are you that you are friends with [friend's name]?").

Friendship stability.   Sociometric interviews were conducted again in the late spring of the school year (May) to determine whether each subject had remained friends with the same partner over time. The procedure used to identify friendships in May was the same as that employed during the prior two assessments (October and January; see methodology described above). Children who had the same friend in May that had been identified in January were scored as having stable friendships (score = 1); those who did not meet this criterion were scored as having unstable friendships (score = 0).

School adjustment indices

Perceived affect in school.   Three additional items were included in the friendship features interview to assess the friend's potential impact on children's feelings about school (i.e., perceived affect in school; alpha = .51). On each of these items, children were asked to indicate how they would feel at school when their friend was present or absent (e.g., "Is school fun when [friend's name] isn't here?").

Loneliness. The Cassidy and Asher (1992) Loneliness and Social Dissatisfaction Questionnaire (LSDQ) was individually administered to children in the fall and spring of the school year to obtain a second measure of children's affective experience in school. To construct a measure of loneliness that was distinct from social dissatisfaction, we created a subscale that included three LSDQ items (those that directly refer to loneliness; e.g., "Are you lonely at school?") and two semantically similar items (i.e., "Is school a lonely place for you?" "Are you sad and alone at school?"). Factor analyses performed on this sample, and other larger samples of kindergarten children ($ns > 400$), show that these five items consistently load on the same factor (see Birch & Ladd, in press; Kochenderfer & Ladd, in press). Scores were created by averaging children's "yes" (2), "sometimes" (1), or "no" (0) responses over these five items (alpha = .75 fall, .78 spring).

Perceived peer support. To measure changes in children's perceptions of social support from classmates, the Perceptions of Peer Social Support Scale (PPSSS) was individually administered to children in both the fall and spring of the school year. Children responded to 16 questions in which they were asked to estimate the extent to which classmates would assist them with a range of emotional and instrumental problems in the classroom (e.g., "Are there kids in your class who would share things like stickers, toys, or games with you?" "Are there kids in your class who would explain the rules to a game if you didn't understand them?"). Children responded yes or no to each item, and if their reply was affirmative, they were asked to indicate whether classmates tended to respond this way "just sometimes" or "a lot of the time." Responses were scored (no = 0, just sometimes = 1, and a lot of the time = 2) and summed across items to create a total perceived peer support score (alpha = .85 fall, .88 spring).

School liking and avoidance. A revised version of the School Liking and Avoidance Questionnaire (SLAQ; Ladd & Price, 1987) was also administered to children during individual interviews to tap differences in their school perceptions (i.e., extent to which children profess to like school), and involvement (i.e., children's expressed desire to avoid school). In this study and others (see Birch & Ladd, in press; Kochenderfer & Ladd, in press), this 14-item scale has consistently factored into a nine-item school liking subscale (e.g., "Do you like being in school?" alpha = .87 fall, .91 spring), and a five-item school avoidance subscale (e.g., "Do you wish you didn't have to come to school?" alpha = .76 fall, .81 spring). Scores for each measure were created by averaging children's "yes" (2), "sometimes" (1), or "no" (0) responses over the items contained in each subscale.

Classroom engagement/independence. Teachers rated children's classroom behavior during the fall and spring of the school year using the Teacher Rating Scale of School Adjustment (TRSSA). The TRSSA is a measure of young children's school adjustment that was developed in collaboration with the teachers who participated in this project and others who were part of a larger longitudinal study of school adjustment. Factor analyses produced several reliable subscales, including a nine-item self-directedness/engagement scale (e.g., "Seeks challenges"; "Works independently"; alpha = .92) that was utilized in this study as a measure of children's involvement in classroom activities. Scores for this scale were calculated by averaging teachers' three-point ratings (doesn't apply = 0; applies sometimes = 1; certainly applies = 2) across all nine items.

Academic readiness and progress. Children's visual and language readiness were assessed during the spring of kindergarten with corresponding subtests of the Metropolitan Readiness Test (MRT; *Metropolitan Readiness Tests,* 1986). Raw scores were used to calculate a visual, language, and quantitative stanine for each child. A measure of children's academic progress was created by asking teachers to rate children's scholastic progress during kindergarten and their readiness for first grade (averaged five-point ratings; alpha = .78).

Procedure

The LSDQ, SLAQ, PPSSS, and MRT, along with the sociometric interviews used to identify children's friendships, were administered during two 40-minute sessions in October and May of the school year. These measures were administered in counterbalanced order. Children completed the FFIYC and an additional sociometric (friendship identification) assessment during a single individual interview that was conducted during January. All child interviews were conducted in a private location near children's classrooms. Before each interview, children were told that their participation was voluntary and that their responses were confidential. After each session, children received some colorful stickers for their participation. Teachers completed the TRSSA twice during kindergarten (fall and spring) and rated children's academic readiness and progress at the close of the school year.

Results

Friendship features interview for young children

Identification of friendship features. To identify subscales that approximated the conceptual structure of the 30-item FFIYC, a principal axis factor analysis with oblique rotation was performed on children's responses. Nine factors with eigen-values greater than 1.0 were extracted that accounted for 68.4% of the item variance. Seven of the nine factors were interpretable – that is, they contained items with moderate to high loadings on the same factor, low cross loadings on other factors, and content that corresponded to one of the designated friendship constructs. The items included on these factors corresponded closely to all of the targeted friendship constructs except companionship; three of the four companionship items loaded with the items intended to tap validation. Also, only two of the three self-disclosure items loaded on the same factor (both referred to sharing negative affect with a friend); the third did not (i.e., sharing secrets with a friend). To achieve greater interpretability, the four companionship items, and two others that failed to load on an interpretable factor or had high cross loadings, were excluded from further analyses. The remaining 24 items are shown in table 1, and the resulting factors were labeled Validation, Aid, Disclosing Negative Affect, Conflict, Exclusivity, Satisfaction, and Affective Climate.

Creation of friendship processes subscales. Subscales were created for each of the five friendship processes by averaging children's scores across items

Table 1   The Friendship Features Interview for Young Children: items

1. If a kid took something that was yours, would (friend's name) tell them to give it back?
2. Does (friend's name) like *you* more than anybody else in your class?
3. Does (friend's name) say you're his (her) friend?
4. Do you feel happy when you're with (friend's name)?
5. Is school fun when (friend's name) is not here?
6. Do you and (friend's name) talk about things that make you sad?
7. Does (friend's name) tell you you're good at things you do in class?
8. When you feel bad about something at school, do you talk to (friend's name) about it?
9. Does (friend's name) tell you that you're good at sports and games?
10. If your teacher yelled at you and it made you feel bad, would (friend's name) make you feel better?
11. Some friends say things that aren't so nice. Does (friend's name) ever say she (he) won't be your friend anymore?
12. Does (friend's name) play mostly with *you* on the playground?
13. If kids were being mean to you, would (friend's name) try to make them stop?
14. Does (friend's name) say nice things to you? (reverse scored)
15. Does (friend's name) mostly do things with *you* at school?
16. If some kids at school were teasing you, would (friend's name) tell them to stop?
17. Some friends boss each other around. Does (friend's name) ever boss you around?
18. Do you have fun when you're with (friend's name) at school?
19. How much do you like being friends with (friend's name)?
20. If (friend's name) wasn't at school one day, would you feel sad?
21. Do you like (friend's name) more than you like any other kids?
22. Is (friend's name) a good friend to you?
23. Some friends make fun of each other. Does (friend's name) ever make fun of you?
24. How glad are you that you're friends with (friend's name)?

that had the highest loadings on the Validation ($M = 1.47$, SD = .64), Aid ($M = 1.42$, SD = .65), Disclosing Negative Affect ($M = .75$, SD = .72), Conflict ($M = .48$, SD = .27), and Exclusivity ($M = 1.35$, SD = .58) factors. Included in table 2 are the structure coefficients assigned to items in the factor analysis and alpha coefficients for each subscale.

Table 2 Friendship processes: subscales, item loadings, and subscale alphas

	Factor loadings				
Subscale (alpha)/item abbreviation	I	II	III	IV	V
I. Validation (.80):					
3. Say you're his (her) friend	.64	...	...	...	...
7. Say you're good in class	.66	...	...	...	...
9. Tell you you're good at sports	.66	...	...	...	...
II. Aid (.81):					
1. Kid took something	...	.57	...	...	...
10. Teacher yelled at you	...	.50	...	...	...
13. Kids were being mean to you	...	.80	...	...	...
16. Kids were teasing you	...	.85	...	...	...
III. Conflict (.65):					
11. Say she (he) won't be your friend	...	...	.70	...	...
14. Say nice things to you (reversed)	...	...	.60	...	...
17. Boss you around	...	...	.31	...	...
23. Make fun of you	...	...	.37	...	...
IV. Exclusivity (.67):					
2. Like you more than anybody	...	...	...	.54	...
12. Play mostly with you	...	...	...	.60	...
15. Mostly do things with you	...	...	...	.67	...
21. You like more than other kids	...	...	...	.42	...
V. Disclosing negative affect (.63):					
6. Talk about sad things	...	...	...	...	.43
8. Talk when you feel bad	...	...	...	...	.70

Relations among the friendship processes subscales.   The scores children received for the five friendship processes subscales were correlated, first for the entire sample and then by gender. As can be seen in table 3, these analyses produced correlations that were low to moderate in magnitude and in expected directions. Scores for Validation, Aid, Disclosure of Negative Affect, and Exclusivity correlated positively with each other but negatively with Conflict. Similar patterns of correlations were obtained for boys and girls, with two exceptions: Aid and Disclosure of Negative Affect were more correlated among boys than girls ($rs = .65$ vs. $.25$, respectively; $z = 3.26$, $p < .01$), and a stronger association was

Table 3   Intercorrelation of the friendship processes subscales

Subscale	V	A	C	E	D
Validation (V)		.47***	−.24*	.44***	.50***
Aid (A)			−.24*	.36***	.45***
Conflict (C)				−.25*	−.08
Exclusiveness (E)					.32**
Disclosing negative affect (D)					

*p < .05; **p < .01; ***p < .001.

found between Aid and Validation for girls than boys (rs = .66 vs. .29, respectively; z = 3.10, p < .01).

Examination of gender differences in friendship processes.   To determine whether boys and girls differed in the way they viewed their friendships, a one-way (gender: male, female) MANOVA was calculated in which the five friendship processes subscales served as variates. The gender effects calculated in this analysis (multivariate and univariate) did not achieve significance, suggesting that, on average, boys' and girls' perceptions of the targeted friendship processes did not differ substantially.

Friendship processes as predictors of friendship satisfaction and stability

Friendship satisfaction.   A friendship satisfaction score was calculated by averaging children's scores across the four items that loaded on this dimension in the factor analysis (alpha = .81). Overall, the level of satisfaction children reported with their friendships was relatively high (scores ranged from .25 to 2.00, M = 1.80, SD = .37), and a one-way ANOVA (gender: male, female) did not reveal gender differences in children's satisfaction scores, F(1, 80) = 1.13, N S.

Correlational and hierarchical regression analyses were used to determine whether children's perceptions of friendship quality (i.e., individual differences in the five perceived friendship processes) were associated with their expressed satisfaction. Satisfaction was significantly correlated with all of the friendship process measures. Children who were more satisfied with their friendships reported higher levels of perceived validation ($r = .39$, $p < .01$), aid ($r = .24$, $p < .03$), disclosure of negative affect ($r = .30$, $p < .01$), and exclusivity ($r = .45$, $p < .01$), and lower levels of conflict ($r = -.34$, $p < .01$). The relative contributions of the friendship process measures were examined in a regression analysis, in which scores for gender, Validation, Aid, Exclusivity, Disclosure of Negative Affect, and Conflict (entered in that order) were used to predict friendship satisfaction. To maintain a favorable ratio of the number of subjects per predictor, scores representing each gender by friendship process interaction term were alternately entered on the final step of each analysis. The scores contributing to each interaction term were centered prior to analysis. The overall regression equation was significant, $R^2 = .31$, $p < .01$, and showed that three of the five process measures made unique contributions to friendship satisfaction: Validation, R^2 increment $= .15$, $p < .01$, Exclusivity, R^2 increment $= .08$, $p < .01$, and Conflict, R^2 increment $= .05$, $p < .01$.

Friendship stability. Examination of the friendship stability scores showed that 50 of the 82 children in the sample (61%) had friendships that were maintained from January to May of the school year. A chi-square analysis revealed that the number of boys and girls who kept or lost friends across this interval did not differ significantly (i.e., unstable: 17 boys, 15 girls; stable: 23 boys, 27 girls).

To determine whether perceived qualities of children's friendships were associated with the stability of their relationships, a discriminant analysis was conducted in which each of the five friendship processes were used to predict the dichotomous stability scores. This analysis produced a significant discriminant function, $\chi^2(5) = 36.40$, $p < .001$, and correctly classified 84.15% of the subjects. (Note: The chance rate for correct classification in a two-category system is 50%.) The measures that produced the highest loadings on this function were Validation (.72) and Conflict (−.63), suggesting that children who tended to perceive their friendships as more validating and less conflictual tended to maintain these relationships over time. Similar results were obtained for separate discriminant function analyses that were calculated for each gender.

Friendship processes as predictors of children's school adjustment

A series of correlational and hierarchical regression analyses were conducted to examine the link between perceived friendship processes

Table 4   Correlations among the school adjustment indices

	PS	L	SL	SA	CE	AP	MV	ML	MQ
Affect in school (AS)	.13	.11	−.07	.06	.08	.15	.13	.30	.22
Peer support (PS)		.09	.08	.03	.07	.01	.00	.15	.07
Loneliness (L)			−.36	.26	−.13	−.17	.01	.05	−.13
School liking (SL)				−.70	.37	.30	.21	.05	−.03
School avoidance (SA)					−.35	−.21	−.21	.02	.01
Classroom engagement (CE)						.69	.57	.37	.46
Academic progress (AP)							.45	.47	.50
Metropolitan visual (MV)								.47	.54
Metropolitan language (ML)									.57
Metropolitan quantitative (MQ)									

Correlations reported are for measures obtained in the spring of the school year; values above .23 are significant at the p < .05 level.

and children's school adjustment. Relations among measures of school adjustment obtained in the spring of the school year are shown in table 4.

A series of regression analyses was conducted in which gender, Validation, Aid, Exclusivity, Disclosure of Negative Affect, and Conflict (entered in that order) were used to predict the scores children received on each of the school adjustment measures in May. The order of entry of the five friendship process measures reflected the extent to which they were endorsed by children as qualities of their friendships (cf. reported subscale means, SDs). Thus, in evaluating the contributions of perceived friendship processes, features that were less commonly attributed to friendships at this age level (e.g., conflict) were evaluated after taking into account those that were more "normative" – that is, features that were more commonly ascribed to friends at this age level (e.g., validation). The scores used to construct each gender × friendship process interaction term were centered, and the resulting terms were entered alternately on the final step of each analysis. For all but the perceived affect in school and achievement measures (i.e., MRT subtests, teacher-rated academic progress measure), a premeasure of children's school adjustment was obtained in the fall of the school year. In the analyses performed on these variables, scores for the premeasure were entered on the first step of the regression in order to determine whether differences in friendship quality were associated with *changes* in children's school adjustment. The results of the regression analyses are shown in table 5.

Perceived affect in school.   Regression analyses (see table 5) revealed that validation accounted for 15% of the variation in children's perceived affect scores, and conflict accounted for an additional 4%. Perceived affect in school was positively correlated with validation ($r = .38, p < .01$) and negatively correlated with conflict ($r = -.31, p < .01$). Aid was also associated with more favorable affect in school; however, in the regression analysis, the statistical contribution of this measure approached but did not achieve significance. Thus, children who reported higher levels of validation and lower levels of conflict in their friendships were more likely to see themselves as having positive feelings while with their friends in school.

Perceived peer support.   Children who saw their friendships as offering higher levels of validation and aid were more inclined to view classmates as supportive over the course of the school year. These two variables correlated positively with perceived peer support ($r = .35, r = .38, ps < .01$, respectively) and, together, accounted for 12% of the residual perceived peer support scores (see table 5). Disclosing negative affect was also associated with gains in perceived peer support, but this measure failed to achieve significance.

Loneliness.   Disclosing negative affect was positively correlated with loneliness ($r = .36, p < .01$) and accounted for 17% of the residual variance in children's loneliness scores (see table 5). Gains in loneliness over the school year were associated with higher levels of self-disclosure (i.e., talk about negative affect) in friendships. Also, a significant gender × conflict interaction term was obtained in the regression analysis. Boys ($r = .55, p < .01$) but not girls ($r = .01$, N.S.) who reported higher levels of conflict in their friendships tended to feel more lonely as the school year progressed.

School liking and avoidance.   As can be seen in table 5, children who perceived their friends as offering higher levels of aid tended to like school more as the year progressed. Higher levels of perceived conflict, especially in boys' friendships, forecasted lower levels of school liking and higher levels of school avoidance. For boys, conflict correlated negatively

Table 5 Results of regression analyses: predicting school adjustment from friendship processes

	Affect in school			Peer support			Loneliness		
	R^2	R^2inc	B	R^2	R^2inc	B	R^2	R^2inc	B
Fall premeasure	...	...	...	.13	.13**	.36	.11	.11	.34
Gender (G)	.00	.00	.02	.14	.01	.08	.12	.01	.12
Validation	.15	.15***	.39	.22	.08**	.29	.12	.00	.04
Aid	.18	.03ᵐ	.21	.26	.04*	.22	.13	.01	−.11
Exclusivity	.18	.00	−.02	.26	.00	−.07	.13	.00	.01
Disclosure	.19	.01	.01	.29	.03ᵐ	.22	.30	.17***	.49
Conflict	.23	.04*	−.21	.29	.00	.05	.32	.02	.13
(G) × Conflict	...	...	...	...	...	...	.37	.05*	−.83

	School liking			School avoidance			Classroom engagement		
Fall premeasure	.23	.23***	.48	.16	.16***	.40	.55	.55***	.74
Gender (G)	.25	.02	.14	.16	.00	−.06	.55	.00	−.02
Validation	.25	.00	.03	.16	.00	.04	.55	.00	.08
Aid	.29	.04*	.23	.17	.01	−.11	.55	.00	.06
Exclusivity	.29	.00	.01	.17	.00	.04	.56	.01	−.11
Disclosure	.30	.01	−.11	.17	.00	.02	.56	.00	−.03
Conflict	.36	.06**	−.28	.20	.03	.18	.56	.00	.02
(G) × Conflict	.41	.05*	.80	.27	.07**	−.94	.60	.04*	.77

	Met-visual			Met-language			Met-quantitative		
Gender (G)	.03	.03	.18	.02	.02	−.12	.00	.00	−.06
Validation	.04	.01	−.10	.04	.02	.14	.00	.00	−.04
Aid	.05	.01	.11	.05	.01	.11	.01	.01	.11
Exclusivity	.11	.06*	−.27	.11	.06*	−.29	.17	.15***	−.45
Disclosure	.12	.01	−.12	.11	.00	.04	.19	.02	−.20
Conflict	.13	.01	.05	.12	.01	.08	.21	.02	.14

	Teacher progress ratings								
Gender (G)	.00	.00	−.03	...	...	...	...	...	...
Validation	.00	.00	−.07	...	...	...	...	...	...
Aid	.02	.02	.15	...	...	...	...	...	...
Exclusivity	.12	.10**	−.36	...	...	...	...	...	...
Disclosure	.12	.00	−.02	...	...	...	...	...	...
Conflict	.13	.01	.08	...	...	...	...	...	...

Fall premeasure = measure of the criterion obtained in the fall of the school year.
ᵐp < .07; *p < .05; **p < .01; ***p < .001.

with school liking ($r = -.62$, $p < .01$) and positively with school avoidance ($r = .54$, $p < .01$). For girls, these same relations were small in magnitude and nonsignificant ($rs = -.15$ and .05, respectively).

Classroom engagement/independence. The gender × conflict interaction term was the only predictor to achieve significance in the regression analysis performed on this measure (see table 5). Perceived conflict in friendship and classroom engagement/independence were negatively correlated for boys ($r = -.33$, $p < .05$) but positively (although non-significantly) correlated for girls ($r = .18$). Thus, for boys, higher levels of perceived conflict in friendship were predictive of lower levels of engagement in classroom activities.

Academic readiness and progress. Perceived exclusivity was the only friendship process subscale that contributed significantly to the prediction of children's academic readiness and progress. Exclusivity correlated negatively with the visual, language, and quantitative subscales of the Metropolitan Readiness Text ($rs = -.26$, $p < .02$; $r = -.12$, N.S., $r = -.35$, $p < .01$, respectively) and with teachers' ratings of children's academic progress ($r = -.28$, $p < .02$). As can be seen in table 5, exclusivity accounted for 10% of the variation in teachers' ratings of children's scholastic progress, and 6%, 6%, and 15% of the variation, respectively, in children's scores on the visual, language, and quantitative subtests of the MRT.

Discussion

The present findings suggest that, when young children are asked to evaluate the quality of their friendships, they are capable of distinguishing among key friendship processes and can provide reliable reports of these features. Support for this conclusion comes from evidence indicating that, on interview items intended to tap differing friendship processes, young children's responses were both differentiated (i.e., less correlated across items representing different friendship processes) and convergent (i.e., more correlated among items tapping the same friendship processes). These findings are consistent with the hypothesis that young children do recognize (i.e., perceive) differences in the quality of their friendships and that individual differences in perceived friendship quality exist at this age level.

The relations that emerged among the five friendship process sub-scales provide important clues about the organization or structure of young children's perceptions of actual friendships. On the one hand, the moderate magnitude of the correlations obtained among these sub-scales suggests that each is tapping a qualitatively distinct feature of children's friendships. On the other hand, the pattern and direction of these correlations suggest that children's perceptions of these processes are not unrelated but, rather, organized in a manner that is consistent with a "reward–cost" model of relationships. For example, when young children perceive their friends to be validating, they are also more likely to see them as helpful (i.e., offering aid), selective in their liking and association (i.e., exclusive toward their partners), and receptive to self-disclosure (i.e., someone with whom to share negative affect). In contrast, when children report higher levels of conflict in their friendships, they are less likely to perceive their partners as engaging in positive processes such as validation, aid, and exclusivity.

As anticipated, the perceptions that young children develop about specific friendship processes were associated with relationship "outcomes," such as friendship satisfaction and stability. Of the five friendship processes investigated here, three were found to make unique contributions to children's friendship satisfaction. Specifically, our data suggest that young children tend to be more satisfied with their friendships when these relationships are perceived to offer higher levels of validation and exclusivity and lower levels of conflict. One inference that is consistent with these findings is that processes such as validation, exclusivity, and conflict carry more weight in young children's overall evaluations of their friendships (i.e., perceived relationship satisfaction) than they do on processes such as self-disclosure or aid. Early friendships, it would appear, tend to be construed more positively when young children perceive them to be relatively self-enhancing (e.g., serving to confirm the self's competence or worth), exclusive (i.e., characterized by possessiveness or restricted liking and association with others) and free of negative interactions (i.e., rejecting, ridiculing, dominating behaviors).

Two of these same processes, validation and conflict, also emerged as significant predictors of friendship stability. Apparently, young children who perceive their friendships to be high on validation and low on conflict are not only more satisfied with these relationships but also more likely to maintain them over time. These findings may help to shed light on the dynamics of early friendships and, in particular, the processes that motivate young children to engage in these relationships and maintain them. Like older children and adults, young children may form and maintain peer relationships because they provide a context for obtaining specific social or instrumental "provisions" (e.g., self-confirmation, security, entertainment, etc.) and for managing salient emotional states (e.g., inducing pleasure or reducing pain). Thus, one way of thinking about children's early friendship motivations is that they are organized around simple reward–cost principles. According to this perspective, young children are more likely to feel satisfied and maintain friendships when they are able to maximize relationship "benefits" and minimize relationship "costs."

Following this logic, validation and conflict may have emerged as the best predictors of friendship satisfaction and stability because of the reward value these processes hold for young children. Compared to the other "positive" friendship processes investigated here (e.g., aid, disclosure of negative affect), validation may have a stronger bearing on friendship satisfaction and stability because it provides young children with direct feedback about the self. For example, friends may seek to maintain relationships with partners who affirm their characteristics and skills because this type of information allows children to "develop and maintain an image of themselves as competent, attractive, and worthwhile" (Asher & Parker, 1989, p. 7). In contrast, conflict between friends may create various "costs" that interfere with relationship satisfaction and stability. Contentious or rejecting behaviors, for example, may disrupt social activities, create aversive emotional states, and reduce children's self-esteem.

Another important aim of this investigation was to examine the relation between perceived friendship quality and children's adjustment, particularly as it might be manifested in school contexts. In this study, perceived friendship processes were examined in relation to several indicators of early school adjustment, including children's school-related affect, perceptions, involvement, and performance. Measures of these adjustment indices were obtained during children's first year in grade school (i.e., kindergarten), a major transition period in the lives of young children (see Ladd, in press).

In exploring the linkage between friendship and adjustment, it was of particular interest to determine whether specific friendship processes make differential contributions to children's school adjustment. In particular, we hypothesized that some friendship processes (e.g., valida-tion, self-disclosure, aid, exclusivity) yield emotional or instrumental resources (i.e., provisions) that empower children to cope successfully with the demands of new school environments. Other processes, such as conflict, were expected to operate as stressors and, therefore, have a negative impact on children's school adjustment.

The findings obtained in this investigation were largely consistent with these premises and begin to illuminate specific patterns of linkage between early friendship processes and children's adjustment in school contexts. As anticipated, conflict was associated with school adjustment difficulties but, surprisingly, this relation was typically stronger for boys than for girls in our sample. Moreover, boys who reported higher levels of conflict in their friendships tended to display a range of adjustment difficulties at school. Specifically, perceived conflict in boys' friendships was associated with declining levels of school involvement, as indexed by children's expressed desire to avoid school and teachers' ratings of classroom engagement. Boys who held this perception also tended to report higher levels of loneliness and lower levels of school liking as the school year progressed. One exception to this pattern of findings was that children of both sexes were less likely to see themselves as having positive affect in school when their friendships were perceived to be conflictual.

One interpretation of these findings is that, when adapting to school, boys are more adversely affected by conflict in their friendships than are girls. Boys' apparent vulnerability in this regard may be attributable to several factors that deserve further attention in future studies. First, although there is evidence to suggest that boys tend to play in larger groups of peers than do girls (Ladd, 1983; Ladd, Price, & Hart, 1990; Waldrop & Halverson, 1975), this tendency toward "extensive" peer relations may be limited to interaction (e.g., play) patterns and not extend to close dyadic ties such as friendship. In fact, data gathered in this investigation produced findings that were consistent with this proposition. A one-factor ANOVA (gender: boys, girls) performed on the number of mutual friends children possessed in their classrooms (including the friend identified for the friendship interview) yielded a significant gender effect, $F(1, 80) = 11.84$, $p < .01$, and showed that girls, on average, possessed a significantly larger number of classroom friendships ($M = 3.14$, SD = 1.08) than did boys ($M = 2.35$, SD = .96). If boys tend to have fewer close dyadic relationships than girls, then they may be more dependent on these ties for essential provisions, and conflict in friendship may take a greater toll on their adjustment. Children may, for example, turn to other friends for support when they are experiencing difficulty in close relationships, and boys may have (on average) fewer such resources in their classrooms.

Second, conflict may have more adverse effects on boys' adjustment because boys and girls differ in the way they resolve conflicts with friends. Even though our data suggest that boys and girls experience similar amounts of conflict in their friendships, it may be the case that girls resolve conflicts more quickly or satisfactorily than boys do. Berndt (1981), for example, has shown that boys are more likely to compete with their friends on tasks that are commonly found in classrooms (e.g., sharing a crayon needed to complete a task) than are girls. If boys are more competitive with friends, they may have more difficulty resolving conflicts. Findings reported by Parker and Asher (1993) provide further support for this hypothesis. These investigators measured conflict resolution as a friendship feature with older children and found that boys report greater difficulty resolving conflicts than do girls. If boys have more difficulty resolving conflicts with friends, then they may also be prone to experience persistent negative interactions or emotional states in their friendships that, over time, become an impediment to involvement in classroom activities or a stimulus for feeling lonely or avoiding school.

Alternatively, other factors may account for the stronger link between conflict and school adjustment for boys. Boys may be more prone to certain behavioral dispositions, such as aggressiveness, that may precipitate difficulties in both contexts. Aggressive interactional styles, for example, may create more conflict in children's friendships and interfere with their school adjustment.

Several "positive" friendship processes emerged as significant predictors of children's early school adjustment. Both validation and aid forecasted gains in children's perceptions of classroom peer support, and measures of these same two processes correlated positively with children's perceptions of their own affect in school (although the increment attributable to aid in the prediction of school affect only approached significance). Aid also forecasted changes in school liking; children who characterized their friendships as offering higher levels of aid tended to like school better as the school year progressed.

These findings are consistent with the hypothesis that friendships yield provisions that affect children's school adjustment and suggest that processes such as validation and aid yield resources that affect the quality of children's emotional life in school. Friends who are perceived to offer higher levels of personal support (e.g., ego validation, affirmation of the self) or interpersonal aid (e.g., help with problematic social situations) may enhance children's feelings of competence and security in school. These benefits or provisions, in turn, may affect not only the emotions children experience in school contexts but also the perceptions they form about specific features of this environment. While our data do not shed light on all of these mechanisms and relations, they do establish a link between two types of friendship processes – validation and aid – and several indicators of children's school adjustment. Specifically, children who see their friendships as a source of validation or aid tend to feel happier in school, see their classmates as supportive, and develop positive school attitudes.

Children's perceptions of self-disclosure and exclusivity in friendships were also related to their school adjustment, but the direction of these relations did not always conform to our initial expectations. Talking with friends about negative affect was associated with *gains* in loneliness over the school year. Although the design of this study does not permit strong inferences about causal priority, this finding raises the possibility that adjustment difficulties may also influence children's friendship processes. It is quite possible, for example, that children who feel increasingly alienated from their classmates (e.g., loneliness due to peer rejection) unburden themselves or seek solace with their friends. Evidence indicating that young children do turn to friends to discuss negative feelings (e.g., fears, concerns) is richly illustrated in research conducted by Gottman and colleagues on the conversations of young friends (see Parker & Gottman, 1989).

Of the friendship perceptions investigated in this study, exclusivity was the only process that was associated with children's academic performance in school, and higher levels of perceived exclusivity were negatively related to children's school readiness and progress. Although additional research is needed to describe the features of exclusive friendships, it is possible that these relationships have properties that interfere with children's academic progress. Friendships that are characterized by high levels of exclusivity may be more intense and possessive and, as a result, limit children's relationships with other classmates and/or distract children from learning and scholastic activities in the classroom. More possessive friendships may restrict children's ties with classmates and, thus, foster weaker support networks in the classroom and negatively affect children's scholastic competence (see Vandell & Hembree, 1994). Similarly, if exclusive friendships are characterized by higher levels of engagement or intensity, then they may demand more of children's time and attention at school or foster activities that distract children from academic instruction or tasks. Teachers, for example, often tell us that they separate close friends in the classroom because they talk too much. As Berndt (1989) has observed, friendships have negative as well as positive features; not all features of children's friendships may have positive effects on their development. Such relations, however, may be context-dependent. Exclusivity, it would appear, may foster friendship satisfaction but interfere with children's academic performance in school.

In considering the relation observed between exclusivity and school performance, we should recognize that our design does not rule out inferences that are consistent with the opposing direction of effect. For example, children who experience academic difficulties in the classroom may seek or cultivate more exclusivity in their friendships. Children who are insecure in the face of academic challenges, for example, may attempt to compensate for these feelings by forming friendships that are more intense (i.e., close) or possessive in nature (i.e., self-focused or self-serving). This possibility should be explored in future studies.

Collectively, these findings extend past research on friendship quality by extending it to younger samples and by mapping young children's perceptions of specific friendship *processes*. Our data suggest that young children can reliably distinguish among differing friendship processes and that their perceptions of these processes are differentially predictive of both relationship and school adjustment outcomes. That is, it would appear that different friendship processes, as they are perceived by young children, make unique contributions to both relationship and school adjustment outcomes. Further, Berndt's (1989) contention that friendships can have detrimental as well as beneficial effects on children's development and adjustment received some support in this investigation.

Another important contribution of this study is that it offers researchers a reliable tool for investigating young children's perceptions of friendship quality. Prior to this, investigators interested in the link between early friendships and adjustment have tended to investigate other aspects of friendship, particularly those identified in the first two levels of Bukowski and Hoza's (1989) model (e.g., participation in friendship, number of friends; see Howes, 1988; Ladd, 1990). Consistent with Bukowski and Hoza's logic, our data suggest that, in addition to these relationship features, it is also important to consider the impact that friendship quality may have on young children's social and emotional adjustment, especially in school settings.

Note

1   Although investigators working with older children have relied on children's perceptions as a means of identifying influential or "very best" friendships (i.e., having children review their friendship nominations and rank them in order of importance or closeness; see Parker & Asher, 1993), our preliminary studies showed that young children often had difficulty distinguishing among their "best" friendships (i.e., ranking their friends reliably) and that data gathered on perceived friendship processes were less differentiated and reliable when ranking strategies were used to identify friendships. Moreover, the stability of early friendships has been found to be an important predictor of children's adjustment and competence during early childhood (see Howes, 1988; Ladd, 1990). Thus, among young children, stability may be a better criterion for identifying important or influential friendships.

References

Asher, S. R., & Parker, J. G. (1989). Significance of peer relationship problems in childhood. In B. Schneider, G. Attili, J. Nadel, & R. Weissberg (Eds.), *Social competence in developmental perspective* (pp. 5–24). Amsterdam: Kluwer.

Berndt, T. J. (1981). Effects of friendship on prosocial intentions and behavior. *Child Development, 52*, 636–643.

Berndt, T. J. (1989). Contributions of peer relationships to children's development. In T. J. Berndt & G. W. Ladd (Eds.), *Peer relationships in child development* (pp. 407–416). New York: Wiley.

Berndt, T. J., Hawkins, J. A., & Hoyle, S. G. (1986). Changes in friendship during a school year: Effects on children's and adolescents' impressions of friendships and sharing with friends. *Child Development, 57*, 1284–1297.

Berndt, T. J., & Ladd, G. W. (1989). *Peer relationships in child development.* New York: Wiley.

Berndt, T. J., & Perry, T. B. (1986). Children's perceptions of friendships as supportive relationships. *Developmental Psychology, 22*, 640–648.

Birch, S. H., & Ladd, G. W. (in press). The teacher–child relationship and children's early school adjustment. *Journal of School Psychology*.

Buhrmester, D., & Furman, W. (1987). The development of companionship and intimacy. *Child Development, 58*, 1101–1113.

Bukowski, W., Boivin, M., & Hoza, B. (1991). The friendship qualities scale: Development and psychometric properties. Unpublished manuscript, Concordia University.

Bukowski, W., & Hoza, B. (1989). Popularity and friendship: Issues in theory, measurement, and outcome. In T. J. Berndt & G. W. Ladd (Eds.), *Peer relationships in child development*. New York: Wiley.

Bukowski, W., & Hoza, B. (1990, April). *Peer relations and loneliness during early adolescence.* Paper presented at the annual meeting of the Society for Research in Adolescence, Atlanta.

Cassidy, J., & Asher, S. R. (1992). Loneliness and peer relations in young children. *Child Development, 63*, 350–365.

Featherman, D. L., & Stevens, G. (1982). A revised socioeconomic index of occupational status: Application and analysis of sex differences in attainment. In R. Hanser (Ed.), *Social structure and behavior: Essays in honor of William Hamilton Sewell* (pp. 141–181). San Diego, CA: Academic.

Furman, W., & Bierman, K. (1983). Developmental changes in young children's conceptions of friendship. *Child Development, 54*, 549–556.

Furman, W., & Buhrmester, D. (1985). Children's perceptions of the personal relationships in their social networks. *Developmental Psychology, 21*, 1016–1021.

Gottman, J. M. (1983). How children become friends. *Monographs of the Society for Research in Child Development, 48*(3, Serial No. 201).

Grotpeter, J. (1994). Relational aggression and friendship: "I'll be your best friend if . . ." Unpublished masters thesis, University of Illinois at Urbana Champaign.

Hartup, W. W., Laursen, B., Stewart, M., & Eastenson, A. (1988). Conflict and the friendship relations of young children. *Child Development, 59*, 1590–1600.

Hartup, W. W., & Sancilio, M. F. (1986). Children's friendships. In E. Schopler & G. B. Mesibov (Eds.), *Social behavior in autism* (pp. 61–80). New York: Plenum.

Howes, C. (1983). Patterns of friendship. *Child Development, 54*, 1041–1053.

Howes, C. (1988). Peer interaction of young children. *Monographs of the Society for Research in Child Development, 53*(1, Serial No. 217).

Kochenderfer, B. J., & Ladd, G. W. (in press). Peer victimization: Cause or consequence of school maladjustment? *Child Development*.

Ladd, G. W. (1990). Having friends, keeping friends, making friends, and being liked by peers in the classroom: Predictors of children's early school adjustment? *Child Development, 61*, 1081–1100.

Ladd, G. W. (in press). Shifting ecologies during the 5–7 year period: Predicting children's adjustment during the transition to grade school. In A. Sameroff & M. Haith (Eds.), *Reason and responsibility: The passage through childhood.* Chicago: University of Chicago Press.

Ladd, G. W., & Kochenderfer, B. J. (in press). Linkages between friendship and adjustment during early school transitions. In W. M. Bukowski, A. F. Newcomb, & W. W. Hartup (Eds.), *The company they keep: Friendship in childhood and adolescence.* New York: Cambridge University Press.

Ladd, G. W., & Price, J. M. (1987). Predicting children's social and school adjustment following the transition from preschool to kindergarten. *Child Development, 58,* 1168–1189.

Ladd, G. W., Price, J. M., & Hart, C. H. (1990). Preschoolers' behavioral orientations and patterns of peer contact: Predictive of social status? In S. R. Asher & J. D. Coie (Eds.), *Peer rejection in childhood.* New York: Cambridge University Press.

Metropolitan Readiness Tests. (1986). New York: Harcourt Brace Jovnovich.

Park, K. A., & Waters, E. (1989). Security of attachment and preschool friendships. *Child Development, 60,* 1076–1081.

Parker, J. G., & Asher, S. R. (1993). Friendship and friendship quality in middle childhood: Links with peer group acceptance and feelings of loneliness and social dissatisfaction. *Developmental Psychology, 29,* 611–621.

Parker, J. G., & Gottman, J. M. (1989). Social and emotional development in a relational context: Friendship interaction from early childhood to adolescence. In T. J. Berndt & G. W. Ladd (Eds.), *Peer relationships in child development.* New York: Wiley.

Sharabany, R., Gershoni, R., & Hofman, J. E. (1981). Girlfriend, boyfriend: Age and sex differences in intimate friendship. *Developmental Psychology, 17,* 800–808.

Thorne, B. (1986). Girls and boys together . . . but mostly apart: Gender arrangements in elementary schools. In W. W. Hartup & Z. Rubin (Eds.), *Relationships and development* (pp. 167–184). Hillsdale, NJ: Erlbaum.

Vandell, D. L., & Hembree, S. E. (1994). Peer social status and friendship: Independent contributors to children's social and academic adjustment. *Merrill-Palmer Quarterly, 40,* 461–477.

Vespo, J. E., & Caplan, M. Z. (1988, March). *Preschoolers' differential conflict behaviors with friends and acquaintances.* Paper presented at the Southeastern Conference on Human Development, Charleston, SC.

Waldrop, M. F., & Halverson, C. F. (1975). Intensive and extensive peer behavior: Longitudinal and cross-sectional analyses. *Child Development, 46,* 19–26.

Weiss, R. (1974). The provisions of social relationships. In Z. Rubin (Ed.), *Doing unto others* (pp. 17–26). Englewood Cliffs, NJ: Prentice-Hall.

SEVEN

Extracurricular Activities

Introduction

Students drop out of school for a variety of reasons such as academic, economic, peer, and personal problems. Educators, policy makers, parents, and researchers have viewed dropping out of school as a serious educational and societal problem. Not only does it limit both economic and social well-being in adulthood, but more concerning is the fact that the adverse effects of dropping out are more intense among the most socioeconomically disadvantaged students. Thus, those students who are most likely to leave school before graduation may be the most harmed by it.

There is an important discrepancy between adults' and adolescents' view of school. While adults evaluate school primarily with respect to their contribution to adolescents' cognitive and career development, adolescents are more likely to view school as an important setting for socializing. When students leave school, researchers need to consider the impact of social experiences at school on their subsequent cognitive, social, and emotional adjustment.

Students' experiences at school vary widely and are dependent on a variety of factors such as their academic progress, the peer group they belong to, and the extracurricular activities they participate in. Studies of high schools suggest that schools are often structured to work best for students who need the least amount of help. For example, academically talented students have more positive experiences at school than less talented students; they are more likely to learn, feel more positive about themselves, receive more attention from teachers, hold more positions of leadership in the school, and participate in more classes that are engaging and challenging. In order to support students staying in school, researchers need to examine the school context and individual processes that may be influencing students' decisions to leave school.

This article by Mahoney and Cairns examines the role of extracurricular activities in protecting students against school dropout. The results of their study suggest that involvement in extracurricular activities may be particularly beneficial for those students who are at the highest risk of dropping out. Such involvement may increase students' commitment to the school by focusing on the students' strengths, while at the same time immersing them in positive school-oriented peer groups. Thus, this article provides evidence to support specific directions for educators, parents, and schools on intervening and preventing school dropout.

Do Extracurricular Activities Protect Against Early School Dropout?

Joseph L. Mahoney and Robert B. Cairns

North American public secondary schools are unique in terms of the number and range of pursuits that they support in the classroom and beyond. In addition to offering a broad academic curriculum, middle schools and high schools encourage students to participate in various extracurricular activities; these include organized sports, special-interest academic pursuits, vocational clubs, supervised student government, newspapers, yearbooks, and various other activities. Extracurricular activities differ from standard courses in school because they are optional, ungraded, and are usually conducted outside the school day in school facilities.

Although "extra" to the curriculum, many activities are closely linked to academic achievement and performance (e.g., math club, French club, national honor society). It seems reasonable to expect that participation in these clubs and organizations should enhance and extend classroom instruction. Other activities – such as football and other interscholastic athletics – have little obvious connection to academic achievement. It has been proposed that participation in the latter nonacademic extracurricular activities may be beneficial nonetheless. Participation could, for example, raise an individual's status within the school, extend her or his social affiliations in the school community (e.g., Csikszentmihalyi, Rathunde, & Whalen, 1993; Eder, 1985; Eder & Parker, 1987; Kinney, 1993), or enable both to occur. The impact would be to render school a more meaningful and attractive experience for students who have experienced few successes in academic subjects.

Do extracurricular activities have beneficial effects for the individual and the school? Or do they simply maintain the status quo and, possibly, offer attractive diversions that compete with serious academic involvement among less competent students (Marsh, 1992)? The second possibility follows from early studies that demonstrate that extracurricular involvement is closely associated with socioeconomic class status, with the exception of athletics (e.g., Coleman, 1961; Hollingshead, 1949). Accordingly, extracurricular activities could consolidate socioeconomic differences outside the classroom that were present within and thereby accentuate socioeconomic divisions.

The theoretical model that guided the present research presupposes that the trajectories of individual lives are supported by a network of influences, for good or for ill (Bronfenbrenner, 1995; Cairns & Cairns, 1994; Magnusson, 1995). Development is viewed as a holistic process involving biological, psychological, and social–environmental influences that become fused over ontogeny (Cairns & Cairns, 1994). Single aspects – whether biological, behavioral, or environmental – gain their meaning through their functional relation with other features and with the whole individual. The effect of any single factor, such as involvement in extracurricular activities, is expected to be relative to the network of constraints that have operated in the past and are likely to operate in the future.

Given these considerations, we anticipated that the influence of extracurricular involvement in the reduction of school dropout would not be evenly distributed across persons. But in contrast to the *attractive diversion* hypothesis, we anticipated that the least competent students would benefit most from extracurricular involvement in terms of dropout reduction.

This expectation reflects two assumptions, one substantive and one statistical. First, we presumed that marginal or at-risk children differ from highly competent ones in terms of the range and breadth of the influences that keep them in school. Hence we expected that extracurricular involvement could shift the balance in the direction of heightened school engagement for children who are marginal or at risk in their school adaptations. In contrast, highly competent children – as judged by social–academic performance in the school – are already firmly embedded in the system and the values that it represents. For these students, extracurricular participance may be redundant insofar as school involvement is concerned. Second, there should be very few early school dropouts among highly competent children, regardless of their participation in optional activities. This low dropout rate would yield a statistical "floor effect" and render it difficult if not impossible to show beneficial effects of extracurricular involvement with respect to dropout. In brief, we propose that an interaction between extracurricular involvement and risk will occur, such that marginal and high-risk boys and girls should show the greatest influence in dropout reduction.

An overview of the educational and psychological literature on the effects of extracurricular activities indicates, curiously, that only modest attention has been given to the effects of extracurricular activities for marginal students (e.g., Brown, 1988; Holland & Andre, 1987). In contrast, a large amount of work has focused on the role of extracurricular activities for the brightest and the most privileged students. Specifically, (*a*) activities and positions of leadership may represent only a small number of individuals (Coleman, 1961; Haensly, Lupkowski, & Edlind, 1986; Hollingshead, 1949; Jacobs & Chase, 1989), (*b*) students of high socioeconomic class tend to report more involvement than lower-class students and show greater leadership and talent within these activities (Csikszentmihalyis, et al. 1993; Hollingshead, 1949), (*c*) girls tend to participate in more activities than boys (Coleman, 1961; Hollingshead, 1949; Jacobs & Chase, 1989), (*d*) those individuals who participate in high profile activities tend to be popular with peers, are school leaders, and may be influential in directing the status norms of the school social system (Coleman, 1961; Eder, 1985; Eder & Parker, 1987; Evans & Eder, 1993; Kinney, 1993), and (*e*) participation in academically linked activities is associated with somewhat higher levels of academic performance and educational attainment (Brown, Kohrs, & Lazzaro, 1991; Marsh, 1992; McNeal, 1995; Otto, 1975; Otto & Alwin, 1977).

Research has shown that extracurricular participation is associated with leadership, academic excellence, and popularity. Because most of these studies have been cross-sectional, it is unclear whether extracurricular involvement contributes to successful school adaptation or is an outcome. For example, extracurricular activities may be more open to highly competent students than to less able ones. Alternatively, competent students may be actively sought out by the institution to participate in the activities and fill leadership roles. Unfortunately, a parallel criticism applies to retrospective accounts of linkages between extracurricular involvement and school dropout, in which autobiographical constructions may confound the sequence and significance of historical events (e.g., Bell, 1967; Ross, 1989). To evaluate the directionality of the relationship between extracurricular activity and school dropout, research should prospectively track individuals beginning at a point in which there were little or no opportunities for extracurricular involvement and prior to dropout.

In this study, we examine the relation of extracurricular involvement to early school dropout. Participants were interviewed annually, and information was obtained from teachers and peers on a range of social and academic dimensions. In addition, annual information on extracurricular involvement was available from school yearbooks. In summary, the three purposes of the study were (a) to describe the normative pattern of extracurricular activity across the years of middle school and high school, (b) to identify persons in the seventh and eighth grades who are marginal or at risk for early school dropout, as determined by configurations of behavioral and academic performance that are based on teacher evaluations, and (c) to assess the relation between extracurricular activity participation and early school dropout across students showing different levels of risk for school dropout. We expected that greater extracurricular activity involvement would be negatively related to early school dropout. We further expected that this effect would be strongest for students at greatest risk for early school dropout.

Method

Participants

The research sample consisted of 392 children (206 girls, 186 boys) who were part of a broader population of 475 participants (227 boys, 248 girls) involved in a longitudinal investigation beginning in 1982–1983 (Cairns & Cairns, 1994). Of this broader sample, two middle schools had adequate accounts of extracurricular participation to be included in this study. As a result, one middle school ($n = 83$) was excluded from the analyses.

The sample was recruited in the 1982–1983 and 1983–1984 school years. In the 1982–1983 school year, all students in the seventh grade in Middle Schools 1 and 2 were invited to participate. In the following year (1983–1984), all seventh grade students in Middle School 2 were invited to participate. The participation rate was approximately 70% across the schools. No significant differences were found between participants and nonparticipants in terms of ethnic status or gender. Twenty-five percent of the participants were African American. The average age was 13 years 4 months in the seventh grade, and 18 years 4 months in the 12th grade. Between 89 and 99% of the original sample of participants were recovered each year.

Participants were interviewed annually for six years, from seventh through twelfth grade. Participants not in school were interviewed in their homes or other locations of their choosing. The interview schedule and assessment measures have been described in detail elsewhere (Cairns & Cairns, 1984, 1994; Cairns, Cairns, Neckerman, Fergusson, & Gariépy, 1989; Cairns, Cairns, Neckerman, Gest, & Gariépy, 1988).

We used school yearbooks to estimate school size. At the beginning of the study, 638 and 444 students were enrolled in Middle Schools 1 and 2. Ninety-two percent of students from Middle Schools 1 and 2 attended High School 1 or High School 2, respectively. The size of these two high schools was approximately 745 students for High School 1 and 570 students for High School 2 at the time of graduation in 1988. The sample as a whole was enrolled in 29 different high schools across the nation, including one penal institution, and one participant was located in South America. At grade 12 in 1987–1988, we interviewed 99% of the original sample (466 of 472 students). Three participants had died during the ensuing years.

Measures

Yearbooks. We obtained information regarding extracurricular involvement for each participant from school yearbooks. These books are published annually in most American middle schools and high schools and are typically available to students for purchase near the end of each school year. Yearbooks are subdivided into several sections including (*a*) individual photographs of students attending the school shown by grade, (*b*) a record and photograph of participants in extracurricular activities, including positions of status within the activity (e.g., president, team captain), (*c*) featured profiles of individual students, and (*d*) descriptions and photographs of other activities portraying the school culture.

High school seniors are commonly given a special summary section that lists their comprehensive extracurricular activity involvement, awards and honors received, and additional achievement information over the entire four years of high school. Yearbook information regarding extracurricular activity participation was submitted annually by the activity advisors and teachers within each school.[1]

One middle school yearbook provided photographs of the children involved in extracurricular activities but failed to include the participants' names. In this case, two researchers fully acquainted with all participants provided the names, using yearbook photographs of the individuals and of the activity participants.

Yearbook information was obtained from two middle schools during the seventh and the eighth grades and from eight of 29 high schools that participants attended during grades 9 through 12. Yearbooks provided complete information for an average of 94% of the sample across grades 7 to 12, ranging from 100% in seventh grade to 88% in 12th grade. Extracurricular activity involvement did not differ significantly between students attending Middle Schools 1 and 2 or High Schools 1 and 2.

Students participated in a total of 64 extracurricular activities during secondary school. Extracurricular information was coded dichotomously, wherein 1 indicated *participation in a given activity*, and 0 indicated *no participation*. Kappa coefficient estimates of reliability for the dichotomous coding were performed on approximately 10% of the sample. For this reliability sample, only two instances of interrater disagreement were noted across all the six grades and 64 activities. Specifically, disagreement occurred for coding of cheerleading involvement in 12th grade ($\kappa = .72$) and track involvement in the 10th grade ($\kappa = .73$). As a result, kappa estimates of reliability averaged .99 across all activities and grades.

The 64 activities were categorized into nine mutually exclusive, nonoverlapping, activity domains including athletics, academics, fine arts, student government, school service activities, press activities, school assistants, vocational activities, and royalty activities (see Appendix). Four independent raters classified each activity into the nine domains described above. Raters were chosen because of their knowledge of both the participant population and the participants' schools as well as their personal experiences as students or teachers in the state the sample represents. Overall agreement on category classification was 92%, with specific domain agreement as follows: academics, 86%; athletics, 97%; fine arts, 100%; student government, 100%; service, 88%; press activities, 83%; school assistants, 94%; vocational activities, 78%; and royalty activities, 100%.

We determined a yearly activity participation score for each participant across each of the 64 activities described above. Yearly scores in each activity were then aggregated across the nine broader activity domains. Finally, each activity domain score was summed to provide an overall score of activity participation for a given year. Thus, the number of activities an individual participated in was accounted for at four levels: (*a*) involvement in specific activities for each year, (*b*) total number of activities participated in during a given year, (*c*) number of activities participated in within each activity domain for each year, and (*d*) total number of activities participated in across all years for each activity domain.

Children who were retained in school for one or more years were included in the study, but participation scores were taken from the non-retained year or years only. For example, if an individual repeated ninth grade, activity information was taken from the original ninth-grade year and not for the repeated year. This decision was based on the overall lack of student participation during a repeated year or years. Of the 44 students who repeated at least one year of school from grades 7 to 12, only four students participated in extracurricular activities during their retained year or years, each in a single activity.

Academic and behavioral competence.   As part of each annual assessment, participants' teachers completed the Interpersonal Competence Scale (ICS; Cairns, Leung, Gest, & Cairns, 1995). The ICS includes 18 items relating to social behavior and academic competence. Each item on the ICS was rated on a seven-point scale in which either end of the scale represents a polar opposite. Positive and negative endpoints of the scale were randomized by item. The ICS has been used with diverse samples and settings and has been demonstrated to be highly reliable across items and consistent over time (Cairns & Cairns, 1994; Cairns et al., 1995).

Three general factors were used in the current study. These factors, followed by specific constituent items in parentheses, include Aggression (gets into trouble, gets into fights, argues), Popularity (popular with boys, popular with girls, lots of friends), Academic Competence (good at spelling, good at math). ICS scores were coded such that higher scores indicate more positive characteristics (i.e., lower aggression, higher popularity, and academic competence; for a further description of psychometric properties, reliability, and factor construction of the ICS, the reader is directed to Cairns et al., 1995).

Early school dropout. To determine dropout rates, we consulted multiple information sources (cf. Cairns, Cairns, & Neckerman, 1989). First, at the end of annual data collection, we visited each school and queried school personnel (including both teachers and school counselors) regarding student enrollment status. Second, each year we examined school enrollment rosters to determine whether a student's name was listed. Third, all students were individually interviewed each year and questioned regarding their school enrollment status. Finally, official commencement lists were used to establish the veridicality of prior enrollment sources.

School dropout was determined to have occurred if a student left school prior to completing the 11th grade. Whether students subsequently reenrolled or completed a General Equivalency Diploma (or equivalent degree) did not alter their initial dropout classification.

Demographic and socioeconomic information. Information concerning parental occupation, place of employment, and student's race was obtained during annual interviews. Parental employment was coded with the Duncan–Featherman scale (Stevens & Featherman, 1981) to provide an index of socioeconomic status (SES). SES was based upon the child's initial interview in the seventh grade. The Duncan–Featherman scale ranges from 0 (unemployed) to 88 (physician, dentist, lawyer). Family SES ranged from 12 to 87, with a mean of 29.8 and median of 25 (e.g., equipment operator, child-care worker, machine operator).

Statistical procedures

Cluster analysis. We chose five factors for the cluster analysis that were linked to several areas of competence and demonstrated a relation to school dropout. These were Socioeconomic Status, Grades Retained (Age), Aggressive Behavior, Academic Performance, and Popularity With Peers.

A variety of studies have shown that SES and poverty are predictors of school failure and dropout (Cairns, Cairns, & Neckerman, 1989; Ekstrom, Goertz, Pollack, & Rock, 1986; Ensminger & Slusarcick, 1992; Frase, 1989; Kaufman, McMillan, & Bradby, 1992). In addition, differences in age, relative to peers, resulting from school retention is a strong predictor of dropout (Cairns, Cairns, & Neckerman, 1989; Kaufman et al., 1992). Finally, school-related behavior in terms of academic performance (Cairns, Cairns, & Neckerman, 1989; Ensminger & Slusarcick, 1992; Kaufman et al., 1992; Simner & Barnes, 1991), aggression (Cairns, Cairns, Neckerman, Fergusson, and Gariépy, 1989; Ensminger & Slusarcick, 1992; Kaufman et al., 1992) and popularity (Cairns, Cairns, & Neckerman, 1989; Kaufman et al., 1992) have been associated with subsequent dropout.

Ethnic status was not included in the computation of the clusters. Although Hispanic and African American students generally have been shown to have higher rates of school dropout, the finding is not universal. In this investigation, African American students had equivalent or marginally lower school-dropout rates than White students, suggesting that the effects of ethnic status may vary as a function of sample, region, and urban–rural differences. Moreover, the effects of ethnic status on school dropout are diminished or eliminated when socioeconomic status is taken into account (Kaufman et al., 1992). Hence we did not include ethnic status as a variable in identifying the clusters, but we report the proportion of African American and White participants who were placed in each cluster.

Following the developmental model outlined above and detailed in other sources (e.g., Bronfenbrenner, 1995; Cairns & Cairns, 1994; Magnusson, 1995), we employed a person-oriented approach to identify homogeneous configurations of individuals who were similar along several dimensions that we deemed relevant for school adaptation. The clustering techniques that we adopted have been described elsewhere (e.g., Bergman, Eklund, & Magnusson, 1992; Bergman & Magnusson, 1992; Cairns, Cairns, & Neckerman, 1989; Gustafson & Magnusson, 1991; Magnusson, 1988; Magnusson & Bergman, 1988). This strategy allowed us to define a starting point, based on differential levels of competence, from which to plot the developmental trajectories of extracurricular activity participation. The relation between activity involvement and early school dropout could then be evaluated with respect to these configurations that were identified in the seventh and eighth grades.

In the cluster analysis for the person-oriented classification, we used the SLEIPNER program for pattern analysis (Bergman & El-Khouri, 1995). The number of cluster solutions was determined by three criteria, namely (*a*) expectations of cluster patterns identified in previous analyses with similar methods and variables (e.g., Cairns, Cairns, & Neckerman, 1989), (*b*) meaningfulness of each additional cluster solution in providing distinctly new and relevant patterns across cluster variables, and (*c*) reduction in error sums of squares and increase in variance accounted for by additional cluster solutions.

We obtained the cluster solutions using Ward's method in the SLEIP-NER program and were subject to an iterative, reclustering procedure. This procedure relocated individuals who were placed in a given cluster, if transferring an individual resulted in a significant reduction of error sums of squares. Iterations proceeded until the cluster solution was stable such that further relocations produced a nonsignificant reduction in error sums of squares. For boys and girls, an eight-cluster solution was identified, each accounting for 58% of variance in cluster variables. (For a further discussion of cluster analytic procedures, the reader is directed to Aldenderfer & Blashfield, 1984; Bergman & Magnusson, 1992; Blashfield & Aldenderfer, 1988; Legendre & Legendre, 1983, pp. 219–259; and Magnusson, 1988.)

We then grouped resulting clusters into three more general levels of competence, namely, high competence, marginal competence, and low competence or at-risk clusters. High competence clusters were characterized by positive scores on the cluster variables and the absence of any extreme negative scores on ratings of academic–behavioral competence. Marginal competence clusters had a mix of one or more positive scores on the cluster variables and one negative score on academic–behavioral competence ratings (e.g., low popularity, low achievement, high aggression). Low competence, at-risk clusters generally showed a profile of negative characteristics across the cluster variables, including high levels of aggression. Unlike the marginal competence clusters, at-risk clusters did not have any academic–behavioral competence ratings in a positive direction (i.e., no redeeming features).

Growth curve analysis. To model activity growth over time for the three competence-based clusters, we used a hierarchical linear model (HLM; Bryk & Raudenbush, 1987; Raudenbush & Chan, 1992). HLM has at least two advantages over traditional linear modeling procedures (e.g., regression; analysis of variance, ANOVA; multivariate analysis of variance, MANOVA): (*a*) HLM provides direct comparisons on the coefficients concerned with polynomial terms (e.g., linear, quadratic, etc.) among subclasses of participants (e.g., competence-based clusters), and (*b*) HLM makes use of all available observations of each participant, avoiding participant deletion resulting from data missing at any time-point (i.e., listwise deletion) common to traditional within-subject analysis (e.g., MANOVA). We used the MIXED procedure in SAS (SAS Institute Inc., 1988) to estimate growth curves separately for boys and girls. A backward elimination strategy was used whereby nonsignificant higher-order parameter and intercept terms were removed in successive steps (Piexoto, 1990).

Results

In this section, we describe the patterns of extracurricular involvement that were observed from middle school through high school and then present the results of our evaluation of the primary hypotheses, conducted with person-oriented longitudinal analyses.

Extracurricular involvement: Gender and ethnic effects

We observed few ethnic differences in overall activity participation, and the differences identified were modest. In this regard, African American students participated in slightly more activities than did White students, that is, ninth-grade difference, $F(1, 342) = 4.62$, $p < .05$. But these differences did not hold for all activity domains. White students were more involved in student government activities than African American students, $F(1, 387) = 3.78$, $p < .05$, whereas African American boys participated in interscholastic sports more often than White boys, $F(1, 387) = 4.65$, $p < .05$.

One striking finding was the number of students who were involved in only one or no activity. An average of 59% of girls and 68% of boys participated in one or no school activities each year. In middle school, only 8% of the boys and 13% of girls participated in more than one activity. During high school, extracurricular involvement increased substantially. Across the ninth through twelfth grades, 48% of boys and 65% of girls participated in more than one activity.

Competence configurations

Cluster analysis provides statistically based homogeneous subsets of individuals across variables of interest. Boys and girls were clustered separately with the broader, population-based sample ($N = 475$). Clustering variables included age and socioeconomic status at grade 7, and mean ICS teacher ratings of academic competence, popularity, and aggression across grades 7 and 8.

Table 1 (top and bottom) shows the final eight-cluster solutions for boys and girls, respectively. These configurations were grouped into three superordinate categories of social–cognitive competence, according to criteria described earlier. For boys, high competence included Clusters 1, 2, and 3; marginal competence included Clusters 4, 5, and 6; and at risk included Clusters 7 and 8. For girls, high competence included Clusters 1, 2, and 3 (same as the boys); marginal competence included Clusters 4 and 5; and at risk included Clusters 6, 7, and 8.

Figure 1 shows growth curve estimates and mean extracurricular involvement for male and female competence clusters across middle school, early high school, and late high school.[2] For boys, growth curve analysis revealed a significant effect for competence, $F(2, 132) = 11.32$, $p < .001$, a quadratic grade effect, $F(2, 132) = 9.36, p < .001$, and a competence $\times$ linear grade interaction, $F(1, 132) = 24.62, p < .001$. The high competent and marginally competent clusters showed a greater increase in activity participation during high school than did the risk clusters. The quadratic trend indicates that activity growth between middle and early high school was greater than between early and late high school.

For female competence-based clusters across the same three age–grade periods, growth curve analysis revealed a significant effect for competence, $F(2, 160) = 6.64$, $p < .01$, a linear grade effect, $F(1, 174) = 90.47$, $p < .001$, and a competence $\times$ linear grade interaction, $F(2, 160) = 6.26, p < .01$. Like the boys, the higher competence clusters for girls showed greater increases than the risk clusters. However, for girls,

Table 1 Person-oriented configurations during middle school

| | | | Cluster variables | | | | | | | | | |
| | | | Age | | ACA | | POP | | AGG | | SES | |
Cluster	n (White/Black)	Description	M	SD	M	SD	M	SD	M	SD	M	SD
Boys												
1	17 (16/1)	High competence – A	12.99	.31	5.43	.97	5.20	.82	2.40	.71	59.65	12.76
2	28 (20/8)	High competence – B	13.02	.46	5.59	.92	4.92	.76	1.73	.59	19.07	6.47
3	36 (24/12)	High competence – C	13.12	.37	4.62	.70	4.88	.47	3.68	.71	22.44	8.61
4	22 (21/1)	Unpopular	13.04	.49	4.37	1.00	3.68	.56	2.55	.83	42.50	11.98
5	9 (8/1)	Aggressive-popular	13.07	.49	3.83	.72	5.05	.79	5.04	.80	51.33	12.27
6	24 (13/11)	Low achievement	13.37	.37	2.80	.86	4.13	.69	2.44	.86	20.63	8.75
7	21 (13/8)	Aggressive risk	13.05	3.39	3.39	.74	3.64	.53	4.68	.64	19.68	8.46
8	24 (15/9)	Multiple risk	14.72	.50	2.95	1.07	3.97	.81	4.90	.87	21.75	10.76
Total sample	186 (133/53)		13.38	.73	4.17	1.33	4.41	.87	3.30	1.38	28.91	17.22
Girls												
1	30 (28/2)	High competence – A	12.91	.25	5.52	.90	4.70	.54	1.88	.76	57.40	11.30
2	44 (36/8)	High competence – B	13.01	.29	5.99	.69	5.73	.51	1.67	.55	32.61	11.81
3	37 (22/15)	High competence – C	13.02	.34	5.59	.79	4.27	.57	1.95	.69	18.87	6.65
4	26 (16/10)	Popular-aggressive	13.01	.30	4.98	.67	5.35	.44	3.41	.57	35.96	13.43
5	13 (8/5)	Low achievement	13.48	.54	2.90	.83	4.47	.51	2.00	.95	22.08	9.96
6	29 (17/12)	Aggressive risk – A	12.83	.31	4.33	.89	4.19	.50	4.11	.85	20.76	9.74
7	11 (6/5)	Aggressive risk – B	14.26	.31	4.16	.61	5.06	.77	4.23	1.08	21.91	10.49
8	8 (5/3)	Multiple risk	14.65	.77	2.72	.83	2.54	.53	5.06	1.13	15.50	3.02
Total sample	206 (143/63)		13.15	5.03	5.03	1.23	4.78	.92	2.64	1.32	30.57	16.78

ACA = academic competence; POP = popularity; AGG = aggression; SES = socioeconomic status.

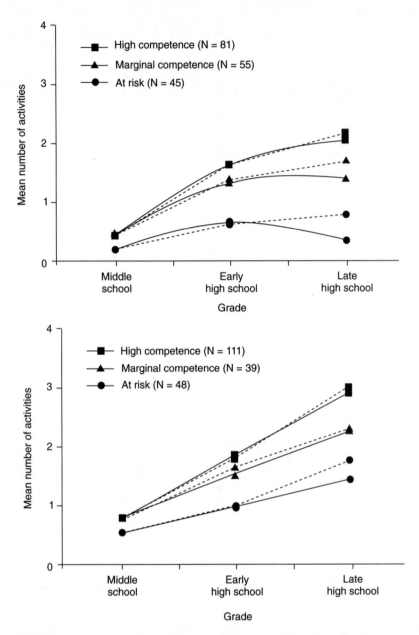

Figure 1 Extracurricular activity involvement as a function of competence and grade for boys (top) and girls (bottom). Solid lines show hierarchical linear model estimated growth curves; dashed lines show sample means.

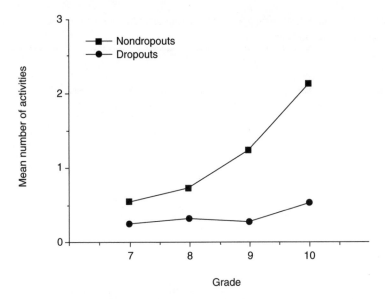

Figure 2   Mean number of extracurricular activities participated in as a
function of dropout status and grade.

a significant quadratic effect was not found, indicating that activity
growth was relatively constant across the three age–grade periods.

Extracurricular activity involvement and school dropout

Sixteen percent of the 392 participants were early school dropouts (27
girls, 34 boys). Dropout rates increased over time. The following number
of participants dropped out for grades 7 to 11: seventh grade, 0; eighth
grade, 3; ninth grade, 13; tenth grade, 16; 11th grade, 29.

To evaluate whether extracurricular involvement would predict early
school dropout, we compared activity participation across grades 7 to
10 for dropouts and nondropouts. Univariate ANOVAs were performed
separately at each grade so as not to confound the number of dropouts
with activity participation. Figure 2 shows the mean number of activities participated in by nondropouts and dropouts. Dropouts participated
in significantly fewer extracurricular activities at all grades, even several
years prior to dropout: seventh grade, $F(1, 389) = 8.41$, $p < .01$; eighth

Table 2 Proportion of dropouts by extracurricular activity involvement and competence for boys and girls

Competence level	Middle school			Early high school		
	No involvement	Up to one activity	More than one activity	No involvement	Up to one activity	More than one activity
Boys						
Competent	.07 (3/42)	.04 (1/28)	.00 (0/11)	.11 (2/19)	.05 (1/19)	.00 (0/39)
Marginal	.26 (7/27)	.05 (1/22)	.00 (0/6)	.27 (3/11)	.13 (2/15)	.00 (0/24)
At risk	.57 (17/30)	.29 (4/14)	1.00 (1/1)	.59 (10/17)	.00 (0/8)	.00 (0/8)
Girls						
Competent	.04 (1/23)	.07 (4/60)	.00 (0/27)	.18 (4/22)	.00 (0/25)	.00 (0/55)
Marginal	.00 (0/10)	.11 (2/19)	.20 (2/10)	.29 (2/7)	.07 (1/15)	.06 (1/16)
At risk	.45 (9/20)	.24 (5/21)	.00 (0/7)	.42 (5/12)	.07 (1/14)	.00 (0/11)

grade, $F(1, 365) = 10.14$, $p < .001$; ninth grade, $F(1, 343) = 15.46$, $p < .001$; and tenth grade, $F(1, 314) = 31.00$, $p < .01$.

We then assessed whether school dropout would differ according to levels of extracurricular involvement and competence. Table 2 shows the proportion of dropouts separately by gender, according to competence clusters and annual extracurricular involvement during middle and early high school. For this analysis, extracurricular involvement was divided into three categories during middle school and early high school; namely, no involvement, one activity, and more than one activity.

During middle school, we identified significant main effects for cluster competence, $F(2, 360) = 29.98$, $p < .001$, and level of activity involvement, $F(2, 360) = 4.24$, $p = .02$. The interaction between cluster competence and activity level did not reach statistical significance, $F(4, 360) = 2.20$, $p = .069$. However, students in the risk clusters showed a significantly higher dropout rate than students in the more competent clusters only in the case of no extracurricular involvement, $F(2, 149) = 20.69$, $p < .001$, or involvement in one activity, $F(2, 161) = 5.99$, $p = .003$. No significant gender interactions were observed. As annual involvement increased, the dropout rates decreased and became similar across the three competence clusters.

Parallel effects were observed in early high school, with somewhat higher levels of significance: cluster competence, $F(2, 319) = 7.26$, $p = .001$; activity level, $F(2, 319) = 30.28$, $p < .001$; and cluster competence

Table 3 Proportion of at-risk dropouts as a function of activity domain and grade

Activity domain	No involvement	Any involvement	Chi-square[a] or Fisher's exact test[b]	p
Middle school				
Fine arts	.40 (27/67)	.35 (9/26)	$\chi^2(1, 93) = .07$	>.10
Athletics	.44 (35/79)	.07 (1/14)	$\chi^2(1, 93) = 5.44$	<.05
Vocational	.40 (36/91)	.00 (0/2)	Fisher's exact	.37
All others combined	.43 (34/79)	.14 (2/14)	$\chi^2(1, 93) = 3.02$	<.10
Early high school				
Fine arts	.27 (15/55)	.07 (1/15)	Fisher's exact	.08
Athletics	.34 (16/47)	.00 (0/23)	$\chi^2(1, 70) = 8.31$	<.01
Vocational	.29 (16/55)	.00 (0/15)	Fisher's exact	.01
All others combined	.30 (16/53)	.00 (0/17)	Fisher's exact	.006

[a] *Chi-square values were computed using Yate's continuity correction.*
[b] *When expected cell frequency <5, Fisher's exact test probabilities are reported.*

by activity level, $F(4, 319) = 5.12$, $p = .001$. There was a large reduction in dropout for students in the risk clusters as activity participation increased. Significant differences between competence clusters were observed only in the case of no activity involvement, $F(2, 85) = 6.23$, $p = .003$. No significant gender interactions were observed. Figure 3 shows the relation between extracurricular involvement and early school dropout as a function of competence clusters, with boys and girls combined. Involvement in extracurricular activities was related to a substantial reduction in school dropout. This effect was strongest for the risk clusters during early high school.

To clarify this finding, risk clusters were compared with respect to participation in each of the nine activity domains and rates of early school dropout (see table 3).[3] Results show that, with the exception of fine arts participation, all domains were associated with reduced rates of early school dropout. This was particularly true for involvement in athletic activities. There were no significant gender interactions for any activity domain. With the exception of one participant, risk students who engaged in any activity domain during early high school graduated from high school.

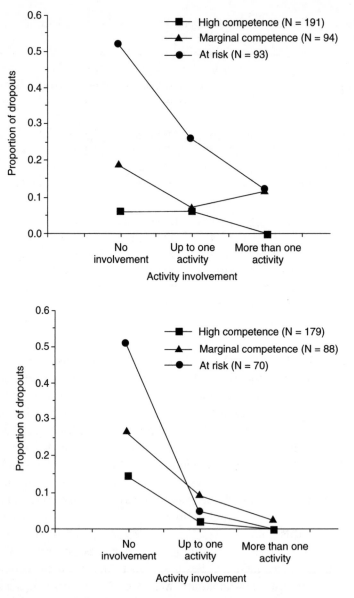

Figure 3 Early school dropout as a function of extracurricular activity involvement and competence during middle school (top) and early high school (bottom).

The cluster methodology also suggests a fresh way to address the relationship between SES and extracurricular activities. Socioeconomic comparisons are usually confounded with differences on other adaptive characteristics (e.g., academic competence, aggressive behavior, popularity). It should be noted that two high competence clusters of boys (i.e., Clusters 1, 2) were similar on multiple characteristics of school adaptation but differed in SES. With these relevant social–academic factors controlled, the socioeconomic difference in activity participation between male Clusters 1 and 2 (see table 1, top) is not significant. A parallel comparison is possible for competent female clusters (i.e., Clusters 1, 2, and 3; see table 1, bottom). These three clusters showed a small but reliable difference in activity participation as a function of SES, $F(4, 312) = 2.87$, $p < .05$.

Discussion

Results indicate that engagement in school extracurricular activities is linked to decreasing rates of early school dropout in both boys and girls. The outcome is observed primarily among students who were at highest risk for dropout.

The association between reduced rates of early school dropout and extracurricular involvement differed according to the competence of the individual. For students in the risk clusters, the associated reduction in dropout was stronger compared with more competent students. It is likely that the relations were not as pronounced for more competent children because they presumably had one or more existing sources of positive connection to the school. The concept that protective factors may differentially moderate the risk–outcome relation as a function of competence has been shown in studies of developmental psychopathology and competence (e.g., Masten et al., 1988; Masten, Morison, Pellegrini, & Tellegen, 1990; Rutter, 1990) and several recent preventive intervention studies, ranging from intellectual development in high-risk infants (Gross, 1990; Gross, Brooks-Gunn, & Spiker, 1992; Infant Health and Development Program, 1990) to depression among unemployed adults (Caplan, Vinokur, Price, & van Ryn, 1989; Price, 1992; Price, van Ryn, & Vinokur, 1992).

In light of the current results, the functions and goals of extracurricular activities should be reconsidered. The exclusionary processes characteristic of some activities (e.g., Coleman, 1961; Eder, 1985; Evans & Eder, 1993; Hollingshead, 1949; Jacobs & Chase, 1989) may work against those students who could benefit most directly from involvement.

But why should participation in a single school extracurricular activity be strongly associated with lower rates of school dropout for students at risk? For students whose prior commitment to the school and its values has been marginal, such participation provides an opportunity to create a positive and voluntary connection to the educational institution. Unlike alternative procedures (e.g., school dropout prevention programs, remedial education), which focus on the deficits of students and serve as a catalyst in the formation of deviant groups, extracurricular activities can provide a gateway into the conventional social networks while, simultaneously, promoting individual interests, achievements, and goals (e.g., Csikszentmihalyi et al., 1993; Eder, 1985; Kinney, 1993; McNeal, 1995). Thus, school dropout may be effectively decreased through the maintenance and enhancement of positive characteristics of the individual that strengthen the student–school connection.

A related question is, why is there a greater associated reduction in school dropout during early high school? One explanation is that the increased diversity of activities offered in high school provides adolescents more opportunity for activity participation suited to their interest–ability (Kinney, 1993). The range of activities included in the domains that risk students most often participated in (athletics, fine arts, and vocational) increased during high school, as did their participation in these domains. Thus, the effect may be stronger in high school because participation increases as a result of greater opportunity, an expanded diversity of activities, or both.

A second explanation would be that the shift from middle school to high school represents a point of developmental transition. Recall that competence was defined by the configuration of variables assessed during middle school. The reorganization of schools, classrooms, teachers, and peer groups that accompanies the transition into high school may provide some students with a turning point by which earlier patterns of adaptation can be transformed. Extracurricular involvement, particularly for persons at risk for dropout, may be one component of that transition that could help shift the balance toward greater engagement in school.

It is also noteworthy that rates of early school dropout were higher in early high school than in middle school. This age-related difference may, in part, reflect that students are required by law to remain in school until the age of 16 years. Students who became committed to dropping out in high school would not be expected to extensively participate in any aspect of formal schooling, including extracurricular activities.

School yearbooks are published annually in most American secondary schools to record the goals of the institution and accomplishments of the students. For the researcher, they constitute a convenient, noninvasive, and public index of each student's participation in extracurricular activities. It is a small irony that the production of yearbooks is itself an extracurricular activity.

Yearbooks are not newspapers, and their content is biased toward recording school-related achievement rather than individual shortcomings. Honors and accomplishments are archived, but failures, delinquencies, and expulsions are not. Despite this bias toward accomplishment, it seems noteworthy that school dropouts could be differentiated from nondropouts by virtue of their absence of involvement in extracurricular activities early on.

It should be recalled, however, that participation was selective. The large number of uninvolved students found in this study is consistent with earlier reports that there is a general inequality of extracurricular participation in American secondary schools. In this investigation, roughly half of the students were not publicly recognized during secondary school, or at least were invisible across the range of extracurricular activities presented in school yearbooks. Using a conservative estimate including only the intact sample at each grade, we found that 59% of girls and 68% of boys showed an average amount of participation in one or no school activities each year. Moreover, the growth curve analysis revealed that participation rates were consistently lower for risk students compared with their more competent counterparts.

The availability of extracurricular activities does not ensure equal opportunity for participation. Why the differential involvement? Possible reasons include the following: (*a*) many activities highlighted in yearbooks require expertise in particular domains (e.g., music, sports, languages, mathematics, science); (*b*) certain school activities require nomination, selection, or election and participation, and status may be maintained by exclusion and gatekeeping (possibly mediated by school personnel, peers, or both); (*c*) some school activities require minimal academic performance (e.g., a "C" average) to be eligible for participation; (*d*) socioeconomic status, although not a general barrier to participation, may influence the types of activities students choose (or are allowed) to participate in as well as the attainment of status within those activities (Coleman, 1961; Hollingshead, 1949; Csikszentmihalyi et al., 1993).

The design of this study followed from a developmental model that called for disaggregation of the sample at the onset of the longitudinal investigation. This step was required to facilitate the tracking of the different developmental pathways that were likely to be adopted. The procedure begins with the assumption that interactions among internal and external characteristics are central to understanding the course of individual human development. In the present research, the technique highlighted the differential outcomes associated with extracurricular involvement, and it could be equally important in subsequent analyses of the success or failure of preventive interventions.

Correlational results provide only weak evidence for causation. This principle holds even when correlational matrices and their sibling analyses (e.g., multiple regression analysis, linear structural equation models) are derived from years of longitudinal study and involves replication across successive time-points and samples. Prior work shows that school dropout is associated with multiple properties of the individual and the social context, and it is very likely that more than a single pathway is involved. Nonetheless, convergent evidence from this study is consistent with the proposition that extracurricular participation helps protect against school dropout for some students. In this regard, the results are consistent with the developmental model of correlated internal and external constraints that guided the research design.

Future research on extracurricular activities should address reasons why some students join extracurricular activities, maintain their participation over time, and the possible reasons why they do not become involved or drop out of the extracurriculum. It would also be of interest to assess whether patterns of participation in school-based extracurricular activities have consequences following formal schooling. Participation in school extracurricular activities may or may not be related to subsequent achievement following formal schooling, depending on the type of activity and the measure of subsequent achievement (Eccles &

Barber, 1995). This finding suggests that research on extracurricular activities should be extended beyond high school to assess the linkages to long-term patterns of adaptation.

Appendix: Extracurricular Activities Participated in from Grades 7 through 12

Asterisks indicate that activity is offered during middle school.

Athletics
Baseball
Basketball*
Cheerleading*
Cross-country
Fellowship of Christian Athletes
Football*
Golf
Grapplelette
Monogram
Pep club*
Softball
Tennis
Track
Volleyball
Wrestling

Assistants
Flag attendant
Food service
Laboratory assistant
Library assistant*
Office assistant

Fine Arts
Art club
Band*
Chorus*
Concert choir

Press
Journalism club
School newspaper*
Photography club
Yearbook*

Vocational
Automobile club
Career club*
Distributive educational club
Future business leaders
Future farmers
Future homemakers
Vocational industrial club

Academics
BETA club
Business club
French club
Future programmers
Future teachers
History club
Junior marshall
National honor society
Science club
Spanish club
Spanish club
Quiz bowl

Service	Bible club
Drama	Civinettes/civitans
Intermediate chorus	Ecology council
Girl's ensemble	Health occupation students
Marching band	Students Against Drunk Drivers
Small ensemble	Young American Society
	Youth Advisory Council
Student Government	
Class officer	*Royalty*
Student council*	Homecoming
Student government association	Prom
	School princess

Notes

1 A comparison of high school yearbook information supplied by school personnel with activity photos in yearbooks revealed a high degree of overlap. Where discrepancy existed, high school photographs typically contained errors of omission, rather than commission. Independent of yearbooks, student participation in many activities was verified through participant interview questions surrounding friendship, social network, and crowd membership.

2 It is noteworthy that the growth curve analysis underestimated the actual mean level of extracurricular activity participation for risk clusters during late high school. We suspect that this finding is due to the higher proportion of dropouts found in the risk clusters. As shown in figure 2, participation rates by students who eventually dropped out of school is significantly lower than those for nondropouts.

3 The following activity domains were grouped together because of the low participation rate among persons in the risk clusters: assistants, service, academics, government, and press. There was no participation in the royalty activities among persons in the risk clusters, so this domain was not included in the analysis.

References

Aldenderfer, M. S., & Blashfield, R. K. (1984). Cluster analysis. In J. L. Sullivan & R. G. Neimi (Series Eds.), *Sage University paper series on quantitative applications in the social sciences* (*Paper series no. 07-044*, 1–88). Beverly Hills, CA: Sage.

Bell, J. W. (1967). A comparison of dropouts and non-dropouts on participation in school activities. *The Journal of Educational Research, 60*, 248–251.

Bergman, L. R., Eklund, G., & Magnusson, D. (1992). Studying individual development: Problems and methods. In D. Magnusson, L. R. Bergman, G. Rudinger, & B. Törestad (Eds.), *Problems and methods in longitudinal research: Stability and change* (pp. 323–326). Cambridge, UK: Cambridge University Press.

Bergman, L. R., & El-Khouri, B. M. (1995). SLEIPNER. *A statistical package for pattern-oriented analysis.* (Version 1.0) [Statistical Package Computer Software]. Stockholm, Sweden: Stockholm University, Department of Psychology.

Bergman, L. R., & Magnusson, D. (1992). Stability and change in patterns of extrinsic adjustment problems. In D. Magnusson, L. R. Bergman, G. Rudinger, & B. Törestad (Eds.), *Problems and methods in longitudinal research: Stability and change* (pp. 323–326). Cambridge, UK: Cambridge University Press.

Blashfield, R. K., & Aldenderfer, M. S. (1988). The methods and problems of cluster analysis. In J. R. Nesselroade & R. B. Cattell (Eds.), *Handbook of multivariate experimental psychology* (2nd ed., pp. 447–473). New York: Plenum.

Bronfenbrenner, U. (1995). The bioecological model from a life course perspective: Reflections of a participant observer. In P. Moen, G. H. Elder, Jr., & K. Lüscher (Eds.), *Examining lives in context: Perspective on the ecology of human development* (pp. 599–618). Washington, DC: American Psychological Association.

Brown, B. B. (1988). The vital agenda for research on extracurricular influence: A reply to Holland and Andre. *Review of Educational Research, 58*, 107–111.

Brown, B. B., Kohrs, D., & Lazzaro, C. (1991, April). *The academic costs and consequences of extracurricular participation in high school.* Paper presented at the meeting of the American Educational Research Association, Chicago, IL.

Bryk, A. S., & Raudenbush, S. W. (1987). Application of hierarchical linear models to assessing change. *Psychological Bulletin, 101*, 147–158.

Cairns, R. B., & Cairns, B. D. (1984). Predicting aggressive patterns in girls and boys: A developmental study. *Aggressive Behavior, 11*, 227–242.

Cairns, R. B., & Cairns, B. D. (1994). *Lifelines and risks: Pathways of youth in our time.* New York: Cambridge University Press.

Cairns, R. B., Cairns, B. D., & Neckerman, H. J. (1989). Early school drop out: Determinants and configurations. *Child Development, 60*, 1437–1452.

Cairns, R. B., Cairns, B. D., Neckerman, H. J., Fergusson, L. L., & Gariépy, J.-L. (1989). Growth and aggression: I. Childhood to early adolescence. *Developmental Psychology, 25*, 320–330.

Cairns, R. B., Cairns, B. D., Neckerman, H. J., Gest, S. D., & Gariépy, J.-L. (1988). Social networks and aggressive behavior: Peer support or peer rejection? *Developmental Psychology, 24*, 815–823.

Cairns, R. B., Leung, M.-C., Gest, S. D., & Cairns, B. D. (1995). A brief method for assessing social development: Structure, reliability, stability, and developmental validity of the Interpersonal Competence Scale. *Behavioral Research and Therapy, 33*, 725–736.

Caplan, R. D., Vinokur, A. D., Price, R. H., & van Ryn, M. (1989). Job seeking, reemployment, and mental health: A randomized field experiment in coping with job loss. *Journal of Applied Psychology, 74*, 759–769.

Coleman, J. S. (1961). *The adolescent society.* New York: Free Press.

Csikszentmihalyi, M., Rathunde, K., & Whalen, S. (1993). *Talented teenagers: The roots of success and failure.* New York: Cambridge University Press.

Eccles, J. L., & Barber, B. L. (1995, May). *Adolescents' activity involvement: Predictors and longitudinal consequences.* In Symposium conducted at the Biennial Meeting of the Society for Research in Child Development, Indianapolis, IN.

Eder, D. (1985). The cycles of popularity: Interpersonal relations among female adolescents. *Sociology of Education, 58*, 154–165.

Eder, D., & Parker, S. (1987). The cultural production and reproduction of gender: The effect of extracurricular activities on peer-group culture. *Sociology of Education, 60*, 200–214.

Ekstrom, R. B., Goertz, M. E., Pollack, J. E., & Rock, D. A. (1986). Who drops out of high school and why? Findings from a national study. *Teachers College Record, 87*, 356–373.

Ensminger, M. E., & Slursarcick, A. L. (1992). Paths to high school graduation or dropout: A longitudinal study of a first-grade cohort. *Sociology of Education, 65*, 95–113.

Evans, C., & Eder, D. (1993). "No Exit": Processes of social isolation in the middle school. *Journal of Contemporary Ethnography, 22*, 139–170.

Frase, M. (1989). Dropout rates in the United States: 1988. *National Center for Educational Statistics Analysis Report.* (DOE Publication No. NCES-89-609). Washington, DC: US Department of Education, Office of Research and Improvement.

Gross, R. T. (1990). A multisite randomized intervention trial for premature, low birthweight infants: The Infant Health and Development Program. In D. E. Rogers & E. Ginzberg (Eds.), *Improving the life chances of children at risk* (pp. 146–161). Boulder, CO: Westview Press.

Gross, R. T., Brooks-Gunn, J., & Spiker, D. (1992). Efficacy of comprehensive early intervention for low birth weight, premature infants and their families: The Infant Health and Development Program. In S. L. Friedman & M. Sigman (Eds.), *Advances in applied developmental psychology: The psychological development of low birthweight children* (Vol. 6, pp. 411–434). Norwood, NJ: Ablex.

Gustafson, S. B., & Magnusson, D. (1991). *Female life careers: A pattern approach.* Hillsdale, NJ: Erlbaum.

Haensly, P. A., Lupkowski, A. E., & Edlind, E. P. (1986). The role of extracurricular activities in education. *The High School Journal, 68,* 110–119.

Holland, A., & Andre, T. (1987). Participation in extracurricular activities in secondary school: What is known, what needs to be known? *Review of Educational Research, 57,* 437–466.

Hollingshead, A. B. (1949). *Elmstown's youth: The impact of social classes on adolescents.* New York: Wiley.

Infant Health and Development Program. (1990). Enhancing the outcomes of low birthweight, premature infants: A multi-site randomized trial. *Journal of the American Medical Association, 263,* 3035–3042.

Jacobs, L. C., & Chase, C. I. (1989). Student participation in and attitudes toward high school activities: Findings from a national study. *The High School Journal, 72,* 175–181.

Kaufman, P., McMillan, M. M., & Bradby, D. (1992). Dropout rates in the United States: 1991. *National Center for Educational Statistical Analysis Report.* (DOE Publication No. NCES-92-129). Washington, DC: US Department of Education, Office of Research and Improvement.

Kinney, D. A. (1993). From nerds to normals: The recovery of identity among adolescents from middle school to high school. *Sociology of Education, 66,* 21–40.

Legendre, L., & Legendre, P. (1983). *Numerical ecology.* New York: Elsevier Scientific.

Magnusson, D. (1988). *Individual development from an interactional perspective: A longitudinal study* (Vol. 1). Hillsdale, NJ: Erlbaum.

Magnusson, D. (1995). Individual development: A holistic, integrated model. In P. Moen, G. H. Elder, Jr., & K. Lüscher (Eds.), *Examining lives in context: Perspective on the ecology of human development* (pp. 19–60). Washington, DC: American Psychological Association.

Magnusson, D., & Bergman, L. R. (1988). Individual and variable-based approaches to longitudinal research on early risk factors. In M. Rutter (Ed.), *Studies of psychosocial risk: The power of longitudinal data* (pp. 45–61). Cambridge, UK: Cambridge University Press.

Marsh, H. W. (1992). Extracurricular activities: Beneficial extension of the traditional curriculum or subversion of academic goals? *Journal of Educational Psychology, 84,* 553–562.

Masten, A. S., Garmezy, N., Tellegen, A., Pellegrini, D., Larkin, K., & Larsen, A. (1988). Competence and stress in school children: The moderating effects of individual and family qualities. *Journal of Child Psychology and Psychiatry*, *29*, 745–764.

Masten, A. S., Morison, P., Pellegrini, D., & Tellegen, A. (1990). Competence under stress: Risk and protective factors. In J. Rolf, A. S. Masten, D. Cicchetti, K. H. Nuechterlein, & S. Weintraub (Eds.), *Risk and protective factors in the development of psychopathology* (pp. 236–256). New York: Cambridge University Press.

McNeal, R. B. (1995). Extracurricular activities and high school dropouts. *Sociology of Education*, *68*, 62–81.

Otto, L. B. (1975). Extracurricular activities in the educational attainment process. *Rural Sociology*, *40*, 162–176.

Otto, L. B., & Alwin, D. F. (1977). Athletics, aspirations, and attainment. *Sociology of Education*, *50*, 102–113.

Piexoto, J. L. (1990). A property of well-formulated polynomial regression models. *The American Statistician*, *44*, 26–30.

Price, R. H. (1992). Psychosocial impact of job loss on individuals and families. *Current Directions in Psychological Science*, *1*, 9–11.

Price, R. H., van Ryn, M., & Vinokur, A. D. (1992). Impact of preventive job search intervention on the likelihood of depression among the unemployed. *Journal of Health and Social Behavior*, *33*, 158–167.

Raudenbush, S. W., & Chan, W.-S. (1992). Growth curve analysis in accelerated longitudinal designs. *Journal of Research in Crime and Delinquency*, *29*, 387–411.

Ross, M. (1989). Relation of implicit theories to the construction of personal histories. *Psychological Review*, *96*, 341–357.

Rutter, M. (1990). Psychosocial resilience and protective factors. In J. Rolf, A. S. Masten, D. Cicchetti, K. H. Nuechterlein, & S. Weintraub (Eds.), *Risk and protective factors in the development of psychopathology* (pp. 181–214). New York: Cambridge University Press.

SAS Institute Inc. (1988). *SAS/STAT user's guide* (6.03 edition). Cary, NC: SAS Institute Inc.

Simner, M. L., & Barnes, M. J. (1991). Relationship between first-grade marks and the high school dropout problem. *Journal of School Psychology*, *29*, 331–335.

Stevens, G., & Featherman, D. C. (1981). A revised sociometric index of socioeconomic status. *Social Science Research*, *10*, 364–395.

Part III

Gender Identity, the Self, and Moral Development

Introduction to Part III

This section considers three different aspects of the self: self-concept, gender, and morality. These represent processes that are referred to as individuation, by which I mean the psychological separation of individuals from the others who are in their social worlds. The goal of each of these articles is to identify key individuation processes and to establish (1) the manner in which an individual establishes a sense of self at different ages (whether it be a self-concept, gender identity, or morality) and (2) how each of these aspects of self contributes to the formation of the individual's unique identity.

These are three areas that are central in the study of social development, and they represent the intersection of social interaction and individuation. Children and adolescents cannot know themselves without a sense of others. Self-concept, gender, and morality are all influenced by interactions with parents, peers, and romantic partners, and are all interrelated. Individuals cannot define themselves and create an identity without an awareness of their own strengths, weaknesses, gender identity, and values. Gender identity and moral values are an important part of one's self-conception. Furthermore, an individual's self-conception may influence his or her commitment to moral concerns. Finally, underlying the development of self, gender, and morality is the importance of cognitive development. With developing cognitive capacities, understanding, definitions, and conceptualizations of self, gender, and morality become more abstract, differentiated, and complex.

EIGHT

Gender Differences

Introduction

Males and females differ psychologically as well as physically. There are, however, differences between sex stereotypes (people's beliefs about the differences between the sexes) and actual sex differences. In 1974, Maccoby and Jacklin published a seminal article examining sex differences. After reviewing more than 1,600 articles pertaining to sex differences, they concluded that there were a number of unfounded beliefs about sex differences in social behavior, including the assumptions that (1) girls are more social than boys, (2) girls are more suggestible than boys, (3) girls have lower self-esteem than boys, and (4) girls are more affected by heredity and boys are more affected by their environment. The one conclusive finding they did make was that boys are more aggressive than girls. These authors concluded that there were very few individual attributes in which there were clear sex differences. Even when sex differences were present, the amount of variance accounted for was small relative to the variance within each sex group.

At the time, Maccoby and Jacklin's article was controversial. Critics argued that they failed to identify sex differences in important characteristics such as empathy, activity, and dominance (where, it was claimed, they do exist, Block, 1976). Whether sex differences appear in assessments of social dispositions (such as empathy and suggestibility) may actually depend on factors such as the measures used, the testing context, the size of the sample, and the age, social class, and background of the participants. This issue still remains controversial.

In this article, Maccoby maintains her belief about the sex differences and extends her work to consider the importance of context, so that, for example, boys and girls may behave differently in same-sex groups than in mixed-sex groups.

References

Block, J. H. (1976). Debatable conclusions about sex differences. *Contemporary Psychology*, *21*, 517–22.

Maccoby, E. E., & Jacklin, C. N. (1974). *The psychology of sex differences*. Stanford, CA: Stanford University Press.

Gender and Relationships:
A Developmental Account

Eleanor E. Maccoby

Historically, the way we psychologists think about the psychology of gender has grown out of our thinking about individual differences. We are accustomed to assessing a wide variety of attributes and skills and giving scores to individuals based on their standing relative to other individuals in a sample population. On most psychological attributes, we see wide variation among individuals, and a major focus of research has been the effort to identify correlates or sources of this variation. Commonly, what we have done is to classify individuals by some antecedent variable, such as age or some aspect of their environment, to determine how much of the variance among individuals in their performance on a given task can be accounted for by this so-called *antecedent* or *independent* variable. Despite the fact that hermaphrodites exist, almost every individual is either clearly male or clearly female. What could be more natural for psychologists than to ask how much variance among individuals is accounted for by this beautifully binary factor?

Fifteen years ago, Carol Jacklin and I put out a book summarizing the work on sex differences that had come out of the individual differences perspective (Maccoby & Jacklin, 1974). We felt at that time that the yield was thin. That is, there were very few attributes on which the average values for the two sexes differed consistently. Furthermore, even when consistent differences were found, the amount of variance accounted for by sex was small, relative to the amount of variation within each sex. Our conclusions fitted in quite well with the feminist zeitgeist of the times, when most feminists were taking a minimalist position, urging that the two sexes were basically alike and that any differences were either illusions in the eye of the beholder or reversible outcomes of social shaping. Our conclusions were challenged as having both overstated the case for sex differences (Tieger, 1980) and for having understated it (Block, 1976).

In the last 15 years, work on sex differences has become more methodologically sophisticated, with greater use of meta-analyses to reveal not only the direction of sex differences but quantitative estimates of their magnitude. In my judgment, the conclusions are still quite similar to those Jacklin and I arrived at in 1974: There are still some replicable sex differences, of moderate magnitude, in performance on tests of mathematical and spatial abilities, although sex differences in verbal abilities have faded. Other aspects of intellectual performance continue to show gender equality. When it comes to attributes in the personality–social domain, results are particularly sparse and inconsistent. Studies continue to find that men are more often agents of aggression than are women (Eagly, 1987; Huston, 1985; Maccoby & Jacklin, 1980). Eagly (1983, 1987) reported in addition that women are more easily influenced than men and that men are more altruistic in the sense that they are more likely to offer help to others. In general, however, personality traits measured as characteristics of individuals do not appear to differ systematically by sex (Huston, 1985). This no doubt reflects in part the fact that male and female persons really are much alike, and their lives are governed mainly by the attributes that all persons in a given culture have in common. Nevertheless, I believe that the null findings coming out of comparisons of male and female individuals on personality measures are partly illusory. That is, they are an artifact of our historical reliance on an individual differences perspective. Social behavior, as many have pointed out, is never a function of the individual alone. It is a function of the interaction between two or more persons. Individuals behave differently with different partners. There are certain important ways in which gender is implicated in social behavior – ways that may be obscured or missed altogether when behavior is summed across all categories of social partners.

An illustration is found in a study of social interaction between previously unacquainted pairs of young children (mean age, 33 months; Jacklin & Maccoby, 1978). In some pairs, the children had same-sex play partners; in others, the pair was made up of a boy and a girl. Observers recorded the social behavior of each child on a time-sampling basis. Each child received a score for total social behavior directed toward the partner. This score included both positive and negative behaviors (e.g., offering a toy and grabbing a toy; hugging and pushing; vocally greeting, inviting, protesting, or prohibiting). There was no overall sex difference in the amount of social behavior when this was evaluated without regard to sex of partner. But there was a powerful interaction between sex of the subject and that of the partner: Children of each sex had much higher levels of social behavior when playing with a same-sex partner than when playing with a child of the other sex. This result is consistent with the findings of Wasserman and Stern (1978) that when asked to approach another child, children as young as age three stopped farther away when the other child was of the opposite sex, indicating awareness of gender similarity or difference, and wariness toward the other sex.

The number of time intervals during which a child was simply standing passively watching the partner play with the toys was also scored. There was no overall sex difference in the frequency of this behavior, but the behavior of girls was greatly affected by the sex of the partner. With other girls, passive behavior seldom occurred; indeed, in girl–girl pairs it occurred less often than it did in boy–boy pairs. However when paired with boys, girls frequently stood on the sidelines and let the boys monopolize the toys. Clearly, the little girls in this study were not more passive than the little boys in any overall, trait-like sense. Passivity in these girls could be understood only in relation to the characteristics of their interactive partners. It was a characteristic of girls in cross-sex dyads. This conclusion may not seem especially novel because for many years we have known that social behavior is situationally specific. However, the point here is that interactive behavior is not just situationally specific, but that it depends on the gender category membership of the participants. We can account for a good deal more of the behavior if we know the gender mix of dyads, and this probably holds true for larger groups as well.

An implication of our results was that if children at this early age found same-sex play partners more compatible, they ought to prefer same-sex partners when they entered group settings that included children of both sexes. There were already many indications in the literature that children do have same-sex playmate preferences, but there clearly was a need for more systematic attention to the degree of sex segregation that prevails in naturally occurring children's groups at different ages. As part of a longitudinal study of children from birth to age six, Jacklin and I did time-sampled behavioral observation of approximately 100 children on their preschool playgrounds, and again two years later when the children were playing during school recess periods (Maccoby & Jacklin, 1987). Same-sex playmate preference was clearly apparent in preschool when the children were approximately four and a half. At this age, the children were spending nearly three times as much time with same-sex play partners as with children of the other sex. By age six and a half, the preference had grown much stronger. At this time, the children were spending 11 times as much time with same-sex as with opposite-sex partners.

Elsewhere we have reviewed the literature on playmate choices (Maccoby, 1988; Maccoby & Jacklin, 1987), and here I will simply summarize what I believe the existing body of research shows:

1   Gender segregation is a widespread phenomenon. It is found in all the cultural settings in which children are in social groups large enough to permit choice.
2   The sex difference in the gender of preferred playmates is large in absolute magnitude, compared to sex differences found when children are observed or tested in nonsocial situations.
3   In a few instances, attempts have been made to break down children's preferences for interacting with other same-sex children. It has been found that the preferences are difficult to change.
4   Children choose same-sex playmates spontaneously in situations in which they are not under pressure from adults to do so. In modern coeducational schools, segregation is more marked in situations that have not been structured by adults than in those that have (e.g., Eisenhart & Holland, 1983). Segregation is situationally specific, and the two sexes can interact comfortably under certain conditions, for example, in an absorbing joint task, when structures and roles are set up by adults, or in nonpublic settings (Thorne, 1986).
5   Gender segregation is not closely linked to involvement in sex-typed activities. Preschool children spend a great deal of their time engaged in activities that are gender neutral, and segregation prevails in these activities as well as when they are playing with dolls or trucks.

6   Tendencies to prefer same-sex playmates can be seen among three-year-olds and at even earlier ages under some conditions. But the preferences increase in strength between preschool and school and are maintained at a high level between the ages of six and at least age 11.

7   The research base is thin, but so far it appears that a child's tendency to prefer same-sex playmates has little to do with that child's standing on measures of individual differences. In particular, it appears to be unrelated to measures of masculinity or femininity and also to measures of gender schematicity (Powlishta, 1989).

Why do we see such pronounced attraction to same-sex peers and avoidance of other-sex peers in childhood? Elsewhere I have summarized evidence pointing to two factors that seem to be important in the preschool years (Maccoby, 1988). The first is the rough-and-tumble play style characteristic of boys and their orientation toward issues of competition and dominance. These aspects of male–male interaction appear to be somewhat aversive to most girls. At least, girls are made wary by male play styles. The second factor of importance is that girls find it difficult to influence boys. Some important work by Serbin and colleagues (Serbin, Sprafkin, Elman, & Doyle, 1984) indicates that between the ages of three and a half and five and a half, children greatly increase the frequency of their attempts to influence their play partners. This indicates that children are learning to integrate their activities with those of others so as to be able to carry out coordinated activities. Serbin and colleagues found that the increase in influence attempts by girls was almost entirely an increase in making polite suggestions to others, whereas among boys the increase took the form of more use of direct demands. Furthermore, during this formative two-year period just before school entry, boys were becoming less and less responsive to polite suggestions, so that the style being progressively adopted by girls was progressively less effective with boys. Girls' influence style was effective with each other and was well adapted to interaction with teachers and other adults.

These asymmetries in influence patterns were presaged in our study with 33-month-old children: We found then that boys were unresponsive to the vocal prohibitions of female partners (in that they did not withdraw), although they would respond when a vocal prohibition was issued by a male partner. Girls were responsive to one another and to a male partner's prohibitions. Fagot (1985) also reported that boys are "reinforced" by the reactions of male peers – in the sense that they modify their behavior following a male peer's reaction – but that their behavior appears not to be affected by a female's response.

My hypothesis is that girls find it aversive to try to interact with someone who is unresponsive and that they begin to avoid such partners. Students of power and bargaining have long been aware of the importance of reciprocity in human relations. Pruitt (1976) said, "Influence and power are omnipresent in human affairs. Indeed, groups cannot possibly function unless their members can influence one another" (p. 343). From this standpoint, it becomes clear why boys and girls have difficulty forming groups that include children of both sexes.

Why do little boys not accept influence from little girls? Psychologists almost automatically look to the nuclear family for the origins of behavior patterns seen in young children. It is plausible that boys may have been more reinforced for power-assertive behavior by their parents, and girls more for politeness, although the evidence for such differential socialization pressure has proved difficult to come by. However, it is less easy to imagine how or why parents should reinforce boys for being unresponsive to *girls*. Perhaps it is a matter of observational learning: Children may have observed that between their two parents, their fathers are more influential than their mothers. I am skeptical about such an explanation. In the first place, mothers exercise a good deal of managerial authority within the households in which children live, and it is common for fathers to defer to their judgment in matters concerning the children. Or, parents form a coalition, and in the eyes of the children they become a joint authority, so that it makes little difference to them whether it is a mother or a father who is wielding authority at any given time. Furthermore, the asymmetry in children's cross-sex influence with their peers appears to have its origins at quite an early age – earlier, I would suggest, than children have a very clear idea about the connection between their own sex and that of the same-sex parent. In other words, it seems quite unlikely that little boys ignore girls' influence attempts because little girls remind them of their mothers. I think we simply do not know why girls' influence styles are ineffective with boys, but the fact that they are has important implications for a variety of social behaviors, not just for segregation.

Here are some examples from recent studies. Powlishta (1987) observed preschool-aged boy–girl pairs competing for a scarce resource. The children were brought to a playroom in the nursery school and were given an opportunity to watch cartoons through a movie-viewer that could only be accessed by one child at a time. Powlishta found that when the two children were alone together in the playroom, the boys got more than their share of access to the movie-viewer. When there was an adult present, however, this was no longer the case. The adult's presence appeared to inhibit the boys' more power-assertive techniques and resulted in girls having at least equal access.

This study points to a reason why girls may not only avoid playing with boys but may also stay nearer to a teacher or other adult. Following up on this possibility, Greeno (1989) brought four-child groups of kindergarten and first-grade children into a large playroom equipped with attractive toys. Some of the quartets were all-boy groups, some all-girl groups, and some were made up of two boys and two girls. A female adult sat at one end of the room and, halfway through the play session, moved to a seat at the other end of the room. The question posed for this study was: Would girls move closer to the teacher when boys were present than when they were not? Would the sex composition of a play group make any difference to the locations taken up by the boys? The results were that in all-girl groups, girls actually took up locations *farther* from the adult than did boys in all-boy groups. When two boys were present, however, the two girls were significantly closer to the adult than were the boys, who tended to remain at intermediate distances. When the adult changed position halfway through the session, boys' locations did not change, and this was true whether there were girls present or not. Girls in all-girl groups tended to move in the opposite direction when the adult moved, maintaining distance between themselves and the adult; when boys were present, however, the girls tended to move *with* the adult, staying relatively close. It is worth noting, incidentally, that in all the mixed-sex groups except one, segregation was extreme; both boys and girls behaved as though there was only one playmate available to them, rather than three.

There are some fairly far-reaching implications of this study. Previous observational studies in preschools had indicated that girls are often found in locations closer to the teacher than are boys. These studies have been done in mixed-sex nursery school groups. Girls' proximity seeking toward adults has often been interpreted as a reflection of some general affiliative trait in girls and perhaps as a reflection of some aspect of early socialization that has bound them more closely to caregivers. We see in the Greeno study that proximity seeking toward adults was *not* a general trait in girls. It was a function of the gender composition of the group of other children present as potential interaction partners. The behavior of girls implied that they found the presence of boys to be less aversive when an adult was nearby. It was as though they realized that the rough, power-assertive behavior of boys was likely to be moderated in the presence of adults, and indeed, there is evidence that they were right.

We have been exploring some aspects of girls' avoidance of interaction with boys. Less is known about why boys avoid interaction with girls, but the fact is that they do. In fact, their cross-sex avoidance appears to be even stronger. Thus, during middle childhood both boys and girls spend considerable portions of their social play time in groups of their own sex. This might not matter much for future relationships were it not for the fact that fairly distinctive styles of interaction develop in all-boy and all-girl groups. Thus, the segregated play groups constitute powerful socialization environments in which children acquire distinctive interaction skills that are adapted to same-sex partners. Sex-typed modes of interaction become consolidated, and I wish to argue that the distinctive patterns developed by the two sexes at this time have implications for the same-sex and cross-sex relationships that individuals form as they enter adolescence and adulthood.

It behooves us, then, to examine in somewhat more detail the nature of the interactive milieus that prevail in all-boy and all-girl groups. Elsewhere I have reviewed some of the findings of studies in which these two kinds of groups have been observed (Maccoby, 1988). Here I will briefly summarize what we know.

The two sexes engage in fairly different kinds of activities and games (Huston, 1985). Boys play in somewhat larger groups, on the average, and their play is rougher (Humphreys & Smith, 1987) and takes up more space. Boys more often play in the streets and other public places; girls more often congregate in private homes or yards. Girls tend to form close, intimate friendships with one or two other girls, and these friendships are marked by the sharing of confidences (Kraft & Vraa, 1975). Boys' friendships, on the other hand, are more oriented around mutual interests in activities (Erwin, 1985). The breakup of girls' friendships is usually attended by more intense emotional reactions than is the case for boys.

For our present purposes, the most interesting thing about all-boy and all-girl groups is the divergence in the interactive styles that develop in them. In male groups, there is more concern with issues of dominance. Several psycholinguists have recorded the verbal exchanges that occur in these groups, and Maltz and Borker (1983) summarized the findings of several studies as follows: Boys in their groups are more likely than girls in all-girl groups to interrupt one another; use commands, threats, or boasts of authority; refuse to comply with another child's demand; give information; heckle a speaker; tell jokes or suspenseful stories; top someone else's story; or call another child names. Girls in all-girl groups, on the other hand, are more likely than boys to express agreement with what another speaker has just said, pause to give another girl a chance to speak, or when starting a speaking turn, acknowledge a point previously made by another speaker. This account indicates that among boys, speech serves largely egoistic functions and is used to establish and protect an individual's turf. Among girls, conversation is a more socially binding process.

In the past five years, analysts of discourse have done additional work on the kinds of interactive processes that are seen among girls, as compared with those among boys. The summary offered by Maltz and Borker has been both supported and extended. Sachs (1987) reported that girls soften their directives to partners, apparently attempting to keep them involved in a process of planning a play sequence, while boys are more likely simply to tell their partners what to do. Leaper (1989) observed children aged five and seven and found that verbal exchanges among girls more often take the form of what he called "collaborative speech acts" that involve positive reciprocity, whereas among boys, speech acts are more controlling and include more negative reciprocity. Miller and colleagues (Miller, Danaher, & Forbes, 1986) found that there was more conflict in boys' groups, and given that conflict had occurred, girls were more likely to use "conflict mitigating strategies," whereas boys more often used threats and physical force. Sheldon (1989) reported that when girls talk, they seem to have a double agenda: to be "nice" and sustain social relationships, while at the same time working to achieve their own individual ends. For boys, the agenda is more often the single one of self-assertion. Sheldon (1989) has noted that in interactions among themselves, girls are *not* unassertive. Rather, girls do successfully pursue their own ends, but they do so while toning down coercion and dominance, trying to bring about agreement, and restoring or maintaining group functioning. It should be noted that boys' confrontational style does not necessarily impede effective group functioning, as evidenced by boys' ability to cooperate with teammates for sports. A second point is that although researchers' own gender has been found to influence to some degree the kinds of questions posed and the answers obtained, the summary provided here includes the work of both male and female researchers, and their findings are consistent with one another.

As children move into adolescence and adulthood, what happens to the interactive styles that they developed in their largely segregated childhood groups? A first point to note is that despite the powerful attraction to members of the opposite sex in adolescence, gender segregation by no means disappears. Young people continue to spend a good portion of their social time with same-sex partners. In adulthood, there is extensive gender segregation in workplaces (Reskin, 1984), and in some societies and some social-class or ethnic groups, leisure time also is largely spent with same-sex others even after marriage. The literature on the nature of the interactions that occur among same-sex partners in adolescence and adulthood is quite extensive and cannot be reviewed here. Suffice it to say in summary that there is now considerable evidence that the interactive patterns found in sex-homogeneous dyads or groups in adolescence and adulthood are very similar to those that prevailed in the gender-segregated groups of childhood (e.g., Aries, 1976; Carli, 1989; Cowan, Drinkard, & MacGavin, 1984; Savin-Williams, 1979).

How can we summarize what it is that boys and girls, or men and women, are doing in their respective groups that distinguishes these groups from one another? There have been a number of efforts to find the major dimensions that best describe variations in interactive styles. Falbo and Peplau (1980) have factor analyzed a battery of measures and have identified two dimensions: one called direct versus indirect, the other unilateral versus bilateral. Hauser et al. (1987) have distinguished what they called *enabling* interactive styles from *constricting* or *restrictive* ones, and I believe this distinction fits the styles of the two sexes especially well. A restrictive style is one that tends to derail the interaction – to inhibit the partner or cause the partner to withdraw, thus shortening the interaction or bringing it to an end. Examples are threatening a partner, directly contradicting or interrupting, topping the partner's story, boasting, or engaging in other forms of self-display. Enabling or facilitative styles are those, such as acknowledging another's comment or expressing agreement, that support whatever the partner is doing and tend to keep the interaction going. I want to suggest that it is because women and girls use more enabling styles that they are able to form more intimate and more integrated relationships. Also I think it likely that it is the male concern for turf and dominance – that is, with not showing weakness to other men and boys – that underlies their restrictive interaction style and their lack of self-disclosure.

Carli (1989) has recently found that in discussions between pairs of adults, individuals are more easily influenced by a partner if that partner has just expressed agreement with them. In this work, women were quite successful in influencing one another in same-sex dyads, whereas pairs of men were less so. The sex difference was fully accounted for by the fact that men's male partners did not express agreement as often. Eagly (1987) has summarized data from a large number of studies on women's and men's susceptibility to influence and has found women to be somewhat more susceptible. Carli's work suggests that this tendency may not be a general female personality trait of "suggestibility" but may reflect the fact that women more often interact with other women who tend to express reciprocal agreement. Carli's finding resonates with some work with young children interacting with their mothers. Mary Parpal and I (Parpal & Maccoby, 1985) found that children were more compliant to a mother's demands if the two had previously engaged in a game in which the child was allowed to give directions that the mother followed. In other words, maternal compliance set up a system of reciprocity in which the child also complied. I submit that the same principle applies in adult interactions and that among women, influence is achieved in part by being open to influence from the partner.

Boys and men, on the other hand, although less successful in influencing one another in dyads, develop group structures – well-defined roles in games, dominance hierarchies, and team spirit – that appear to enable them to function effectively in groups. One may suppose that the male directive interactive style is less likely to derail interaction if and when group structural forces are in place. In other words, men and boys may *need* group structure more than women and girls do. However, this hypothesis has yet to be tested in research. In any case, boys and men in their groups have more opportunity to learn how to function within hierarchical structures than do women and girls in theirs.

We have seen that throughout much of childhood and into adolescence and adulthood as well, people spend a good deal of their social time interacting with others of their own gender, and they continue to use distinctive interaction styles in these settings. What happens, then, when individuals from these two distinctive "cultures" attempt to interact with one another? People of both sexes are faced with a relatively unfamiliar situation to which they must adapt. Young women are less likely to receive the reciprocal agreement, opportunities to talk, and so on that they have learned to expect when interacting with female partners. Men have been accustomed to counterdominance and competitive reactions to their own power assertions, and they now find themselves with partners who agree with them and otherwise offer enabling responses. It seems evident that this new partnership should be easier to adapt to for men than for women. There is evidence that men fall in love faster and report feeling more in love than do women early in intimate relationships (Huston & Ashmore, 1986). Furthermore, the higher rates of depression in females have their onset in adolescence, when rates of cross-sex interaction rise (Nolen-Hoeksema, in press). Although these phenomena are no doubt multidetermined, the asymmetries in interaction styles may contribute to them.

To some degree, men appear to bring to bear much the same kind of techniques in mixed-sex groups as they are accustomed to using in same-sex groups. If the group is attempting some sort of joint problem solving or is carrying out a joint task, men do more initiating, directing, and interrupting than do women. Men's voices are louder and are more listened to than women's voices by both sexes (West & Zimmerman, 1985); men are more likely than women to lose interest in a taped message if it is spoken in a woman's rather than a man's voice (Robinson & McArthur, 1982). Men are less influenced by the opinions of other group members than are women. Perhaps as a consequence of their greater assertiveness, men have more influence on the group process (Lockheed, 1985; Pugh & Wahrman, 1983), just as they did in childhood. Eagly and colleagues (Eagly, Wood, & Fishbaugh, 1981) have drawn our attention to an important point about cross-sex interaction in groups: The greater resistance of men to being influenced by other group members is found only when the men are under surveillance, that is, if others know whether they have yielded to their partners' influence attempts. I suggest that it is especially the monitoring by other *men* that inhibits men from entering into reciprocal influence with partners.

When other men are present, men appear to feel that they must guard their dominance status and not comply too readily lest it be interpreted as weakness.

Women's behavior in mixed groups is more complex. There is some work indicating that they adapt by becoming more like men – that they raise their voices, interrupt, and otherwise become more assertive than they would be when interacting with women (Carli, 1989; Hall & Braunwald, 1981). On the other hand, there is also evidence that they carry over some of their well-practiced female-style behaviors, some-times in exaggerated form. Women may wait for a turn to speak that does not come, and thus they may end up talking less than they would in a women's group. They smile more than the men do, agree more often with what others have said, and give nonverbal signals of attentiveness to what others – perhaps especially the men – are saying (Duncan & Fiske, 1977). In some writings this female behavior has been referred to as "silent applause."

Eagly (1987) reported a meta-analysis of behavior of the two sexes in groups (mainly mixed-sex groups) that were performing joint tasks. She found a consistent tendency for men to engage in more task behavior – giving and receiving information, suggestions, and opin-ions (see also Aries, 1982) – whereas women are more likely to engage in socioemotional behaviors that support positive affective relations within the group. Which style contributes more to effective group process? It depends. Wood, Polek, and Aiken (1985) have compared the performance of all-female and all-male groups on different kinds of tasks, finding that groups of women have more success on tasks that require discussion and negotiation, whereas male groups do better on tasks where success depends on the volume of ideas being generated. Overall, it appears that *both* styles are productive, though in different ways.

There is evidence that women feel at a disadvantage in mixed-sex interaction. For example, Hogg and Turner (1987) set up a debate between two young men taking one position and two young women taking another. The outcomes in this situation were contrasted with a situation in which young men and women were debating against same-sex partners. After the cross-sex debate, the self-esteem of the young men rose, but that of the young women declined. Furthermore, the men liked their women opponents better after debating with them, whereas the women liked the men less. In other words, the encounter in most cases was a pleasurable experience for the men, but not for the women. Another example comes from the work of Davis (1978), who set up get-acquainted sessions between pairs of young men and women. He found that the men took control of the interaction, dictating the pace at which intimacy increased, whereas the women adapted themselves to the pace set by the men. The women reported later, however, that they had been uncomfortable about not being able to control the sequence of events, and they did not enjoy the encounter as much as the men did.

In adolescence and early adulthood, the powerful forces of sexual attraction come into play. When couples are beginning to fall in love, or even when they are merely entertaining the possibility of developing an intimate relationship, each is motivated to please the other, and each sends signals implying "Your wish is my command." There is evidence that whichever member of a couple is more attractive, or less in love, is at an advantage and is more able to influence the partner than vice versa (Peplau, 1979). The influence patterns based on the power of interpersonal attraction are not distinct in terms of gender; that is, it may be either the man or the woman in a courting relationship who has the influence advantage. When first meeting, or in the early stages of the acquaintance process, women still may feel at some disadvantage, as shown in the Davis study, but this situation need not last. Work done in the 1960s indicated that in many couples, as relationships become deeper and more enduring, any overall asymmetry in influence diminishes greatly (Heiss, 1962; Leik, 1963; Shaw & Sadler, 1965). Most couples develop a relationship that is based on communality rather than exchange bargaining. That is, they have many shared goals and work jointly to achieve them. They do not need to argue over turf because they have the same turf. In well-functioning married couples, both members of the pair strive to avoid conflict, and indeed there is evidence that the men on average are even more conflict-avoidant than the women (Gottman & Levenson, 1988; Kelley et al., 1978). Nevertheless, there are still carry-overs of the different interactive styles males and females have acquired at earlier points in the life cycle. Women seem to expend greater effort toward maintaining harmonious moods (Huston & Ashmore, 1986, p. 177). With intimate cross-sex partners, men use more direct styles of influence, and women use more indirect ones. Furthermore, women are more likely to withdraw (become silent, cold, and distant) and/or take unilateral action in order to get their way in a dispute (Falbo & Peplau, 1980), strategies that we suspect may reflect their greater difficulty in influencing a male partner through direct negotiation.

Space limitations do not allow considering in any depth the next set of important relationships that human beings form: that between parents and children. Let me simply say that I think there is evidence for the following: The interaction styles that women have developed in interaction with girls and other women serve them well when they become mothers. Especially when children are young, women enter into deeper levels of reciprocity with their children than do men (e.g., Gleason, 1987; Maccoby & Jacklin, 1983) and communicate with them better. On the other hand, especially after the first two years, children need firm direction as well as warmth and reciprocity, and fathers' styles may contribute especially well to this aspect of parenting. The relationship women develop with young children seems to depend very little on whether they are dealing with a son or a daughter; it builds on maternal response to the characteristics and needs of early childhood that are found in both boys and girls to similar degrees. Fathers, having a less intimate relationship with individual children, treat young boys and girls in a somewhat more gendered way (Siegal, 1987). As children approach middle childhood and interact with same-sex other children, they develop the interactive styles characteristic of their sex, and their parents more and more interact with them as they have always done with same-sex or opposite-sex others. That is, mothers and daughters develop greater intimacy and reciprocity; fathers and sons exhibit more friendly rivalry and joking, more joint interest in masculine activities, and more rough play. Nevertheless, there are many aspects of the relationships between parents and children that do not depend on the gender of either the parent or the child.

Obviously, as the scene unfolds across generations, it is very difficult to identify the point in the developmental cycle at which the interactional styles of the two sexes begin to diverge, and more important, to identify the forces that cause them to diverge. In my view, processes within the nuclear family have been given too much credit – or too much blame – for this aspect of sex-typing. I doubt that the development of distinctive interactive styles has much to do with the fact that children are parented primarily by women, as some have claimed (Chodorow, 1978; Gilligan, 1982), and it seems likely to me that children's "identification" with the same-sex parent is more a consequence than a cause of children's acquisition of sex-typed interaction styles. I would place most of the emphasis on the peer group as the setting in which children first discover the compatibility of same-sex others, in which boys first discover the requirements of maintaining one's status in the male hierarchy, and in which the gender of one's partners becomes supremely important. We do not have a clear answer to the ultimate question of why the segregated peer groups function as they do. We need now to think about how it can be answered. The answer is important if we are to adapt ourselves successfully to the rapid changes in the roles and relationships of the two sexes that are occurring in modern societies.

References

Aries, E. (1976). Interaction patterns and themes of male, female, and mixed groups. *Small Group Behavior, 7,* 7–18.

Aries, E. J. (1982). Verbal and nonverbal behavior in single-sex and mixed-sex groups: Are traditional sex roles changing? *Psychological Reports, 51,* 127–134.

Block, J. H. (1976). Debatable conclusions about sex differences. *Contemporary Psychology, 21,* 517–522.

Carli, L. L. (1989). Gender differences in interaction style and influence. *Journal of Personality and Social Psychology, 56,* 565–576.

Chodorow, N. (1978). *The reproduction of mothering.* Berkeley, CA: University of California Press.

Cowan, C., Drinkard, J., & MacGavin, L. (1984). The effects of target, age and gender on use of power strategies. *Journal of Personality and Social Psychology, 47,* 1391–1398.

Davis, J. D. (1978). When boy meets girl: Sex roles and the negotiation of intimacy in an acquaintance exercise. *Journal of Personality and Social Psychology, 36,* 684–692.

Duncan, S., Jr., & Fiske, D. W. (1977). *Face-to-face interaction: Research, methods and theory.* Hillsdale, NJ: Erlbaum.

Eagly, A. H. (1983). Gender and social influence. *American Psychologist, 38,* 971–981.

Eagly, A. H. (1987). *Sex differences in social behavior: A social role interpretation.* Hillsdale, NJ: Erlbaum.

Eagly, A. H., Wood, W., & Fishbaugh, L. (1981). Sex differences in conformity: Surveillance by the group as a determinant of male nonconformity. *Journal of Personality and Social Psychology, 40,* 384–394.

Eisenhart, M. A., & Holland, D. C. (1983). Learning gender from peers: The role of peer group in the cultural transmission of gender. *Human Organization, 42,* 321–332.

Erwin, P. (1985). Similarity of attitudes and constructs in children's friendships. *Journal of Experimental Child Psychology, 40*, 470–485.

Fagot, B. I. (1985). Beyond the reinforcement principle: Another step toward understanding sex roles. *Developmental Psychology, 21*, 1097–1104.

Falbo, T., & Peplau, L. A. (1980). Power strategies in intimate relationships. *Journal of Personality and Social Psychology, 38*, 618–628.

Gilligan, C. (1982). *In a different voice: Psychological theory and women's development*. Cambridge, MA: Harvard University Press.

Gleason, J. B. (1987). Sex differences in parent–child interaction. In S. U. Phillips, S. Steele, & C. Tanz (Eds.), *Language, gender and sex in comparative perspective* (pp. 189–199). Cambridge, UK: Cambridge University Press.

Gottman, J. M., & Levenson, R. W. (1988). The social psycho-physiology of marriage. In P. Roller & M. A. Fitzpatrick (Eds.), *Perspectives on marital interaction* (pp. 182–200). New York: Taylor & Francis.

Greeno, C. G. (1989). Gender differences in children's proximity to adults. Unpublished doctoral dissertation, Stanford University, Stanford, CA.

Hall, J. A., & Braunwald, K. G. (1981). Gender cues in conversation. *Journal of Personality and Social Psychology, 40*, 99–110.

Hauser, S. T., Powers, S. I., Weiss-Perry, B., Follansbee, D. J., Rajapark, D., & Greene, W. M. (1987). The constraining and enabling coding system manual. Unpublished manuscript.

Heiss, J. S. (1962). Degree of intimacy and male–female interaction. *Sociometry, 25*, 197–208.

Hogg, M. A., & Turner, J. C. (1987). Intergroup behavior, self stereotyping and the salience of social categories. *British Journal of Social Psychology, 26*, 325–340.

Humphreys, A. P., & Smith, P. K. (1987). Rough and tumble friendship and dominance in school children: Evidence for continuity and change with age in middle childhood. *Child Development, 58*, 201–212.

Huston, A. C. (1985). The development of sex-typing: Themes from recent research. *Developmental Review, 5*, 1–17.

Huston, T. L., & Ashmore, R. D. (1986). Women and men in personal relationship. In R. D. Ashmore & R. K. Del Boca (Eds.), *The social psychology of female–male relations*. New York: Academic Press.

Jacklin, C. N., & Maccoby, E. E. (1978). Social behavior at 33 months in same-sex and mixed-sex dyads. *Child Development, 49*, 557–569.

Kelley, H. H., Cunningham, J. D., Grisham, J. A., Lefebvre, L. M., Sink, C. R., & Yablon, G. (1978). Sex differences in comments made during conflict in close relationships. *Sex Roles, 4*, 473–491.

Kraft, L. W., & Vraa, C. W. (1975). Sex composition of groups and pattern of self-disclosure by high school females. *Psychological Reports, 37*, 733–734.

Leaper, C. (1989). The sequencing of power and involvement in boys' and girls' talk. Unpublished manuscript (under review), University of California, Santa Cruz.

Leik, R. K. (1963). Instrumentality and emotionality in family interaction. *Sociometry, 26,* 131–145.

Lockheed, M. E. (1985). Sex and social influence: A meta-analysis guided by theory. In J. Berger & M. Zelditch (Eds.), *Status, attributions, and rewards* (pp. 406–429). San Francisco, CA: Jossey-Bass.

Maccoby, E. E. (1988). Gender as a social category. *Developmental Psychology, 26,* 755–765.

Maccoby, E. E., & Jacklin, C. N. (1974). *The psychology of sex differences.* Stanford, CA: Stanford University Press.

Maccoby, E. E., & Jacklin, C. N. (1980). Sex differences in aggression: A rejoinder and reprise. *Child Development, 51,* 964–980.

Maccoby, E. E., & Jacklin, C. N. (1983). The "person" characteristics of children and the family as environment. In D. Magnusson & V. L. Allen (Eds.), *Human development: An interactional perspective* (pp. 76–92). New York: Academic Press.

Maccoby, E. E., & Jacklin, C. N. (1987). Gender segregation in childhood. In H. W. Reese (Ed.), *Advances in child development and behavior* (Vol. 20, pp. 239–288). New York: Academic Press.

Maltz, D. N., & Borker, R. A. (1983). A cultural approach to male–female miscommunication. In John A. Gumperz (Ed.), *Language and social identity* (pp. 195–216). New York: Cambridge University Press.

Miller, P., Danaher, D., & Forbes, D. (1986). Sex-related strategies for coping with interpersonal conflict in children aged five and seven. *Developmental Psychology, 22,* 543–548.

Nolen-Hoeksema, S. (in press). *Sex differences in depression.* Stanford, CA: Standford University Press.

Parpal, M., & Maccoby, E. E. (1985). Maternal responsiveness and subsequent child compliance. *Child Development, 56,* 1326–1334.

Peplau, A. (1979). Power in dating relationships. In J. Freeman (Ed.), *Women: A feminist perspective* (pp. 121–137). Palo Alto, CA: Mayfield.

Powlishta, K. K. (1987, April). *The social context of cross-sex interactions.* Paper presented at biennial meeting of the Society for Research in Child Development, Baltimore, MD.

Powlishta, K. K. (1989). Salience of group membership: The case of gender. Unpublished doctoral dissertation, Stanford University, Stanford, CA.

Pruitt, D. G. (1976). Power and bargaining. In B. Seidenberg & A. Snadowsky (Eds.), *Social psychology: An introduction* (pp. 343–375). New York: Free Press.

Pugh, M. D., & Wahrman, R. (1983). Neutralizing sexism in mixed-sex groups: Do women have to be better than men? *American Journal of Sociology, 88,* 746–761.

Reskin, B. F. (Ed.). (1984). *Sex segregation in the workplace: Trends, explanations and remedies.* Washington, DC: National Academy Press.

Robinson, J., & McArthur, L. Z. (1982). Impact of salient vocal qualities on causal attribution for a speaker's behavior. *Journal of Personality and Social Psychology, 43,* 236–247.

Sachs, J. (1987). Preschool boys' and girls' language use in pretend play. In S. U. Phillips, S. Steele, & C. Tanz (Eds.), *Language, gender and sex in comparative perspective* (pp. 178–188). Cambridge, UK: Cambridge University Press.

Savin-Williams, R. C. (1979). Dominance hierarchies in groups of early adolescents. *Child Development, 50,* 923–935.

Serbin, L. A., Sprafkin, C., Elman, M., & Doyle, A. (1984). The early development of sex differentiated patterns of social influence. *Canadian Journal of Social Science, 14,* 350–363.

Shaw, M. E., & Sadler, O. W. (1965). Interaction patterns in heterosexual dyads varying in degree of intimacy. *Journal of Social Psychology, 66,* 345–351.

Sheldon, A. (1989, April). *Conflict talk: Sociolinguistic challenges to self-assertion and how young girls meet them.* Paper presented at the biennial meeting of the Society for Research in Child Development, Kansas City.

Siegal, M. (1987). Are sons and daughters treated more differently by fathers than mothers? *Developmental Review, 7,* 183–209.

Thorne, B. (1986). Girls and boys together, but mostly apart. In W. W. Hartup & L. Rubin (Eds.), *Relationships and development* (pp. 167–184). Hillsdale, NJ: Erlbaum.

Tieger, T. (1980). On the biological basis of sex differences in aggression. *Child Development, 51,* 943–963.

Wasserman, G. A., & Stern, D. N. (1978). An early manifestation of differential behavior toward children of the same and opposite sex. *Journal of Genetic Psychology, 133,* 129–137.

West, C., & Zimmerman, D. H. (1985). Gender, language and discourse. In T. A. van Dijk (Ed.), *Handbook of discourse analysis: Vol. 4. Discourse analysis in society* (pp. 103–124). London: Academic Press.

Wood, W., Polek, D., & Aiken, C. (1985). Sex differences in group task performance. *Journal of Personality and Social Psychology, 48,* 63–71.

NINE

Self-Concept

Introduction

Self-concept, one of the oldest research subjects in the social sciences, has been proposed as a mediator of social adjustment and psychological well-being among children and adults (Kazdin, 1988). Despite the fact that the theoretical and clinical importance of self-concept have been well established, problems with operationalization and measurement of self-concept are numerous. These problems include a lack of theoretical consensus, little construct validity, and a substantial influence of social desirability – i.e., people will often answer questions in terms of some "ideal" respondent, rather than in terms of what they really think or feel. Traditionally, researchers in this area have defined self-concept as a unidimensional construct, highlighting the global nature of self-esteem (Coopersmith, 1967). Unfortunately, this model has only scant support in the literature.

More recently, researchers have proposed a multidimensional approach to the study of self-concept in children (Marsh, 1987). According to this approach, self-concept can best be described as a pyramid with a general self-concept at the apex, several intermediate-level self-concepts (including academic and nonacademic self-concepts), and, nested under these intermediate levels, specific domains of self-concept.

Self-concept development is a gradual process. In young children, it is related to tangible and observable events such as the child's physical appearance, possessions, environment, and favorite activities. With increasing age, conceptions of self move from concrete ideas to more abstract psychological constructs (I am smart) and become even more abstract in adolescence (I am smart at school but not when it comes to understanding others).

Marsh, Craven, and Debus provide an elegant study that examines four questions: (1) Does self-concept become more differentiated with age? (2) Is self-concept stable over time? (3) Are there age and gender differences in self-concept? (4) Is there a relationship between the teacher's views of students' self-concept and students' views of their own self-concept?

In addition to the theoretical contribution of this article, there are several methodological strengths. First, there is a demonstration of how to test the reliability and the validity of a measure. Second, the study collected measures from two different informants, the students and their teachers. Third, two cohorts of students were studied to determine whether the results would be similar for different groups. Finally, the study was longitudinal, allowing the experimenters to examine the stability of the findings over time.

References

Coopersmith, S. (1967). *The antecedents of self-esteem.* San Francisco: W. H. Freeman.

Kazdin, A. E. (1988). Childhood depression. In E. J. Mash & L. G. Terdal (eds), *Behavioral assessment of childhood disorders* (2nd edn, pp. 157–95). New York: Guilford Press.

Marsh, H. W. (1987). The hierarchical structure of self-concept: An application of hierarchical confirmatory analysis. *Journal of Educational Measurement.* *24,* 17–39.

Structure, Stability, and Development of Young Children's Self-Concepts: A Multicohort–Multioccasion Study

Herbert W. Marsh, Rhonda Craven,
and Raymond Debus

Introduction

Research on self-concept development continues to be focused predominantly on middle childhood and adolescent years (e.g., Dusek & Flaherty, 1981; Harter, 1985, 1986; Hattie, 1992; Stipek, 1981; Stipek & MacIver, 1989; Wigfield, 1994; Wigfield, Eccles, MacIver, Reuman, & Midgley, 1991), but there has been increasing attention given to the structure and development of self-concept in very young children (Byrne, 1996; Eccles, Wigfield, Harold, & Blumenfeld, 1993; Harter, 1983, 1985, 1986; Harter & Pike, 1984; Marsh, Craven, & Debus, 1991). A major focus of this research has been to clarify the emergence and progressive differentiation of more specific facets of self-concept in the early childhood years. Innovative approaches in developing measures and procedures for their administration to young children below the age of eight years (Byrne, 1996; Harter & Pike, 1984; Marsh et al., 1991) have contributed to changing perspectives on the emergence of a more differentiated structure of self-concept.

Predictions about how self-concept and its factorial structure evolve with age have been proposed from a variety of theoretical perspectives. Shavelson, Hubner, and Stanton (1976) hypothesized that self-concept becomes more differentiated with age. Marsh (1985, 1990; Marsh, Barnes, Cairns, & Tidman, 1984), expanding on the Shavelson et al.

hypothesis, proposed that self-concepts of very young children are consistently high but that with increasing life experience children learn their relative strengths and weaknesses so that with increasing levels of age, mean levels of self-concept decline, individual self-concept becomes more differentiated, and self-concept becomes more highly correlated with external indicators of competence (e.g., skills, accomplishments, and self-concepts inferred by significant others). Markus and Wurf (1987) noted that the structure of self depends on both the information available to an individual and the cognitive ability to process this information. Reflecting changes in the cognitive ability to process self-relevant information, Harter (1983, 1985) proposed that self-concept becomes increasingly abstract with age, shifting from concrete descriptions of behavior in early childhood, to trait-like psychological constructs (e.g., popular, smart, good looking) in middle childhood, to more abstract constructs during adolescence. According to her conceptual model, the concept of a global self-worth did not evolve before the age of about eight. Eccles et al. (1993; also see Wigfield & Eccles, 1992) developed an expectancy-value model of academic choice in which self-perceptions of competency and task value ratings in different domains form the basis of subsequent academic choice and have recently examined the domain specificity of responses by very young children. Based on earlier research (e.g., Nicholls, 1979; Parsons & Ruble, 1977; Stipek & MacIver, 1989), Eccles et al. proposed that the declines in mean levels of competency self-ratings reflected an optimistic bias for very young children and increased accuracy in responses by young children as they grow older.

For older children, there have been considerable advances in the quality of self-concept research due to stronger theoretical models, and the development of multidimensional measurement instruments based on theoretical models (see Byrne, 1984, 1996; Harter, 1983, 1985, 1986; Marsh, 1990, 1993a; Marsh & Craven, 1997; Marsh & Hattie, 1996). These advances have not, however, been fully applied to research with young children in part because psychometrically strong, multidimensional instruments have not been developed for young children (see Harter, 1983; Marsh & Craven, 1997; Marsh et al., 1991; Stipek & MacIver, 1989; Wylie, 1989). As proposed by Harter (1983, 1985; Harter & Pike, 1984), the effective measurement of self-concept with very young children may require simplified item contents or pictorial representations, simplified response formats, and individually based interviews instead of conventional paper-and-pencil tests that are group administered. Perhaps, as appears to have been the case for research with older children, progress in theory, research, and practice for very young children will be stimulated by the development of better multidimensional measurement instruments.

The Multidimensionality of Self-Concept Responses by Young Children

In this section, three issues are discussed that form the basis of this study: (1) how-best to measure self-concept for young children to study the development of a differentiated factor structure of self-concept, (2) substantive developmental issues such as age differences and the development of gender differences in self-concept responses by young children, and (3) the accuracy of self-concept inferred by significant others and how this varies with age.

Measurement of young children's self-concepts

Harter and Pike (1984) developed an instrument to measure self-concept scales (physical, cognitive, peers, and maternal) using items represented by parallel verbal statements and pictures. They found that below age eight children either did not understand general self-worth items or did not provide reliable responses, prompting them to exclude this scale from their instrument. Their exploratory factor analyses supported only two scales: competence (incorporating the physical and cognitive scales) and social acceptance (incorporating the peer and maternal scales). The authors noted that the factor structure was less differentiated than typically found for older children and that there was no differentiation among competencies in specific areas, thus supporting the frequently noted assumption that the structure becomes more differentiated with age. Their failure to support their a priori four-factor structure, however, provides a weak basis of inference about the structure of self-concept, particularly when they did not use confirmatory factor analysis (CFA) that allows the researcher to specify the model to be tested (e.g., Marsh & Hocevar, 1985). Marsh et al. (1991) suggested that the failure to separate even the physical and academic components that are so robust in responses by slightly older students was surprising. They noted, for example, that correlations among the physical and academic scales reported by Harter and Pike (rs of .43–.56) did not approach 1.0 even after correction for unreliability and that there was support for their differentiation in relation to other criteria reported by Harter and Pike (e.g., teacher ratings, choice behavior, being held back a grade). Finally, even support for their conclusion that self-concept becomes more differentiated with age was not strong in that Harter and Pike neither reported administering their instrument to older children nor offered any evidence that self-concept became more differentiated within the four-to-seven age range that they considered. In summary, the Harter and Pike interpretation of their results may be unduly pessimistic about the ability of very young children to differentiate among multiple dimensions of self-concept, and it may be premature to conclude that children at this age level can identify only two broad components of self.

Marsh et al. (1991) described a new, adaptive procedure for assessing multiple dimensions of self-concept for kindergarten, first-, and second-year students aged five to eight. They explored pictorial self-concept instruments like that developed by Harter and Pike (1984) but found that the juxtaposition of the pictures and verbal explanations seemed more confusing to young students than the verbal presentations alone. The critical component of their study was the individualized interview format used to collect SDQ-I (Self Description Questionnaire) responses. There was an initial concern that the 64-item SDQ-I instrument would be too long for these very young children, but items near the end were more effective than earlier items. Apparently children learned to respond appropriately so that they were responding more appropriately to items at the end of the instrument than to items at the beginning of the instrument. This observation has important implications for the typically short instruments used with young children. Based on CFAs, Marsh et al. found support for all eight SDQ-I scales, including the Esteem scale at each year level. However, with increasing age the SDQ-I factors became more differentiated as inferred from the decreasing size of factor correlations. They also reported gender differences for this very young group of children that were largely consistent with extrapolations from earlier research with older children.

Based on an expectancy-value model, Eccles and her colleagues (Eccles, Adler, & Meece, 1984; Eccles et al., 1993; Wigfield et al., 1997) focused on how expectancy (self-perceptions of competency, expectations of future success, and self-efficacy) combine with task value to influence academic choice. Their competency-related beliefs in specific activities (how good they are, how good they are relative to others, how good they are relative to other activities, expectations of future success, ability to master new skills) were closely related to the self-concept construct. Eccles et al. (1993) provided further support for the multidimensionality of self-concept for young children, finding that children in grades 1, 2, and 4 differentiated math, reading, music, and sports self-concepts (self-perceived competency ratings). In exploratory factor analyses of responses to items from all four domains and both the competency and task value components, four domain-specific factors were clearly evident for each age group. The CFAs of competency and task value ratings conducted separately for each domain provided supported the separation of task and competency ratings, although no CFAs of competency ratings from different domains were reported. Consistent with research with older children (e.g., Eccles & Wigfield, 1995), there was no evidence that children distinguished between different competency-related beliefs (e.g., self-perceived skills and expectations for future success).

Wigfield et al. (1997), using a cohort-sequential longitudinal design (see Baltes & Nesselroade, 1979), assessed three age cohorts (students in grades 1, 2, and 4) in each of three successive years. This allowed them to compare age differences due to cohort differences with true longitudinal comparisons and to evaluate stability over time for responses by the same children. Consistent with previous research (e.g., Marsh, 1989) they found that perceived competency declined with age, and these effects were reasonably consistent over domain and across cohort and longitudinal comparisons. There was also a consistent pattern in test–retest stability coefficients in which stability over time was low for the youngest children and grew steadily with age, although these comparisons were complicated to some extent by age-related differences in reliability. Wigfield et al. reported predicted gender differences (favoring boys in math and sport, favoring girls in music and reading), but found few interactions with gender and either cohort or time of measurement. Instead, consistent with Marsh (1989) and Marsh et al. (1991), they found that gender differences emerged early and were reasonably consistent over age. Finally, teacher and parent ratings of competence collected at each time of measurement showed little systematic relation to self-ratings for the youngest children but were substantially related to self-perceptions for the oldest children. For example, only teacher ratings of sport were significantly related to self-perceptions in Years 1 and 2, whereas teacher ratings in all four domains were significantly related to self-perceptions in Years 5 and 6. Interestingly, in contrast to children's self-perceptions, teacher and parent ratings of competence did not vary as a function of age. Wigfield et al. concluded that very young children have more optimistic self-perceptions of their own competence whereas older children have more realistic self-perceptions.

In the last decade there were two major reviews of self-concept measures (Byrne, 1996; Wylie, 1989) for different age groups. Both reviewers noted a large number of different instruments available for very young children but concluded that only two were sufficiently developed to warrant consideration: the Harter and Pike (1984) instrument discussed earlier and the Joseph (1979) instrument that relies on items from a variety of different domains to infer a global, undifferentiated self-concept and so is of limited relevance to our concern about the multidimensional structure of self-concept. Both reviewers noted that there was a paucity of psychometric evidence (reliability, stability, factor structure) for either of these instruments and the evidence that was available was not particularly encouraging. Essentially no further development of either instrument was reported by Byrne beyond that described seven years earlier by Wylie (1989). Although Byrne (1996) did not consider the Marsh et al. (1991) study in her chapter on measures for very young children, she did review the SDQ-I in another chapter devoted to measures for somewhat older, preadolescent children, concluding that (Byrne, 1996, p. 117) "there is absolutely no doubt that the SDQ-I is clearly the most validated self-concept instrument available for use with preadolescent children." Byrne specifically noted the effectiveness of the Marsh et al. (1991) study in adapting the SDQ-I for use with very young children, emphasizing that the psychometric properties based on this single study were stronger than those based on any of the instruments specifically designed for very young children.

Age and gender differences in responses by very young children

Age differences. In her classic review, Wylie (1979) reported that age differences in overall or total self-concept were small and inconsistent.

In his subsequent review and empirical analyses of 12,000 responses from the SDQ normative archives, Marsh (1989) reported that there was a reasonably consistent pattern of self-concepts declining from a young age through early adolescence, leveling out, and then increasing at least through early adulthood. These age differences were, however, small and differed somewhat depending on the particular scale. For example, Marsh et al. (1984) reported that the initially very high Parents self-concept ratings remained high across the early preadolescent period but fell sharply during the adolescent period. More recently, Chapman and Tunmer (1995) also reported that Reading self-concept declined with age based on a cross-sectional study of very young children as did the Marsh et al. (1991) and Wigfield et al. (1997) studies described earlier. Marsh and Craven (1997) argued that whereas young children have extremely high self-concepts, they develop more realistic appraisals of their relative strengths and weaknesses with age and this added experience is apparently incorporated into their self-concepts. Hence, with increasing life experience, self-concept in specific domains should become more differentiated, more accurately reflecting the child's relative strengths and weaknesses.

Crain (1996) recently reviewed development and age differences in self-concept but concluded that the typical poor quality of measurement instruments used in studies of very young children undermined extrapolations from that research. Crain, however, specifically highlighted the important contributions of the Marsh et al. (1991, p. 403) study, emphasizing that this research cast doubt on previous research for this age group but concluded that "certainly, further examination of very young children's multidimensional self-concept is a fruitful topic for further research." In particular, she highlighted the need for longitudinal research to elucidate changes in the structure, development, and stability of young children's self-concepts over time.

Whereas most research on age and development effects in self-concept has focused on mean differences, Shavelson et al. (1976) proposed age and developmental differences in the structure of self-concept. They hypothesized that self-concept becomes more differentiated with age but offered no clear rationale for evaluating this hypothesis. Marsh (1989; Marsh et al., 1991) operationalized this hypothesis to mean that correlations among SDQ scales become smaller with age and tested this hypothesis with responses to the three SDQ instruments. For responses by very young children, correlations decreased in size from kindergarten to Year 1, and from Year 1 to Year 2. For preadolescent responses, correlations decreased from Year 2 to Year 3, and to lesser extents between Years 3 and 4, and between Years 4 and 5. For responses by older preadolescents, adolescents, and late adolescents, no further declines in the correlations were found. Thus, these data support the Shavelson et al. hypothesis that self-concept becomes differentiated with age for very young children, but not for responses by older children. Perhaps differentiation in self-concept reaches some optimal point at which social comparison processes and cognitive abilities are adequately developed rather than after a cumulative period of life experiences. However, as in most studies of self-concept development, researchers relied on cross-sectional age comparisons rather than stronger tests of differences over time for the same cohort or more sophisticated designs that allow simultaneous cross-sectional and longitudinal comparisons.

Gender differences.   Historically, studies of gender differences in self-concept have focused primarily on global or total scores. Early reviews (e.g., Maccoby & Jacklin, 1974; Wylie, 1979) reported little or no gender differences, but Feingold (1994) compared results from three meta-analyses of gender differences in personality variables including self-esteem that each demonstrated small differences (effect sizes of .10 to .16) favoring males.

Consistent with Wylie's (1979) suggestion, Marsh (1989) reported that these reasonably small differences in total scores reflect larger, counterbalancing gender differences in specific components of self-concept. Based on normative archive responses to the three SDQ instruments (covering the preadolescent to young adult age range), he reported statistically significant but small gender differences in most SDQ scales, some favoring girls but more favoring boys. Total self-concept scores favored boys, although gender explained only 1% of the variance. The gender differences in specific scales tended to be consistent with traditional gender stereotypes: (1) boys had higher self-concepts for Physical Ability, Appearance, Math, Emotional Stability, Problem Solving, and Esteem; (2) girls tended to have higher self-concepts for Verbal/Reading, School, Honesty/Trustworthiness, and Religion/Spiritual Values; and (3) there were no gender differences for the Parents scale in any of the three data sets. Gender differences in the social scales, however, were not fully consistent with traditional gender stereotypes favoring girls. These gender differences in self-concept are broadly consistent with gender stereotypes, but the small effects suggest, perhaps, that this influence on self-concept is diminishing. Marsh (1989) also found that age × gender interactions were typically small, except for Appearance (very young girls had higher Appearance self-concepts than boys, but older girls had much lower Appearance self-concepts). Apparently, gender stereotypes have already affected self-concepts by preadolescence, and these effects are relatively stable from preadolescence to at least early adulthood. Subsequent research with even younger children (Eccles et al., 1993; Marsh et al., 1991) further supports the suggestion that gender stereotypes affect self-concepts of children at very young ages. In a recent review of gender differences in self-concept, Crain (1996, p. 412) also concluded that there are "differences in domain-specific self-concepts of boys and girls that tend to run along gender-stereotypic lines." However, she argued that the gender differences were typically not of sufficient size to be of substantive significance and that societal changes in the role of women may alter the pattern of gender differences in multiple dimensions of self-concept.

Inferred self-concept ratings

Self-concept ratings inferred by others are used to determine how accurately self-concept can be assessed by external observers and to validate self-concept responses. For teachers, being able to infer self-concept accurately is particularly important for understanding and responding to their students. When multiple dimensions of self-concept are represented by both self-ratings and inferred ratings, multitrait–multimethod (MTMM) analyses (Campbell & Fiske, 1959; Marsh & Grayson, 1995) provide tests of the construct validity of the responses. *Convergent validity* is inferred from substantial correlations between self-ratings and inferred ratings on matching self-concept traits. *Discriminant validity* provides a test of the distinctiveness of self–other agreement and of the multidimensionality of the self-concept facets; it is inferred from the lack of correlation between nonmatching traits.

In eight MTMM studies, Marsh (1988, 1990) demonstrated significant agreement between multiple self-concepts inferred by primary school teachers and student responses to the SDQ-I. The mean correlation between student and teacher ratings across all scales was $r = .30$, but agreement was strongest where the teachers could most readily make relevant observations (math, .37; reading, .37; school, .33; physical ability, .38; and, perhaps, peer relations .29). Student–teacher agreement was lower on Relations with Parents (.17) and Physical Appearance (.16). Marsh and Craven (1991) extended this research in a comparison of the abilities of elementary school teachers, mothers, and fathers to infer multiple self-concepts of preadolescent children. Responses by mothers and by fathers were slightly more accurate than those by teachers, but all three groups were more accurate in their inferences about Physical Ability, Reading, Mathematics, and School self-concepts than other specific scales or Esteem. Self–other agreement in this study tended to be better than has been found in other research, but this apparently reflects the fact that children and significant others all completed the complete SDQ-I instrument (in contrast to studies described earlier in which teachers infer self-concepts of all students in their class using a single-item summary rating of each SDQ-I scale whereas students complete multi-item scales). Nevertheless, the self–other agreement reported by Marsh and Craven was still much less than values reported in studies with older participants. For example, in MTMM studies of university students and "person in the world who knew them best" (Marsh, Barnes, & Hocevar, 1985; Marsh & Byrne, 1993), self–other agreement was very high (mean $r = .57$), and four of the scales had self–other correlations over .75. The authors speculated that self–other agreement was so good because (1) the participants were older and thus knew themselves better and based their self-responses on more objective, observable criteria, (2) both participants and significant others made their responses on the same well-developed instrument based on multi-item scales, and (3) the significant others in these studies knew the participants better than the observers in most research. These results imply that external observers are best able to infer self-concepts when respondents are older and the multidimensionality of self-concept is taken into account.

The juxtaposition of the self–other agreement studies for different age groups also provides at least indirect support for the proposal that with increasing age and life experience children learn their relative strengths and weaknesses so that their self-concepts become more differentiated and more highly correlated with external indicators, including self-concepts inferred by significant others (also see Wigfield et al., 1997). A fuller evaluation of this proposal, however, requires CFA models based on longitudinal data for very young children. For example, particularly strong support for this proposal would be the demonstration that ratings by an external observer at T1 contribute directly to the prediction of self-concept ratings of the child at T2 beyond what can be predicted by the child's self-concept ratings at T1. In this sense, ratings by the external observer are able to predict changes in the child's self-concept over time because the child's self-concept is likely to change in the direction of being more consistent with external criteria used by the observer at T1 (i.e., becoming more "realistic").

The present investigation

Marsh et al. (1991) provided a promising advance in the measurement of very young children's self-concepts and in clarifying the emergence and progressive differentiation of specific facets of self-concept for this age group. Due in part to limitations in self-concept research with very young children, reviewers (e.g., Byrne, 1996; Crain, 1996) noted the important contributions of this study but also emphasized the need to follow up this research with longitudinal studies more appropriate for evaluating the development of self-concept. In response to such concerns, the present investigation is based on the Marsh et al. (1991) study but expands on the empirical and theoretical implications of that earlier research in a number of ways. In particular, the earlier study was based on a single wave of data from three age cohorts so that developmental implications relied primarily on cross-sectional comparisons. Here we used a multicohort–multioccasion (MCMO) design with two waves of data collected one year apart with the same children in each of three age cohorts. Based on these data, we contrasted cross-sectional (multiple age cohort) comparisons with true longitudinal (multiple occasion) comparisons. This provides a much stronger basis for evaluating age-related differences in reliability, dimensionality, and gender differences that were the focus of the earlier research, and for evaluating stability over time. In addition, self-concept ratings inferred by teachers are included in the present investigation. This additional source of information allows the evaluation of the accuracy of teacher's inferred self-concept ratings, an examination of how relations between inferred and actual ratings vary with age cross-sectionally and longitudinally, and an evaluation of the proposal that young children's self-concept becomes more predictable with age. More specifically, in addition to building on the earlier research by providing further psychometric support for the use of the individually administered SDQ-I with young children, the present investigation is designed to (1) test the Shavelson et al. (1976) hypothesis that self-concept becomes more differentiated with age and to provide more specific data on how the factor structure of self-concept varies over time for children aged five to eight, (2) evaluate the stability of young children's self-concepts over time, (3) evaluate gender and age differences for young children longitudinally as well as cross-sectionally, and (4) evaluate how teacher ratings of the self-concepts of their students relate to students' own self-concept ratings and how these relations vary with age. From a practical perspective the ability to measure the self-concepts of young children and elucidate developments in self-concept over time enables early childhood practitioners to understand young children better, to identify an accurate basis for assessment, and to provide an outcome measure for a variety of interventions. Hence this research has the potential to advance self-concept theory, research, and practice.

Method

Sample

The sample considered in this study is a total of 396 students who at T1 were enrolled in kindergarten ($n = 127$, M age = 5.4, $SD = .4$) Year 1 ($n = 139$, M age = 6.3, $SD = .4$), and Year 2 ($n = 130$, M age = 7.4, $SD = .5$). The participants came primarily from middle-class families and attended one of three schools in suburban metropolitan Sydney, Australia, that agreed to participate in the study. Although these students were a year older and enrolled in Years 1, 2, and 3 at T2, we refer to the age cohorts as kindergarten, Year 1, and Year 2. Because of the focus of this study on longitudinal comparisons, responses from 98 children who had data at T1 but not T2 were excluded. This attrition was due to normal absences on the day the materials were administered and the typical mobility of families in this region of metropolitan Sydney.

Instrument: The SDQ-I

The SDQ-I (Marsh, 1988, 1990) is based on the Shavelson et al. (1976) model and is designed for preadolescents (SDQ-I). Research (see Marsh,

1988, 1990, 1993a; Marsh & Craven, 1997) has shown that (1) factor analyses have consistently identified each a priori SDQ-I factor, (2) the reliability of each scale is generally in the .80s and .90s whereas correlations among the factors are quite small (median *rs* less than .20), and (3) the self-concept responses are consistently correlated with external validity criteria (e.g., self-concepts in matching areas inferred by significant others, academic achievement indicators, age, gender, locus of control, self-attributions for the causes of academic successes and failures, physical fitness and participation in sports, and self-concept enhancement interventions). This research provides strong support for the construct validity of responses to the SDQ instruments for children as young as ten or, perhaps, eight (see reviews by Byrne, 1996; Hattie, 1992; Wylie, 1989).

The SDQ-I (Marsh, 1988) is designed to measure eight self-concept scales that are summarized in the Appendix. Three total scores can also be formed on the basis of these scales: academic self-concept (the average of reading, mathematics, and school self-concept scales), nonacademic self-concept (the average of physical, appearance, peer, and parent relations self-concept scales), and total self (the average of academic and nonacademic total scales). Each of the eight SDQ-I scales was defined by responses to eight positively worded items. On the standard SDQ-I there are an additional 12 negatively worded items. Because previous research has shown that children have trouble responding appropriately to the negatively worded items, they are not included in the scores derived from the SDQ-I. For purposes of the individually administered SDQ-I used here, the negatively worded items were excluded altogether. As described below, the response scale typically used with the SDQ-I was also altered for purposes of just the individually administered responses.

As part of the study, teachers at T1 rated each of their students only on the eight SDQ-I scales, based on a single summary item representing each scale instead of the multiple items representing each scale actually completed by students. Teachers were given a single page of instructions containing a brief definition of each SDQ-I scale, a list of all the students in their class with eight columns next to each student's name corresponding to the eight SDQ-I scales, and instructions about how to complete the survey. Teachers were instructed to make judgments of each child's self-concept based on the student's own feelings about himself or herself (i.e., to infer their students' self-concepts) using a nine-point (1 = poor to 9 = high) response scale.

Procedures

Procedures for the administration of the standard SDQ-I (see Marsh, 1988) were adjusted to enable the modified SDQ-I to be administered as an individual interview and are described in greater detail by Marsh et al. (1991). The interviewers were 110 university students in a primary teacher education program who already had experience working with young children. All interviewers were given a two-hour training program and subsequently tested children from each of the three age groups as part of a class assignment. At each participating school a group of interviewers simultaneously conducted interviews with all students from a particular class. The testing was conducted using an individual, one-on-one interview style format. Each testing session began with a brief set of instructions assuring participants of the confidentiality of their responses and presenting four example items. After reading each example item the interviewer asked the child if he or she understood the sentence. If the child did not understand the sentence, the interviewer explained the sentence further, paraphrasing any words the child did not understand, ascertained that the child understood the sentence, re-read the sentence, and requested a response. The interviewer initially asked the child to respond "yes" or "no" to the sentence to indicate whether the sentence was true or false as a description of the child. If the child initially responded "yes," the interviewer then asked the child if he or she meant "yes always" or "yes sometimes." If the child initially responded "no," the interviewer then asked the child if he or she meant "no always" or "no sometimes." The second response probe was stated for every response even when it was answered in the initial response (e.g., the child said "yes always" instead of "yes"), thus providing a check on the accuracy of the child's initial response. After the child successfully responded to example items and any questions were answered, the interviewers then read aloud each of the 64 positively worded SDQ-I items. The child was encouraged to seek clarification of any item they did not understand. If the child stated that the item was not understood, the interviewer explained the meaning of the item further and ascertained that the child understood the sentence before readministering the item. If the child indicated that he or she understood the sentence but could not decide whether to respond yes or no, the interviewer recorded a response of 3, halfway between the responses of "no sometimes" and "yes sometimes." Because this occurred infrequently and children were not told of this option, this middle category was used very infrequently. Halfway through the administration of the SDQ-I items the interviewer asked the child to do some physical activities for a brief period before proceeding to administer the remaining 32 items. This procedure was intended to cater to young children with short attention spans.

Statistical analyses

The statistical analyses consisted of an evaluation of the psychometric properties (internal consistency reliability, stability over time, and factor structure) of the self-concept responses, of gender and age differences in the self-concept ratings, and of relations between self-concept ratings and self-concept inferred by teachers. All analyses were conducted with SPSS (Norusis, 1993), including the CFAs that were conducted with the SPSS version of LISREL (Jöreskog & Sörbom, 1989).

As in other SDQ research (e.g., Marsh, 1988; Marsh & Hocevar, 1985) factor analyses were conducted on item-pair scores (or parcels) in which the first two items in each scale are averaged to form the first item pair, the next two items are used to form the second pair, and so forth. Analysis of 32 item pairs instead of 64 individual items is advantageous because this strategy substantially reduces the number of measured variables and because the responses to item pairs tend to be more reliable, to be more normally distributed, and to have less idiosyncratic variance than do individual items. The CFAs were conducted with the SPSS version of LISREL 7 (Jöreskog & Sörbom, 1989) using maximum likelihood estimates derived from covariance matrices based on pairwise deletion for missing data. A detailed description of CFA is beyond the scope of the present investigation and is available elsewhere (e.g., Bollen, 1989; Byrne, 1989; Jöreskog & Sörbom, 1989; Pedhazur & Schmelkin, 1991). Following Marsh, Balla, and Hau (1996) and McDonald and Marsh (1990), we emphasize the relative noncentrality index (RNI) to evaluate goodness of fit but also present the chi-square test statistic and *df* that allow the calculation of other indexes of fit. Whereas there are no precise standards for what values of indices such as these are needed for an "acceptable" fit, typical guidelines are that the RNI should be greater than .9. However, model comparison is also facilitated by positing a partially nested ordering of models in which the parameter estimates for a more restrictive model are a proper subset of those in a more general model (for further discussion, see Bentler, 1990). In the present application, for example, a model in which factor loadings are constrained to be invariant across the three age cohorts is nested under a model in which there are no such invariance constraints of the factor loadings. The fit indices for alternative models, however, can be compared whether or not the particular models are nested. Whereas tests of statistical significance and indices of fit aid in the evaluation of the fit of a model, there is ultimately a degree of subjectivity and professional judgment in the selection of a "best" model.

Although a variety of different CFAs is considered in the results, the SDQ-I self-concept factors are always inferred from multiple indicators of the latent construct. For gender and for teacher-inferred self-concept ratings for each SDQ-I scale, however, there is only a single indicator of each latent construct. In each case, single-indicator latent variables were assumed to be measured without error. Whereas this strategy is reasonable for gender, there is likely to be error in the teacher ratings. Whereas it is reasonable to incorporate a plausible estimate of measurement error into the analysis that would automatically increase correlations between teacher ratings and other constructs, the present strategy is conservative in relation to showing that teacher ratings are related to student responses.

In most applications of CFA, a priori models typically assume that the residual variance (uniqueness plus random error, hereafter referred to as uniquenesses) associated with each measured variable is independent of residual variances associated with other measured variables. However, when the same items are administered to the same participants on multiple occasions, it is likely that the uniquenesses associated with the matching measured variables are correlated. If there are substantial correlated uniquenesses that are not included in the model, then the estimated correlations between the corresponding latent constructs will be positively biased. In the present application, for example, this would result in a positively biased estimate of the test–retest stability coefficient relating responses to the same latent variable on two occasions. This situation is not specific to CFA studies, and Marsh (1993b) demonstrated that stability coefficients can exceed 1.0 when disattenuated for measurement error. However, the inclusion of correlated uniquenesses in CFAs provides a test for these correlated uniquenesses and a control for what would otherwise be a positive bias. Because of this problem, test–retest stability correlations are likely to be negatively biased because they do not take into account measurement error and, perhaps, positively biased because they do not control for correlated uniquenesses. This complexity is likely to be compounded when, as in the present investigation, comparisons are made between different age cohorts where the size of measurement errors and, perhaps, the correlated uniquenesses are likely to vary with age. Because of these complications, a potentially important contribution of the present investigation is to evaluate age cohort differences in test–retest stability coefficients with latent variable models that incorporate appropriate control for measurement error and test for correlated uniquenesses.

In preliminary analyses, the inclusion of these correlated uniquenesses was supported by modestly better fits to the data and, in particular, because their exclusion would positively bias the test–retest stability coefficients. Whereas stability coefficients were smaller when correlated uniquenesses were included (table 4), the differences were typically small. Across all 32 sets of analyses (eight SDQ-I scales for total, kindergarten, Year 1, and Year 2), the difference between the two stability correlation estimates never exceeded .06 and typically was much smaller, suggesting that the inclusion of correlated uniquenesses in this study was not a critical issue. To facilitate the substantive import of the results, only the models with correlated uniquenesses are presented along with the more conservative estimates of test–retest correlations based on these models.

Results

Internal consistency, stability, and distinctiveness

We begin with a preliminary overview of psychometric results based on traditional approaches that also serve as an advance organizer to more sophisticated CFA approaches. Because our major thrust is on the CFA results, these preliminary results are summarized only briefly.

Internal consistency. Coefficient α estimates of reliability tended to increase with age, based on both cross-sectional and longitudinal comparisons (table 1). For example, the median α varied from .74 (T1 K) to .85 (T2 Year 2) for the three age cohorts (table 1). This pattern was evident in the mean and median αs for the cross-sectional, between-

Table 1 Coefficient alpha estimates of reliability at Time 1 (T1) and Time 2 (T1), T1/T2 stability correlation, correlations among all and selected scales, and SDs of the scale scores for each grade level and the total sample

Scores	Kind (n = 127)			Year 1 (n = 139)			Year 2 (n = 130)			Total (n = 396)		
	T1	T2	T12	T1	T2	T12	T1	T2	T12	T1	T2	T12
Reliability and stability:												
Total scores:												
Nonacademic	.83	.88	.43	.88	.88	.35	.86	.89	.54	.86	.88	.44
Academic	.89	.91	.36	.92	.89	.29	.91	.91	.54	.91	.91	.40
Total	.93	.94	.45	.95	.93	.29	.94	.93	.57	.94	.93	.43
Scale scores:												
Physical	.52	.70	.49	.71	.72	.43	.69	.78	.49	.65	.73	.46
Appearance	.74	.82	.36	.83	.87	.40	.86	.88	.43	.82	.86	.41
Peers	.77	.75	.27	.79	.77	.27	.80	.84	.52	.78	.79	.36
Parents	.66	.71	.32	.72	.69	.39	.69	.74	.50	.70	.72	.39
Read	.78	.85	.26	.85	.80	.24	.83	.88	.59	.82	.85	.37
Math	.78	.81	.20	.85	.83	.28	.85	.90	.45	.83	.85	.32
School	.70	.81	.39	.82	.85	.28	.84	.85	.46	.79	.84	.38
Esteem	.75	.73	.27	.79	.71	.25	.74	.75	.33	.76	.72	.28
Median scale score	.74	.78	.29	.80	.79	.28	.82	.85	.48	.79	.82	.38
Mean scale score	.71	.77	.32	.80	.78	.32	.79	.83	.47	.77	.80	.37
Distinctiveness of scales:												
Mean of all rs	.45	.45	.22	.50	.40	.13	.39	.31	.21	.44	.38	.18
Mean of seven select rs	.45	.36	.23	.48	.36	.14	.30	.19	.13	.41	.30	.16
SD of eight SDQ scales	.38	.43		.42	.45		.49	.55		.43	.48	

Presented under each column are the coefficient alpha estimates of reliability at Time 1 (T1) and Time 2 (T2), and the test–retest correlation between matching scales at T1 and T2 (T12). Under the heading "Distinctiveness," the mean of all rs refers to the mean of all off-diagonal correlations in the 8 × 8 matrix of correlations at T1, T2, or T12 (i.e., nonmatching correlations between T1 and T2 responses). Mean of seven selected rs refers to the mean of seven correlations predicted a priori to be smallest. The SDs of the eight SDQ scales reflect the extent to which children give the similar (lower SDs) or different (higher SDs) mean responses to the different SDQ scales.

group comparison of different age cohorts and particularly for T1 to T2 longitudinal comparisons within each age cohort and for the total sample. Thus, for example, median α was lowest for kindergarten responses (.74 for T1, .78 for T2), followed by Year 1 (.80 for T1, .79 for T2), and largest for the Year 2 responses (.82 for T1, .85 for T2). This pattern is also reasonably consistent for the individual scales, although αs for T1 and T2 responses at Year 2 do not differ systematically. Interestingly, a major exception to this pattern was for Esteem, where reliability estimates did not seem to be consistently related to either cross-sectional or longitudinal age differences.

In contrast to the scale scores, the total (total academic, total non academic, and total self) scores were more reliable (αs from .83 to .95) and these αs did not vary systematically as a function of cross-sectional or longitudinal age comparisons. The total scores were more reliable than the individual scores because they were based on so many more responses. However, the lack of consistent age differences in αs for total scores was in marked contrast to the individual scores (except for the Esteem scale, which may be more like the total scores in that its intent was to infer an overall evaluation of self). This pattern of results, increasing internal consistency estimates of reliability with age for specific self-concept scales but not for global and total scores, implied that older children were more clearly differentiating among the specific components of self-concept. Because this issue was of central concern to the present investigation, it was the focus of subsequent analyses.

Stability over time. As expected, test–retest stability correlations based on scale scores were all statistically significant and tended to increase with age (see correlations between T1 and T2 measures, labeled T12 in table 1). Across the eight scales, the stability coefficients for the oldest, Year 2 students (mean $r = .47$) were higher than the coefficient based on the total sample (mean $r = .37$). However, stability coefficients for the kindergarten (mean $r = .32$) and Year 1 (mean $r = .32$) samples were similar.

Discriminant validity and distinctiveness. In table 2 all correlations between T1 and T2 scale scores are presented for each year group to evaluate the discriminant validity of the self-concept responses. Adapting the terminology of MTMM analyses (Campbell & Fiske, 1959; Marsh

Table 2 Correlations between Time 1 and Time 2 responses for kindergarten (K), Year 1, and Year 2 students and for the total sample

Variables	Physical	Appearance	Peers	Parents	Reading	Math	School	General
Physical:								
K	**.49***	.10	.13	.05	.23*	.20*	.26*	.14
1	**.43***	.09	.11	.11	.14	.20*	.23*	.11
2	**.49***	.13	.21*	.21*	.14	.10	.16	.14
T	**.46***	.12*	.15*	.11*	.16*	.17*	.22*	.13*
Appearance:								
K	.24*	**.36***	.11	.26*	.31*	.16	.23*	.27*
1	.17*	**.40***	.21*	.10	.13	.02	.08	.21*
2	.16	**.43***	.38*	.27*	.12	.12	.21*	.27*
T	.18*	**.41***	.24*	.18*	.17*	.10	.18*	.24*
Peers:								
K	.30*	.21*	**.27***	.25*	.23*	.20*	.24*	.33*
1	.10	.00	**.27***	.30*	.02	.06	.06	.17*
2	.11	.07	**.52***	.23*	.21*	.10	.11	.19*
T	.16*	.09	**.36***	.25*	.15*	.12*	.13*	.23*
Parents:								
K	.28*	.24*	.23*	**.32***	.31*	.28*	.29*	.31*
1	.09	.08	.22*	**.39***	.11	.10	.14	.21*
2	.01	.18*	.31*	**.50***	.37*	.25*	.38*	.18*
T	.13*	.15*	.25*	**.39***	.27*	.21*	.26*	.24*
Reading:								
K	.12	.29*	.08	.12	**.26***	.14	.29*	.30*
1	.12	.14	.17	.09	**.24***	.20*	.16	.14
2	.07	−.06	.24*	.20*	**.59***	.10	.24*	.09
T	.09	.11*	.17*	.10*	**.37***	.14*	.24*	.17*
Math:								
K	.25*	.20*	.11	.18*	.33*	**.20***	.33*	.21*
1	.30*	.09	.03	−.01	.08	**.28***	.21*	.05
2	.13	.17*	.28*	.23*	.22*	**.45***	.27*	.10
T	.22*	.16*	.15*	.11*	.21*	**.32***	.27*	.12*
School:								
K	.24*	.33*	.16	.32*	.34*	.20*	**.39***	.35*
1	.18*	−.01	.09	.05	.09	.20*	**.28***	.14
2	.15	.17	.29*	.32*	.46*	.24*	**.46***	.23*
T	.18*	.17*	.19*	.19*	.29*	.21*	**.38***	.24*
General:								
K	.28*	.18*	.16	.24*	.31*	.11	.25*	**.27***
1	.25*	.14	.16	.26*	.14	.13	.18*	**.25***
2	.15	.20*	.47*	.42*	.34*	.21*	.26*	**.33***
T	.23*	.17*	.25*	.28*	.26*	.15*	.23*	**.28***

Stability coefficients, correlations between T1 and T2 responses to the same SDQI scale, are in bold.
* p < .05.

& Grayson, 1995), the stability coefficients (coefficients in bold in the main diagonal of table 2) were viewed as convergent validities, and the different occasions were taken to be the multiple methods. From this perspective, one indication of discriminant validity was to compare each stability coefficient (convergent validities) with the other 14 coefficients in the same row and column for that age cohort. Across the eight scales there were a total of $8 \times 14 = 112$ comparisons each for the kindergarten, Year 1, Year 2, and total samples. The stability coefficients were larger than the comparison coefficient for all 112 comparisons based on the total sample, and for 109, 109, and 91 of 112 comparisons based on responses for children from Year 2, Year 1, and kindergarten, respectively. For each year group considered separately, there was at least one failure (i.e., one comparison coefficient that was larger than the convergent validity) for one scale (Esteem) for Year 2 responses, two scales (Esteem, Peers) for Year 1 responses, and four scales (Esteem, Peers, Reading, Math) for kindergarten responses. Overall, these results provide strong support for the discriminant validity of the self-concept responses but also support the prediction that discriminant validity increases with age.

Marsh (1989) proposed an alternative approach to evaluating how the distinctiveness of the self-concept traits vary with age. He argued that some of the scales (e.g., Reading and School) should be substantially correlated whereas others (e.g., Physical and Reading) should not. Based on previous research and theory, he selected seven correlations that he predicted to be the lowest. Based on the assumption that self-concept becomes more differentiated with age, he reasoned that the difference in the mean of the selected correlations and mean of all correlations should increase with age. Here we extended this logic to evaluations of longitudinal differences in correlations for the same age cohort on different occasions as well as cross-sectional differences between age cohorts like those considered by Marsh (1989). At T1, the mean of the selected *r*s compared to the mean of all *r*s (see table 1) did not differ for kindergarten students, was slightly lower for Year 1 students, and was clearly lower for Year 2 students. Although both the means of all *r*s and selected *r*s tended to decrease over time, the decrease was larger for the mean of *r*s selected a priori to be lower. For each age cohort, the difference between the mean of the selected *r*s and the mean of all *r*s was larger at T2 than T1. Hence, these comparisons based on the cross-sectional and particularly the longitudinal comparisons supported the hypothesis that self-concept becomes more differentiated with age.

Alternatively, distinctiveness can be operationalized as the extent to which children give the same or similar mean responses to all scales (lower distinctiveness) or give different mean responses to different scales (higher distinctiveness). Following Marsh (1989), this was operationalized as the *SD* of the eight SDQ scale scores, computed separately for each of the 3 (age cohort) × 2 (time) combinations. The results (table 1) provided a clear pattern in which responses became more differentiated (larger *SD*s) with age based on both cross-sectional age-cohort comparisons and longitudinal comparisons. These results provided clear support for the proposal that SDQ responses become more differentiated with age.

Factor structure

Confirmatory factor analysis provides a particularly powerful tool for evaluating the factor structure underlying responses by these young children. Results from separate CFAs conducted for responses at T1 and T2 were summarized in table 3. For each CFA, a very restrictive a priori model was posited in which each measured variable was allowed to load on only one factor and uniquenesses associated with each variable were assumed to be uncorrelated. The factor solutions were well defined in that both solutions were fully proper, goodness of fit was reasonable (RNI = .916 and .901 for T1 and T2, respectively), and all factor loadings were statistically significant and substantial (varying from .45 to .85). Although the factor correlations were also substantial, varying from .25 to .81, none approached 1.0 even though they have been corrected for measurement error. Of particular interest was the comparison of the parameter values for the T1 and T2 solutions. Factor loadings tended to be larger for T2 than T1 (22 were larger, eight were smaller, and two were the same in table 3) whereas factor correlations tended to be smaller at T2 than T1 (22 were smaller, four were larger, and two were the same in table 3). These higher factor loadings were consistent with earlier findings that T2 responses were more reliable, whereas the lower factor correlations were consistent with earlier findings that T2 scales were better differentiated.

Marsh et al. (1991) were also concerned with a possible fatigue effect in asking very young children to respond to so many self-concept items.

They found, however, that factor loadings tended to be larger for items near the end of the SDQ than those near the start. They interpreted this to mean that there was a warmup effect, whereby young children learned to respond appropriately, rather than a fatigue effect. There was support for this conclusion based on both T1 and T2 factor solutions (table 3). The factor loadings were larger for the last measured variable than the first measured variable for all eight factors in the T1 solution and for seven of eight factors in the T2 solution. For both T1 and T2 solutions the median factor loadings increased steadily for indicators 1 (.58 and .66 for T1 and T2, respectively), 2 (.66 and .70), 3 (.70 and .72), and 4 (.74 and .74). These results suggest a substantial warmup effect that was particularly evident at T1 but that was still evident at T2. Whereas the factor loadings were systematically larger for the T2 solution, the difference was primarily due to the higher loadings for measured variables from the first half of the SDQ-I.

Summarized in table 4 are a series of four models fit separately for each SDQ scale. Separate one-factor congeneric factor models were used to assess the unidimensionality of responses for each scale at T1 and T2, respectively (those labeled T1 and T2). For the total sample, these one-factor models provided a very good fit for T1 and T2 responses (RNIs vary from .96 to 1.0). The RNIs were also high for analyses of each age cohort considered separately, with the possible exception of kindergarten responses to the Physical and Appearance scales (RNIs of .86 and .84, respectively).

Also summarized in table 4 are two-factor models fit to the T1 and T2 responses for each scale (those labeled T1/T2 in table 4). These models were used to assess whether two factors – one for T1 responses and one for T2 responses – adequately fit the data and to define an optimal estimate of the correlation between the two factors – the T1/T2 stability coefficient. These stability coefficients in table 4 are all substantially larger than those based on scale scores considered earlier (table 1). This follows because the correlations in table 4 were corrected for measurement error (and the inclusion of correlated uniquenesses had only a small effect). However, the pattern of differences observed in table 1 was evident in table 4 as well. Thus, for example, stability coefficients were reasonably similar for kindergarten (median $r = .32$) and Year 1 (median $r = .34$) students, but those for Year 2 were substantially larger (median $r = .55$).

Table 3 Separate factor solutions for responses at Time 1 (T1) and Time 2 (T2)

Scale	Physical T1	Physical T2	Appearance T1	Appearance T2	Peers T1	Peers T2	Parents T1	Parents T2	Reading T1	Reading T2	Math T1	Math T2	School T1	School T2	General T1	General T2	Uniquenesses T1	Uniquenesses T2
Factor loadings:																		
Physical:																		
1	.48	.58	0	0	0	0	0	0	0	0	0	0	0	0	0	0	.76	.67
2	.46	.68	0	0	0	0	0	0	0	0	0	0	0	0	0	0	.79	.54
3	.65	.71	0	0	0	0	0	0	0	0	0	0	0	0	0	0	.58	.49
4	.65	.62	0	0	0	0	0	0	0	0	0	0	0	0	0	0	.58	.61
Appearance:																		
1	0	0	.60	.70	0	0	0	0	0	0	0	0	0	0	0	0	.64	.52
2	0	0	.67	.79	0	0	0	0	0	0	0	0	0	0	0	0	.56	.37
3	0	0	.74	.79	0	0	0	0	0	0	0	0	0	0	0	0	.45	.38
4	0	0	.74	.71	0	0	0	0	0	0	0	0	0	0	0	0	.46	.50
Peers:																		
1	0	0	0	0	.62	.67	0	0	0	0	0	0	0	0	0	0	.62	.55
2	0	0	0	0	.71	.70	0	0	0	0	0	0	0	0	0	0	.50	.51
3	0	0	0	0	.68	.66	0	0	0	0	0	0	0	0	0	0	.54	.57
4	0	0	0	0	.73	.66	0	0	0	0	0	0	0	0	0	0	.46	.57
Parents:																		
1	0	0	0	0	0	0	.53	.57	0	0	0	0	0	0	0	0	.71	.68
2	0	0	0	0	0	0	.43	.42	0	0	0	0	0	0	0	0	.82	.83
3	0	0	0	0	0	0	.70	.71	0	0	0	0	0	0	0	0	.51	.50
4	0	0	0	0	0	0	.72	.80	0	0	0	0	0	0	0	0	.49	.36

Reading:

Item	PA·T1	PA·T2	Peers·T1	Peers·T2	Parents·T1	Parents·T2	Reading·T1	Reading·T2	Math·T1	Math·T2	School·T1	School·T2	General·T1	General·T2	2nd·T1	2nd·T2
1	0	0	0	0	0	0	.72	.74	0	0	0	0	0	0	.49	.45
2	0	0	0	0	0	0	.76	.85	0	0	0	0	0	0	.42	.28
3	0	0	0	0	0	0	.78	.82	0	0	0	0	0	0	.40	.33
4	0	0	0	0	0	0	.80	.79	0	0	0	0	0	0	.37	.38

Math:

Item	PA·T1	PA·T2	Peers·T1	Peers·T2	Parents·T1	Parents·T2	Reading·T1	Reading·T2	Math·T1	Math·T2	School·T1	School·T2	General·T1	General·T2	2nd·T1	2nd·T2
1	0	0	0	0	0	0	0	0	.58	.65	0	0	0	0	.66	.58
2	0	0	0	0	0	0	0	0	.70	.74	0	0	0	0	.51	.45
3	0	0	0	0	0	0	0	0	.83	.84	0	0	0	0	.32	.29
4	0	0	0	0	0	0	0	0	.79	.82	0	0	0	0	.38	.32

School:

Item	PA·T1	PA·T2	Peers·T1	Peers·T2	Parents·T1	Parents·T2	Reading·T1	Reading·T2	Math·T1	Math·T2	School·T1	School·T2	General·T1	General·T2	2nd·T1	2nd·T2
1	0	0	0	0	0	0	0	0	0	0	.58	.72	0	0	.66	.48
2	0	0	0	0	0	0	0	0	0	0	.65	.71	0	0	.57	.50
3	0	0	0	0	0	0	0	0	0	0	.70	.70	0	0	.51	.52
4	0	0	0	0	0	0	0	0	0	0	.78	.76	0	0	.39	.42

General:

Item	PA·T1	PA·T2	Peers·T1	Peers·T2	Parents·T1	Parents·T2	Reading·T1	Reading·T2	Math·T1	Math·T2	School·T1	School·T2	General·T1	General·T2	2nd·T1	2nd·T2
1	0	0	0	0	0	0	0	0	0	0	0	0	.45	.55	.70	.80
2	0	0	0	0	0	0	0	0	0	0	0	0	.62	.65	.58	.61
3	0	0	0	0	0	0	0	0	0	0	0	0	.73	.74	.45	.47
4	0	0	0	0	0	0	0	0	0	0	0	0	.70	.70	.51	.51

Factor correlations:

(each cell shows T1 and T2 values)

	Physical Appearance	Peers	Parents	Reading	Math	School
Physical Appearance						
Peers	.41 .41					
Parents	.55 .48	.59 .55				
Reading	.40 .35	.46 .47	.53 .58			
Math	.52 .27	.47 .36	.58 .40	.49 .33		
School	.52 .48	.61 .40	.58 .32	.40 .34	.57 .38	
General	.57 .41	.75 .69	.69 .51	.56 .39	.75 .39	.78 .61

Separate factor analyses of responses for T1 and T2 are summarized in completely standardized form. All parameters with the value of 0 were fixed a priori and not estimated as part of the analysis.

Table 4 Psychometric properties (goodness of fit, reliability, test–retest correlation) for each scale: total sample and each year group separately

Scales	Total (n = 393)				K (n = 127)				Year 1 (n = 139)				Year 2 (n = 130)			
	χ^2	df	RNI	Stabil corr	χ^2	df	RNI	Stabil corr	χ^2	df	RNI	Stabil corr	χ^2	df	RNI	Stabil corr
Physical:																
T1	5.63	2	.98	...	5.93	2	.86	...	.28	2	1.02	...	6.00	2	.97	...
T2	12.86	2	.97	...	4.53	2	.97	...	8.94	2	.94	...	3.37	2	.99	...
T1/T2	42.14	15	.96	.601	34.18	15	.87	.798	20.54	15	.98	.523	16.57	15	.99	.573
Appearance:																
T1	33.82	2	.93	...	16.04	2	.84	...	2.31	2	1.00	...	9.97	2	.96	...
T2	24.29	2	.96	...	17.81	2	.89	...	8.47	2	.97	...	1.06	2	1.00	...
T1/T2	73.46	15	.95	.494	52.75	15	.85	.484	29.56	15	.97	.433	16.30	15	1.00	.492
Peers:																
T1	2.55	2	1.00	...	4.43	2	.98	...	.13	2	1.01	...	.72	2	1.01	...
T2	12.62	2	.97	...	1.93	2	1.00	...	5.62	2	.97	...	5.94	2	.98	...
T1/T2	30.40	15	.98	.451	13.15	15	1.01	.295	22.56	15	.98	.350	17.76	15	.99	.651
Parents:																
T1	8.82	2	.97	...	3.81	2	.97	...	.16	2	1.02	...	10.46	2	.92	...
T2	14.41	2	.96	...	5.68	2	.96	...	12.17	2	.91	...	.53	2	1.01	...
T1/T2	37.18	15	.97	.459	15.94	15	.99	.401	29.59	15	.94	.436	19.53	15	.98	.587

Reading:																
T1	18.19	2	.98	...	9.73	2	.95	...	2.69	2	1.00	...	5.13	2	.99	...
T2	11.23	2	.99	...	3.18	2	1.00	...	3.05	2	.99	...	3.67	2	1.00	...
T1/T2	57.49	15	.97	.417	27.98	15	.97	.312	24.65	15	.98	.247	27.20	15	.98	.637
Math:																
T1	7.85	2	.99	...	2.53	2	1.00	...	2.12	2	1.00	...	7.82	2	.98	...
T2	12.31	2	.98	...	15.47	2	.92	...	4.79	2	.99	...	12.66	2	.97	...
T1/T2	30.05	15	.99	.356	29.70	15	.95	.244	13.27	15	1.00	.307	32.10	15	.97	.462
School:																
T1	.42	2	1.00	...	.78	2	1.02	...	.38	2	1.01	...	.13	2	1.01	...
T2	25.33	2	.96	...	17.57	2	.88	...	4.59	2	.99	...	6.83	2	.98	...
T1/T2	39.51	15	.98	.483	31.63	15	.92	.551	8.77	15	1.02	.337	27.05	15	.97	.542
Esteem:																
T1	1.07	2	1.00	...	.01	2	1.02	...	1.26	2	1.00	...	3.56	2	.99	...
T2	3.66	2	.99	...	.08	2	1.02	...	2.94	2	.99	...	2.97	2	.99	...
T1/T2	33.93	15	.97	.299	15.81	15	1.00	.317	33.31	15	.94	.219	14.85	15	1.00	.417

T1 = Time 1, T2 = Time 2, df = degrees of freedom, RNI = relative noncentrality index, Stabil corr = test–retest correlation for analyses of T1/T2 responses. Congeneric one-factor models were conducted for T1 and T2 responses for the total sample and for each year group (kindergarten, Year 1, Year 2) and evaluated in relation to RNI. Two-factor models (with correlated uniquenesses relating responses to the same measured variables administered at T1 and T2) were then conducted for T1/T2 responses, and these are summarized by RNIs and test–retest correlations.

Multiple group comparisons: Invariance over age cohorts

In analyses summarized in this section, structural equation path models relating gender and teacher inferred ratings (of their students' self-concepts) to T1 and T2 self-concept ratings were evaluated for each SDQ-I scale. Critical issues were the influence of gender and teacher ratings (collected at T1) on T1 self-concept responses and whether these variables had an additional direct effect on T2 self-concept ratings beyond the effects that were mediated by T1 self-concept. If gender influenced T2 self-concept directly, then there would be evidence that the gender differences were changing with age. If T1 teacher ratings directly affected T2 self-concept, then there would be support for the proposal that students' self-concepts became more predictable with age.

In CFA studies with multiple groups, it is possible to test the invariance (equality) of any one, any set, or all parameter estimates across the multiple groups. Here we evaluated the invariance of various sets of parameters across the multiple age groups (table 5). In the least restrictive Model 1 (table 6), no parameters were constrained to be equal across the three age cohorts, and this model provided a good fit for each of the SDQ scales. In Model 2 the factor loadings relating the T1 and T2 self-concept ratings to their latent construct were constrained to be invariant across the three age cohorts. Although this model resulted in a significantly poorer fit in a strict statistical sense for a few scales, all the RNIs were .92 or greater. In Model 3 all parameter estimates were constrained to be invariant across the three age cohorts, and this model resulted in significantly poorer fits for all of the SDQ scales. In Model 4, the invariance constraints on the uniquenesses were relaxed so that the uniquenesses were estimated separately for each age cohort. This resulted in a substantially improved fit relative to the model with all parameters constrained to be invariant. Whereas the fit of Model 4 was statistically poorer than that of Model 1 (with no invariance constraints) for several of the scales, all of the RNIs were .94 or greater.

In Models 5–7, the invariance of selected structural parameters of particular interest were evaluated. In each model, the uniquenesses were independently estimated in each age cohort (as in Model 4) along with an additional set of parameters. Tests of statistical significance were used to evaluate whether freeing the additional parameters led to an improved fit to the data compared to Model 4.

In Model 5, the constraint requiring the stability coefficients leading from T1 self-concept to T2 self-concept to be invariant across the three age-cohort groups was relaxed. This led to a statistically significant ($p < .05$) improvement in fit for two scales (Parents, Reading) and marginally improved fits ($p < .10$) in two other scales. For all four of these scales, the stability coefficient increased with age.

In Model 6, the invariance constraints on path coefficients leading from teacher ratings and gender to T1 and T2 self-concept were relaxed. However, the change in chi-square was not even marginally significant for any of the SDQ scales. Finally, in Model 7, the invariance constraint on the correlation between teacher ratings and gender was relaxed. Here again, however, these constraints were not even marginally significant for any of the SDQ scales.

Based on these results summarized in table 5, Model 4 (with all parameters invariant across the age cohorts except for the uniquenesses) was selected as the best fitting model and selected parameter estimates from this model are presented in table 6. For each SDQ scale, correlations between gender, teacher ratings, T1 self-concept, and T2 self-concept are presented first. These are followed by path coefficients leading from gender and teacher ratings to T1 and T2 self-concept, and from T1 self-concept to T2 self-concept. The stability coefficients leading from T1 self-concept to T2 self-concept tended to be somewhat smaller than those in table 4 because the effects of gender and teacher ratings have been removed. However, the differences were not large, and the pattern of results was very similar.

Gender differences.   Gender differences (table 6) were represented as simple correlations between gender and self-concept and as path coefficients based on the path model. Path coefficients leading from gender to T1 and T2 Physical self-concept were both significant, implying that differences favoring boys were increasing with time. Consistent with this observation, the simple correlation between gender and T2 Physical self-concept was larger than the corresponding correlation with T1 Physical self-concept.

For Appearance self-concept, gender was positively correlated with T1 self-concept but was not significantly related to T2 self-concept.

Table 5 Invariance tests conducted on path model

Scale	Model 1 All free χ^2	TLI	RNI	Model 2 Fact load invar χ^2	TLI	RNI	Model 3 All inv χ^2	TLI	RNI
df	93			105 (13)[a]			141 (48)[a]		
Phys	159.6	.88	.92	169.9	.90	.92	234.5**	.89	.88
Appr	167.3	.91	.94	196.2**	.90	.92	256.9**	.90	.90
Peer	118.7	.96	.97	139.8**	.95	.96	190.9**	.95	.94
Prnt	118.9	.94	.96	137.9*	.93	.94	311.8**	.72	.71
Read	141.3	.95	.97	152.0	.96	.97	236.9**	.94	.94
Math	145.9	.94	.96	155.7	.95	.96	257.4**	.92	.91
Schl	127.8	.95	.97	155.6**	.94	.95	214.3**	.93	.93
Estm	118.8	.95	.97	138.0	.94	.96	209.9**	.91	.91

Model 4 Uniq (U) free χ^2	TLI	RNI	Model 5 U & stabil free χ^2	TLI	RNI	Model 6 U & paths fr χ^2	TLI	RNI	Model 7 U & TR/sex corr free χ^2	TLI	RNI
125 (32)[a]			123 (2)[b]			117 (8)[b]			123 (2)[b]		
189.6**	.91	.92	189.3	.91	.92	182.4	.91	.92	189.4	.91	.92
216.0**	.92	.92	215.9	.91	.92	208.5	.91	.92	214.5	.91	.92
162.1**	.96	.96	156.3*	.96	.96	155.9	.95	.96	161.1	.95	.96
164.2**	.93	.93	156.9*	.94	.94	156.7	.92	.93	163.0	.93	.93
192.9**	.95	.96	170.8*	.97	.97	180.5	.95	.96	192.7	.95	.95
175.9**	.96	.96	170.3*	.96	.97	170.4	.95	.96	175.6	.96	.96
173.1**	.95	.95	170.6	.95	.95	163.9	.95	.95	172.9	.95	.95
157.7**	.95	.96	157.0	.95	.95	150.7	.95	.95	156.8	.95	.95

Phys = physical, Appr = appearance, Peer = peers, Prnt = parents, Read = reading, Math = mathematics, Schl = school, Estm = esteem. Alternative models were specified such that all parameters were free (i.e., no invariance constraints were imposed; Model 1); factor loadings were invariant across groups (Model 2); all parameters were invariant across groups (Model 3; total invariance); only uniquenesses were free (Model 4); uniqueness and self-concept stability coefficients were free (Model 5); uniquenesses and paths leading from teacher ratings and gender to T1 and T2 self-concept were free (Model 6); and uniquenesses and correlations between teacher ratings and gender were free (Model 7).

[a] Tests of statistical significance compared this model with no invariance constraints (TOT FR), and the value in parentheses is the difference in df for the two tests.

[b] Tests of statistical significance compared this model with U FR, and the value in parentheses is the difference in df for the two tests.

*p < .10; **p < .05.

Whereas the path from gender to T1 Appearance was significantly positive, the path from gender to T2 Appearance was nonsignificantly negative. Consistent with Marsh (1989), this suggests that the differences in favor of girls at T1 may decline with age.

For Reading self-concept, correlations between gender and self-concept were marginally significant at T1 and T2 ($p < .10$), but neither path coefficient from gender to self-concept was significant. For Math self-concept, the path from gender to T1 self-concept was nonsignificant whereas the path to T2 self-concept was significantly negative. This implied that the gender differences in favor of boys were increasing over time. For all other SDQ scales there are neither significant correlations nor significant path coefficients relating gender to self-concept.

Although not the major focus of the present investigation, it was also interesting to note that the pattern of gender differences in teacher ratings of students' self-concepts were reasonably consistent with those observed in student ratings. Whereas teachers inferred no gender differences in Math self-concept favoring boys at T1, the corresponding gender difference in T1 self-concept ratings was also nonsignificant. Although teachers inferred boys to have higher Physical self-concepts than girls, the size of the gender differences was much smaller than observed in student self-concept ratings.

Teacher inferred self-concept ratings.   The most interesting results in table 6, perhaps, were correlations and path coefficients leading from teacher ratings of students' self-concepts and students' actual self-concepts. For all but one of the SDQ scales, T1 teacher ratings were more highly correlated with T2 self-concept ratings than with T1 self-concept ratings. Consistent with this observation, teacher ratings contributed to the prediction of T2 self-concept ratings beyond the contribution of T1 self-concept ratings for six of eight SDQ scales – all but Appearance and Reading. For Reading self-concept, teacher inferences were more accurate than any other scales at T1 and all of the relation between teacher ratings and T2 Reading self-concept was mediated by T1 self-concept. Teacher inferences of Appearance self-concept were not significantly related to either T1 or T2 self-concept ratings by students. Particularly because T1 teacher ratings and T1 self-concept ratings by students were collected at the same time (near the end of the school year), it is particularly noteworthy that teacher ratings were more highly correlated with T2 student ratings collected a year later when students had a new teacher. These results provided clear support for the hypothesis that

Table 6 Path coefficients (pc) and correlations (*r*) relating Time 1 and Time 2 self-concept (T1, T2), teacher ratings of self-concept (TR), and gender (Gend) for each self-concept factor

Variables		T1	T2	TR	Gender
Physical:					
T1	*r*				
T2	*r*	.65**			
TR	*r*	.14**	.31**		
Gend	*r*	−.42**	−.48**	−.09*	
T1	pc	0	0	.10	.41**
T2	pc	.52**	0	.22**	.25*
Appearance:					
T1	*r*				
T2	*r*	.48**			
TR	*r*	.04	.08		
Gend	*r*	.11**	.02	.11*	
T1	pc	0	0	.03	.11**
T2	pc	.48**	0	.06	−.04
Peers:					
T1	*r*				
T2	*r*	.46**			
TR	*r*	.14**	.30**		
Gend	*r*	.05	.06	−.03	
T1	pc	0	0	.14**	.05
T2	pc	.42**	0	.24**	.05
Parents:					
T1	*r*				
T2	*r*	.47**			
TR	*r*	−.06	.13**		
Gend	*r*	.08	.08	.01	
T1	pc	0	0	−.06	.08
T2	pc	.48**	0	.16**	.04
Reading:					
T1	*r*				
T2	*r*	.44**			
TR	*r*	.23**	.16**		
Gend	*r*	.09*	.08*	.07	
T1	pc	0	0	.23**	.08
T2	pc	.42	0	.06	.04

Table 6   *Continued*

Variables		T1	T2	TR	Gender
Math:					
T1	r				
T2	r	.37**			
TR	r	.14**	.16**		
Gend	r	−.05	−.12**	.00	
T1	pc	0	0	.14**	−.04
T2	pc	.34**	0	.11**	−.10**
School:					
T1	r				
T2	r	.48**			
TR	r	.13**	.19**		
Gend	r	.06	.05	.11**	
T1	pc	0	0	.12**	.05
T2	pc	.46**	0	.13**	.01
Esteem:					
T1	r				
T2	r	.34**			
TR	r	.12**	.19**		
Gend	r	.09	−.01	.09*	
T1	pc	0	0	.12**	.08
T2	pc	.32**	0	.16**	−.05

Path coefficients (pc) and correlations relating the major constructs based on the path model in which uniquenesses were freely estimated for each age group, but all other coefficients (including those presented here) were constrained to be invariant across age groups (see table 3).
$*p < .10$; $**p < .05$.

student self-concept ratings grew more predictable with time – that they were less likely to make idiosyncratic self-ratings and were more likely to base their self-concept ratings on criteria like those used by external observers.

The effects of gender, age cohort, and time on multiple dimensions of self-concept

Here we simultaneously evaluated age differences with cross-sectional comparisons and longitudinal comparisons of the same age cohort on different occasions based on an MCMO design. The critical comparisons involved cross-sectional comparisons based on the multiple age cohorts, longitudinal comparisons based on responses by the same cohort on the multiple occasions (T1 and T2), and age cohort × occasion interactions that tested the consistency of longitudinal comparisons over the different age cohorts. This MCMO design was operationalized as a 3 (age cohort) × 2 (gender) × 2 (time) design in which time was a within-subjects (repeated-measures) effect whereas age cohort and gender were between-subjects effects (see table 7). The main effects of age cohort and time provided alternative (cross-sectional and longitudinal) tests of the effect of age. If there was no effect of age, then the main effects of age cohort, time, and their interaction should all be nonsignificant. If the effect of age was linear, then the effects of both age and time should both be significant, but the age cohort × time interaction should be non-significant. However, if the effect of age was nonlinear, then there may be main and interaction effects that would require a careful evaluation of the means for each cohort/time combination. In the present investigation the comparison of the cohort and time effects was facilitated because each age cohort differed from the next cohort by one year and the time interval in the longitudinal comparisons was also one year. The construct validity of interpretations of age differences would be strengthened if these tests provided consistent results. The main effect of gender provided a test of gender differences averaged across age cohorts and time. However, the gender × age cohort interaction and the gender × time interaction each provided alternative tests of the consistency of the gender effects over age.

Particularly in developmental research there is an apparent preference for longitudinal comparisons that also allow researchers to evaluate test–retest stability over time. Ultimately, however, mean differences based on cross-sectional comparisons and longitudinal comparisons are both legitimate approaches to evaluating age differences. Because there are potential strengths and weaknesses in both strategies, the best solution is to combine both types of comparison in the MCMO design. However, particularly when sample sizes are modest, an overreliance on simplistic tests of statistical significance can be counterproductive. Thus, for example, a marginally significant (longitudinal) time effect and a marginally nonsignificant (cross-sectional) age cohort effect may actually reflect the underlying age difference in a very consistent manner. For this reason, it is critical to evaluate the consistency in the pattern, direction, and size of age differences inferred from longitudinal and cross-sectional comparisons, particularly when only one of the comparisons is significant or there is an age cohort × time interaction.

Age differences.   The main effects of either age cohort or time were statistically significant for Appearance, Parents, and School, whereas the age cohort × time interaction effect was significant for Reading. For Appearance, there was a statistically significant decline in self-concept that was evident in both the cross-sectional (age cohort) and longitudinal (time) indicators of age differences. Because the time × age cohort interaction was not significant, the decline in Appearance over time did not vary as a function of the age cohort. For School self-concept, there was a decline in self-concept with age cohort and a marginal decline (*p* = .07) with time. Whereas the differences were not large, they were reasonably consistent across the two indicators of age differences.

For Parents self-concept, there was a significant age cohort effect that interacted with time, but no main effect of time. Considering both age cohort and time means, self-concept was stable for kindergarten (4.46) and Year 1 (4.44 for both T2 from the kindergarten cohort and T1 for the Year 1 cohort), increased between Year 1 and Year 2, and then was stable over Year 2 and Year 3 (means of 4.56, 4.58, 4.57 for the T2 cohort of Year 1 and both times for the Year 2 cohort). In this case, there was a reasonably consistent pattern of results when both age cohort and times within each cohort were evaluated simultaneously.

For Reading self-concept, there were no significant effects of either age cohort or time, but there was a significant interaction between these two effects. Considering all six means constituting the three age cohorts and two times, there appeared to be an "inverted u" effect in which self-concept increased across the first two age cohorts and over time within each of these age cohorts, and then decreased from the second age cohort to the third age cohort and over time within the third age cohort. Again, there was a reasonably consistent pattern of age differences when means for each age cohort and times within each age cohort were considered simultaneously.

Gender differences.   There were significant main effects (*p* < .05) for Physical self-concept (favoring boys), Parents (favoring girls), and Reading self-concept (favoring girls) and a marginal gender difference (*p* = .08) in Math self-concept (favoring boys). Because some differences

Table 7 Effects of gender, year in school, and time on multiple dimensions of self-concept

| | K (n = 127) | | | | Time 1 (n = 139) | | | | Time 2 (n = 130) | | | | p values for tests of significance | | | | | | |
| | Time 1 | | Time 2 | | Time 1 | | Time 2 | | Time 1 | | Time 2 | | Gend | Year | | Time | | | |
Scale and gender	M	SD	M	SD	M	SD	M	SD	M	SD	M	SD	(G)	(Y)	G×Y	(T)	T×G	T×Y	T×G×Y
Physical:																			
Male	4.50	.43	4.61	.43	4.53	.52	4.59	.49	4.62	.41	4.52	.50	.00	.31	.14	.06	.01	.16	.47
Female	4.27	.47	4.17	.59	4.24	.53	4.10	.55	4.12	.46	3.97	.58							
Total	4.39	.46	4.40	.55	4.37	.54	4.33	.58	4.39	.50	4.27	.61							
Appearance:																			
Male	4.11	.70	4.10	.72	4.01	.82	3.94	.83	3.96	.74	3.89	.79	.28	.00	.52	.01	.16	.91	.73
Female	4.36	.53	4.17	.70	4.12	.61	3.93	.80	3.96	.76	3.86	.74							
Total	4.23	.63	4.13	.71	4.07	.71	3.93	.81	3.96	.75	3.88	.76							
Peers:																			
Male	4.24	.67	4.16	.74	4.20	.71	4.17	.67	4.17	.76	4.16	.70	.23	.58	.85	.25	.93	.70	.97
Female	4.33	.64	4.25	.49	4.29	.63	4.23	.57	4.19	.59	4.19	.71							
Total	4.29	.65	4.20	.63	4.25	.67	4.20	.62	4.18	.69	4.17	.70							
Parents:																			
Male	4.36	.54	4.43	.56	4.39	.64	4.55	.49	4.58	.45	4.50	.59	.04	.02	.82	.24	.55	.03	.05
Female	4.57	.40	4.44	.49	4.47	.40	4.57	.37	4.59	.35	4.66	.33							
Total	4.46	.49	4.44	.53	4.44	.52	4.56	.43	4.58	.40	4.57	.49							

	M	SD	M	SD	M	SD	M	SD	M	SD	M	SD	p	p	p	p	p	p	p
Reading:																			
Male	4.20	.69	4.35	.79	4.40	.65	4.45	.50	4.24	.79	4.01	.91	.03	.14	.06	.74	.93	.00	.31
Female	4.40	.56	4.39	.59	4.32	.67	4.43	.57	4.48	.51	4.33	.62							
Total	4.30	.64	4.37	.70	4.36	.66	4.44	.54	4.35	.68	4.16	.80							
Math:																			
Male	4.26	.66	4.21	.74	4.23	.77	4.34	.57	4.11	.85	4.15	.90	.08	.50	.63	.82	.34	.69	.44
Female	4.10	.75	4.13	.78	4.14	.74	4.10	.72	4.18	.68	4.03	.80							
Total	4.18	.71	4.17	.76	4.18	.75	4.21	.66	4.14	.77	4.09	.85							
School:																			
Male	4.14	.62	4.03	.79	4.13	.71	4.14	.59	3.92	.82	3.84	.84	.18	.04	.28	.07	.79	.44	.76
Female	4.21	.60	4.15	.64	4.10	.69	4.09	.75	4.15	.59	3.98	.64							
Total	4.17	.61	4.09	.72	4.12	.70	4.11	.68	4.02	.73	3.91	.75							
Esteem:																			
Male	4.12	.69	4.24	.57	4.25	.64	4.29	.50	4.23	.64	4.25	.53	.33	.86	.43	.99	.10	.94	.59
Female	4.35	.52	4.26	.62	4.28	.57	4.25	.53	4.27	.44	4.23	.40							
Total	4.23	.62	4.25	.59	4.27	.60	4.27	.51	4.25	.55	4.24	.47							
Total:																			
Male	4.24	.46	4.26	.47	4.27	.53	4.31	.40	4.23	.49	4.17	.48		.81	.26	.61	.17	.38	.80
Female	4.32	.42	4.24	.47	4.24	.45	4.22	.42	4.24	.36	4.15	.36							
Total	4.28	.44	4.25	.47	4.26	.48	4.26	.42	4.24	.43	4.16	.43							

For each self-concept scale and the total score a 2 (time) × 3 (year in school) × 2 (gender) analysis of variance was conducted in which time was a repeated measures (within-subject) variable and gender and year in school were between-subjects variables; p values for each effect are presented.

favored girls whereas others favored boys, the differences in the total score were not statistically significant. Interestingly, there were no significant differences in Esteem even though research reviewed earlier based on older participants typically reported significant differences favoring males (Marsh, 1989).

Of particular interest was the question of whether gender differences were consistent over cross-sectional and longitudinal age comparisons. For Physical self-concept there was a significant gender × time interaction ($p < .01$) in which gender differences favoring boys are larger at T2 than T1 for each of the three age cohorts. Although not statistically significant ($p = .14$), there was a similar pattern of results for the gender × age cohort interaction. For each time, gender differences favoring boys were smallest in kindergarten, intermediate for Year 1, and largest at Year 2. Whereas no other interaction effects involving gender were statistically significant at the traditional $p < .05$ level, there were marginal effects for Reading (gender × age cohort; $p = .06$). For Reading self-concept, the expected gender difference favoring girls was evident in Year 2 and, to a lesser extent, in kindergarten, but not in Year 1. These differences, however, were consistent over time, suggesting that the marginal effect may have been an idiosyncratic cohort difference.

In summary, gender differences for even these very young children appeared to be consistent with those found by older participants – favoring girls in Parents and Reading, favoring boys in Physical and, to a lesser extent, Math. Furthermore, except for Physical self-concept, there was no clear indication that the age differences observed here varied with either cross-sectional or longitudinal differences in age. For Physical self-concept, gender differences favoring boys increased significantly with the longitudinal indicator of age and increased marginally ($p = .14$) with the cross-sectional indicator of age. Whereas the age cohort effect on Physical self-concept may not warrant consideration on its own, at least the direction of the effect was consistent with the longitudinal effect.

Discussion

This research addresses a variety of converging theoretical perspectives, particularly our earlier work based on the original Shavelson et al. (1976) model (e.g., Marsh, 1985, 1990; Marsh et al., 1984; Marsh &

Hattie, 1996) and work by Eccles and colleagues (Eccles et al., 1993; Wigfield & Eccles, 1992; Wigfield et al., 1997) based in part on earlier research (e.g., Nicholls, 1979; Parsons & Ruble, 1977; Stipek & MacIver, 1989). Marsh (1990) proposed that self-concepts of very young children are consistently high but that with increasing life experience children learn their relative strengths and weaknesses so that with increasing levels of age, mean levels of self-concept decline, individual self-concepts become more differentiated, and self-concept becomes more highly correlated with external indicators of competence (e.g., skills, accomplishments, and self-concepts inferred by significant others). Similarly, Eccles et al. (1993) proposed that the declines in mean levels of competency self-ratings reflected an optimistic bias for very young children and increased accuracy in responses by young children as they grow older and become more realistic. A number of the empirical trends evaluated here provide new and continuing support for these theoretical predictions – support for the factor structure of multidimensional self-concept responses and the increasing distinctiveness of the different self-concept components, longitudinal and cross-sectional age comparisons, accuracy of teacher-inferred self-concept ratings.

Factor structure and distinctiveness

From both a theoretical and a practical perspective, the most important finding of this study, perhaps, was the clearly differentiated factor structure for these very young children. The results from T2 replicated the results from T1 in that each of the a priori factors was clearly defined. The T2 results were, perhaps, stronger than the T1 results in that the factor loadings tended to be larger, the factors tended to be more distinct, the factors tended to be more reliable, and relations with T1 teacher ratings tended to be larger. Because the children were one year older at T2 than T1, the stronger results at T2 were not unexpected. However, particularly given problems in obtaining clearly defined factor structures for very young children – based in part on the typically poor quality of extant measurement instruments for this age group (e.g., Byrne, 1996; Crain, 1996; Wylie, 1989) – these results are very encouraging.

This distinctiveness of self-concept factors and how this varies with age is an important theoretical concern that has received inadequate attention in developmental self-concept research. The size of correlations between self-concept factors decreased across cross-sectional age cohorts and decreased over time for longitudinal comparisons. This pattern of results was evident in comparisons based on raw scale scores and comparisons based on latent factor correlations in the CFAs. However, Marsh (1989) proposed that correlations between some components of self-concept should be substantial whereas others should be small. Support for the increasing distinctiveness of SDQ factors based on correlations selected a priori to be small was particularly strong. The average size of these selected correlations did not differ from the average size of all correlations for the youngest children at T1, but the differences steadily increased over age cohorts and over time within each age cohort. In an alternative operationalization of distinctiveness, the *SD* of the eight self-concept scale scores was computed for each child at T1 and T2. These *SD*s showed a clear pattern of increasing distinctiveness (higher *SD*s) over age cohorts and over time within age cohorts. The consistent pattern of results for the various comparisons of age differences in the size of correlations and the size of *SD*s supported the conclusion that self-concepts became more distinct with age for the age range considered here. Finally, based on the MTMM studies in which multiple occasions were taken to be the multiple methods, support for the discriminant validity of the SDQ-I factors improved with age. We interpreted these various results to mean that young children were better able to distinguish between their relative strengths and weaknesses due to gaining life experience that comes with age, and that this was reflected in their self-concept responses.

Stability and change in the development of self-concept

The theoretical perspectives summarized earlier suggest that self-concepts should decline with age at least through the early adolescent period, and there seems to be reasonable support for these predictions based on responses by older children. The present investigation offered a potentially important contribution due to the MCMO design coupled with the good psychometric properties for responses by very young children. For four of eight individual scales (Physical, Peers, Math, Esteem) there were no age differences for either cross-sectional or longitudinal comparisons. The strongest and most consistent effect was for Appearance self-concept in that both cross-sectional and longitudinal comparisons indicated that self-concept declined with age. Similarly, both cross-sectional and longitudinal comparisons showed that School self-concept declined with age. Reading self-concept showed an initial increase followed by a decline that was also consistent across cross-sectional and longitudinal comparisons. Parents self-concept was particularly interesting in that it showed a significant increase in self-concept with age, although the nature of the trend differed somewhat for T1 and T2 responses (see table 7). These results were not fully consistent with expectations that self-concept will decline during these early years based on responses by somewhat older children (Marsh, 1989). In particular, the *increase* in Parents self-concept ran counter to expectations, although Marsh et al. (1984; Marsh, 1989) found that there was no significant decline in Parents self-concept responses during early adolescence even though responses to this scale were highest of all SDQ scales. Even though these differences in Parents responses were significant, the sizes of the differences were very small (table 1). For other scales, there is a general tendency for decreasing self-concept with age cohort and time, but these differences were smaller than expected.

Developmental changes in the predictability of self-concept responses

The theoretical proposals summarized earlier suggested that self-concepts of young children become more predictable with age – more closely aligned with external indicators such as objective accomplishments and the perspectives of significant others. The inclusion of teacher ratings was a new and important feature because self–other agreement on multiple dimensions of self-concept has rarely been considered for children this young or has been found to be nonsignificant (also see Wigfield et al., 1997). Here we found that teacher ratings were significantly related to all self-concept domains except Appearance, a domain in which self–other agreement is typically lowest for all ages and is nonsignificant for preadolescent children (Marsh, 1989; Marsh & Craven, 1991). Furthermore, the significant self–other agreement between teacher and student ratings reported here was likely to underestimate the true relation because teachers were asked to complete a single summary rating for each domain rather than the multi-item ratings completed by students. These results provided important new support for the construct validity of self-concept ratings by very young children.

The longitudinal comparisons of relations between teacher ratings of students' self-concept and students' actual self-concepts also supported the proposal that young children's self-concepts were becoming more predictable as they grew older. Teacher ratings collected at T1 were significantly related to students' ratings at T1 and T2. Logically – particularly given that the ratings were collected near the end of the school year – it might be expected that the T1 teacher ratings should be more highly correlated with T1 student ratings than T2 student ratings, and the effects of T1 teacher ratings on T2 self-concepts should be mediated by T1 self-concept ratings. This follows in that T1 teacher ratings and T1 self-concepts were collected at the same time (when the teacher had been the teacher of the student for almost a year), whereas at T2 each child typically had a new teacher who had taught the child for almost a year. However, T1 teacher ratings were more highly related to T2 self-concepts than to T1 self-concepts, and the direct effects of T1 teacher ratings were significant on T2 self-concept in addition to the effect mediated through T1 self-concepts.

Gender differences

Although not directly implicated in theoretical predictions summarized earlier, the hypothesis that gender differences evolve with age (Marsh, 1989; Marsh et al., 1991; Wigfield et al., 1997) has received surprisingly little support. Instead, researchers have found a gender stereotypic pattern of gender differences that is surprisingly consistent over age. Because of the past difficulties in measuring self-concepts with very young children, the present investigation had the potential of making an important contribution in this area. The gender differences observed here were reasonably consistent across the different analyses and reasonably consistent with extrapolations from research based on older children. There were, however, some interesting differences based on these results and extrapolations from earlier research – the higher Appearance self-concepts for very young girls (compared to typical differences favoring boys for older students), the lack of gender differences favoring girls in School self-concepts, the lack of gender differences favoring boys in Esteem, and perhaps the lack of gender differences favoring girls in Peer self-concept. Nevertheless, except for Physical self-concept, the gender differences and age × gender interactions observed here were modest, and this was consistent with previous research suggesting that gender differences are surprisingly stable over age. It was also interesting to note that the pattern of gender differences in student self-concept ratings was reasonably consistent with those based on teacher-inferred self-concept ratings.

Potential strengths and weaknesses of the measurement procedure

Results of the present investigation provided stronger support for the construct validity of self-concept responses than those based on other instruments designed for very young children reviewed by Byrne (1996) or Wylie (1989). Thus, it is relevant to speculate on the potential strengths and weaknesses in the instrument and administration procedure.

The individual interview-style administration was an important feature of the strategy used here that Marsh et al. (1991) showed to be more effective than group administration procedures – even when the items were read aloud to students. However, this administration procedure required much more time than the typical group administration procedure. Many of the statistical procedures used here required reasonably large sample sizes. For present purposes, the sample sizes used here were not overly large, and even larger sample sizes would have been desirable. Hence, the individual administration procedure coupled with moderately large sample sizes were important strengths of the present investigation, but they also represented a potential limitation in the added resources required to collect the data.

The test administration was conducted by a large number of different undergraduate teacher education students with some classroom experience who were given a two-hour training program. The training included an instructional video of the instrument actually being administered and trial administrations. These results suggested that the testing procedures are easily mastered by relatively inexperienced test administrators. However, even stronger results might have been obtained if the administration had been done by a small number of more highly trained professionals.

Self-concept instruments for young children sometimes combine the use of verbal cues and pictures, but our preliminary research suggested that the pictures were counterproductive – distracting young children from the verbal content of the items. Whereas these results are only suggestive, it would be of interest to pursue these preliminary findings with more fully developed instruments that use a pictorial format.

A significant difference between this study and most other research with very young children was the length of the questionnaire – 64 items. Whereas we were initially concerned with a potential fatigue effect such that the quality of responses for items near the end of the instrument deteriorated, we actually found that these items were psychometrically stronger – not weaker. Across all items from the different scales, there was a clear progression of increasing factor loadings for items presented in first, second, third, and fourth quarters of the instrument. There was support for this effect at T1 and T2, although the effect was stronger at T1 when children were younger and had not previously completed the instrument. In fact, the larger T2 factor loadings – compared to T1 factor loadings – were largely due to the stronger performance of items in the first half of the instrument at T2. These results have important implications for early childhood researchers in that the use of short instruments may be counterproductive and may account for some of the difficulties researchers have in obtaining responses from very young children that yield good psychometric properties.

The items used in this study were from a well-established instrument (see reviews of the SDQ-I by Byrne, 1996; Hattie, 1992; Wylie, 1989), but one that was designed for somewhat older children. A potential limitation of this strategy was that the wording of some of the items (e.g., those using the term "mathematics") was overly complex for some of these very young children. However, this potential limitation was apparently offset by the flexibility of the individual administration procedure in which the meaning of any item could be explained to a child who did not understand the item. Instruments specifically designed for very young children like those reviewed by Byrne (1996) and Wylie (1989) have typically not been used with older children. Hence it is not clear whether apparent problems with at least some of these instruments are inherent in the instruments instead of – or in addition to – their use with very young students. If an instrument is not effective with a population slightly older than the target population, it is unlikely to be effective with very young children.

Appendix: Summary of the Eight Self-Concept Scales on the Self-Description Questionnaire

Physical Ability: Student perceptions of their skills and interest in sports, games, and physical activities.

Physical Appearance: Student perceptions of their physical attractiveness, how their appearance compares with that of others, and how others think they look.

Peer Relationships: Student perceptions of how easily they make friends, their popularity, and whether others want them as a friend.

Parent Relationships: Student perceptions of how well they get along with their parents, whether they like their parents, and the extent to which they feel parental acceptance and approval.

Reading: Student self-perceptions of their ability, enjoyment of, and interest in reading.

Math: Student self-perceptions of their ability, enjoyment of, and interest in mathematics.

School: Student self-perceptions of their ability, enjoyment of, and interest in school subjects in general.

Esteem: Student self-perceptions of themselves as effective, capable individuals who have self-confidence and self-respect and are proud and satisfied with the way they are.

References

Baltes, P. B., & Nesselroade, J. R. (Eds.). (1979). *Longitudinal research in the study of behavior and development*. New York: Academic Press.

Bentler, P. M. (1990). Comparative fit indices in structural models. *Psychological Bulletin, 107*, 238–246.

Bollen, K. A. (1989). *Structural equations with latent variables*. New York: Wiley.

Byrne, B. M. (1984). The general/academic self-concept nomological network: A review of construct validation research. *Review of Educational Research, 54*, 427–456.

Byrne, B. M. (1989). *A primer of LISREL: Basic applications and programming for confirmatory factor analytic models*. New York: Springer Verlag.

Byrne, B. (1996). *Measuring self-concept across the life span: Issues and instrumentation.* Washington, DC: American Psychological Association.

Campbell, D. T., & Fiske, D. W. (1959). Convergent and discriminant validation by the multitrait–multimethod matrix. *Psychological Bulletin, 56,* 81–105.

Chapman, J. W., & Tunmer, W. E. (1995). Development of children's reading self-concepts: An examination of emerging subcomponents and their relation with reading achievement. *Journal of Educational Psychology, 87,* 154–167.

Crain, R. M. (1996). The influence of age, race, and gender on child and adolescent multidimensional self-concept. In B. A. Bracken (Ed.), *Handbook of self-concept: Developmental, social, and clinical considerations* (pp. 395–420). New York: Wiley.

Dusek, J. B., & Flaherty, J. F. (1981). The development of self-concept during adolescent years. *Monographs of the Society for Research in Child Development, 46*(4, Serial No. 191).

Eccles, J. S., Adler, T. F., & Meece, J. L. (1984). Sex differences in achievement: A test of alternative theories. *Journal of Personality and Social Psychology, 46,* 26–43.

Eccles, J. S., & Wigfield, A. (1995). In the mind of the actor: The structure of adolescents' achievement task values and expectancy-related beliefs. *Personality and Social Psychology Bulletin, 21,* 215–225.

Eccles, J. S., Wigfield, A., Harold, R. D., & Blumenfeld, P. (1993). Age and gender differences in children's self- and task perceptions during elementary school. *Child Development, 64,* 830–847.

Feingold, A. (1994). Gender differences in personality: A meta-analysis. *Psychological Bulletin, 116,* 429–456.

Harter, S. (1983). Developmental perspectives on the self-system. In E. M. Hetherington (Ed.), P. H. Mussen (Series Ed.), *Handbook of child psychology: Vol. 4. Socialization, personality, and social development* (4th ed., pp. 275–385). New York: Wiley.

Harter, S. (1985). Competence as dimensions of self-evaluation: Toward a comprehensive model of self-worth. In R. L. Leahy (Ed.), *The development of self* (pp. 55–122). New York: Academic Press.

Harter, S. (1986). Processes underlying the construction, maintenance, and enhancement of self-concept in children. In S. Suls & A. Greenwald (Eds.), *Psychological perspectives of the self* (Vol. 3, pp. 136–182). Hillsdale, NJ: Erlbaum.

Harter, S., & Pike, R. (1984). The pictorial scale of perceived competence and social acceptance for young children. *Child Development, 55,* 1969–1982.

Hattie, J. (1992). *Self-concept.* Hillsdale, NJ: Erlbaum.

Jöreskog, K. G., & Sörbom, D. (1989). *LISREL 7: A guide to the program and applications.* Chicago: SPSS.

Joseph, B. W. (1979). *Pre-school and Primary Self-Concept Screening Test: Instruction manual.* Chicago: Stoelting.

Maccoby, E. E., & Jacklin, C. N. (1974). *The psychology of sex differences.* Stanford, CA: Stanford University Press.

Markus, H., & Wurf, E. (1987). The dynamic self-concept: A social psychological perspective. *Annual Review of Psychology, 38,* 299–337.

Marsh, H. W. (1985). Age and sex effects in multiple dimensions of preadolescent self-concept: A replication and extension. *Australian Journal of Psychology, 37,* 197–204.

Marsh, H. W. (1988). *Self Description Questionnaire: A theoretical and empirical basis for the measurement of multiple dimensions of preadolescent self-concept: A test manual and a research monograph.* San Antonio, TX: Psychological Corp.

Marsh, H. W. (1989). Age and sex effects in multiple dimensions of self-concept: Preadolescence to early-adulthood. *Journal of Educational Psychology, 81,* 417–430.

Marsh, H. W. (1990). A multidimensional, hierarchical model of self-concept: Theoretical and empirical justification. *Educational Psychology Review, 2,* 77–172.

Marsh, H. W. (1993a). Academic self-concept: Theory measurement and research. In J. Suls (Ed.), *Psychological perspectives on the self* (Vol. 4, pp. 59–98). Hillsdale, NJ: Erlbaum.

Marsh, H. W. (1993b). Stability of individual differences in multiwave panel studies: Comparison of simplex models and one-factor models. *Journal of Educational Measurement, 30,* 157–183.

Marsh, H. W., Balla, J. R., & Hau, K. T. (1996). An evaluation of incremental fit indices: A clarification of mathematical and empirical processes. In G. A. Marcoulides & R. E. Schumacker (Eds.), *Advanced structural equation modeling techniques* (pp. 315–353). Hillsdale, NJ: Erlbaum.

Marsh, H. W., Barnes, J., Cairns, L., & Tidman, M. (1984). The Self Description Questionnaire (SDQ): Age effects in the structure and level of self-concept for preadolescent children. *Journal of Educational Psychology, 76,* 940–956.

Marsh, H. W., Barnes, J., & Hocevar, D. (1985). Self–other agreement on multidimensional self-concept ratings: Factor analysis and multitrait–multimethod analysis. *Journal of Personality and Social Psychology, 49,* 1360–1377.

Marsh, H. W., & Byrne, B. M. (1993). Confirmatory factor analysis of multitrait–multimethod self-concept data: Between-group and within-group invariance constraints. *Multivariate Behavioral Research, 28,* 313–349.

Marsh, H. W., & Craven, R. G. (1991). Self–other agreement on multiple dimensions of preadolescent self-concept: The accuracy of inferences by teachers, mothers, and fathers. *Journal of Educational Psychology, 83,* 393–404.

Marsh, H. W., & Craven, R. G. (1997). Academic self-concept: Beyond the dust-bowl. In G. Phye (Ed.), *Handbook of classroom assessment: Learning, achievement and adjustment.* San Diego, CA: Academic Press.

Marsh, H. W., Craven, R. G., & Debus, R. L. (1991). Self-concepts of young children aged 5 to 8: Their measurement and multidimensional structure. *Journal of Educational Psychology, 83,* 377–392.

Marsh, H. W., & Grayson, D. (1995). Latent-variable models of multitrait–multimethod data. In R. H. Hoyle (Ed.), *Structural equation modeling: Issues and applications* (pp. 177–198). Newbury, CA: Sage.

Marsh, H. W., & Hattie, J. (1996). Theoretical perspectives on the structure of self-concept. In B. A. Bracken (Ed.), *Handbook of self-concept.* New York: Wiley.

Marsh, H. W., & Hocevar, D. (1985). The application of confirmatory factor analysis to the study of self-concept: First and higher order factor structures and their invariance across age groups. *Psychological Bulletin, 97,* 562–582.

McDonald, R. P., & Marsh, H. W. (1990). Choosing a multivariate model: Noncentrality and goodness of fit. *Psychological Bulletin, 107,* 247–255.

Nicholls, J. (1979). Development of perceptions of own attainment and causal attributions of success and failure in reading. *Journal of Educational Psychology, 71,* 94–99.

Norusis, M. J. (1993). *SPSS for Windows.* Chicago: SPSS.

Parsons, J. E., & Ruble, D. N. (1977). The development of achievement-related expectancies. *Child Development, 48,* 1075–1079.

Pedhazur, E. J., & Schmelkin, L. P. (1991). *Measurement, design and analysis: An integrated approach.* Hillsdale, NJ: Erlbaum.

Shavelson, R. J., Hubner, J. J., & Stanton, G. C. (1976). Validation of construct interpretations. *Review of Educational Research, 46,* 407–441.

Stipek, D. J. (1981). Children's perceptions of their own and their classmates' ability. *Journal of Educational Psychology, 73,* 404–410.

Stipek, D. J., & MacIver, D. (1989). Developmental change in children's assessment of intellectual competence. *Child Development, 60,* 521–538.

Wigfield, A. (1994). Expectancy-value theory of achievement motivation: A development perspective. *Educational Psychology Review, 6,* 49–78.

Wigfield, A., & Eccles, J. S. (1992). The development of achievement task values: A theoretical analysis. *Developmental Review, 12,* 265–310.

Wigfield, A., Eccles, J. S., MacIver, D., Reuman, D. A., & Midgley, C. (1991). Transitions during early adolescence: Changes in children's domain specific self-perceptions and general self-esteem across the transition to junior high school. *Developmental Psychology, 27,* 552–565.

Wigfield, A., Eccles, J. S., Yoon, K. S., Harold, R. D., Arbreton, A. J., Freedman-Doan, C., & Blumenfeld, P. C. (1997). Changes in children's competence beliefs and subjective task values across the elementary school years: A three-year study. *Journal of Educational Psychology, 89,* 451–469.

Wylie, R. C. (1979). *The self-concept* (Vol. 2). Lincoln: University of Nebraska Press.

Wylie, R. C. (1989). *Measures of self-concept.* Lincoln: University of Nebraska Press.

TEN

Moral Reasoning

Introduction

One important developmental task is learning right from wrong. Moral development involves learning the rules and conventions about what individuals should do in their interactions with others. There are three aspects of morality: (1) moral reasoning – how individuals think about rules of ethical conduct; (2) moral self-evaluation – how individuals feel about moral issues; (3) moral behavior – how individuals behave when confronted with moral dilemmas. These aspects reflect the cognitive, affective, and behavioral components of morality, respectively.

Early in development, children are faced with the dilemma of satisfying their own needs or meeting the demands and restrictions placed on them by their parents and society. With age, these conflicts change from basic "dos and don'ts" that are learned by rote, such as remembering to say please and thank you, don't take the cookie, etc., to more complex and abstract rules, such as that it is wrong to steal or to endanger another person's well-being. As they develop, children learn to control their behavior by adopting standards of conduct for themselves and feeling guilt when they fail to meet these standards. They develop into adolescents and adults who can appreciate the logic behind society's rules, which are based on considerations of mutual respect for others.

This article by Smetana, Killen, and Turiel examines the concept of moral reasoning, with particular reference to Jean Piaget, Lawrence Kohlberg, and Carol Gilligan. Piaget and Kohlberg pioneered studies of moral reasoning, thereby presenting a cognitive perspective of moral development. Piaget (1932) argued that as children develop they become more sophisticated in their moral reasoning due to their increased cognitive capacities and the experience of negotiating conflict resolutions with peers. Kohlberg (1986) agreed with Piaget, and extended Piaget's notions by identifying six stages of moral reasoning.

In brief, these six stages can be characterized as (1) avoiding punishment, (2) seeking rewards, (3) gaining approval or disapproval, (4) conforming to society's rules and laws, (5) accepting the principles of the community, and (6) acting according to personal conscience. Kohlberg proposed that these stages are universal (i.e., they are found in all societies), occur in sequence, and are age related. For example, children younger than age nine tend to reason at the level of stages 1 and 2; adolescents reason at stages 3 and 4, and adults may operate at stages 5 and 6.

Critics of Kohlberg argue that his theory does not relate moral reasoning to behavior, does not take into account cultural differences, and is male biased. With respect to the latter point, Gilligan (1982) proposed that the theory needs to incorporate individuals' relationships and connectedness with others. This can be considered a "caring perspective," and it has been argued that it is much more typically found in women than in men. Smetana et al.'s article includes an examination of gender differences in moral reasoning.

References

Gilligan, C. (1982). *In a different voice*. Cambridge, MA: Harvard University Press.

Kohlberg, L. (1986). A current statement on some theoretical issues. In S. Modgil & C. Modgil (eds), *Lawrence Kohlberg*. Philadelphia: Falmer.

Piaget, J. (1932). *The moral judgement of the child*. New York: Harcourt Brace Jovanovich.

Children's Reasoning about Interpersonal and Moral Conflicts

Judith G. Smetana, Melanie Killen,
and Elliot Turiel

A complex and vexing problem for moral theory and research on social development is the connection between interpersonal relationships and particularistic or generalized moral obligations. Interpersonal and moral considerations are important aspects of social interactions that can be in conflict. On the one hand, it is recognized that persons in close relationships (e.g., friends, family) have special obligations to each other. On the other hand, concerns with issues like justice, rights, and welfare are thought to entail obligations that often transcend particular interpersonal ties. For example, from the moral point of view, there are problems with favoritism in the distribution of goods, or with granting certain rights to and ensuring the welfare of only some people (such as friends, family, or members of one's racial and ethnic group) and not others. At the same time, subordinating the interests of close relations in favor of abstract moral claims of strangers is problematic, certainly from a subjective perspective, and perhaps from an ethical one (Scheffler, 1988; Williams, 1981).

The link between interpersonal relationships and considerations of justice, rights, or welfare has been considered in several approaches to social and moral development (e.g., Damon, 1977; Selman, 1980). In particular, there is an ongoing debate regarding how to best characterize the development of justice and interpersonal concerns. Gilligan (1982) has argued that Kohlberg's (1969, 1971) formulation of stages of moral development fails to adequately distinguish a morality of justice from a morality of care in interpersonal concerns and that, in Kohlberg's sequence, the latter is relegated to lower stages. Gilligan and her colleagues (e.g., Gilligan & Attanucci, 1988) propose that interpersonal concerns and justice constitute two distinct types of moral orientation linked to gender, and that each type can take a different developmental trajectory in different individuals. For the most part, morality in males is dominated by concerns with justice and rights; for females it is dominated by concerns with care in interpersonal relationships.[1]

In the present research, we explored the proposition that concerns with interpersonal relationships and justice coexist within individuals (males and females) across development, and that the ways they are applied or coordinated may partially depend on parameters of the situation in which judgments are made. This perspective is adopted from research demonstrating that children form domains of social knowledge, including morality (justice, rights, welfare), social convention, and psychological issues (Nucci, 1981; Smetana, 1985; Turiel, 1983; Turiel, Smetana, & Killen, 1991). The research indicates that individuals hold heterogeneous social orientations and coordinate and weigh different situational features when evaluating situations that entail social conflicts.

For most people, maintaining and fostering interpersonal relationships is a central social consideration. However, judgments about justice or welfare can apply to persons in close relationships and to those with lesser or no interpersonal ties. Therefore, concerns with interpersonal relations can be in conflict with justice, rights, or welfare considerations in at least two ways. Justice or welfare considerations can conflict with an interpersonal concern that is morally neutral or even negative (e.g., giving priority to a friend in distributing resources when a stranger has a more just claim). There also can be a conflict in the application of justice or welfare considerations in interpersonal and impersonal relationships (e.g., choosing between helping a sibling or a stranger when both are in need). If interpersonal and justice considerations do coexist in males and females, then we would expect that the ways these considerations are applied by them will, at least in part, depend on the situation (e.g., the nature of the relationship, the salience of an injustice). For instance, in situations in which the justice considerations are not in strong conflict with interpersonal considerations, females and males might give priority to justice and rights over interpersonal concerns, whereas in other situations, they might give priority to maintaining interpersonal relationships over justice. Our proposition, therefore, differs from the proposition that features of the situations (for instance, the type of dilemma) interact with subjects' gender in influencing responses of justice or care (Miller & Luthar, 1989; Pratt et al., 1988; Rothbart et al., 1986; Walker et al., 1987), as well as the proposition that the moral status of each type of orientation is culturally determined (Miller, Bersoff, & Harwood, 1990).

Two studies were undertaken in the present research. One aim was to ascertain if females and males differentiate justice concerns from concerns with maintaining and fostering interpersonal relationships, and if their judgments are influenced by situational features. In this regard, we distinguished among maintenance of relationships, concerns with welfare (avoiding harm to others), and justice or rights. It should be noted, therefore, that this research was not designed as a direct test of Gilligan's hypotheses since our definition of interpersonal concerns differs somewhat from hers. Gilligan's care orientation focuses primarily on positive responsiveness to others (though her definition does include a concern with maintaining relationships). Study 1 examined interpersonal concerns in the context of avoiding harm or unfairness to others. This was done in order to assess whether children differentiate justice and concerns with maintaining relationships.

In Study 1, the situations initially presented to children posed justice or rights considerations in conflict with interpersonal expectations (from a close friend) serving motives of self-interest. Therefore, in these situations justice and rights considerations were in conflict with interpersonal expectations which did not have compelling welfare, justice, or rights components. In addition, the salience of each type of consideration was systematically varied either by changing the interpersonal relationship (from close friend to sibling to acquaintance) or by changing the magnitude of the violation of justice or rights. It was expected that females and males would give priority to the justice or rights considerations in the initially presented situations, and that their judgments would change in accord with shifts in the salience of the situational components.

Study 2 included stronger conflicts between justice and claims of an interpersonal nature by presenting situations in which the interpersonal expectations were positive in their intent and goals (not motivated by self-interest). Study 2 more directly pertains to Gilligan's care orientation than Study 1, since concerns with welfare, justice, and rights could be applied to interpersonal relations and impersonally. Our expectation was that situational features would be more important than gender in children's justice or interpersonal considerations.

Study 1

One aim of Study 1 was to ascertain whether, in certain situations, both males and females make judgments based primarily on justice and rights, even in interpersonal contexts. Toward this end, children were presented with hypothetical situations which posed the possibility of committing a transgression to maintain a friendship by furthering the self-interest of the friend. For each of two types of transgression, unequal distribution (fairness) and stealing (property rights), children were presented with a conflict (referred to as the Initial Situation), and their evaluations and reasoning were assessed. A further aim of Study 1 was to determine whether judgments are influenced by changes in the salience of the interpersonal or fairness/rights components. The salience of the components in each situation were systematically varied by presenting children with different information.

The interpersonal components of the situations were varied by altering only the type of relationship depicted. In one variation, the interpersonal relationship was described as between acquaintances (thus decreasing the salience), and in the other, the relationship was described as involving siblings (thus increasing the salience). The salience of the fairness or rights components was varied by changing the magnitude of the transgression. In the situation pertaining to unequal distribution, the salience of the fairness component was increased by depicting the transgression as more severe than in the Initial Situation, whereas in the stealing situation, the transgression was depicted as less severe. As previous research has shown that stealing is evaluated as more wrong than unequal distribution (Smetana, 1981; Smetana, Kelly, & Twentyman, 1984), this was done to counterbalance differences between the two situations in the magnitude of the transgression depicted. Second, the type of transgression was varied to assess additional fairness or rights transgressions. Thus, in one variation, physical harm was pitted against maintaining a friendship, whereas in the other variation a trust violation was pitted against maintaining a friendship.

Subjects evaluated what the story protagonist should do and provided justifications for their choices. In addition, the ways that children weighed the different alternatives were also examined by coding whether children discussed both fairness/rights and the interpersonal choices in making their judgments or whether they considered only one alternative. This was done as a further test of the hypothesis that children separate and distinguish between fairness/rights and interpersonal issues.

It was expected that in the Initial Situations, children would generally judge that fairness or rights considerations should have priority over friendship expectations. However, in situations in which the interpersonal considerations were more salient (e.g., the sibling condition) and/or the fairness/rights components were less salient, it was expected that children would give priority to maintaining the interpersonal relationship. Finally, it was expected that children would give priority to justice/rights when these considerations were made more salient.

Method

Subjects

Subjects in this study were 48 children evenly divided into eight males and eight females at the third, sixth, and ninth grades (mean ages = 8.40, 11.38, 14.38 years, respectively). Subjects, who were middle class and from different ethnic groups, came from one elementary school and one junior high school in the San Francisco Bay area.

Procedure

Each subject was individually administered questions pertaining to two hypothetical situations by a female interviewer who was blind to the hypotheses of the study. The interviews took approximately 35 minutes and were tape-recorded and transcribed. Each situation began with an initial description of a conflict between a fairness or rights precept and an expectation from a friend (the Initial Situation). The story descriptions, questions, and salience variations are summarized in table 1. Story 1 depicts a child who is requested by a friend to distribute candy

Table 1   Story themes and conditions for Study 1

Sharing story

Initial Situation: Bob brings candy to share with everyone. His close friend George does not want Bob to give candy to Tim. George and Tim do not get along and Tim has been picking on George.

Interpersonal condition – Acquaintance: Bob is asked by an acquaintance (who does not get along with Tim) to not share with Tim.

Interpersonal condition – Sibling: Bob is asked by his brother (who does not get along with Tim) to not share with Tim.

Greater Need condition: Bob, who is in charge of distributing lunches, does not give one to Tim because he had picked on George.

Physical Harm condition: Bob inflicts physical harm on Tim to please George.

Stealing story

Initial Situation: Pat asks her close friend Diane to steal a set of pens accessible to Diane and needed by Pat.

Interpersonal condition – Acquaintance: Diane is asked by an acquaintance to take pens.

Interpersonal condition – Sibling: Diane is asked by her sister to take pens.

Less Need condition: Diane is asked to take a pack of gum for her friend.

Trust condition: Diane is asked to break a promise in order to engage in an activity with her friend.

---

unequally. Story 2 depicts a child who is asked by a friend to steal for her. For the Initial Situations, subjects were asked to make judgments as to what the protagonist should do and why. Then, subjects were asked about two interpersonal variations of the Initial Situation: whether the transgression should be done (*a*) for an acquaintance and (*b*) for a sibling (referred to as the Acquaintance and Sibling conditions, respectively). Finally, subjects were presented with two variations in fairness and rights that increased the magnitude of the transgressions. First, the amount of need was varied. In the distributive justice story, a situation of greater need of distribution (increased salience of fairness) was described, and in the stealing story, a situation of less need for the goods (increased salience of property rights) was described (Greater Need and Less Need conditions, respectively). In another variation, the type of act was changed to depict physical harm (instead of distributive justice) and violating a trust (instead of stealing). These changes in the type of act were made to include more than one stimulus item for each story (Physical Harm and Trust Violation conditions, respectively). For each story, five sets of judgments and justifications were obtained (table 1).

Coding and reliability

Responses were coded using three systems developed for this study but based on previous work (Davidson, Turiel, & Black, 1983; Killen, 1990). Twelve protocols, four from subjects at each grade level, were randomly selected to refine the coding systems. The coders, all of whom were females, were unaware of the study's hypotheses and subjects' gender. First, *judgments* as to what the protagonist should do were coded dichotomously as (1) affirming the choice of fairness (sharing) or rights (not stealing), or (2) affirming the interpersonal choice. The second coding, referred to as *coordination of components*, assessed the extent to which children integrated different choices when evaluating the conflicts. Responses were coded into two categories: a focus on both considerations and a focus on only one element. Third, *justifications* for choices were coded into five categories: (*a*) *fairness–welfare*: fairness ("it's not fair"), physical welfare ("she'll get hurt"), and psychological welfare ("he'll feel bad"); (*b*) *interpersonal*: maintain friendship/familial relationships or establish friendship ("it's the best thing to do so that they can stay friends"); (*c*) *psychological*: dispositional or personality characteristics of an actor as basis for evaluating an act ("if he doesn't give the candy to George he will become a greedy person and grow up to be mean"); (*d*) *conventional*: violation of a social norm ("he would be breaking the school rule"); and (*e*) *personal*: act within individual jurisdiction ("he can do whatever he wants; it's up to him to decide"). In coding justifications, we followed the procedure used in previous research (Davidson et al., 1983) of combining fairness and welfare responses (welfare is defined as acts that negatively affect another's physical or psychological well-being). There were no differences on the major study variables (age, sex, or condition) between fairness and welfare responses. In Story 1, fairness and welfare responses occurred in equal frequencies. Story 2 resulted in greater use of fairness (79%) than welfare (21%) responses.

Interrater reliability between two coders using 12 protocols in coding judgments, coordination of components, and justifications (using Cohen's kappa) was .80, .83, and .82, respectively.

Results

Judgments

Table 2 displays the percentage of children at each age who gave priority to sharing equally (Story 1) and not stealing (Story 2) for each
condition. Responses for each story were analyzed by a 3 (grade) × 2
(sex) × 5 (salience condition) repeated-measures analysis of variance
(ANOVA) with condition as the repeated measure. Responses were
arcsine-transformed to correct for nonnormality, which may sometimes
occur with the use of percentages (Winer, 1971). In these and other
analyses, Duncan multiple-range tests and Bonferroni *t* tests were performed to test for significant between-subjects and within-subjects
effects, respectively.

Story 1: Sharing. As can be seen in table 2, for the most part the majority of subjects gave priority to the act of sharing (83% in the Initial Situation; 87% overall). However, responses did vary by salience condition,
$F(4,164) = 13.98, p < .0001$. As expected, Bonferroni *t* tests showed that
greater priority was given to avoiding the transgression in the Physical

Table 2   Responses (in %) affirming sharing and not stealing

	Grade 3		Grade 6		Grade 9		
Story and condition	Males	Females	Males	Females	Males	Females	Total
Sharing story:							
Initial Situation	100	88	63	88	86	75	83
Interpersonal – Acquaintance	75	100	88	100	100	100	94
Interpersonal – Sibling	88	75	63	100	43	75	74
Greater Need	100	88	88	100	86	100	94
Physical Harm[a]	100	100	88	100	100	100	98
Stealing story:							
Initial Situation	88	75	13	75	14	38	51
Interpersonal – Acquaintance	100	100	75	100	71	88	89
Interpersonal – Sibling	88	75	13	88	43	50	60
Less Need	100	100	63	88	71	63	81
Trust Violation[b]	88	88	50	25	0	0	43

[a] *The Physical Harm condition was in place of sharing.*

[b] *The Trust Violation condition was in place of not stealing.*

Harm condition (98%) than in the Initial Situation (83%) or in the Sibling condition (74%; p's $< .005$). In addition, greater priority was given to sharing in the Greater Need condition (94%) than in the Sibling condition ($p < .005$). There were no significant main effects for sex (females $= 93\%$; males $= 84\%$) or grade (91%, 88%, and 87% for third, sixth, and ninth grades, respectively), and sex did not interact significantly with condition or grade.

Story 2: Stealing.   As with sharing, there was a main effect for salience condition, $F(4,164) = 15.16$, $p < .0001$. As expected, Bonferroni t tests indicated that children more frequently gave priority to the prescription against stealing in the Acquaintance condition (89%) or in the Less Need condition (81%) than when asked to steal by a friend as described in the Initial Situation (51%; p's $< .005$). In addition, children more frequently judged it wrong to steal in the Acquaintance condition than in the Sibling condition (60%), or to break a promise in the Trust Violation condition (43%; p's $< .005$). Children also judged it more wrong to steal in the Less Need condition than to break a promise in the Trust Violation condition ($p < .005$). There was no significant main effect for sex (males $= 58\%$, females $= 70\%$ giving priority to not stealing). However, responses varied by grade, $F(2,41) = 17.80$; $p < .0001$. Third graders gave greater priority to not stealing than did sixth and ninth graders (90%, 59%, 44%, respectively).

There was a significant grade $\times$ condition interaction, $F(8,164) = 2.21$, $p < .05$. In the Initial Situation, third graders gave greater priority to not stealing than did sixth or ninth graders, $F(2,41) = 6.68$, $p < .01$. In the Trust Violation condition, third graders more frequently judged it wrong to break a promise than did sixth or ninth graders, and sixth graders more frequently judged it wrong to break a promise than did ninth graders, $F(2,41) = 23.39$, $p < .0001$. Furthermore, in the Less Need condition, third graders gave greater priority to not stealing than did ninth graders, $F(2,41) = 3.19$, $p < .05$. A similar finding was obtained for the Sibling condition, which approached significance, $F(2,41) = 3.00$, $p < .06$.

Coordination of components

In order to assess whether subjects considered the two components in arriving at their choices, analyses were performed on the percentage of responses entailing a consideration of both fairness/rights and interpersonal components. A 3 (grade) × 2 (sex) × 5 (salience condition) repeated-measures ANOVA with condition as the repeated measure was performed separately upon arcsine-transformed responses for each story.

Story 1: Sharing.   The majority of responses (72% overall) indicated a consideration of the two components in making judgments, although this varied by salience condition, as indicated by a significant main effect, $F(4,164) = 8.15$, $p < .0001$. Subjects more frequently considered both fairness and interpersonal components in the Initial Situation (92%) and the Sibling condition (81%) than in the Greater Need condition (50%).

Sex was not significant in this analysis. However, age differences were obtained. Sixth and ninth graders considered both components to a greater extent than did third graders, $F(2,41) = 10.30$, $p < .001$ (79%, 84%, 52%, respectively). A grade × condition interaction, $F(8,164) = 3.24$, $p < .05$, indicated that differences occurred in the Acquaintance condition, $F(2,41) = 8.89$, $p < .001$, the Greater Need condition, $F(2,41) = 6.87$, $p < .01$, and the Physical Harm condition, $F(2,41) = 5.54$, $p < .01$. In the Acquaintance and Physical Harm conditions, sixth and ninth graders considered both elements to a greater extent than did third graders (82%, 94%, 37% in the Acquaintance condition; 88%, 72%, 37% in the Physical Harm condition); in the Greater Need condition, ninth graders considered both elements to a greater extent than did third graders (80%, 19%).

Story 2: Stealing.   In this story, too, the majority of responses (63%) indicated a consideration of both components. A main effect for salience condition, $F(4,164) = 7.77$, $p < .0001$, revealed that subjects considered both components to a greater extent in the Initial Situation (91%) than in the Acquaintance, Sibling, Less Need, and Trust Violation conditions (55%, 66%, 51%, 51%, respectively; p's $< .0001$). A main effect for grade, $F(2,41) = 6.23$, $p < .01$, indicated that, as with the previous story, sixth and ninth graders considered both components to a greater extent than did third graders (72%, 72%, 45%, respectively).

Justifications

The justifications were separated by subjects' choices in the stories. Table 3 presents the percentage of justification categories used by subjects at

Table 3 Justifications (in %) affirming sharing and not stealing

		Sharing story			Stealing story		
	Grade:	3	6	9	3	6	9
Initial Situation:							
Fairness–welfare		60	33	40	69	44	23
Interpersonal		18	12	13	12	0	3
Psychological		18	33	30	0	0	3
Other		0	0	0	0	0	3
Interpersonal – Acquaintance:							
Fairness–welfare		57	72	43	75	66	53
Interpersonal		14	9	50	9	6	23
Psychological		11	9	0	16	16	6
Other		0	3	7	0	0	0
Interpersonal – Sibling:							
Fairness–welfare		47	41	26	59	25	37
Interpersonal		25	16	10	0	6	3
Psychological		9	22	23	22	19	3
Other		0	9	0	0	0	0
Need:[a]							
Fairness–welfare		92	69	73	91	69	80
Interpersonal		2	3	3	0	0	0
Psychological		3	19	7	3	6	0
Other		0	0	10	6	0	0
Physical Harm/Trust Violation:[b]							
Fairness–welfare		71	49	76	75	31	0
Interpersonal		15	9	10	6	0	0
Psychological		15	34	12	3	6	0
Other		0	0	0	3	0	0

[a] *This condition depicted greater need for the sharing story and Lesser Need for the not stealing story.*
[b] *The Physical Harm condition was in place of sharing and the Trust Violation condition was in place of not stealing.*

each grade and for each condition for the choice to share and not steal. (Because there were so few sex differences, responses for boys and girls are combined). Since conventional and personal justifications were used infrequently, they were combined into an Other category and dropped from further analysis. Each justification could have been used with either choice in the story (e.g., the interpersonal justification for a sharing choice or a fairness–welfare justification for an interpersonal choice). The table shows that three categories (fairness–welfare, interpersonal, and psychological) were primarily used for the sharing and not stealing choices. For each story, separate 3 (grade) × 2 (sex) × 5 (salience condition) repeated-measures multivariate analyses of variance (MANOVAs) were performed on the arcsine-transformed proportions of responses in the fairness–welfare, interpersonal, and psychological categories.[2]

Three categories (fairness–welfare, interpersonal, and personal choice) were used in explaining the interpersonal choices of not sharing and not stealing. Given their low frequency, however, these data were not statistically analyzed.

Story 1: Sharing. The MANOVA revealed differences in justifications for the choice of sharing, $F(2,38) = 43.96$, $p < .0001$; overall, fairness–welfare justifications (54%) were used more frequently than interpersonal (12%) or psychological (20%) justifications (p's $< .0001$). There was a significant main effect for salience condition in justifications on the MANOVA, $F(8,32) = 10.03$, $p < .0001$. Bonferroni t tests revealed that children more frequently used welfare–fairness justifications in the conditions with increased salience of the fairness component: they were used more in the Greater Need and Physical Harm conditions than in the Initial Situation (p's $< .0001$) and in the Greater Need condition than in the Sibling condition ($p < .0001$). Children more frequently used interpersonal justifications in the Initial Situation and the Acquaintance condition than in the Greater Need condition (p's $< .005$). Psychological justifications were used more frequently in the Initial Situation than in the Acquaintance or Greater Need conditions (p's $< .005$). Finally, the MANOVA also revealed a significant salience condition × grade interaction in justifications, $F(16,64) = 3.04$, $p < .001$. There were grade × condition interactions for fairness–welfare justifications, $F(8,168) = 2.93$, $p < .01$, and interpersonal justifications, $F(8,168) = 2.97$, $p < .01$. In the Initial Situation, third graders gave more fairness–welfare justifications than did sixth or ninth graders, $F(2,44) = 6.62$, $p < .01$, whereas in the Physical Harm condition, third and ninth graders gave more fairness–welfare justifications than did sixth graders, $F(2,44) = 4.08$, $p < .05$. In the Acquaintance condition, ninth graders gave more interpersonal justifications than did third or sixth graders,

$F(2,42) = 5.33$, $p < .01$. No sex differences in justifications were obtained.

Story 2: Stealing.   The justifications for the choice of not stealing paralleled the sharing choice in that the fairness–welfare justification was used more often than the others, as indicated by significant differences, among justifications, $F(2,40) = 124.73$, $p < .0001$ fairness–welfare = 50%; interpersonal = 3%; psychological = 5%). The MANOVA also revealed a main effect for grade, $F(4,80) = 6.26$, $p < .001$. Third graders more frequently justified the wrongness of stealing on the basis of fairness–welfare concerns than did sixth or ninth graders, $F(2,44) = 8.51$, $p < .0001$. Finally, the MANOVA revealed a significant main effect for salience condition, $F(8,34) = 5.63$, $p < .0001$. Children more frequently used welfare–fairness justifications in the Less Need condition than in the Initial Situation or the Acquaintance condition, p's $< .005$. Children more frequently used interpersonal justifications in the Acquaintance condition than in the Greater Need condition, p's $< .005$.

Discussion

Study 1 demonstrates that children of both genders make judgments about justice and rights both in situations in which justice or rights considerations were in minimal conflict with interpersonal considerations (e.g., the Initial Situations) and in situations in which the salience of the fairness–rights and interpersonal considerations were varied (to shift the balance between the two components). For most conditions, the majority of children gave priority to the fairness and rights choices over meeting the expectations of a friend, and their fairness and welfare justifications were consonant with their evaluations. There were no gender differences in the use of either fairness or welfare justifications.

The study also demonstrated that females and males take into consideration interpersonal concerns, and that they are attended to situational features. With regard to stealing, children gave greater priority to interpersonal relationships and judged it more acceptable to violate rights for a friend or a sibling than for an acquaintance. In turn, the salience of the fairness and rights components influenced children's judgments and reasoning. For instance, when the need to share was increased (Greater Need condition in Story 1) or when the transgressions would result in physical harm, most children subordinated the interpersonal consideration. Similarly, when a child was asked by a friend to steal something of lesser need (Story 2), most subjects did not give priority to the interpersonal consideration. Reasoning in these situations was consistent with evaluations since children used fairness–welfare justifications to an even greater extent in the conditions with increased salience of the justice or rights components.

Based on previous research (Davidson et al., 1983; Smetana, 1985; Turiel, 1983), justifications pertaining to welfare and rights were combined in these analyses and compared to interpersonal justifications, which pertained primarily to maintaining friendships. This differs from previous research more directly testing Gilligan's hypotheses, where reasoning regarding care and interpersonal relations has been combined (e.g., Gilligan & Attanucci, 1988; Lyons, 1983; Miller & Luthar, 1989; Rothbart et al., 1986; Walker et al., 1987). It is possible that this procedure underestimated the prevalence of "care" responses in our sample. However, our conclusions are based on the findings for judgments as well as justifications, and it is important to note the congruence between them.

Analyses of the coordination of components represent a more fine-grained assessment of whether children are cognizant of each component than assessments of judgments. In some conditions, children of all the ages and both genders considered both components in their judgments. However, the finding that with age children become more consistent in considering both components when the two are placed in greater conflict must be interpreted cautiously. These findings may reflect an increased cognitive capacity to coordinate components in situations with greater conflicts, or they may simply reflect an increased ability to express judgments about the two components. In any event, the findings are consistent with Walker et al. (1987), who found that individuals at higher levels of moral development evidenced substantial amounts of both response and rights orientations in their reasoning. If our results were to reflect changes in cognitive capacities, it would indicate that, with age, children take more aspects of the situation into account in making judgments. More generally, the extent to which children evaluated both components varied according to the different salience conditions. Considered in conjunction with the results from the analysis of judgments, Study 1 suggests that children focused solely on

justice and rights only in situations where those claims were most compelling (e.g., in situations of greater need) and in situations where
the interpersonal claims were less convincing (e.g., the Acquaintance
condition).

Study 1 primarily ascertained that female and male children reason
on the basis of justice, rights, and welfare when those considerations are
in conflict with self-interested interpersonal expectations from friends or
siblings. The study did not address how children make judgments and
reason about conflicts in which the interpersonal expectations have
legitimacy and in which acts are performed to be helpful, kind, or con-
siderate to another (rather than to avoid losing a friendship). Furthermore, since the order of conditions was not varied in Study 1, it is
possible that the effects found for salience conditions were due to repeatedly asking children the same questions. Finally, the results may be
unreliable due to the small sample size. Study 2 was designed to address
these issues.

Study 2

Study 1 established that the availability of either interpersonal or justice
concepts does not differ by gender and provided a context for additional
research on judgments about compelling conflicts between the two types
of considerations. It is possible that females are more oriented than
males to interpersonal considerations with positive intent and goals, as
others (Rothbart et al., 1986) have claimed. There is no indication of
this, however, from Study 1. Our hypothesis, instead, as noted earlier, is
that the application of both justice and interpersonal concerns depends
on elements of the situation.

The stimulus situations in Study 2 posed conflicts between justice or
rights and interpersonal relationship calling for helpful or kind acts. Subjects were posed with situations in which an interpersonal act that
benefits a friend or sibling entails unfairness or violation of rights toward
an acquaintance or stranger. It is important to note that these stimulus
situations (unlike Study 1) involve conflicts between welfare in interpersonal contexts, on the one hand, and impartial justice and rights considerations on the other. This comparison should be kept in mind when
interpreting our terminology (for simplicity's sake we continue to refer to
the components as interpersonal and justice/rights).

Three stories were used in Study 2. One depicted a brother's attempt to care for his vulnerable younger sister; by helping his sister the boy's action would result in unfair treatment of another female. In the second story, a girl chooses between (*a*) meeting a sick friend's request to help her complete a task to win a science fair contest, and (*b*) a boy's claim that doing so would violate the fairness of the competition. The third story was a conflict between welfare and property rights modeled after situations used by Kohlberg (1969) and Gilligan (1982), but adjusted to be more comprehensible to children. The conflict revolved around the choice to steal in order to protect the physical welfare of a sibling. We hypothesized that judgments and justifications would vary by the situation and that there would be no gender differences.

The methods of this study were similar to those of Study 1. Subjects were asked to judge and provide justifications about an Initial Situation. Then they were presented with conditions varying the salience of justice/rights and interpersonal components. Because Study 2 had three stories instead of two, the moral and interpersonal components were each varied in one condition (rather than two) to reduce the demands on the subjects. Since Study 1 indicated that nearly all children gave priority to justice/rights in the Acquaintance condition, this condition was dropped in Study 2. The interpersonal conditions thus either depicted a friend or a sibling, depending on the relationship described in the Initial Situation. This, in turn, was varied to control for order effects in each story. The justice/rights conditions in the three stories varied in depicting situations of greater need, a different act (lying), and a rule violation.

Method

Subjects

A different sample of subjects from those in Study 1, consisting of 76 children (39 males and 37 females), was used in Study 2. There were 13 males and 11 females at the third grade, 14 males and 12 females at the sixth grade, and 12 males and 14 females at the ninth grade (mean ages = 9.08, 12.10, 14.92 years, respectively). As in Study 1, they were of mixed ethnicity and middle class. They were recruited from two elementary schools and two junior high schools in the San Francisco Bay area.

Procedure

Subjects were individually administered questions about three hypothetical situations, presented in counterbalanced order, by two females who were blind to the hypotheses of the study. The interview took about 40 minutes and was tape-recorded and transcribed. The story descriptions, question, and variations in the components are summarized in table 4. The first two stories (referred to as the music club and science club stories) depict conflicts between fairness and welfare in

Table 4 Story themes and conditions for Study 2

Music club story

Initial Situation: Sam, the leader of an afterschool club, lets his younger sister join the club to stop other children from teasing her. There is only space for one new member, and another girl is more deserving.

Interpersonal condition – Friend: Sam lets a friend into the club instead of another more deserving person.

Greater Need condition: The other girl would lose all her friends and be very unhappy if she were not in the club.

Science project story

Initial Situation: Amy is too sick to work on her science fair project and asks her best friend Sally to help her finish it. John, who is also competing in the science fair, thinks it would be unfair to have someone else help Amy on her project.

Interpersonal condition – Sibling: Sally is asked by her younger sister to finish the work.

Rule Violation condition: The contest has an explicit rule prohibiting obtaining help.

Hurt brother story

Initial Situation: Walking home with his brother Jimmy, Marvin trips and cuts his leg. Very worried about his brother and not having enough money to call their mother, Jimmy goes to a store, but the storeowner won't let him use his phone. Jimmy takes $10 lying on the register to make a phone call to their mother.

Interpersonal condition – Friend: It is Jimmy's friend who is hurt rather than his brother.

Lying condition: Jimmy lies to the storeowner, telling him the $10 belongs to him.

---

interpersonal relationships, and the third (the hurt brother story) depicts a conflict between protecting the physical welfare of a sibling and theft (the violation of property rights served interpersonal and welfare ends).

The situations were presented in the same way as in the previous study. To prevent fatigue because of an additional story, only one interpersonal and one justice/rights condition were presented for each story (see table 4). Since the Initial Situations in two stories depicted sibling relationships, the relationship was varied to depict a friendship. The Initial Situation of the other story described a friendship relationship, and therefore in the interpersonal condition, a sibling relationship was described. Each story also had a different variation in the magnitude of the fairness or rights component. In the music club story, the salience of the fairness component was increased by describing a situation of greater need on the part of the girl than the sister. In the science project story, the fairness condition included the existence of an explicit rule prohibiting help for the contestants. In the hurt brother story, the type of act was varied to depict a lie in conjunction with theft. As in Study 1, for each condition the child was asked to judge what the protagonist should do and why. Thus, for each of three stories, three sets of judgments and justifications were obtained.

Coding and reliability

The three coding schemes from Study 1 were used. The first was a dichotomous assessment of *judgments* as to what the protagonist should do. The second was an assessment of the extent to which children integrated different choices when evaluating the conflicts (the *coordination of components* coding), with responses coded into two categories (focus on both components and focus on only one component). *Justifications* were coded using the same categories as in Study 1, with the addition of a *pragmatic* category (retribution or fear of punishment) that had not been given by subjects in Study 1. There were no age, sex, or condition effects in the comparisons of fairness and welfare justifications. Fairness and welfare justifications were used in each of the stories; they were mainly divided in accordance with choices in the stories. Interrater reliability, calculated as kappa coefficients between two coders scoring 20 protocols, was .86, .80, and .85 for judgments, coordination of components, and justifications, respectively.

Results

Judgments

Table 5 displays the percentage of children at each age who gave priority to the fairness or rights choices (i.e., not admitting the sister in the music club story, not helping the friend in the science project story, and not taking the money in the hurt brother story). The analyses were conducted on the percentage of children at each age who gave priority to the fairness or rights choices (i.e., not admitting the sister in the music club story, not helping the friend in the science project story, and not taking the money in the hurt brother story). Arcsine-transformed responses for each story were analyzed by 3 (grade) × 2 (sex) × 3 (salience condition) repeated-measure ANOVAs with condition as the repeated measure. Again, Duncan multiple-range tests and Bonferroni *t* tests were used to test significant effects.

Story 1: The music club story. As seen in table 5, subjects were evenly split in their choices for the Initial Situation (51% and 49%) and the Greater Need condition (54% and 46%). However, responses did vary by

Table 5 Responses (in %) endorsing the noninterpersonal choice (not admitting sister/not taking money/not helping friend)

	Grade 3		Grade 6		Grade 9		
Story and condition	*Males*	*Females*	*Males*	*Females*	*Males*	*Females*	*Total*
Music club story:							
Initial Situation	23	55	57	25	75	71	51
Interpersonal – Friend	85	100	93	92	100	100	95
Greater Need	23	55	64	33	75	71	54
Hurt brother story:							
Initial Situation	62	73	50	33	58	64	57
Interpersonal – Friend	77	73	29	42	50	64	55
Lying	85	100	86	83	92	100	91
Science project story:							
Initial Situation	15	18	36	8	17	36	22
Interpersonal – Sibling	15	9	21	8	17	29	17
Rule Violation	92	91	79	75	92	86	84

salience condition, $F(2,140) = 42.26$, $p < .0001$. The interpersonal condition (Friend rather than Sibling) resulted in more frequent affirmation of the fairness choice (95%). There was also an age shift in the affirmation of the fairness choice. A main effect for grade, $F(2,70) = 4.92$, $p < .01$, indicated that ninth graders were more likely to give priority to fairness than third or sixth graders (82%, 57%, 61%, respectively). The main effect for sex was not significant, but there was a significant grade × sex interaction, $F(2,70) = 3.66$, $p < .05$. Third-grade males gave less priority to the fairness choice than did sixth- or ninth-grade males, $F(2,36) = 5.43$, $p < .01$ (44%, 71%, 83%, respectively), whereas the sixth-grade females gave less priority to the fairness choice than did ninth-grade females, $F(2,34) = 3.27$, $p < .05$.

Story 2: The science project story. Table 5 shows that for the science project story only a minority of subjects gave priority to the fairness choice in the Initial Situation (22%) and the interpersonal condition (17%), but this varied by condition, $F(2,140) = 105.59$, $p < .0001$. When helping the friend involved violating a rule, subjects more frequently judged it wrong to help (84%) than in the other conditions (p's $< .005$). These findings held for males and females across ages; there were no other significant main effects or interactions.

Story 3: Hurt brother story. In this situation, too, there was a main effect for salience condition, $F(2,140) = 3.09$, $p < .05$. A greater proportion of children judged it wrong to steal in the Lying condition (91%) than in the Initial Situation (57%) or the interpersonal condition (55%). There was a main effect for grade, $F(2,70) = 3.29$, $p < .05$. Duncan multiple-range tests indicated that third graders more frequently gave priority to not stealing than did sixth graders. No significant differences for gender were obtained.

Coordination of components

Three (grade) × 2 (sex) × 3 (salience condition) repeated-measures ANOVAS with condition as the repeated measure were performed separately on the arcsine-transformed responses for each story. There were differences in consideration of components among the stories and between conditions within stories. In the music club story the majority of children at all ages (91%) considered both components.

There were no main effects or interactions for sex, grade, or salience condition.

The science project story produced an increased use of two components with grade, as it interacted with condition. A main effect for salience condition, $F(2,140) = 11.28$, $p < .0001$, indicated that subjects considered both components more in the Initial Situation (65%), which depicted a friendship relationship, than in the interpersonal (Sibling) condition (43%) or in the Rule Violation condition (31%). There was a significant grade × salience condition interaction, $F(2,70) = 4.06$, $p < .01$. Sixth and ninth graders more frequently considered both components of the Initial Situation than did third graders, $F(2,70) = 4.83$, $p < .01$ (77%, 77%, 42%, respectively).

In the hurt brother story, no grade or sex differences were obtained. A main effect for salience condition, $F(2,140) = 30.95$, $p < .0001$, indicated that subjects were less likely to consider two components in the Lying condition (13%) than in the Initial Situation (58%) or the interpersonal (Friend) condition (58%).

Justifications

The percentages of use of justification categories are presented in tables 6 and 7 as separated by subjects' choices in the stories. Since the conventional, personal, psychological, and pragmatic justification categories were used infrequently for the fairness choice, they were combined into an Other category (as discussed below, in a few conditions these were a substantial amount). In addition, the interpersonal category for the fairness or rights choices was used infrequently (see table 6). Therefore, only the fairness–welfare justifications for the fairness choice were analyzed, using a 3 (grade) × 2 (sex) × 3 (salience condition) repeated-measure ANOVA. Since the frequency of interpersonal justifications was substantial in some conditions in Study 2, separate 3 (grade) × 2 (sex) × 3 (salience condition) repeated-measures MANOVAs were performed on the arcsine-transformed proportions of fairness–welfare and interpersonal justifications given for the interpersonal choice in each story. Few pragmatic justifications were given for the interpersonal choice, and thus they were not included in these analyses.

As we did in reporting justification category analyses in Study 1, we only highlight the major findings. For the music club story there were

Table 6 Justifications (in %) affirming the noninterpersonal choice

	Music club story			Hurt brother			Science project		
Grade:	3	6	9	3	6	9	3	6	9
Initial Situation:									
Fairness–welfare	45	42	73	45	33	53	14	27	16
Interpersonal	2	0	0	0	0	0	0	0	0
Other	1	1	0	24	29	9	4	4	5
Interpersonal:[a]									
Fairness–welfare	93	83	96	28	11	40	9	16	23
Interpersonal	2	12	0	0	9	4	0	0	0
Other	0	0	0	42	19	19	0	2	9
Moral:[b]									
Fairness–welfare	24	34	73	26	37	42	31	46	46
Interpersonal	4	20	2	0	0	2	0	0	0
Other	12	0	8	68	49	45	56	38	44

[a] *The interpersonal condition pertained to Friends in the music club story and hurt brother story, and to Siblings in the science project story.*
[b] *The moral condition pertained to Greater Need in the music club story, to Lying in the hurt brother story, and to Rule Violation in the science project story.*

no sex differences in the use of fairness–welfare justifications for the fairness choice. There were main effects for grade, $F(2,64) = 7.61, p < .001$, and salience condition, $F(2,128) = 40.00, p < .001$, as well as a grade × salience condition interaction, $F(4,128) = 2.64, p < .05$. Bonferroni t tests indicated that children used the fairness–welfare category more in the condition where the interpersonal component was less salient (interpersonal condition with a Friend; 91%) than in the Initial Situation (53%) and the Greater Need condition (44%). Second, across conditions, ninth graders used the fairness–welfare category more than did the younger subjects. The interaction reflects that in the Initial Situation ninth graders used the fairness–welfare category more than did sixth graders, $F(2,67) = 3.34, p < .05$, whereas in the Greater Need condition ninth graders used it more than did all the younger subjects, $F(2,69) = 9.79, p < .001$.

The MANOVA performed on justifications given for the interpersonal choice revealed a significant effect for type of justification, $F(1,64) =$

Table 7   Justifications (in %) affirming the interpersonal choices

	Music club story			*Hurt brother*			*Science project*		
Grade:	3	6	9	3	6	9	3	6	9
Initial Situation:									
Fairness–welfare	29	35	19	26	37	38	74	46	72
Interpersonal	21	22	8	4	2	0	8	17	7
Interpersonal:[a]									
Fairness–welfare	4	4	4	14	43	37	34	27	39
Interpersonal	0	0	0	11	14	0	34	50	20
Pragmatic	0	0	0	6	5	0	5	5	5
Moral:[b]									
Fairness–welfare	36	32	13	0	13	2	10	13	8
Interpersonal	23	13	4	0	0	0	2	2	2

[a] *The interpersonal condition pertained to Friends in the music club story and hurt brother story, and to Siblings in the science project story.*
[b] *The moral condition pertained to Greater Need in the music club story, to Lying in the hurt brother story, and to Rule Violation in the science project story.*

9.42, $p < .01$. Children used fairness–welfare justifications (20%) more than interpersonal justifications (4%) for the interpersonal choice. The MANOVA also revealed a salience condition × sex interaction in justifications, $F(2,64) = 5.36, p < .01$. The fairness–welfare category was used more by females than males for the interpersonal choice in the Greater Need condition, $F(1,68) = 4.19, p < .05$.

For the science project story, there were no sex or grade effects in use of the fairness–welfare category for the fairness choice, as shown in table 6. The only differences obtained were a main effect for salience condition on the MANOVA, $F(2,116) = 11.44, p < .0001$. The fairness–welfare category was used more in the Rule Violation condition (41%) than in the Initial Situation (19%) or the interpersonal (Sibling) condition (16%), p's $< .001$. Children justified the interpersonal choices (as shown in table 7) on the basis of fairness–welfare (36%) more than interpersonal concerns (16%), as indicated by a main effect for type of justification on the MANOVA, $F(1,58) = 17.74, p < .0001$. There were no sex or age effects.

In the hurt brother story, there was a somewhat different pattern of justifications than in the other stories. As shown in table 6, there was substantial use of the pragmatic, conventional, and psychological categories (grouped as Other) in justifying the fairness choice. Furthermore, there were no main effects or interactions in the use of fairness–welfare justifications for the fairness choice. As shown in table 7, however, there were differences between justifications for the interpersonal choice, $F(1,51) = 26.45, p < .0001$. Fairness–welfare (25%) was used more than interpersonal (3%) justifications ($p < .001$). There was also a main effect for salience condition in justifications, $F(2,50) = 14.20, p < .0001$. There was more use of the fairness–welfare category in the Initial Situation (34%) and in the interpersonal condition (32%) than in the Lying condition (7%; p's $< .001$).

Discussion

It appears that when children are faced with conflicts between fairness and positive interpersonal expectations, they make interpersonal choices to a greater extent than when the expectations are motivated by self-interest. Overall, children gave greater priority to interpersonal choices in Study 2 than in Study 1. Moreover, no gender differences were found in Study 2.

As in Study 1, a main finding of this study is that both females and males made judgments that accounted for situational features of the stories. There were differences between stories, as well as differences in accord with shifts in the salience of the interpersonal or fairness/rights considerations. In the science project story, children clearly gave priority to the interpersonal considerations. In the other two stories, children were nearly equally divided in their choices of whether to care for a sibling or meet other fairness or rights considerations.

It also appears that each of the stories tapped somewhat different judgments. In the music club story, both males and females (and especially the younger ones) were responsive to the need to care for a vulnerable younger sister. However, children gave greater priority to helping a sister than helping a friend in similar circumstances. Children of both genders were especially responsive to the interpersonal expectations in the competitive context of the science project story since most of them, unlike in the music club story, judged it acceptable to help either a sibling or a friend. Perhaps lower priority was placed on impersonal fairness in this situation because the context of competition was not seen as including equal rights. Another difference between these two stories was that shifts in salience of the fairness or rights components resulted in children giving it greater priority only in the science project story (the Rule Violation condition).

The purpose of the hurt brother story was to assess judgments and justifications in the type of conflict used in previous discussions of gender differences. Again, no gender differences were found. Children were evenly divided in their choices regarding a sibling and a friend. There was the expected difference in salience condition; children were less likely to give priority to the interpersonal expectation when the protagonist lied as a means to help the sibling. The types of justifications used in this story indicate that it was perceived as more complex than the other stories. This story implicated additional considerations, such as the violation of laws and the possibility of punishment, and produced substantial use of pragmatic, conventional, and psychological justifications (grouped as Other). Children's perceptions of complexity in this story may account for the disparate and conflicting results obtained by other researchers using stories of this type (e.g., Baumrind, 1986; Gilligan, 1982; Walker, 1984, 1986a). That is, our results indicate that in these stories children perceive components from different domains (e.g., legal issues, sanctions), in addition to, for example, justice and care components. In the absence of systematic delineation of such components, it is possible that their salience varied from one study to another and, if so, might account for conflicting results.

The absence of gender differences in the story choices was paralleled by an absence of gender differences in justifications. Children primarily used fairness–welfare justifications to support their choices, especially in conditions with an increased salience of fairness or rights (as was also found in Study 1). It was also found that children reasoned about their interpersonal choices with fairness-welfare justifications more than interpersonal justifications. This indicates that, for both genders, interpersonal expectations are perceived to include fairness and welfare components. It should be stressed that, as in Study 1, males and females used fairness justifications to an equal extent as welfare justifications (the two were grouped in the analyses into one general category).

Finally, the main age-related findings in this study were consistent with those of Study 1. Although children of all ages were able to consider both components in some of their judgments, older children did so with greater consistency than the younger ones in the Science Project story. However, there were no significant age differences in the coordination of components in the other stories.

General Discussion

The findings of the two studies are complementary. Together, they demonstrate that children of both genders consider interpersonal relationships and justice, welfare, and rights. Moreover, in both studies children's judgments and reasoning shifted in accordance with situational variations. In Study 1, females and males generally favored the obligations of justice and rights over self-interested interpersonal expectations. It appears, therefore, that at least by middle childhood children have formed concepts of justice and rights that they apply to a range of social situations. At the same time, the concepts of justice and rights are not rigidly applied. Study 1 demonstrated that children also take interpersonal components into account, and that changes in the salience of one or the other component lead to changes in the ways they are applied.

The findings of Study 2 showed that children are responsive to more positive interpersonal expectations than those depicted in Study 1. In the context of interpersonal concerns with positive intent and goals, males and females make similar judgments and use similar reasoning categories. It must be stressed that we are not claiming that these studies demonstrate that no gender differences exist in moral orientations. More studies would be needed to even consider the possibility. Rather, we have obtained evidence that both males and females make judgments of justice, rights, and welfare, judge the necessity of maintaining interpersonal relationships, and apply concepts of justice, rights, and welfare to interpersonal relations and recognize potential conflicts between the two. The features of a situation have a bearing on how it is approached and resolved.

It also should be noted that our studies had a different focus from most recent studies of gender differences (Baumrind, 1986; Gilligan, 1982; Walker, 1984, 1986a). We examined whether and how children use interpersonal and justice considerations in a series of situational contexts. The other studies have focused on general age-related shifts in "moral" reasoning through analyses of judgments about situations in which the interpersonal and justice components are not clearly specified or manipulated (e.g., through story comparisons or salience variations).

Therefore, the exact implications of our results for formulations (Damon, 1977; Kohlberg, 1969; Selman, 1980) of stages or levels of moral judgment about particular conflicts or dilemmas are uncertain. The findings of our studies, however, do suggest that there are not clear-cut individual or group differences regarding concerns with justice, welfare, and rights, on the one hand, and concerns with interpersonal relations, on the other hand. Each type of concern coexists in individuals' social judgments and reasoning.

Notes

1 Gilligan's (1977, 1982) propositions have led to a number of investigations and reanalyses of existing data. Lyons (1983) reports data supporting Gilligan's propositions, although her scoring system has been criticized by Walker, de Vries, and Trevethan (1987); other studies using Lyons's scoring system on small samples (Gilligan & Attanucci, 1988) suggest that most adults use both orientations, but that females are more likely to focus on care, and males are more likely to focus on justice. Based on an extensive review and meta-analysis of studies using Kohlberg's assessments, Walker (1984) concludes that the overall pattern of studies provides no evidence for the sex differences suggested by Gilligan. (Walker's conclusions have been questioned by Baumrind [1986]; also see Walker's [1986a] rebuttal.) Several studies (Pratt, Golding, & Hunter, 1984; Walker, 1986b, 1989; Walker et al., 1987) examining the justice versus care orientation as scored within Kohlberg's system failed to find support for the predicted pattern of sex differences. Gibbs, Arnold, and Burkhart (1984) found no overall stage differences between males and females, but they interpret significant differences in the types of reasons males and females at Stage 3 endorse as consistent with Gilligan's thesis. Finally, several studies have found that type of dilemma (e.g., hypothetical vs. real-life), rather than gender, influences justice and care responses (Pratt, Golding, Hunter, & Sampson, 1988; Rothbart, Hanley, & Albert, 1986), although other studies found more equivocal support for such differences (Ford & Lowery, 1986; Wlaker, 1989; Walker et al., 1987). These two sets of studies, however, found no sex differences within orientations.

2 Analyses of covariance indicated that all significant effects remained statistically significant with story choice controlled.

References

Baumrind, D. (1986). Sex differences in moral reasoning: Response to Walker's (1984) conclusions that there are none. *Child Development, 57,* 511–521.

Damon, W. (1977). *The social world of the child.* San Francisco: Jossey-Bass.

Davidson, P., Turiel, E., & Black, A. (1983). The effects of stimulus familiarity on the use of criteria and justifications in children's social reasoning. *British Journal of Developmental Psychology, 1,* 49–65.

Ford, M. R., & Lowery, C. R. (1986). Gender differences in moral reasoning: A comparison of the use of justice and care orientations. *Journal of Personality and Social Psychology, 50,* 777–783.

Gibbs, J. C., Arnold, K. D., & Burkhart, J. E. (1984). Sex differences in the expression of moral judgment. *Child Development, 55,* 1040–1043.

Gilligan, C. (1977). In a different voice: Women's conceptions of self and of morality. *Harvard Educational Review, 47,* 481–517.

Gilligan, C. (1982). *In a different voice: Psychological theory and women's development.* Cambridge, MA: Harvard University Press.

Gilligan, C., & Attanucci, J. (1988). Two moral orientations: Gender differences and similarities. *Merrill-Palmer Quarterly, 34,* 223–237.

Killen, M. (1990). Children's evaluations of morality in the context of peer, teacher–child, and familial relations. *Journal of Genetic Psychology, 151,* 395–410.

Kohlberg, L. (1969). Stage and sequence: The cognitive-developmental approach to socialization. In D. A. Goslin (Ed.), *Handbook of socialization theory and research* (pp. 347–480). Chicago: Rand McNally.

Kohlberg, L. (1971). From is to ought: How to commit the naturalistic fallacy and get away with it in the study of moral development. In T. Mischel (Ed.), *Cognitive development and epistemology* (pp. 151–235). New York: Academic Press.

Lyons, N. (1983). Two perspectives: On self, relationships, and morality. *Harvard Educational Review, 53,* 125–145.

Miller, J. G., Bersoff, D. M., & Harwood, R. L. (1990). Perceptions of social responsibilities in India and in the United States: Moral imperatives or personal decisions? *Journal of Personality and Social Psychology, 58,* 33–47.

Miller, J. G., & Luthar, S. (1989). Issues of interpersonal responsibility and accountability: A comparison of Indians' and Americans' moral judgments. *Social Cognition, 7,* 237–261.

Nucci, L. P. (1981). The development of personal concepts: A domain distinct from moral or societal concepts. *Child Development, 52,* 114–121.

Pratt, M. W., Golding, G., & Hunter, W. J. (1984). Does morality have a gender? Sex, sex role, and moral judgment relationships across the adult lifespan. *Merrill-Palmer Quarterly, 30,* 321–340.

Pratt, M. W., Golding, G., Hunter, W., & Sampson, R. (1988). Sex differences in adult moral orientations. *Journal of Personality*, 56, 373–391.

Rothbart, M. K., Hanley, J., & Albert, M. (1986). Gender differences in moral reasoning. *Sex Roles*, 15, 645–653.

Scheffler, S. (1988). Agent-centered restrictions, rationality, and the virtues. In S. Scheffler (Ed.), *Consequentialism and its critics* (pp. 243–260). New York: Oxford University Press.

Selman, R. L. (1980). *The growth of interpersonal understanding: Developmental and clinical analyses*. New York: Academic Press.

Smetana, J. G. (1981). Preschool children's conceptions of moral and social rules. *Child Development*, 52, 1333–1336.

Smetana, J. G. (1985). Preschool children's conceptions of transgressions: The effects of varying moral and conventional domain-related attributes. *Developmental Psychology*, 21, 18–29.

Smetana, J. G., Kelly, M., & Twentyman, C. T. (1984). Abused, neglected, and nonmaltreated children's conceptions of moral and social-conventional rules. *Child Development*, 55, 277–287.

Turiel, E. (1983). *The development of social knowledge: Morality and convention*. Cambridge: Cambridge University Press.

Turiel, E., Smetana, J. G., & Killen, M. (1991). Social contexts in social cognitive development. In W. M. Kurtines & J. L. Gewirtz (Eds.), *Handbook of moral behavior and development* (Vol. 2, pp. 307–332). Hillsdale, NJ: Erlbaum.

Walker, L. J. (1984). Sex differences in the development of moral reasoning. *Child Development*, 55, 677–691.

Walker, L. J. (1986a). Sex differences in the development of moral reasoning: A rejoinder to Baumrind. *Child Development*, 57, 522–526.

Walker, L. J. (1986b). Experiential and cognitive sources of moral development in adulthood. *Human Development*, 29, 113–124.

Walker, L. J. (1989). A longitudinal study of moral reasoning. *Child Development*, 60, 157–166.

Walker, L. J., de Vries, B., & Trevethan, S. D. (1987). Moral stages and moral orientation in real-life and hypothetical dilemmas. *Child Development*, 58, 842–858.

Williams, B. (1981). *Moral luck*. Cambridge: Cambridge University Press.

Winer, B. J. (1971). *Statistical principles in experimental design*. New York: McGraw-Hill.

Introduction to Part IV

We see and hear about the aggressive nature of our society on a daily basis. As a result, few topics have had as much theoretical and empirical attention as aggressive behavior. The most common reason for referral to children's mental health or counseling services is for aggressive or antisocial behavior (Offord et al., 1987), and in about 5 percent of individuals, aggressive behavior begins early and is a primary precursor to chronic antisocial behavior in adulthood. For these individuals, there is an increased risk of social and other problems in adulthood, including psychiatric problems, substance abuse, chronic unemployment, divorce, a range of physical disorders, motor vehicle accidents, dependence on welfare systems, and generalized reduced levels of attainment and competence in adulthood (Caspi, Elder, & Bem, 1987).

Aggressive behavior and its associated problems are not only chronic, but are often transmitted across generations (Huesmann, Eron, Lefkowitz, & Walder, 1984). Aggressive behavior also can have severe effects on its victims, such as siblings, peers, parents, teachers, and strangers too. The monetary costs of aggression are high: aggressive children generate lifelong costs because they are involved in multiple systems such as mental health, juvenile justice, special education, and social services. Interrupting this pattern of behavior is a critical issue.

The articles in this section consider gender differences in the manifestations and development of aggressive behavior, the role of the family in predicting aggressive behaviors, and how aggression can be prevented.

References

Caspi, A., Elder, G. H., & Bem, D. J. (1987). Moving against the world: Life course patterns of explosive children. *Developmental Psychology, 23,* 308–13.

Huesmann, L. R., Eron, L. D., Lefkowitz, M. M., & Walder, L. O. (1984). Stability of aggression over time and generations. *Developmental Psychology, 20,* 1120–34.

Offord, D. R., Boyle, M. H., Szatmari, P., Rae-Grant, N. I., Links, P. S., Cadman, D. T., Byles, J. A., Crawford, J. W., Blum, H. M., Byrne, C., Thomas, H., & Woodward, C. A. (1987). Ontario Child Health Study: II. Six-month prevalence of disorder and rates of service utilization. *Archives of General Psychiatry, 44,* 832–6.

ELEVEN

Forms of Aggression

Introduction

The problem of aggressive behavior in girls has often been overlooked. Recently, researchers have made recommendations for a different perspective than that typically used with boys, in order to understand the problems of aggressive girls. They argue that the definition of aggression needs to be expanded from the traditional perspective of physical assault to include the behaviors that typically comprise girls' attacks, including verbal aggression (Bjorkqvist, Osterman, & Kaukiainen, 1992), aggression directed at peer relationships, and aggression directed at damaging self-esteem and/or social status (Crick & Grotpeter, 1995). A current school of thought is that girls are more likely to be indirectly aggressive, while boys are more likely to be physically aggressive. However, although girls may use more indirect than physical aggressive strategies, these two forms of aggression co-occur in both girls and boys.

With the expanding definition of aggression, a controversy has arisen over how to measure girls' aggression, and how to identify those girls with serious problems. Crick argues that more comprehensive assessments are needed, which should be sensitive to the diversity of acts that may be considered aggressive, and to the changing nature of girls' aggression over time. Furthermore, she argues that there is a need to look for girls' aggression in different contexts than boys' aggression. Without examining the specific forms of girls' aggression and assessing this aggression within close relationships, girls' problems may be overlooked, underestimated, and untreated. Crick demonstrates that girls act aggressively in different ways than boys, and that relationally aggressive girls are at risk for negative outcomes that include internalizing (e.g., fear of being bad) and externalizing (e.g., being bad) behavior problems.

References

Bjorkqvist, K., Osterman, K., & Kaukiainen, A. (1992). The development of direct and indirect aggressive strategies in males and females. In K. Bjorkqvist & P. Niemela (eds), *Of mice and women: Aspects of female aggression* (pp. 51–64). New York: Academic Press.

Crick, N., & Grotpeter, J. (1995). Relational aggression, gender, and social–psychological adjustment. *Child Development, 66*, 710–22.

Engagement in Gender Normative Versus Nonnormative Forms of Aggression: Links to Social–Psychological Adjustment

Nicki R. Crick

Because of its deleterious effects on children's development, childhood aggression has been one of the most widely studied adjustment problems in the past several decades. Although hundreds of studies, books, and journals have been dedicated to the topic, past work on aggression has been limited in two important ways: (*a*) aggressive boys have received most of the research attention, whereas aggressive girls have often been excluded from relevant studies, and (*b*) forms of aggression that are salient to boys have been emphasized, whereas forms that are salient to girls have largely been ignored (Bjorkqvist & Niemela, 1992; Cowan & Underwood, in press; Crick & Grotpeter, 1995; Robins, 1986). The present research was designed to address these issues through the study of aggressive children of both sexes and through the assessment of aggressive behaviors that are prevalent among girls (relational aggression) as well as those that are prevalent among boys (overt aggression).

Past research on childhood aggression has focused largely on the study of *overt aggression*, behaviors that harm others through physical damage or through the threat of such damage. Research on the prevalence of overt aggression has demonstrated that boys are significantly more overtly aggressive than are girls (Berkowitz, 1993; Block, 1983; Parke & Slaby, 1983), a finding that has led to a focus on male samples in studies of childhood aggression. As a result, we presently know significantly less about overtly aggressive girls (Bjorqvist & Niemela, 1992; Crick & Grotpeter, 1995; Robins, 1986). Study of overtly aggressive girls, in addition to overtly aggressive boys, is important for several reasons. First, there is evidence that the aggression "gender gap" is narrowing (Loeber, 1990; Robins, 1986; US Department of Justice, 1990). Research indicates that, between 1965 and 1987, the frequency of aggressive acts committed by minors in the United States increased steadily for both sexes. However, the frequency for girls increased at a faster rate than that of boys, narrowing the male:female ratio from 11:1 in 1965 to 8:1 in 1987 (US Department of Justice, 1990). These findings indicate that overtly aggressive behavior problems are increasing at a relatively rapid rate among girls. This fact, combined with evidence that overtly aggressive children are at risk for serious adjustment problems (Eron, 1992; Parker & Asher, 1987; Serbin, Peters, McAffer, & Schwartzman, 1991), indicates an increasing risk of developmental problems for young girls as well as increasing levels of risk for our society as a whole (e.g., in the form of increased crime rates, high-school dropout rates, and adolescent pregnancy rates). Thus, it is important to increase our understanding of overtly aggressive girls.

To adequately address the issue of aggression among girls, it is also important to consider other forms of aggression in addition to overt forms. In recent research, a relational form of aggression has been identified in which harm to others occurs through manipulation or control of their relationships with others (e.g., threatening to withdraw acceptance or friendship as a way to control others; using social exclusion or rumor spreading as a form of retaliation; Crick & Grotpeter, 1995). In contrast to physical aggression in which physical damage is the instrument of harm (e.g., pushing or hitting) or verbal aggression in which the instrument of harm is psychological abuse (e.g., verbal insults), *relational aggression* includes behaviors in which relationships specifically serve as the vehicle of harm.

Recent studies indicate that in contrast to overt aggression, girls exhibit significantly higher levels of relational aggression than do boys (Cairns, Cairns, Neckerman, Ferguson, & Gariépy, 1989; Crick & Grotpeter, 1995; Feshbach, 1969; Lagerspetz, Bjorkqvist, & Peltonen, 1988). In addition, a study of extreme groups of relationally and overtly aggressive children has shown that aggressive boys and girls are identified with almost equal frequency when relational as well as overt forms of aggression are assessed (Crick & Grotpeter, 1995). These findings indicate that both girls and boys are aggressive and that past estimates of prevalence have been biased by the failure to assess forms of aggression salient to girls.

Past research has shown that both overt and relational aggression are independently related to social–psychological maladjustment (e.g., Bukowski & Newcomb, 1984; Coie & Dodge, 1983; Coie & Kupersmidt, 1983; Crick & Grotpeter, 1995). However, additional research is needed in this area for several reasons. First, past research on the relation between overt aggression and social–psychological adjustment, although extensive, has focused primarily on the study of boys. Thus, we presently have relatively little empirical information regarding the social–psychological risk status of overtly aggressive girls (Robins, 1986; Yoshikawa, 1994). Second, research on the relation between relational aggression and adjustment is limited to a few studies (by comparison, hundreds of studies have assessed this relation for overtly aggressive children). Third, no studies have been conducted yet that have evaluated the relative contributions of overt aggression and relational aggression in children's social–psychological adjustment both within and across genders.

It is possible that particular combinations of gender and aggression form (e.g., being an overtly aggressive girl vs. being a relationally aggressive girl) are related to unique patterns of social–psychological risk. For example, Crick and Dodge (1994) have recently proposed that overtly aggressive girls and relationally aggressive boys may be more seriously at risk for social–psychological maladjustment than relationally aggressive girls and overtly aggressive boys because of the nonnormative nature of their behavior relative to their gender group. Gender atypical behavior (e.g., overt aggression exhibited by girls) is likely to incur more social sanctions and negative sentiments from peers and adults than is behavior that is relatively extreme in frequency or intensity but gender normative (e.g., overt aggression exhibited by boys). This situation may result in greater severity of social–psychological problems (e.g., higher levels of maladjustment) for children who engage in gender atypical aggression (e.g., these children may become more socially rejected or excluded because peers view their behavior as unusual for their gender).

Further, significant differences may exist not only in the severity of adjustment difficulties but also in the types of adjustment problems associated with gender normative versus gender atypical aggression. Past research has shown that overt aggression is often associated with cognitive and affective patterns that are externalizing in nature (e.g., blaming others for one's failures, holding unrealistically positive views of the self; denying psychological discomfort or social maladjustment; Boivin, Thomassin, & Alain, 1989). This pattern is similar, although exaggerated in form, to the one that is stereotypical of the male population as a whole (e.g., see Block, 1983, for a review; Crick & Ladd, 1993; Franke & Hymel, 1984). In contrast, initial evidence indicates that relational aggression is associated with attributes that are internalizing in nature (reporting relatively high levels of psychological distress, holding negative self-perceptions; Crick & Grotpeter, 1995). This pattern is more stereotypical of the female population in general (Block, 1983; Crick & Ladd, 1993; Franke & Hymel, 1984).

The potential moderating role of gender has not been adequately addressed in past studies of the relation between aggression and social–psychological adjustment. As a result, researchers do not know whether engagement in aggressive behavior that is gender atypical (e.g., overt aggression for girls or relational aggression for boys) is associated with types of adjustment difficulties that are gender atypical (externalizing attributes for girls; internalizing attributes for boys) or gender normative (internalizing attributes for girls, externalizing attributes for boys). It is possible that the relations between aggression and adjustment found in past research have been biased by a focus on overtly aggressive groups. For example, the overtly aggressive groups identified in past studies may have exhibited externalizing attributes partly because the group members were primarily boys. Whether overtly aggressive girls would also exhibit an externalizing pattern (in which case adjustment would be most related to aggression form), an internalizing pattern (in which case adjustment would be most related to gender), or a combination of these two patterns is not clear. Similarly, it is not clear whether relationally aggressive males would exhibit an adjustment pattern that is similar to other boys (externalizing) or to relationally aggressive girls (internalizing).

In the present research, the role of aggression form (overt versus relational) in predicting severity and type of social–psychological maladjustment was evaluated within and across gender through the comparison of the internalizing and externalizing adjustment difficulties experienced by overtly aggressive boys, overtly aggressive girls, relationally aggressive boys, relationally aggressive girls, and nonaggressive boys and girls. In addition, because some of the aspects of adjustment assessed have been shown to vary with age (e.g., depression), the possible moderating role of grade was also taken into account. To identify adequate numbers of children in each of the identified groups, it was necessary to recruit and assess a relatively large sample of children.

Method

Participants

A total of 1,166 third through sixth graders (578 boys and 588 girls) from 12 elementary schools in several small to moderately sized towns in central Illinois participated in this research. Approximately 15% of the sample was African American, 84% was Caucasian, and 1% represented other ethnic groups. The socioeconomic status (SES) of the families of the participating children was estimated to range from lower SES to middle SES, with most families at the lower end of this continuum.[1] Every child needed parental consent to participate (consent rate was 80.4%).

Assessment of overt and relational aggression

A peer nomination instrument developed in past research was used to assess relational and overt aggression (Crick, 1995; Crick & Grotpeter, 1995; Grotpeter & Crick, 1996). This measure consists of three subscales, two of which assess aggressive behavior. The Overt Aggression subscale consists of five items (e.g., children who hit, kick, or punch others; children who say mean things to other kids to insult them or put them down). The Relational Aggression subscales consists of five items (e.g., children who try to make other kids not like a certain person by spreading rumors about them or talking behind their backs; children who tell their friends that they will stop liking them unless the friends do what they say). The other subscale, Prosocial Behavior, consists of four items (e.g., children who say and do nice things for others), and these items serve as positively toned filler items.

During the administration of the peer nomination instrument, children were provided with a class roster and were asked to nominate up to three classmates who best fit the behavioral descriptions provided for each of the items on the measure. The number of nominations children received from peers for each of the items on these subscales was then standardized within each classroom. The standardized scores for the items of a subscale were then summed to yield a total subscale score.

Both of the aggression subscales have been shown to be highly reliable in past research, with Cronbach's alpha ranging from .82 to .89 for the Relational Aggression subscale and from .94 to .97 for the Overt Aggression subscale for the three previously described samples; test–retest reliability over a four-week interval was $r = .82$ and $r = .90$ (Crick, 1996) for the Relational Aggression and Overt Aggression subscales, respectively. Also, factor analysis of the peer nomination measure has confirmed the existence of two separate factors for Relational and Overt Aggression, both with eigenvalues greater than 1.0 and high factor loadings (ranging from .73 to .91) and insubstantial cross loadings (Crick & Grotpeter, 1995). Further, the correlation between the Overt and Relational Aggression scales has been shown to be moderate ($r = .54$ to .57; Crick & Grotpeter, 1995; Grotpeter & Crick, 1996).

Assessment of social–psychological adjustment

Teacher reports.   Teacher reports of children's internalizing and externalizing problems were measured with the teacher form of the Child Behavior Checklist (CBCL), an instrument with demonstrated reliability and validity (Achenbach & Edelbrock, 1981, 1991a, 1991b). Each of the items on this instrument describes maladaptive behaviors. The response scale for each item ranges from 0 (*not true of this child*) to 2 (*very true or often true of this child*). This instrument includes two general adjustment scales, internalizing (e.g., fears she or he might do something bad; cries a lot) and externalizing (e.g., argues a lot; doesn't seem to feel guilty after misbehaving), and only the 69 items that assess these two constructs were included in the present research (i.e., although the complete CBCL consists of 118 items, only the 69 internalizing and externalizing items were rated by the participating teachers). Children's average internalizing and externalizing scores were used in subsequent analyses. For the present sample, Cronbach's alpha was .89 and .97 for the internalizing and externalizing scales, respectively.

Self-reports. The short form of the Weinberger Adjustment Inventory (WAI; Weinberger & Schwartz, 1990), a measure with favorable psychometric properties (e.g., Cronbach's alpha ranging from .70 to .90 for each subscale; high test–retest reliability; evidence for construct validity) was used to assess self-reports of adjustment problems. The WAI measure consists of 37 items and two subscales, Psychological Distress and Self-Restraint. Specifically, the Psychological Distress subscale (items assess anxiety, depression, low self-esteem, and low well-being; e.g., I often feel sad or unhappy; I'm not very sure of myself) was used as an index of children's perceptions of their own internalizing difficulties, and the Self-Restraint subscale was used as an index of children's perceptions of their own externalizing difficulties (items assess impulse control problems, inability to suppress anger, lack of consideration for others, and lack of responsibility; e.g., people who get me angry better watch out; I do things without giving them enough thought). Responses to each item on the scale range from 1 (*not at all true*) to 5 (*always true*).[2] For the present sample, Cronbach's alpha was .81 and .85 for the Psychological Distress and Self-Restraint scales, respectively. Children's average distress and restraint scores were used in subsequent analyses.

Administration procedures

The previously described peer assessment and self-report instruments were completed by participants during one 60-minute group assessment session conducted within children's classrooms. This session was conducted by trained graduate and undergraduate research assistants, who employed standardized procedures. During each session, children were trained in the use of the response scales prior to administration of the instruments. Also, each item of every instrument was read aloud by the administrator and repeated as necessary to ensure understanding of item content. Administration assistants were also available to answer children's questions. To recognize the participants' contribution to the project, children were given small, school-related items at the end of the group session (e.g., pencils, erasers). Teachers completed the CBCL for each of their participating students within one to four weeks of the administration of the peer assessment and self-report sessions.

Results

Psychometric properties of the aggression measure and identification of aggression groups

To assess the psychometric properties of the peer nomination measure for the present sample, a factor analysis (varimax rotation) was first conducted on children's scores for each item. This analysis yielded the three predicted factors (see table 1). Specifically, Overt Aggression accounted for 50.6% of the variation (eigenvalue = 7.1), Relational Aggression accounted for 17.6% of the variation (eigenvalue = 2.5), and Prosocial Behavior accounted for 10.4% of the variation (eigen-

Table 1   Factor loadings for the peer nomination instrument

	Factor		
Item	*Overt Aggression*	*Relational Aggression*	*Prosocial Behavior*
Hits, kicks, punches others	.90		
Says mean things to insult others or put them down	.79		
Pushes and shoves others	.90		
Tells other kids that they will beat them up unless the kids do what they say	.90		
Calls others mean names	.82		
Tries to make other kids not like a certain person by spreading rumors about them		.72	
When mad, gets even by keeping the person from being in their group of friends		.80	
Tells friends they will stop liking them unless friends do what they say		.76	
When mad at a person, ignores them or stops talking to them		.83	
Tries to keep certain people from being in their group during activity or play time		.70	
Good leader			.80
Does nice things for others			.86
Helps others			.90
Cheers up others			.87

value = 1.4). Loadings ranged from .70 to .90, and all crossloadings were below .43.

In contrast to the results of Crick and Grotpeter (1995), no items substantially crossloaded for this sample and, thus, no items were dropped from the measure in subsequent analyses. Thus, children's scores for the five overt aggression items and for the five relational aggression items were summed to create two total aggression scores. Cronbach's alpha was .96 for the Overt Aggression scale and .88 for the Relational Aggression scale. (The correlation between the two aggression scales was $r = .63$, $p < .001$.[3])

Children's Relational Aggression scores and Overt Aggression scores were used both as continuous variables in subsequent analyses and as a means to identify groups of aggressive versus nonaggressive children. Specifically, children with Overt Aggression scores 1 *SD* above the sample mean were considered overtly aggressive ($n = 161$, 130 boys and 31 girls), and children with scores below this criterion were considered nonovertly aggressive ($n = 955$, 423 boys and 532 girls). Similarly, children with Relational Aggression scores 1 *SD* above the sample mean were considered relationally aggressive ($n = 179$, 71 boys and 108 girls), and children with scores below this criterion were considered nonrelationally aggressive ($n = 937$, 483 boys and 453 girls).

Gender and age-related grade differences in aggression

To assess gender and age-related grade differences in the dimensions of relational and overt aggression, two 2 (gender) × 2 (grade: third/fourth vs. fifth/sixth) analyses of variance (ANOVAs) were conducted in which children's aggression scores served as the dependent variables. Results for Overt Aggression revealed significant effects of gender, $F(1, 1164) = 177.4$, $p < .001$, indicating that boys ($M = 1.53$, $SD = 5.01$) were viewed by peers as significantly more overtly aggressive than were girls ($M = -1.68$, $SD = 3.00$). Results for Relational Aggression also revealed significant effects of gender, $F(1, 1164) = 6.0$, $p < .05$, indicating that girls ($M = .28$, $SD = 4.24$) were perceived by peers to be significantly more relationally aggressive than boys ($M = -.30$, $SD = 3.70$). No significant grade differences were obtained in these two sets of analyses.

Social–psychological adjustment, aggression, and gender

To assess aggression group and gender differences in children's social–psychological adjustment, two 2 (Overt Aggression group) × 2 (Relational Aggression group) × 2 (gender) × 2 (grade: third/fourth vs. fifth/sixth) by 2 (adjustment type: internalizing vs. externalizing) ANOVAs were conducted with adjustment type serving as a within-subjects variable. In the first analysis, teachers' reports of children's adjustment served as the dependent variables, and in the second, children's self-reports were used. For significant effects reported below that do not involve the adjustment type variable, the dependent variable reflects a combination of externalizing and internalizing problems (for teacher reports) or a combination of Psychological Distress and Self-Restraint difficulties (for self-reports). This dependent variable is referred to below as *maladjustment* because it reflects a combination of psychological and behavioral symptoms. Significant interaction effects were investigated further with Duncan post hoc tests.

Teacher reports of children's adjustment. Analyses of children's teacher-report adjustment scores based on the CBCL yielded a significant main effect of Overt Aggression, $F(1, 1073) = 45.6$, $p < .001$, and a marginally significant effect of Relational Aggression, $F(1, 1073) = 3.6$, $p < .06$. Specifically, teachers viewed overtly aggressive children ($M = .99$, $SD = .61$) and relationally aggressive children ($M = .81$, $SD = .61$) as more maladjusted than their nonovertly ($M = .44$, $SD = .46$) and nonrelationally ($M = .42$, $SD = .43$) aggressive peers, respectively (see above for a description of the maladjustment variable).

These analyses also yielded a number of significant interaction effects. First, an interaction of Relational Aggression and Overt Aggression was obtained, $F(1, 1073) = 8.5$, $p < .001$. Post hoc analyses ($p < .05$) showed that children who exhibited both Overt and Relational Aggression ($M = 1.05$, $SD = .64$) were viewed by their teachers as significantly more maladjusted than overtly aggressive children, ($M = .93$, $SD = .59$), relationally aggressive children, ($M = .60$, $SD = .50$), and nonaggressive children ($M = .40$, $SD = .42$). In addition, overtly aggressive children were significantly more maladjusted than relationally aggressive and nonaggressive children. And, relationally aggressive children were perceived by teachers as significantly more maladjusted than nonaggressive children.

An interaction effect of Relational Aggression, Overt Aggression, and grade was also found, $F(1, 1073) = 6.3$, $p < .01$ (see table 2 for cell means and standard deviations). Post hoc analyses ($p < .05$) showed that, according to teacher reports, older children who exhibited both Relational and Overt Aggression were significantly more maladjusted than all other groups except that their scores did not differ from younger, overtly aggressive children. Also, younger, overtly aggressive children were significantly more maladjusted than nonaggressive children (younger and older), relationally aggressive children (younger and older), and older, overtly aggressive children. Further, overtly aggressive children (older and younger) were significantly more maladjusted than relationally aggressive children and nonaggressive children. Younger, relationally aggressive children were significantly more maladjusted than older, relationally aggressive children and nonaggressive children. And, older, relationally aggressive children were significantly more maladjusted than nonaggressive children.

Analyses also yielded a significant interaction of relational aggression and gender, $F(1, 1073) = 4.4$, $p < .05$. Post hoc analyses ($p < .05$)

Table 2 Teacher-rated adjustment scores by Overt Aggression group, Relational Aggression group, and grade

	Adjustment score	
Group and age	M	SD
Nonaggressive		
Younger	0.39	0.43
Older	0.41	0.41
Overtly aggressive		
Younger	1.03	0.63
Older	0.83	0.55
Relationally aggressive		
Younger	0.68	0.52
Older	0.53	0.47
Overtly and relationally aggressive		
Younger	0.95	0.60
Older	1.14	0.67

Younger refers to third and fourth graders, and older refers to fifth and sixth graders.

showed that teachers perceived relationally aggressive boys ($M = 1.00$, $SD = .65$) to be significantly more maladjusted than relationally aggressive girls ($M = .68$, $SD = .55$), nonrelationally aggressive boys ($M = .53$, $SD = .50$), and nonrelationally aggressive girls ($M = .35$, $SD = .39$). Further, relationally aggressive girls were viewed as significantly more maladjusted than nonaggressive boys and girls. And, nonrelationally aggressive boys were perceived to be significantly more maladjusted than nonrelationally aggressive girls.

Teacher reports of adjustment also yielded an interaction effect between Overt Aggression and gender, $F(1, 1073) = 11.8$, $p < .01$. Post hoc tests ($p < .05$) revealed that teachers viewed overtly aggressive girls ($M = 1.12$, $SD = .61$) as significantly more maladjusted than overtly aggressive boys ($M = .96$, $SD = .62$), nonovertly aggressive boys ($M = .47$, $SD = .47$), and nonovertly aggressive girls ($M = .37$, $SD = .39$). In addition, overtly aggressive boys were reported to be significantly more maladjusted than nonovertly aggressive children. Finally, nonovertly aggressive boys were viewed as significantly more maladjusted than nonovertly aggressive girls.

Analyses of children's teacher-report adjustment scores also yielded several additional significant effects involving the within-subjects variable, adjustment type. First, a significant main effect of adjustment type was obtained, $F(1, 1073) = 137.6$, indicating that, in general, children were viewed by teachers as more externalizing ($M = .27$, $SD = .37$) than internalizing ($M = .23$, $SD = .23$). In addition, a significant interaction of Overt Aggression and adjustment type was obtained. Post hoc tests ($p < .05$) revealed that overtly aggressive children were significantly more externalizing ($M = .73$, $SD = .47$) than nonovertly aggressive children ($M = .19$, $SD = .28$)[4] and also were significantly more externalizing than internalizing ($M = .26$, $SD = .22$). However, a significant interaction of Overt Aggression, gender, and adjustment type, $F(1, 1073) = 8.4$, $p < .01$, indicated significant gender differences in these relations (see table 3 for cell means and standard deviations). Specifically, post hoc tests ($p < .05$) of teacher-reported adjustment scores revealed that overtly aggressive girls were significantly more externalizing than all other groups, including overtly aggressive boys. Overtly aggressive boys were significantly more externalizing than all other groups (except overtly aggressive girls). Overtly aggressive children of both sexes were more externalizing than internalizing. Also, in sharp contrast to overtly aggressive girls, nonovertly aggressive girls

Table 3 Teacher-rated internalizing and externalizing scores by gender and Overt Aggression group

	Internalizing score		Externalizing score	
Group and gender	M	SD	M	SD
Nonovertly aggressive				
Boys	.23	.25	.24	.31
Girls	.22	.22	.15	.24
Overtly aggressive				
Boys	.25	.23	.71	.46
Girls	.28	.19	.84	.49

were significantly less externalizing than all other groups, including nonovertly aggressive boys.

A significant interaction of Relational Aggression, Overt Aggression, and adjustment type was also obtained, $F(1, 1073) = 4.2$, $p < .05$. Post hoc analyses ($p < .05$; see table 4 for cell means and standard deviations) indicated that relationally aggressive children were rated by teachers as significantly more externalizing and significantly more internalizing than their nonaggressive peers.[5] In addition, children who exhibited both forms of aggression were significantly more externalizing than all other groups, including overtly aggressive children. All other significant mean differences reflected findings already described above.

Self-reports of adjustment. Analyses of children's self-report adjustment scores from the WAI yielded a significant main effect of Overt Aggression, $F(1, 1150) = 16.6$, $p < .001$, indicating that overtly aggressive children ($M = 5.4$, $SD = 1.3$) reported significantly higher levels of maladjustment (i.e., a combined variable reflecting relatively low Self-Restraint and high Distress) than that of their nonovertly aggressive peers ($M = 4.7$, $SD = 1.2$). Several significant interaction effects were also obtained. The first involved the interaction of Relational Aggression, Overt Aggression, and gender, $F(1, 1150) = 7.7$, $p < .01$ (see table 5 for cell means and standard deviations). Post hoc analyses ($p < .05$) of the means of the Relational Aggression group × Overt Aggression group ×

Table 4 Teacher-reported internalizing and externalizing scores by Overt Aggression group and Relational Aggression group

	Internalizing score		Externalizing score	
Group	M	SD	M	SD
Nonaggressive ($n = 894$)	.22	.23	.18	.27
Relationally aggressive ($n = 98$)	.27	.23	.32	.34
Overtly aggressive ($n = 85$)	.25	.23	.68	.43
Overtly and relationally aggressive ($n = 89$)	.27	.22	.77	.50

Table 5 Self-reported adjustment scores by Overt Aggression group, Relational Aggression group, and gender

	Adjustment score	
Group and gender	M	SD
Nonaggressive		
Boys ($n = 421$)	4.84	1.18
Girls ($n = 473$)	4.50	1.12
Overtly aggressive		
Boys ($n = 80$)	5.33	1.27
Girls ($n = 5$)	5.92	2.18
Relationally aggressive		
Boys ($n = 15$)	4.70	1.18
Girls ($n = 83$)	4.93	1.15
Overtly and relationally aggressive		
Boys ($n = 62$)	5.72	0.97
Girls ($n = 27$)	4.91	1.52

Higher scores reflect higher levels of adjustment difficulties.

gender interaction indicated that overtly aggressive girls and relationally plus overtly aggressive boys reported significantly higher levels of maladjustment than did all other groups. Overtly aggressive boys reported significantly more maladjustment than did relationally aggressive girls, overtly aggressive girls, and nonaggressive boys. Finally, relationally aggressive girls, relationally plus overtly aggressive girls, and nonaggressive boys reported significantly more maladjustment than nonaggressive girls.

These analyses also yielded a significant interaction of Overt Aggression and adjustment type, $F(1, 1150) = 9.7$, $p < .01$. Post hoc analyses ($p < .05$) conducted on the means of Overt Aggression group × adjustment type interaction showed that overtly aggressive children reported significantly more difficulties with Self-Restraint ($M = 2.89$, $SD = .78$) than did nonovertly aggressive children ($M = 2.26$, $SD = .71$), and they reported significantly more difficulties with Self-Restraint than with Psychological Distress ($M = 2.53$, $SD = .74$).

Finally, a significant interaction of gender and adjustment type was obtained, $F(1, 1150) = 14.6$, $p < .001$. Post hoc tests ($p < .05$) conducted on the interaction means revealed that, relative to girls ($Ms = 2.12$, 2.47; $SDs = .68$, .68, respectively), boys reported significantly more difficulties with Self-Restraint ($M = 2.60$, $SD = .75$) and fewer problems with Psychological Distress ($M = 2.40$, $SD = .68$). In addition, boys reported significantly more Self-Restraint problems than Psychological Distress difficulties, whereas girls exhibited the opposite pattern.

Discussion

This study provides new information about the moderating role of gender in the links between childhood aggression and social–psychological adjustment. Further, the findings described here provide additional support for gender differences in the expression of aggressive behavior (i.e., relational vs. overt aggression).

As hypothesized, results revealed significant links between aggression and social–psychological maladjustment. Specifically, overtly aggressive children were shown to be significantly more externalizing than their peers (on the basis of teacher and self-reports), whereas relationally aggressive children were found to be significantly more internalizing (teacher reports). These patterns are highly consistent with past research (e.g., Coie & Dodge, 1983; Crick & Grotpeter, 1995). However, in addition to these linkages, relationally aggressive children were also shown in the present research to be significantly more externalizing than their peers (teacher reports). This link has never been evaluated in prior studies (i.e., only the association between internalizing problems and relational aggression has been assessed in prior investigations). These findings extend past research by demonstrating that relationally aggressive children may exhibit externalizing problems such as impulsivity, defiant behaviors, or other blaming tendencies in addition to internalizing problems such as sadness, anxiety, or somatic complaints. Although the externalizing difficulties of relationally aggressive children have not been specifically studied in the past, the present results are consistent with findings from two prior studies (Crick, 1995; Grotpeter, Crick, & Bigbee, 1996) in which it was demonstrated that relationally aggressive children exhibit hostile attributional biases. That is, similar to overtly aggressive children (see Crick & Dodge, 1994, for a review), relationally aggressive children are likely to blame peers for negative social outcomes in which they are involved, a pattern that is consistent with externalizing tendencies.

Results of this research also provide the first evidence regarding the role of gender normative versus gender nonnormative forms of aggression in children's adjustment. Specifically, findings demonstrate that engagement in gender nonnormative forms of aggression (i.e., overt aggression for girls and relational aggression for boys) is associated with significantly higher levels of social–psychological maladjustment than is engagement in gender normative aggression for both boys and girls. These findings indicate that, as hypothesized, the severity of aggressive children's adjustment difficulties depends on both gender and aggression form. In contrast, these findings also indicate that the type of adjustment difficulties children exhibit (i.e., internalizing, externalizing, or both) is associated with aggression form but not with gender. That is, for each form of aggression, aggressive children of both sexes exhibit the same pattern (or type) of adjustment difficulties (i.e., internalizing and externalizing problems for relationally aggressive children; externalizing and self-restraint problems for overtly aggressive children). However, boys and girls who exhibit a particular form of aggression differ significantly in the severity of their adjustment difficulties. It seems likely that the greater difficulties associated with gender nonnormative aggression may be due at least partially to greater exposure to sanctions imposed for these behaviors by peers, parents, teachers, and others. Past research has demonstrated that boys approve more of overt aggression than do girls (Huesmann, Guerra, Zelli, & Miller, 1992), and they report it be more common in their peer groups than do girls (Crick, Bigbee, &

Howes, 1996). In contrast, girls report relational aggression to be more common in their peer groups than do boys (Crick et al., 1996). It seems likely that children who violate these gender norms may place themselves at risk for a greater degree of intolerance, rejection, and negativity from others than children who aggress in ways that are considered more "acceptable" within their respective gender peer groups. And this negative treatment from others may exacerbate children's adjustment difficulties.

The previously described findings demonstrate the importance of research on understudied groups of aggressive children (i.e., those who engage in gender nonnormative forms of aggression such as overtly aggressive girls) through the use of complex research designs. Although the significance of this type of research has been proposed by a number of investigators over the past few years (e.g., Robins, 1986; Zahn-Waxler, 1993), relatively little empirical evidence has been available to bolster their recommendations. Although such research poses practical constraints and difficulties (e.g., large sample sizes are needed to adequately evaluate the relevant factors), it clearly has the potential to significantly enhance our theoretical understanding of the role of gender in children's behavioral and psychological development. Perhaps more importantly, this type of research also has the potential to generate knowledge that could benefit aggressive children who are not typically the focus of most intervention efforts (i.e., overtly aggressive girls, relationally aggressive girls and boys). The present findings provide evidence for the assertion by Zahn-Waxler (1993) that understanding the source of the sterotypic gender differences in internalizing (typically viewed as a female difficulty) and externalizing (typically viewed as a male difficulty) and their relation to children's conduct problems is likely to be a complex and multifaceted process. Increasing our knowledge of these issues will likely require the use of relatively difficult methodological approaches. For example, adequate assessment of the role of parents (or siblings) in the socialization of aggression would ideally require assessment of both male and female parents (or siblings) of aggressive and nonaggressive children of both genders within each of four aggression groups (nonaggressive, relationally aggressive, overtly aggressive, relationally and overtly aggressive) studied over time.

It is important to note that the gender differences in the aggression–adjustment relation reported here might vary if different adjustment outcomes were assessed, or if children of different ages were included as participants. Future research on these issues is needed to evaluate the degree to which the present findings generalize to other circumstances, and the degree to which they depend on factors that were not assessed here. It is also important to note that in this study, the findings discussed above for relationally aggressive boys (i.e., that they are more maladjusted than relationally aggressive girls and nonaggressive children) were obtained for teacher reports of adjustment but not for self-reports. It is possible that the lack of findings for self-reports reflects a tendency on the part of relationally aggressive children to underreport their behavioral difficulties, a trend noted in prior research (e.g., Crick & Grotpeter, 1995). Further attention to multi-informant assessment of adjustment in future research seems warranted. Finally, development of observational measures of relational aggression (and comparison of results obtained with observation vs. peer reports) will also be a significant avenue for future research efforts. The results obtained here should help to generate further attention to these, and similar, issues to promote a better understanding of the role of gender and aggression in children's development.

Notes

1   Socioeconomic status was estimated on the basis of informal information provided by the school districts regarding the percentage of children eligible for the free lunch program and through prior research experience in the relevant districts.

2   The response scale used in this instrument represents a simplification of the response scales used by Weinberger and Schwartz (1990). The original instrument included two different response scales, one of which participants use for the first half of the items and the second of which they use for the last half. In a prior study with these original response scales, I found them to be confusing to some children of the ages included here. Thus, I adapted them in the present research to make them easier for children to understand.

3   The correlations for the present sample between Prosocial Behavior and Relational Aggression ($r = -.27$, $p < .001$) and between Prosocial Behavior and Overt Aggression ($r = -.38$, $p < .001$) are low to moderate and indicate that prosocial behavior and aggression (both forms) are not highly overlapping constructs. These findings are consistent with past research that has demonstrated that prosocial behavior contributes information about future

adjustment above and beyond that predicted by relational and overt aggression (Crick, 1996).

4 Comparison of these means with those provided by Achenbach & Edelbrock (1991b, Appendix B, pp. 204–207) indicates that the average externalizing score for the overtly aggressive group in this sample was above the clinical average for both boys and girls.

5 Comparison of these means with those provided by Achenbach & Edelbrock (1991b, Appendix B, pp. 204–207) indicates that the average externalizing score for the relationally aggressive group in this sample was above the average for Achenbach's female clinical sample and was very close to the average when compared with his male clinical sample (only 1 raw score point below the clinical average). Additionally, the average internalizing score for the relationally aggressive group was within 2 raw score points of both the male and female clinical sample norms.

References

Achenbach, T. M., & Edelbrock, C. S. (1981). Behavioral problems and competencies reported by parents of normal and disturbed children aged four through sixteen. *Monographs of the Society for Research in Child Development*, *46* (1, Serial No. 188).

Achenbach, T. M., & Edelbrock, C. S. (1991a). *Manual for the Child Behavior Checklist/4–18 and 1991 Profile*. Burlington: University of Vermont, Department of Psychiatry.

Achenbach, T. M., & Edelbrock, C. S. (1991b). *Manual for the Teacher's Report Form and 1991 Profile*. Burlington: University of Vermont, Department of Psychiatry.

Berkowitz, L. (1993). *Aggression: Its causes, consequences, and control*. New York: Academic Press.

Bjorkqvist, K., & Niemela, P. (1992). New trends in the study of female aggression. In K. Bjorkqvist & P. Niemala (Eds.), *Of mice and women: Aspects of female aggression* (pp. 1–15), New York: Academic Press.

Block, J. H. (1983). Differential premises arising from differential socialization of the sexes: Some conjectures. *Child Development*, *54*, 1335–1354.

Boivin, M., Thomassin, L., & Alain, M. (1989). Peer rejection and self-perceptions among early elementary school children: Aggressive rejectees vs. withdrawn rejectees. In B. H. Schneider, G. Attili, J. Nadel, & R. P. Weissberg (Eds.), *Social competence in developmental perspective*. Norwell, MA: Kluwer Academic.

Bukowski, W. M., & Newcomb, A. F. (1984). Stability and determinants of sociometric status and friendship choice: A longitudinal perspective. *Developmental Psychology*, *20*, 941–952.

Cairns, R. B., Cairns, B. D., Neckerman, H. J., Ferguson, L. L., & Gariépy, J. L. (1989). Growth and aggression: 1. Childhood to early adolescence. *Developmental Psychology, 25,* 320–330.

Coie, J. D., & Dodge, K. A. (1983). Continuities and changes in children's social status: A five-year longitudinal study. *Merrill-Palmer Quarterly, 29,* 261–281.

Coie, J. D., & Kupersmidt, J. B. (1983). A behaviroal analysis of emerging social status in boys' playgroups. *Child Development, 54,* 1400–1416.

Cowan, B., & Underwood, M. (in press). A developmental investigation of social aggression among children. *Developmental Psychology.*

Crick, N. R. (1995). Relational aggression: The role of intent attributions, feelings of distress, and provocation type. *Development and Psychopathology, 7,* 313–322.

Crick, N. R. (1996). The role of relational aggression, overt aggression, and prosocial behavior in the prediction of children's future social adjustment. *Child Development, 67,* 2317–2327.

Crick, N. R., Bigbee, M. A., & Howes, C. (1996). Gender differences in children's normative beliefs about aggression: How do I hurt thee? Let me count the ways. *Child Development, 67,* 1003–1014.

Crick, N. R., & Dodge, K. A. (1994). A review and reformulation of social-information-processing mechanisms in children's social adjustment. *Psychological Bulletin, 115,* 74–101.

Crick, N. R., & Grotpeter, J. K. (1995). Relational aggression, gender, and social–psychological adjustment. *Child Development, 66,* 710–722.

Crick, N. R., & Ladd, G. W. (1993). Children's perceptions of their peer experiences: Attributions, loneliness, social anxiety, and social avoidance. *Developmental Psychology, 29,* 244–254.

Eron, L. D. (1992). Gender differences in violence: Biology and/or socialization? In K. Bjorkqvist & P. Niemela (Eds.), *Of mice and women: Aspects of female aggression* (pp. 89–97). New York: Academic Press.

Feshbach, N. D. (1969). Sex differences in children's modes of aggressive responses toward outsiders. *Merrill-Palmer Quaterly, 15,* 249–258.

Franke, S., & Hymel, S. (1984, May). *Social anxiety in children: The development of self-report measures.* Paper presented at the biennial meeting of the University of Waterloo Conference on Child Development, Waterloo, Ontario, Canada.

Grotpeter, J. K., & Crick, N. R. (1996). Relational aggression, overt aggression, and friendship. *Child Development, 67,* 2328–2338.

Grotpeter, J. K., Crick, N. R., & Bigbee, M. A. (1996). Because they're being mean: Intent attributions of relationally and overtly aggressive and victimized children. Manuscript submitted for publication.

Huesmann, L. R., Guerra, N. G., Zelli, A., & Miller, L. (1992). Differing normative beliefs about aggression for boys and girls. In K. Bjorkvist & P. Niemela

(Eds.), *Of mice and women: Aspects of female aggression.* New York: Academic Press.

Lagerspetz, K. M. J., Bjorkqvist, K., & Peltonen, T. (1988). Is indirect aggression more typical of females? Gender differences in aggressiveness in 11–12 year-old children. *Aggressive Behavior, 14,* 403–414.

Loeber, R. (1990). Development and risk factors of juvenile antisocial behavior and delinquency. *Clinical Psychology Review, 10,* 1–41.

Parke, R. D., & Slaby, R. G. (1983). The development of aggression. In P. H. Mussen (Series Ed.) & E. M. Hetherington (Vol. Ed.), *Handbook of child psychology: Vol. 4. Socialization, personality, and social development* (4th ed., pp. 547–642). New York: Wiley.

Parker, J., & Asher, S. R. (1987). Peer acceptance and later personal adjustment: Are low-accepted children at risk? *Psychological Bulletin, 102,* 357–389.

Robins, L. N. (1986). The consequences of conduct disorder in girls. In D. Olweus, J. Block & M. Radke-Yarrow (Eds.), *Development of antisocial and prosocial behavior: Research, theories, and issues.* New York: Academic Press.

Serbin, L. A., Peters, P. L., McAffer, V. J., & Schwartzman, A. E. (1991). Childhood aggression and withdrawal as predictors of adolescent pregnancy, early parenthood, and environmental risk for the next generation. *Canadian Journal of Behavioural Science, 23,* 318–331.

US Department of Justice, Federal Bureau of Investigation (1990, April). *Age-specific arrest rates and race-specific arrest rates for selected offenses, 1965–1988.* Washington, DC: Government Printing Office.

Weinberger, D. A., & Schwartz, G. E. (1990). Distress and restraint as superordinate dimensions of self-reported adjustment: A typological perspective. *Journal of Personality, 58,* 381–417.

Yoshikawa, H. (1994). Prevention as cumulative protection: Effects of early family support and education on chronic delinquency and its risks. *Psychological Bulletin, 115,* 28–54.

Zahn-Waxler, C. (1993). Warrior and worriers: Gender and psychopathology. *Development and Psychopathology, 5,* 79–89.

TWELVE

Development of Antisocial Behavior

Introduction

Researchers consistently have established that the incidence and prevalence of violent and serious delinquency reaches a peak during adolescence, and is more frequent among males than females (Moffitt, 1993). Furthermore, the majority of crimes are committed by a relatively small number of offenders. Involvement in juvenile offending, however, does not suddenly appear in adolescence. There is overwhelming consensus among researchers that antisocial behavior develops in an orderly fashion. Perhaps one of the more comprehensive understandings of the development, course, and stability of aggressive behavior can come from a developmental perspective.

Research on the etiology, course, and sequelae of aggressive behavior is extremely complex. Moffitt (1993) suggests that there are multiple contributors to aggressive behavior outcomes within any individual, and that the relevant causal processes may vary among individuals. As a consequence there is heterogeneity in the manifestations of aggressive behavior and the underlying causes, as well as numerous pathways to any particular manifestation of aggressive behavior. Aggressive and antisocial behavior is a developmental trait that may begin early and continue throughout the lifespan. A developmental perspective of aggressive behavior seeks to explain both the stability and the changes in form that characterize the trajectories of antisocial individuals over time.

Patterson and his colleagues have spent many years observing boys who are aggressive and studying their interactions with parents, peers, and romantic partners. In this article they summarize their model of the development of aggressive behavior based on a social learning and developmental perspective. The model considers how family interactions may serve inadvertently to support aggressive behavior and how these negative styles of interaction are transferred and generalized to the school setting. With increasing age, there are increasing consequences of aggressive behaviors.

Reference

Moffitt, T. E. (1993). The neuropsychology of conduct disorder. *Development and Psychopathology*, 5, 135–51.

A Developmental Perspective on Antisocial Behavior

G. R. Patterson, Barbara D. DeBaryshe,
and Elizabeth Ramsey

In 1986, more than 1.4 million juveniles were arrested for nonindex crimes (e.g., vandalism, drug abuse, or running away) and almost 900,000 for index crimes (e.g., larceny–theft, robbery, or forcible rape; Federal Bureau of Investigation, 1987). The United States spends more than $1 billion per year to maintain our juvenile justice system. The yearly cost of school vandalism alone is estimated to be one-half billion dollars (Feldman, Caplinger, & Wodarski, 1981). These statistics are based on official records and may represent only a fraction of the true offense rate. Data on self-reported delinquent acts indicate that police records account for as little as 2% of the actual juvenile law violations (Dunford & Elliott, 1982).

Of course, not all costs can be counted in dollars and cents. Antisocial children are likely to experience major adjustment problems in the areas of academic achievement and peer social relations (Kazdin, 1987; Walker, Shinn, O'Neill, & Ramsey, 1987; Wilson & Herrnstein, 1985). Follow-up studies of antisocial children show that as adults they ultimately contribute disproportionately to the incidence of alcoholism, accidents, chronic unemployment, divorce, physical and psychiatric illness, and the demand on welfare services (Caspi, Elder, & Bem, 1987; Farrington, 1983; Robins, 1966; Robins & Ratcliff, 1979).

Antisocial behavior appears to be a developmental trait that begins early in life and often continues into adolescence and adulthood. For many children, stable manifestations of antisocial behavior begin as early as the elementary school grades (see Farrington, Ohlin, & Wilson, 1986; Loeber, 1982; and Olweus, 1979, for reviews). As Olweus noted, stability coefficients for childhood aggression rival the figures derived for the stability of IQ. Findings that early behaviors such as temper tantrums and grade school troublesomeness significantly predict adolescent and adult offenses suggest the existence of a single underlying continuum. If early forms of antisocial behavior are indeed the forerunners of later antisocial acts, then the task for developmental psychologists is to determine which mechanisms explain the stability of antisocial behavior and which control changes over time.

From a policy standpoint, a serious social problem that is predictable and understandable is a viable target for prevention. The purpose of this article is to present an ontogenic perspective on the etiology and developmental course of antisocial behavior from early childhood through adolescence. Evidence is presented in support of the notion that the path to chronic delinquency unfolds in a series of predictable steps. This model is presented in detail by Patterson, Reid, and Dishion (in press). In this model, child behaviors at one stage lead to predictable reactions from the child's social environment in the following step. This leads to yet further reactions from the child and further changes in the reactions from the social environment. Each step in this action–reaction sequence puts the antisocial child more at risk for long-term social maladjustment and criminal behavior.

A Developmental Progression for Antisocial Behavior

Basic training in the home

There is a long history of empirical studies that have identified family variables as consistent covariates for early forms of antisocial behavior and for later delinquency. Families of antisocial children are characterized by harsh and inconsistent discipline, little positive parental involvement with the child, and poor monitoring and supervision of the child's activities (Loeber & Dishion, 1983; McCord, McCord, & Howard, 1963).

Two general interpretations have been imposed on these findings. Control theory, widely accepted in sociology (Hirschi, 1969), views harsh discipline and lack of supervision as evidence for disrupted parent–child bonding. Poor bonding implies a failure to identify with parental and societal values regarding conformity and work. These omissions leave the child lacking in internal control. Several large-scale surveys provide correlational data consistent with this hypothesis. The correlations show that youths who have negative attitudes toward school, work, and authority tend to be more antisocial (Elliott, Huizinga, & Ageton, 1985; Hirschi, 1969). The magnitude of these correlations tends to be very small. Because the dependent and independent variables are often provided by the same agent, it is difficult to untangle the contribution of method variance to these relations.

In contrast, the social–interactional perspective takes the view that family members directly train the child to perform antisocial behaviors (Forehand, King, Peed, & Yoder, 1975; Patterson, 1982; Snyder, 1977; Wahler & Dumas, 1984). The parents tend to be noncontingent in their use of both positive reinforcers for prosocial and effective punishment for deviant behaviors. The effect of the inept parenting practices is to permit dozens of daily interactions with family members in which coercive child behaviors are reinforced. The coercive behaviors are directly reinforced by family members (Patterson, 1982; Snyder, 1977; Snyder & Patterson, 1986). While some of the reinforcement is positive (attend, laugh, or approve), the most important set of contingencies for coercive behavior consists of escape-conditioning contingencies. In the latter, the child uses aversive behaviors to terminate aversive intrusions by other family members. In these families, coercive behaviors are functional. They make it possible to survive in a highly aversive social system.

As the training continues, the child and other family members gradually escalate the intensity of their coercive behaviors, often leading to high-amplitude behaviors such as hitting and physical attacks. In this training, the child eventually learns to control other family members through coercive means. The training for deviant behaviors is paralleled by a lack of training for many prosocial skills. Observations in the homes of distressed families suggest that children's prosocial acts are often ignored or responded to inappropriately (Patterson, 1982; Patterson et al., in press; Snyder, 1977). It seems that some families produce children characterized by not one, but two problems. They have antisocial symptoms and they are socially unskilled.

A series of structural equation modeling studies by Patterson and his colleagues support the theory that disrupted parent practices are causally related to child antisocial behavior. They used multiple indicators to define parental discipline and monitoring practices, child coercive behavior in the home, and a cross-situational measure of the child antisocial trait. In four different samples, involving several hundred grade school boys, the parenting practices and family interaction constructs accounted for 30–40% of the variance in general antisocial behavior (Baldwin & Skinner, 1988; Patterson, 1986; Patterson, Dishion, & Bank, 1984; Patterson et al., in press). Forgatch (1988) used a quasi-experimental design based on data from families referred for treatment of antisocial boys. She showed that changes in parental discipline and monitoring were accompanied by significant reductions in child antisocial behavior. There were no changes in antisocial child behavior for those families who showed no changes in these parenting skills.

Social rejection and school failure

It is hypothesized that coercive child behaviors are likely to produce two sets of reactions from the social environment. One outcome is rejection by members of the normal peer group, and the other is academic failure.

It is consistently found that antisocial children show poor academic achievement (Hawkins & Lishner, 1987; Wilson & Herrnstein, 1985). One explanation for this is that the child's noncompliant and under-controlled behavior directly impedes learning. Classroom observations of antisocial children show they spend less time on task than their non-deviant peers (Shinn, Ramsey, Walker, O'Neill, & Steiber, 1987; Walker et al., 1987). Earlier classroom observation studies showed that they were also deficient in academic survival skills (e.g., attending, remaining in seat, answering questions) necessary for effective learning (Cobb, 1972; Cobb & Hops, 1973; Hops & Cobb, 1974). Two studies showed a significant covariation between antisocial behavior and failure to complete homework assignments (Dishion, Loeber, Stouthamer-Loeber, & Patterson, 1983; Fehrmann, Keith, & Reimers, 1987).

The association between antisocial behavior and rejection by the normal peer group is well documented (Cantrell & Prinz, 1985; Dodge, Coie, & Brakke, 1982; Roff & Wirt, 1984). Experimental studies of group formation show that aggressive behavior leads to rejection, not the reverse (Coie & Kupersmidt, 1983; Dodge, 1983). Rejected children are also deficient in a number of social–cognitive skills, including peer group entry, perception of peer group norms, response to provocation, and interpretation of prosocial interactions (Asarnow & Calan, 1985; Dodge, 1986; Putallaz, 1983).

It is often suggested that academic failure and peer rejection are causes rather than consequences of antisocial behavior. However, a stronger case may be made that antisocial behavior contributes to these negative outcomes. For example, some investigators have predicted that successful academic remediation will lead to a reduction in antisocial behavior (e.g., Cohen & Filipczak, 1971). However, it has been repeatedly demonstrated that programs improving the academic skills of antisocial youths have not achieved reductions in other antisocial symptoms (Wilson & Herrnstein, 1985); similar findings have been obtained for social skills training (Kazdin, 1987).

Deviant peer group membership

Antisocial behavior and peer group rejection are important preludes to deviant peer group membership (Dishion, Patterson, & Skinner, 1988; Snyder, Dishion, & Patterson, 1986). These analyses also suggest that lax parental supervision also accounts for unique variance to the prediction of deviant peer affiliation.

A large number of studies point to the peer group as the major training ground for delinquent acts and substance use (Elliott et al., 1985; Hirschi, 1969; Huba & Bentler, 1983; Kandel, 1973). Peers are thought to supply the adolescent with the attitudes, motivations, and rationalizations to support antisocial behavior as well as providing opportunities to engage in specific delinquent acts. There are, however, only a small number of studies designed to investigate the hypothesized training process. One study in an institutional setting showed that delinquent peers provided considerable positive reinforcement for deviant behavior and punishment for socially conforming acts (Buehler, Patterson, & Furniss, 1966).

It seems, then, that the disrupted family processes producing antisocial behavior may indirectly contribute to later involvement with a deviant peer group. This particular product may function as an additional determinant for future antisocial behavior. In effect, the deviant peer group variable may be thought of as a positive feedback variable that contributes significantly to maintenance in the process. Common adult

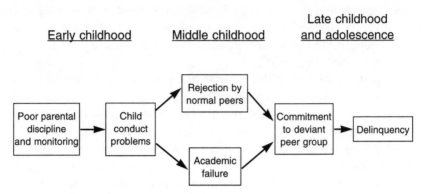

Figure 1   A developmental progression for antisocial behavior.

outcomes for highly antisocial youths include school dropout, uneven employment histories, substance abuse, marital difficulties, multiple offenses, incarceration, and institutionalization (Caspi et al., 1987;Huesmann, Eron, Lefkowitz, & Walder, 1984; Robins & Ratcliff, 1979).

Figure 1 depicts the relaton among the concepts discussed up to this point.

Some Implications of the Development Perspective

Early versus late starters

Boys starting their criminal career in late childhood or early adolescence are at the greatest risk of becoming chronic offenders (Farrington, 1983; Loeber, 1982). Studies of prison populations have shown that recidivists are generally first arrested by age 14 or 15, whereas one-time offenders are first arrested at a later age (Gendreau, Madden, & Leipciger, 1979). Farrington found that boys first arrested between ten and twelve years of age average twice as many convictions as later starters (Farrington, Gallagher, Morley, St. Ledger, & West, 1986); this comparison holds into early adulthood.

One implication of the aforementioned developmental perspective is that early forms of age-prototypic antisocial behavior may be linked to the early onset of official juvenile offenses. Following this logic, the child who receives antisocial training from the family during the preschool and elementary school years is likely to be denied access to positive socialization forces in the peer group and school.

On the other hand, the late starter would be someone committing his or her first offense in middle to late adolescence. This individual lacks the early training for antisocial behaviors. This implies that he or she has not experienced the dual failure of rejection by normal peers and academic failure.

Only about half the antisocial children become adolescent delinquents, and roughly half to three quarters of the adolescent delinquents become adult offenders (Blumstein, Cohen, & Farrington, 1988; Farrington, 1987; Robins & Ratcliff, 1979). At some point in late adolescence, the incidence of delinquent acts as a function of age group begins to drop; the drop continues into the late 20s. One interpretation of these data is that many of the delinquent offenders drop out of the process. We assume that many of these dropouts are late starters, but more research is clearly needed to specify what factors determine the probability of an individual's dropping out of the antisocial training process. A proper developmental theory of antisocial behavior must delineate not only the variables that lead a child into the process but those that cause some of them to drop out of it.

Contextual Variables for Family Disruption

Because parent–child interaction is a central variable in the etiology of antisocial behavior, it is important to determine why a minority of parents engage in highly maladaptive family management practices. A number of variables, which shall be referred to as disruptors, have negative effects on parenting skill. These variables also correlate with the probability of children's antisocial behavior. Thus, the effect of disruptors on children's adjustment is indirect, being mediated through perturbations in parenting. Potential disruptors include a history of antisocial behavior in other family members, demographic variables representing disadvantaged socioeconomic status, and stressors – such as marital conflict and divorce – that hamper family functioning.

Antisocial parents and grandparents

There is a high degree of intergenerational similarity for antisocial behavior (Farrington, 1987; Robins & Ratcliff, 1979). As a predictor of adult antisocial personality, having an antisocial parent places the child at significant risk for antisocial behavior; having two antisocial parents puts the child at even higher risk (Robins & Earls, 1985). Concordance across three generations has also been documented (Elder, Caspi, & Downey, 1983; Huesmann et al., 1984; Robins, West, & Herjanic, 1975).

There is considerable evidence that parental discipline practices may be an important mediating mechanism in this transmission. Our set of findings shows that antisocial parents are at significant risk for ineffective discipline practices. Ineffective discipline is significantly related to risk of having an antisocial child. For example, Elder et al. (1983) found a significant relation between retrospective accounts of grandparental explosive discipline and paternal irritability. Irritable fathers tended to use explosive discipline practices with their own children who tended to exhibit antisocial behavior. Patterson and Dishion (1988) also found a significant correlation between retrospective reports of grandparental explosive reactions in the home and parental antisocial traits. Furthermore, the effect of the parents' antisocial trait on the grandchildren's antisocial behavior was mediated by parental discipline practices.

Family demographics

Demographic variables such as race, neighborhood, parental education, income, and occupation are related to the incidence of antisocial behavior, particularly in its more severe forms (Elliott et al., 1985; Rutter & Giller, 1983; Wilson & Herrnstein, 1985). We presume that the effect of social class on child adjustment is mediated by family management practices.

The empirical findings linking social class to parenting practices are not consistent. But, in general, middle-class parents seem more likely to use reasoning and psychological methods of discipline, allow their children more freedom of choice and self-direction, show egalitarian parenting styles, express positive affect toward their children, verbalize, and support cognitive and academic growth (Gecas, 1979; Hess, 1970).

Lower-class parents are more likely to use physical discipline, be controlling of their child's behavior, exhibit authoritarian parenting styles, and engage in less frequent verbal and cognitive stimulation.

The findings from the at-risk sample at the Oregon Social Learning Center are in keeping with the trends in the literature (Patterson et al., in press). Uneducated parents working in unskilled occupations were found to be significantly less effective in discipline, monitoring, problem solving, positive reinforcement, and involvement.

Family stressors

Stressors impinging on the family such as unemployment, family violence, marital discord, and divorce are associated with both delinquency (Farrington, 1987) and child adjustment problems in general (Garmezy & Rutter, 1983; Hetherington, Cox, & Cox, 1982; Rutter, 1979). Although stressors may well have direct and independent effects on child behavior, we assume that the major impact of stress on child adjustment is mediated by family management practices. If the stressors disrupt parenting practices, then the child is placed at risk for adjustment problems. For example, in the case of divorce, postseparation behavior problems occur with diminished parental responsiveness, affection, and involvement, and increased parental punitiveness and irritability (Hetherington et al., 1982; Wallerstein & Kelley, 1981). Structural equation modeling using data from a large sample of recently separated families provided strong support for the relation among stress, disrupted discipline, and antisocial behavior for boys (Forgatch, Patterson, & Skinner, in press).

We assume that antisocial parents and parents with marginal child-rearing skills are perhaps most susceptible to the disrupting effects of stressors and socioeconomic disadvantage. Elder, Caspi, and Nguyen (in press) described this interaction as an *amplifying effect*. External events are most disabling to those individuals who already exhibit negative personality traits or weak personal resources because stressors amplify such problems in adjustment. The interaction between the aforementioned disruptors and parental susceptibility is presented in figure 2.

When antisocial parents or parents with minimal family management skills are faced with acute or prolonged stress, nontrivial disruptions in family management practices are likely to occur. It is these

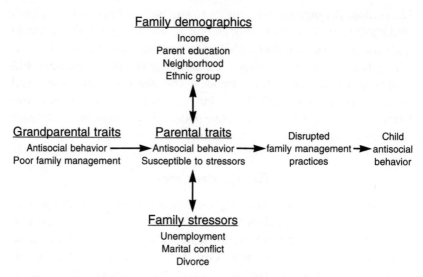

Figure 2   Disruptors of effective parenting.

disruptions that are thought to place the child at risk for adjustment problems. A recent study by Snyder (1988) provided strong support for the mediational hypothesis. Roughly 20 hours of observation collected in the homes of three mother–child dyads showed significant covariation across days between stress and both disrupted maternal discipline and maternal irritability. Days characterized by high stress prior to the observation showed higher rates of disrupted behavior for the mother and increased child problem behaviors. A similar covariation was shown in the study by Wahler and Dumas (1984).

Is Prevention a Possibility?

Reviews of the literature summarizing efforts to intervene with antisocial adolescents invariably lead to negative conclusions (Kazdin, 1987; Wilson & Herrnstein, 1985). At best, such interventions produce short-term effects that are lost within a year or two of treatment termination. For example, efforts to apply behavior modification procedures in a halfway house setting (Achievement Place) showed no treatment effects after youths returned to their homes and communities (Jones, Weinrott, & Howard, 1981). Similarly, systematic parent training for families of delinquent adolescents produced reductions in offenses, but this effect did not persist over time (Marlowe, Reid, Patterson, Weinrott, & Bank, 1988).

Successful intervention appears to be possible for preadolescents, with parent-training interventions showing the most favorable outcomes (Kazdin, 1987). Parent training refers to procedures in which parents are given specific instructions in ways to improve family management practices (e.g., Forehand, Wells, & Griest, 1980; Patterson, Reid, Jones, & Conger, 1975). As shown in the review by Kazdin (1987), the parent-training programs have been evaluated in a number of random assignment evaluation studies including follow-up designs (six-month to four-year intervals). In general, the findings support the hypothesis that parent training is effective when applied to younger antisocial children. That several major studies failed to show a treatment effect led most investigators to conclude that parent-training techniques *and* soft clinical skills are necessary for effective treatment. Current intervention studies have expanded their scope to include teaching academic and social–relational skills in addition to parent training. In order to alter both the problem child's lack of social skills and his or her antisocial symptoms, it seems necessary to design these more complex interventions.

We believe that prevention studies are now feasible. It seems reasonable to identify children in the elementary grades who are both antisocial and unskilled. Successful programs would probably include three components: parent training, child social-skills training, and academic remediation.

References

Asarnow, J. R., & Calan, J. R. (1985). Boys with peer adjustment problems: Social cognitive processes. *Journal of Consulting and Clinical Psychology, 53,* 80–87.

Baldwin, D. V., & Skinner, M. L. (1988). A structural model for antisocial behavior: Generalization to single-mother families. Manuscript submitted for publication.

Blumstein, A., Cohen, J., & Farrington, D. P. (1988). Criminal career research: Its value for criminology. *Criminology, 26,* 1–35.

Buehler, R. E., Patterson, G. R., & Furniss, J. M. (1966). The reinforcement of behavior in institutional settings. *Behavior Research and Therapy, 4,* 157–167.

Cantrell, V. L., & Prinz, R. J. (1985). Multiple predictors of rejected, neglected, and accepted children: Relation between sociometric status and behavioral characteristics. *Journal of Consulting and Clinical Psychology, 53*, 884–889.

Caspi, A., Elder, G. H., & Bem, D. J. (1987). Moving against the world: Life course patterns of explosive children. *Developmental Psychology, 23*, 308–313.

Cobb, J. A. (1972). The relationship of discrete classroom behavior to fourth grade academic achievement. *Journal of Educational Psychology, 63*, 74–80.

Cobb, J. A., & Hops, H. (1973). Effects of academic skill training on low achieving first graders. *Journal of Educational Research, 63*, 74–80.

Cohen, H. L., & Filipczak, J. (1971). *A new learning environment.* San Francisco: Jossey Bass.

Coie, J. D., & Kupersmidt, J. B. (1983). A behavioral analysis of emerging social status in boys' groups. *Child Development, 54*, 1400–1416.

Dishion, T. J., Loeber, R., Stouthamer-Loeber, M., & Patterson, G. R. (1983). Social skills deficits and male adolescent delinquency. *Journal of Abnormal Child Psychology, 12*, 37–54.

Dishion, T. J., Patterson, G. R., & Skinner, M. L. (1988). Peer group selection processes from middle childhood to early adolescence. Manuscript in preparation.

Dodge, K. A. (1983). Behavioral antecedents of peer social status. *Child Development, 54*, 1386–1399.

Dodge, K. A. (1986). A social information processing model of social competence in children. In M. Perlmutter (Ed.), *Minnesota symposium on child psychology* (Vol. 18, pp. 77–125). Hillsdale, NJ: Erlbaum.

Dodge, K. A., Coie, J. D., & Brakke, N. P. (1982). Behavior patterns of socially rejected and neglected preadolescents: The roles of social approach and aggression. *Journal of Abnormal Child Psychology, 10*, 389–410.

Dunford, F. W., & Elliott, D. S. (1982). *Identifying career offenders with self-reported data* (Grant No. MH27552). Washington, DC: National Institute of Mental Health.

Elder, G. H., Jr., Caspi, A., & Downey, G. (1983). Problem behavior in family relationships: A multigenerational analysis. In A. Sorensen, F. Weinert, & L. Sherrod (Eds.), *Human development: Interdisciplinary perspective* (pp. 93–118). Hillsdale, NJ: Erlbaum.

Elder, G. H., Jr., Caspi, A., & Nguyen, T. V. (in press). Resourceful and vulnerable children: Family influences in stressful times. In R. K. Silbereisen & K. Eyferth (Eds.), *Development in context: Integrative perspectives on youth development.* New York: Springer.

Elliott, D. S., Huizinga, D., & Ageton, S. S. (1985). *Explaining delinquency and drug use.* Beverly Hills, CA: Sage.

Farrington, D. P. (1983). Offending from 10 to 25 years of age. In K. T. Van Dusen & S. A. Mednick (Eds.), *Prospective studies of crime and delinquency* (pp. 17–37). Boston: Kluwer-Nijhoff.

Farrington, D. P. (1987). Early precursors of frequent offending. In J. Q. Wilson & G. C. Loury (Eds.), *From children to citizens: Vol. III. Families, schools, and delinquency prevention* (pp. 27–51). New York: Springer-Verlag.

Farrington, D. P., Gallagher, B., Morley, L., St. Ledger, R. J., & West, D. J. (1986). Cambridge study in delinquent development: Long term follow-up. Unpublished annual report, Cambridge University Institute of Criminology, Cambridge, England.

Farrington, D. P., Ohlin, L. E., & Wilson, J. Q. (1986). *Understanding and controlling crime: Toward a new research strategy*. New York: Springer-Verlag.

Federal Bureau of Investigation. (1987). *Crime in the United States: Uniform crime reports, 1986*. Washington, DC: Government Printing Office.

Fehrmann, P. G., Keith, T. Z., & Reimers, T. M. (1987). Home influences on school learning: Direct and indirect effects of parental involvement in high school grades. *Journal of Educational Research, 80*, 330–337.

Feldman, R. A., Caplinger, T. E., & Wodarski, S. S. (1981). The St. Louis conundrum: Prosocial and antisocial boys together. Unpublished manuscript.

Forehand, R., King, H. E., Peed, S., & Yoder, P. (1975). Mother–child interactions: Comparison of a non-compliant clinic group and a non-clinic group. *Behaviour Research and Therapy, 13*, 79–85.

Forehand, R., Wells, K., & Griest, D. (1980). An examination of the social validity of a parent training program. *Behavior Therapy, 11*, 488–502.

Forgatch, M. S. (1988, June). *The relation between child behaviors, client resistance, and parenting practices*. Paper presented at the Earlscourt Symposium on Childhood Aggression, Toronto.

Forgatch, M. S., Patterson, G. R., & Skinner, M. (in press). A mediational model for the effect of divorce on antisocial behavior in boys. In E. M. Hetherington (Ed.), *The impact of divorce and step-parenting on children*. Hillsdale, NJ: Lawrence Erlbaum.

Garmezy, N., & Rutter, M. (Eds.). (1983). *Stress, coping, and development in children*. New York: McGraw Hill.

Gecas, V. (1979). The influence of social class on socialization. In W. R. Burr, R. Hill, F. I. Nye, & I. L. Reiss (Eds.), *Contemporary theories about the family* (Vol. 1, pp. 365–404). New York: Free Press.

Gendreau, P., Madden, P., & Leipciger, M. (1979). Norms and recidivism rates for social history and institutional experience for first incarcerates: Implications for programming. *Canadian Journal of Criminology, 21*, 1–26.

Hawkins, J. D., & Lishner, D. M. (1987). Schooling and delinquency. In E. H. Johnson (Ed.), *Handbook on crime and delinquency prevention* (pp. 179–221). New York: Greenwood Press.

Hess, R. D. (1970). Social class and ethnic influences on socialization. In P. H. Mussen (Ed.), *Charmichael's manual of child psychology* (Vol. 2, pp. 457–558). New York: Wiley.

Hetherington, E. M., Cox, M., & Cox, R. (1982). Effects of divorce on parents and children. In M. Lamb (Ed.), *Nontraditional families* (pp. 233–288). Hillsdale, NJ: Erlbaum.

Hirschi, T. (1969). *Causes of delinquency.* Berkeley, CA: University of California Press.

Hops, H., & Cobb, J. A. (1974). Initial investigations into academic survival-skill training, direct instruction, and first-grade achievement. *Journal of Educational Psychology, 66,* 548–553.

Huba, G. J., & Bentler, P. M. (1983). Causal models of the development of law abidance and its relationship to psychosocial factors and drug use. In W. S. Laufer & J. M. Day (Eds.), *Personality theory, moral development and criminal behavior* (pp. 165–215). Lexington, MA: Lexington Books.

Huesmann, L. R., Eron, L. D., Lefkowitz, M. M., & Walder, L. O. (1984). Stability of aggression over time and generations. *Developmental Psychology, 20,* 1120–1134.

Jones, R. R., Weinrott, M. R., & Howard, J. R. (1981). The national evaluation of the Teaching Family Model. Unpublished manuscript, Evaluation Research Group, Eugene, OR.

Kandel, D. B. (1973). Adolescent marijuana use: Role of parents and peers. *Science, 181,* 1067–1081.

Kazdin, A. E. (1987). Treatment of antisocial behavior in children: Current status and future directions. *Psychological Bulletin, 102,* 187–203.

Loeber, R. (1982). The stability of antisocial and delinquent child behavior: A review. *Child Development, 53,* 1431–1446.

Loeber, R., & Dishion, T. J. (1983). Early predictors of male delinquency: A review. *Psychological Bulletin, 94,* 68–99.

Marlowe, H. J., Reid, J. B., Patterson, G. R., Weinrott, M. R., & Bank, L. (1988). Treating adolescent multiple offenders: A comparison and follow up of parent training for families of chronic delinquents. Manuscript submitted for publication.

McCord, W., McCord, J., & Howard, A. (1963). Familial correlates of aggression in nondelinquent male children. *Journal of Abnormal and Social Psychology, 62,* 79–93.

Olweus, D. (1979). Stability of aggressive reaction patterns in males: A review. *Psychological Bulletin, 86,* 852–875.

Patterson, G. R. (1982). *A social learning approach: 3. Coercive family process.* Eugene, OR: Castalia.

Patterson, G. R. (1986). Performance models for antisocial boys. *American Psychologist, 41,* 432–444.

Patterson, G. R., & Dishion, T. J. (1988). Multilevel family process models: Traits, interactions, and relationships. In R. Hinde & J. Stevenson-Hinde (Eds.), *Relationships within families: Mutual influences* (pp. 283–310). Oxford: Clarendon Press.

Patterson, G. R., Dishion, T. J., & Bank, L. (1984). Family interaction: A process model of deviancy training. *Aggressive Behavior, 10,* 253–267.

Patterson, G. R., Reid, J. B., & Dishion, T. J. (in press). *Antisocial boys.* Eugene, OR: Castalia.

Patterson, G. R., Reid, J. B., Jones, R. R., & Conger, R. E. (1975). *A social learning approach to family intervention: Vol 1. Families with aggressive children.* Eugene, OR: Castalia.

Putallaz, M. (1983). Predicting children's sociometric status from their behavior. *Child Development, 54,* 1417–1426.

Robins, L. N. (1966). *Deviant children grown up: A sociological and psychiatric study of sociopathic personality.* Baltimore: Williams & Wilkins.

Robins, L. N., & Earls, F. (1985). A program for preventing antisocial behavior for high-risk infants and preschoolers: A research prospectus. In R. L. Hough, P. A. Gongla, V. B. Brown, & S. E. Goldston (Eds.), *Psychiatric epidemiology and prevention: The possibilities* (pp. 73–84). Los Angeles: Neuropsychiatric Institute.

Robins, L. N., & Ratcliff, K. S. (1979). Risk factors in the continuation of childhood antisocial behavior into adulthood. *International Journal of Mental Health, 7*(3–4), 96–116.

Robins, L. N., West, P. A., & Herjanic, B. L. (1975). Arrests and delinquency in two generations: A study of black urban families and their children. *Journal of Child Psychology and Psychiatry, 16,* 125–140.

Roff, J. D., & Wirt, R. D. (1984). Childhood aggression and social adjustment as antecedents of delinquency. *Journal of Abnormal Child Psychology, 12,* 111–116.

Rutter, M. (1979). Protective factors in children's responses to stress and disadvantage. In M. W. Kent & J. E. Rolfe (Eds.), *Primary prevention of psychopathology: 3. Social competence in children.* Hanover, NH: University Press of New England.

Rutter, M., & Giller, H. (1983). *Juvenile delinquency: Trends and perspectives.* New York: Penguin Books.

Shinn, M. R., Ramsey, E., Walker, H. M., O'Neill, R. E., & Steiber, S. (1987). Antisocial behavior in school settings: Initial differences in an at-risk and normal population. *Journal of Special Education, 21,* 69–84.

Snyder, J. J. (1977). Reinforcement analysis of interaction in problem and nonproblem families. *Journal of Abnormal Psychology, 86,* 528–535.

Snyder, J. J. (1988). An intradyad analysis of the effects of daily variations in maternal stress on maternal discipline and irritability: Its effects on child deviant behaviors. Manuscript in preparation.

Snyder, J. J., Dishion, T. J., & Patterson, G. R. (1986). Determinants and consequences of associating with deviant peers during preadolescence and adolescence. *Journal of Early Adolescence, 6*(1), 20–43.

Snyder, J. J., & Patterson, G. R. (1986). The effects of consequences on patterns of social interaction: A quasi-experimental approach to reinforcement in natural interaction. *Child Development, 57,* 1257–1268.

Wahler, R. G., & Dumas, J. E. (1984). Family factors in childhood psychopathology: Toward a coercion neglect model. In T. Jacob (Ed.), *Family interaction and psychopathology.* New York: Plenum Press.

Walker, H. M., Shinn, M. R., O'Neill, R. E., & Ramsey, E. (1987). Longitudinal assessment and long-term follow-up of antisocial behavior in fourth-grade boys: Rationale, methodology, measures, and results. *Remedial and Special Education, 8,* 7–16.

Wallerstein, J. S., & Kelley, J. B. (1981). *Surviving the breakup: How children and parents cope with divorce.* New York: Basic Books.

Wilson, J. Q., & Herrnstein, R. J. (1985). *Crime and human nature.* New York: Simon & Schuster.

THIRTEEN

Prevention of Conduct Disorders

Introduction

Because of the heavy burden of suffering generated by aggressive behavior, the development of effective prevention and intervention techniques is essential. In a review of the literature on prevention programs, Yoshikawa (1994) suggested that the following factors are essential to the development of successful prevention programs targeting aggressive behavior: (1) programs should be ecological in design, targeting family interactions, peer groups, the school setting, and the neighborhood; (2) programs should target urban and low-income populations because these groups have a higher incidence both of crime and of the multiple risk factors for aggression; (3) programs should run a minimum of two years; (4) because of sensitive periods in development, programs should be implemented in the first five years of life. Intervening in this early period of life does not negate the importance of later prevention and treatment. Rather, early intervention may reduce the risk of later aggressive behavior. Further, by intervening early, there are fewer contexts that may need to be targeted.

Coie and Jacobs make this point in their examination of the contexts that require intervention with increasing age. Basing their argument on a developmental model of aggression, they point out that interventions need to address individual characteristics that are related to aggressive behavior, as well as parenting and family management practices, peer groups, the school environment, and the neighborhood. All of these components play a role in the development, maintenance, and termination of aggressive behavior.

References

Yoshikawa, H. (1994). Prevention as cumulative protection: Effects of early family support and education on chronic delinquency and its risks. *Psychological Bulletin, 115*, 28–54.

The Role of Social Context in the Prevention of Conduct Disorder

John D. Coie and Marlene R. Jacobs

A rapidly growing literature is now available describing our range of current knowledge about the etiology, life course, and treatment of conduct disorder (CD). At the same time, a host of ongoing longitudinal research programs continuously refine the developmental models we currently employ to describe its emergence and maintenance over time. This paper springs from the same basic premises that are outlined in John Reid's paper in this volume [Reid, 1993] and shares his conclusion that the more we learn about the nature of CD, the more it is evident that preventive measures represent the most practical and effective approach to reducing CD. We also share Reid's conclusions about the importance of developmental transitions in the timing of prevention activity and agree with his analysis of individual and family factors that must be addressed. In our commentary on the future directions for the prevention of CD, we will use Reid's paper as a point of departure and attempt to build a case for considering the importance of larger contextual influences on the problem of CD. In the process, we discuss what we perceive as important societal changes that may have a bearing on the prevalence and maintenance of CD and ways in which current models developed across the last 30 or 40 years do not adequately incorporate many of these secular transformations.

Reemphasis on Reid's Major Points

A substantial body of longitudinal research consistently demonstrates that the trajectory for continued conduct problems tends to be initiated early. Without intervention, children who are diagnosed with CD are likely to become trapped in a snowballing pattern of negative interactions with family members, teachers, and peers. Their possibilities for adaptive change become increasingly narrow over time as they consistently alienate themselves from many essential socializing influences and supports. By failing to learn prosocial alternatives to antisocial behavior and becoming ensnared in a deviant life-style by the consequences of their own behavior, these children increasingly restrict their already limited options for change. As a result, CD is likely to continue from childhood into adolescence and adulthood, to become increasingly resistant to change with advancing age, and to remain impervious to even the most current intervention efforts (Kazdin, 1987).

Fortunately, we have reached the point where longitudinal research has enabled us to identify those at high risk for serious adolescent CD. Loeber et al. (1993) demonstrate that the reliable identification of high-risk groups can be made as early as school entry. In addition to the successful identification of high-risk children, an understanding of the developmental process underlying CD has emerged from a variety of research endeavors as well. These discoveries make it plausible to consider seriously how prevention programs might best be designed and implemented. The social interactional model, initially put forth by G. R. Patterson (1982) and his colleagues, successfully molds a comprehensive network of hypotheses regarding the correlated social variables of conduct-disordered children and their families and represents the dominant perspective that individual characteristics interact with family and environmental conditions to place some children at identifiable high risk for CD by the time they enter school.

In school, antisocial behavior inevitably interferes with learning by reducing the time such children spend engaged in on-task assignments. To make matters worse, high-risk children are likely to attend schools in which there is a high density of other high-risk children (Rutter, Maughan, Mortimore, Ouston, & Smith, 1979), generating an even more chaotic atmosphere. Meanwhile, the coercive behavioral style of CD children is likely to elicit severe peer disapproval. Over time, classmates become increasingly mistrustful of these volatile children (Dodge, 1980) and respond to them in ways that increase the likelihood of their even greater use of instrumental coercion and aggression. The failing, disliked, and antisocial child is ultimately left with few social settings that provide any form of reinforcement. As a result, similarly deviant peers begin to drift together and may actually serve to encourage each other's existing antisocial tendencies while modeling and shaping new forms of problematic behavior. Over time, these accumulating consequences of the child's personality and academic problems, both singly and in interaction with each other, reduce the options for adaptive change.

An inherent implication of this developmental model is that methods of prevention must change across time as new risk mediators enter the clinical picture over the course of development. One benefit of constructing a sound developmental model is the ability to use it as a tool to predict those points at which particular preventive measures stand the best chance of making a difference. As Reid points out, our current model suggests that two major transition periods are most amenable to prevention efforts – initial school entry and transition to middle school. Both points represent major changes in both individual responsibilities and the broader social context and, thus, provide a significant window of opportunity for a restructuring of potential risk factors and skills deficits. Although some risk factors persist across development, others are specific to discrete developmental periods. Thus, prevention programs geared toward school entry should incorporate a focus that is specifically designed to fit the challenges of this early transition, whereas those preventive efforts designed for the passage to middle school should incorporate their own pertinent strategies.

Focusing on the Implications of Social Context

Reid's paper, which effectively summarizes a broad spectrum of empirical and theoretical findings, reveals an important bias in the focus of most current analyses of CD. The majority of research in this domain tends to highlight those individual characteristics of the child and immediate family that are thought to contribute to the emergence and maintenance of CD. Not surprisingly then, most existing treatment and prevention programs are designed to intervene on the individual level in an attempt to modify targeted aspects of the child's or parents' cognitive and behavioral patterns. Many of these approaches, as Reid points out, appear to hold some promise.

It is at this point, however, that we would like to propose a slightly broader perspective on CD and attempt to incorporate Bronfenbrenner's (1977) conceptualization of contextual "levels" into current approaches toward prevention. We will argue that while individual characteristics of the child (e.g., poor self-control, impulsivity, aggression, inability to delay gratification) and the parents (e.g., inconsistent and harsh disciplining practices, insufficient supervision, lack of warmth) have always played a central role in our developmental models of CD, research from a variety of sources collectively suggests that the child's broader social context is a crucial determinant of its emergence, manifestation, and maintenance, as well. The goal of this paper is to describe some of the contextual aspects of CD that tend to be underrepresented in the developmental literature, with a specific focus on the ways in which the social context can be altered to facilitate prevention designs.

Early School Years

Current developmental models of CD strongly emphasize the importance of the family in fostering behavior problems in the early childhood period. While parents clearly play a dominant socializing role during this phase of life, it is important to consider the emerging influence of the peer context as well. A close examination of theoretical descriptions as well as empirical data suggests that even at a young age the peer social fabric often directly supports CD by reinforcing aggressive and coercive behaviors. By recognizing this more subtle source of contextual influence, we are able to paint a more comprehensive picture of CD and to understand more readily why aggressive and coercive behavior is often so resistant to change.

According to Patterson's (1982) coercion model, children who successfully coerce their parents into providing short-term payoffs in the immediate home situation are inadvertently "trained" to employ an interactional style that they expect to work in similar ways in later social encounters at school. As a result, such children quickly extend their aggressive and socially incompetent behavioral repertoire to the peer group. Once initiated, the coercive behavioral style escalates even further through the very same negative reinforcement processes that Patterson describes in the context of parent–child interactions. All too often in the world of peers, might does make right. Peers inadvertently reinforce the aggressive child's use of threats and physical force to achieve personal goals by backing down and allowing them to succeed (Coie, Dodge, Terry, & Wright, 1991; Patterson, Littman, & Bricker, 1967). As a result, aggressive children are more inclined than non-aggressive children to believe that aggression has positive functional consequences (Perry, Perry, & Rasmussen, 1986). Thus, while Reid accurately points out the serious and negative long-term consequences of aggressive behavior, what needs to be emphasized here are the imme-diate gratifications that trap these aggressive children into patterns of behavior that have immediately rewarding outcomes but lead to long-term maladaptive consequences. Significant and tangible advantages are attached to the kinds of excessive aggression that are simultaneously linked to more subtle expressions of peer rejection. Thus, the social context in the early school years plays an important role in fostering and maintaining maladaptive behaviors despite their ultimately detrimental consequences.

In addition to directly reinforcing coercive behaviors by allowing aggressive children to successfully meet their goals by such means, the peer group can contribute to the maintenance of socially maladaptive behavior in other ways, as well. One possibility is that peers, for a variety of reasons, fail to give aggressive children clear feedback about their coercive behavior. We know from aggressive dyad data, for example, that reactive aggressors tend not to agree that they are actually the real aggressors in social interactions, even when unbiased observers cannot identify the supposed "provocation" to which these aggressive children are reacting (Coie et al., 1991). Instead, these boys appear to feel per-petually threatened or assaulted by their targets and actually see them-selves as victims who are merely protecting themselves from a hostile environment. This slanted view of the social milieu, particularly char-acteristic of reactive aggressors, is undoubtedly central to the main-tenance of such maladaptive behavior (Dodge & Coie, 1987).

The fact that aggressive rejected children appear to feel justified in their coercive behavior paints only part of the picture. Not only do they often believe that they are reacting to a real threat when they aggress toward others, these children also appear somewhat oblivious to what other children feel about them and their aggressive tendencies (Patterson, Kupersmidt, & Griesler, 1990). While a large body of empirical work links aggressive behavior to peer rejection (see Coie, Dodge, & Kupersmidt, 1990, for a review), it has been conjectured that aggressive children do not realize that their behavior has such negative consequences. This hypothesis suggests that some aggressive children continue to function in ways that elicit peer disapproval because they lack the ability to compare themselves accurately with other children and subsequently misperceive their own degree of acceptance within the peer group. To the extent that the actions of the peer group allow conduct-disordered children to form inaccurate perceptions that blind them to their significant adjustment problems, they essentially serve to reduce motivation for constructive change.

Evidence from a variety of sources corroborates the hypothesis that aggressive-rejected children do, indeed, process social information differently than nonaggressive-rejected children and may be less skillful at interpreting subtle cues about their behavior. For example, aggressive-rejected children, in contrast to their nonaggressive counterparts, report that they are no more lonely or socially dissatisfied than average status children (Parkhurst & Asher, 1992). In fact, aggressive-rejected children actually report positive beliefs about their relations with peers (Rabiner, Keane, & Mackinnon, in press) and are no more concerned than average status children about being humiliated or rejected. Instead, these children tend to overestimate their competence in more domains than either withdrawn-rejected or average children and, particularly, overestimate their degree of social competence in a way that directly contrasts with the perceptions of nonaggressive children (Patterson et al., 1990).

Not only might peers tolerate the social misperceptions of aggressive children, the group might further contribute to their lack of status awareness by simply failing to provide them with the feedback they need in order to realize that their behavior is unacceptable. Peers may choose to withhold negative feedback from aggressive-rejected children out of fear of retaliation (Coie et al., 1991) or because it seems like more trouble than it is worth to interact with them at all. Thus, a lack of awareness of the negative consequences of their actions may be less the result of misinterpretation of cues than a real absence of information altogether.

The bottom line, regardless of how the misperception generates itself, is that aggressive children do not appear to experience many negative consequences of their behavior. Instead, the social context actually facilitates the maintenance of their negative interactional repertoire through immediate short-term gain while shielding the aggressor from the quite serious long-term repercussions. The net result is that the social context in the early school years creates a framework in which conduct-disordered children can thrive, without providing them with clear reasons to change their coercive behavioral style.

Implications for Prevention

Considering the influence of the early school environment and peer dynamics on the intransigence of conduct-disordered behavior, it seems clear that prevention programs must take the broader social context into consideration if the hope is to make an appreciable and long-lasting difference in the lives of those children deemed to be at risk. Unfortunately, most of our current prevention programs focus exclusively on parent or child training without also extending their efforts to the school or the peer context.

To be sure, directly intervening with the child and family is both advantageous and necessary. Parent training that focuses on changing contingencies for the child's behavior, breaking the pattern of coercive interchanges, and improving monitoring skills allows for a more healthy interaction between parent and child. Meanwhile, child training designed to bolster social problem solving, emotional recognition training, anger control, prosocial skills building and remedial academic tutoring will provide conduct-disordered children with some of the basic skills they need to succeed both at home and at school. It is important to realize, however, that while parent and child training represent the necessary foundation for any effective preventive effort, they may not be sufficient on their own. Given that conduct problems usually are manifested in many settings and in the context of multiple determinants, preventive intervention must be comprehensive and attentive not only to the child and the immediate family but also to the natural pay-off matrices embedded in the peer group and the classroom environment. This can be achieved by program components that aim to change both the peer environment at school and the individual child's readiness to respond to these contextual changes.

Truly comprehensive prevention programs must work with teachers to alter the peer context in the classroom. Although the true root of disruptive child behavior in the early school years may be fostered by coercive family processes, characteristics of the classroom context undoubtedly add important elements to the equation. Specifically, teachers often promote the maintenance of negative child behaviors by providing inconsistent or inappropriate reinforcement schedules. Observations suggest that teacher reinforcement for positive behavior is rare while admonishments directed toward the problematic students occur with greater frequency and are often noncontingent upon student behavior (Strain, Lambert, Kerr, Stagg, & Lenkner, 1983).

Changing the school climate thus poses a necessary challenge to preventive efforts. An important first step involves restructuring the pay-off matrix within the classroom. Teachers should be trained to respond to students in ways that will consistently reinforce desired behaviors while discouraging the types of maladaptive behaviors that, left unchecked, will tend to cycle and escalate. If teachers can succeed in eliciting greater compliance and on-task behavior of all children, they will reduce the overall chaos of the classroom environment and limit the distractions that are particularly likely to encourage high-risk children to misbehave. Especially in classrooms with a high concentration of such children, training in how to provide a positive peer climate and supportive classroom atmosphere can go a long way toward fostering a context less conducive to conduct problems.

Programs to achieve these goals for the classroom environment already exist and there is evidence that they can be successful (Werthamer-Larsson, Kellam, & Wheeler, 1991). The use of group contingencies for good behavior can be an effective way to use peer group pressure to bring aggressive outliers into line. The part of the problem that still requires some solution is how to convey the message to young children that their seemingly effective aggressive behavior is costing them in terms of peer regard. Sensitive teachers may be able to convey this through classroom discussions that allow children to express their feelings about coercive behavior (without labeling specific peers) and to lead them in thinking of ways they can, as a group, discourage this kind of behavior.

Some children will be better prepared than others to respond to these efforts to change the peer social context. This means that some of our individually oriented prevention components need to address these differences in ways that are not achieved by conventional social skills or problem-solving packages. Since the social context of the early school years appears to provide a variety of short-term benefits for aggressive and other inappropriate behaviors, one promising focus for preventive efforts, for example, involves training young children to delay gratification. In essence, conduct-disordered children tend to opt for immediate gratification in the form of acquiring a desired toy, standing in the front of the line, or otherwise getting their way rather than attempting to delay these short-term desires in lieu of the more long-term goal of positive peer relations. By providing these children with the skills necessary to visualize, plan, and maintain long-term patterns of goal-directed behavior, it might be possible to decrease their maladaptive actions (e.g., Mischel, 1974, 1981). Targeted interventions designed to teach self-regulatory cognitions and restructuring techniques in a step-by-step format may offer an effective alternative.

A related goal of prevention programs should be an explicit emphasis on the social status consequences of behavior. If conduct-disordered children are unaware of or inaccurate in the perception of their negative social status (as already described), then it stands to reason that delayed gratification holds little meaning for them. After all, if these children believe that they have nothing to lose by acting on their immediate impulses and nothing to gain by forgoing them, their choice seems obvious. Making aggressive children aware that they do pay a price for their actions – that aggressive leads to social disapproval – makes a careful consideration of their goals more likely. This is a difficult undertaking and one that requires sensitivity. It can be combined with our earlier suggestion of teacher-led classroom discussions of reactions to coercive behavior by means of private conversations between the teacher and specific children. When they are aware of the negative social consequences attached to cheating, lying, fighting, or refusing to take turns, aggressive children may be more likely to forgo the small rewards such behaviors provide with an eye toward the larger prize of social acceptance and comradery.

Middle School Years

As in the case of the early school years, transition to middle school engenders a host of contextual variables that appear to facilitate and often intensify problematic behavior. In fact, the middle school years represent a particularly precarious period because conduct problems that may be viewed as merely troublesome or hard to manage in early childhood begin to take on more serious, and often permanent, implications over time. Thus, the dangers of delinquency, substance abuse, school dropout, and teenage pregnancy become very real concerns for high-risk children during this stage of development.

Current developmental models of CD emphasize the gradual reduction of parental influence as the peer group becomes a principal influence in the maintenance of deviant behavior during the middle school years. The dominant perspective on the processes underlying CD in middle childhood, termed control theory (Hirshi, 1969), suggests that delinquent behavior and conduct problems are more likely to result when an individual's bonds to society (including the family, the school system, and the community as a whole) are significantly weakened or broken. One significant effect of a weak bond to societal values is the enhanced importance of delinquent friends (Hawkins & Weiss, 1985). As a joint result of rejection from the mainstream peer culture and negligent parental monitoring of their activities, aggressive children are thought to drift into deviant peer networks. Once these initially deviant children have banded together, the potential for even further aggression and conduct problems is likely to increase exponentially. In fact, a number of recent studies have highlighted the influence of deviant peer associations in adolescent delinquency (e.g., Cairns, Cairns, & Neckerman, 1989; Dishion, Patterson, Stoolmiller, & Skinner, 1991; Elliot, Huizinga, & Ageton, 1985).

Taken as a whole, control theory provides a compelling account of how problematic behavior plays itself out in adolescence, why CD children associate with deviant peers, and how the deviant peer group feeds into further behavioral problems. Notwithstanding its explanatory utility, however, it is important to consider the limits of control theory as a universal model for CD. First, a central tenant of this paradigm is that conduct-disordered children are "deviant" from mainstream culture and are therefore thrown into each other's company by mutual default. This assumption may not hold true in all contexts. Indeed, it is likely that in certain settings aggressive or otherwise "deviant" behaviors are actually quire normative and, possibly, even adaptive.

Furthermore, control theory assumes that strong bonds with family or community act to buffer children from the influence of deviant peers as well as from the subsequent risks linked to association with them. How well does this assumption fare in contexts where the values and norms of families, communities, or even the entire cultural climate appear to endorse violence and coercion as an effective means of personal expression and conflict resolution? Clearly, parental and peer group influences are not the only variables involved in the maintenance and reinforcement of CD in middle childhood. It is at this point that the child's contacts beyond the immediate family begin to expand. As a result, the larger social context – including the influence of the local neighborhood as well as more all-encompassing cultural values and expectations – plays an enormous role in molding the behavior of adolescents. Both proximal and distal effects of these contextual influences begin early and become deeply ingrained, suggesting the necessity of focusing on the neighborhood and broader cultural milieu in future preventive efforts.

The Impact of the Neighborhood

Considerable evidence indicates that a variety of diverse problem behaviors (e.g., drinking, illicit drug use, delinquency, teenage pregnancy) interact and are associated with each other in adolescent samples. This finding has led some researchers to suggest that all of these phenomena may comprise a single behavioral syndrome (Donovan & Jessor, 1985). Epidemiological research demonstrates that the individuals themselves also cluster and that behavioral problems and their negative consequences echo throughout entire neighborhoods as part of a continuous cycle of social disintegration (Wilson, 1987). Poverty and its associated sequelae have become increasingly concentrated in inner-city neighborhoods (Lynn & McGeary, 1990). Given the convergence of risk factors, it would appear difficult not to be influenced by the interwoven strands of crime, violence, unemployment, and lack of opportunity that virtually have taken over many disadvantaged communities. Researchers who examine community-level differences have consistently found associations between poverty and high rates of violence (Beasley & Antunes, 1974; Mlandenka & Hill, 1976). Violence has been linked to other poverty-related characteristics, as well, including limited social resources, weak intergenerational ties in families and communities, low organizational participation in community life, accessibility of guns, and drug traffic distribution (Sampson, 1993). Children growing up in areas characterized by these sorts of problems are likely to model their self-defense and conflict-resolving behaviors on the violent actions that surround them and to perceive violence as an accepted and appropriate response (Owens & Straus, 1975). In contexts such as these, supposedly "deviant" behavior becomes not only normative, but mandated; aggression becomes synonymous with survival.

Given the fact that behavioral norms may well be consistent with aggressive tactics in those samples where poverty, social stress, racial prejudice, and crime rates are high, it is imperative that we be careful in generalizing from one context to another. Control theory is meant to describe the emergence of behavior that deviates from mainstream standards or values. Because "deviance" must be defined in relation to its normative context, this theory cannot adequately model the development of CD in those settings in which aggressive behavior prevails. Indeed, the whole concept of "deviant peer group" loses its clarity when violence is pervasive. We need to design preventive models with different structures for those contexts where violent behavior is the rule rather than the exception.

Research from our own ongoing longitudinal study provides an interesting perspective on the dynamics of peer networks, peer status, and delinquent/aggressive behavior in a high poverty, high crime, inner-city sample (Coie, Terry, & Zakriski, 1992). A cohort of children were followed from third through ninth grade, with peer sociometrics, behavioral ratings, peer social network, and police report data collected for approximately 800 subjects. The best models for predicting eighth- and ninth-grade delinquency did not show any significant influence of deviant peer associations in eighth grade, once police contacts prior to eighth grade were controlled statistically. Furthermore, in contrast with data on younger children, eighth-grade social preference scores had a *positive* relation to deviant peer associations. These findings imply that deviant children do not associate with each other merely because they are rejected by everyone else. On the contrary, it appears that association with deviant peers directly contributes to higher status; hanging out with "deviant" peers actually makes adolescents more likable in this particular social context!

These findings do not fit with current models derived from control theory and suggest that delinquency and conduct problems are not necessarily related to either low social preference or subsequent deviant peer associations. It is possible that methodological peculiarities account for some of the differences in the results of this study and those cited in support of the impact of deviant peer associations. Setting methodological issues aside, however, it appears likely that some of the inconsistency between our data and those that support control theory represent real differences in the processes underlying peer dynamics and conduct problems and are related to aspects of the social context.

One possible interpretation of our findings is that in the most disadvantaged segments of urban communities, there is no critical mass of stable, achievement-oriented families to provide neighborhood cohesion, sanctions against maladaptive behavior, and support for basic community institutions. Without practical connections to mainstream society, these neighborhoods become isolated and are left to fend for themselves. Stressed and discouraged families are surrounded by others in similar straits, leading to a concentration of the persistently poor, unskilled, and unemployed. Support for this hypothesis can be found in a study specifically designed to examine the differences between high- and low-risk neighborhoods (Garbarino & Sherman, 1980). Results suggested a potent "concentration effect." That is, those who needed the most tended to be clustered together in settings that most had to struggle to meet those needs. In short, high-risk neighborhoods emerged as a conglomeration of very "needy" families competing for drastically limited social resources. The problems of individual families were found to be compounded rather than ameliorated by the neighborhood context. Furthermore, this "concentration" of poverty and its related social problems is associated with interpersonal violence. In a recent study in a Chicago public school, 75% of boys and 70% of girls surveyed had seen someone shot (Shakoor & Chalmers, 1991). As a result of the convergence of aggressive tendencies in such high-risk neighborhoods, many of the role models for children and adolescents living in such communities reinforce a positive stance toward the use of violence.

It is important to express, however, that blanket stereotypes can never adequately describe a collection of families as diverse as those who reside in disadvantaged communities. Without doubt, there are many families who do not contribute to the violence and chaos that surround them, who worry about the effects of a "bad" neighborhood on their kids, and who actively battle against its negative influences. A growing literature on "contestation" (Malson, 1992), or the deliberate efforts of concerned parents to provide their children with values and experiences different from those imposed by the immediate context, provides further evidence that competent parents see themselves as a beleaguered minority in their communities. Violence and delinquency are not perceived as deviant in any statistical sense. Instead, in certain high-risk neighborhoods it is the "contestors" who stand alone as they desperately endeavor to barricade their children from the negative role models and distorted pay-off matrices that they cannot control (Furstenberg, 1990).

In short, it may be the case that some neighborhoods are deeply enmeshed in a social context that turns the conventional dynamics of peer networks, social status, and delinquency on its head. When an entire community is besieged by violence, being aggressive or disruptive may represent not merely the path of least resistance but also the path of opportunity for children growing up in its midst. Within these communities, violence often is perceived as the only effective method for overcoming the many barriers to advancement. As a result, peer pressure and the desire to be accepted by friends actually may foster the sorts of behaviors that characterize CD and are typically considered deviant in more mainstream settings.

While underprivileged children may be represented disproportionately in the CD population (West, 1982), it should be stressed that disadvantaged communities do not hold a monopoly on the increased violence, juvenile behavior problems, and delinquency that have emerged in recent years. Instead, disadvantaged populations simply magnify problems that permeate all social and economic strata. Statistics show an upsurge of violence and delinquency occurring on the national level. FBI data chronicle a 22.2% increase in arrests for murder of those individuals under the age of 18 between 1983 and 1987. Aggravated assault jumped 18.6% and rape increased by 14.6% in this same age bracket. The escalations are occurring despite the overall decline in the total number of teenagers in the United States since 1983 (Toufexis, 1989).

These statistics represent only the tip of the iceberg and do not even touch upon the more mundane sorts of aggressive outbursts and losses of control that typically get children into trouble at home and in school. As a whole, American society seems to have adopted a greater tolerance for violence, and this attitude is reflected not only in the increase of high-profile crimes but also in the tendency of our youth to resort more readily to aggressive tactics in their everyday interactions. The frequency of violent portrayals in the media (Heath, Bresdin, & Rinaldi, 1989), the growing availability of guns and other weapons to young people, and the corresponding increase in firearm-related homicides for young people (Fingerhut & Kleinman, 1989) all contribute to the message that the current level of violence is something we are prepared to live with. Surrounded by this convergent sanctioning of violence from multiple arenas, children naturally learn that losing one's temper or striking out at others is an acceptable, if not typical, method of making one's way in the world.

Notwithstanding other influences, the media alone exerts an enormous impact on the values and expectations of children. Violent movies, TV shows, comic books, song lyrics, and even the behavior of volatile sports heroes may lead young "consumers" to believe that aggressive strategies are to be emulated. Children's exposure to violent portrayals in the media has been linked to perceptions of the world as an evil and frightening place (Singer, Singer, & Rapaczynski, 1984), which may lead some children to believe that violent responses are required to protect oneself in the course of daily living. Furthermore, exposure to television violence has been found to lead to emotional desensitization, making viewers less likely to respond both physiologically and behaviorally to aggression in others (Slaby & Quaforth, 1980).

Research on the relationship between exposure to media violence and aggressive behavior is overwhelmingly supportive of the relationship between viewing aggressive behavior and acting aggressively (Heath et al. 1989), although there is debate, for example, over such issues as the degree to which both media exposure and aggressive behavior are related to poor parental supervision or the degree to which bidirectional causality leads highly aggressive children to deliberately select violent material to watch. Notwithstanding the complex nature of intervening variables and bidirectional effects, several research reviews (e.g., Heath et al., 1989; Huesmann & Malamuth, 1986) conclude that at least some children exposed to media depictions of aggression are more likely to act aggressively afterward than they otherwise would have. Despite this demonstrated link between TV violence and aggressive behavior, American media continue to capitalize on the reckless and the violent, inadvertently training children to behave in these ways.

Implications for Prevention

Perhaps the most important point to be taken from this discussion of CD in the middle school years is that the impact of social context takes on even greater importance as children extend their social horizons beyond the immediate family. The world of peers takes on an importance that has been obvious to developmentalists for a long time. What is less obvious is that the dynamics of peer culture may have changed very significantly in many inner-city, high-poverty areas of our society. These changes require us to rethink the task of prevention in those schools that most need it.

Most current CD prevention programs operate under the assumption that high-risk children are those who are aggressive, disruptive, and subsequently rejected by the peer group. Therefore, the primary focus of such programs is geared toward various forms of social skills and anger control training. If, as our data suggests, aggression is actually related to popularity in some contexts, traditional preventive measures probably are not a sufficient means of addressing the problem. If CD is being reinforced by peers, then intervention must operate on the peer network to modify the reinforcement contingencies it affords. Even if we were to be successful with earlier prevention work with high-risk youth, the transition to middle school would place these same youth at marked risk once more, because of the absence of compelling social reference groups. Only by teaching the entire peer group, as well as the community in which it is embedded, to resolve conflict without violence can we hope to alter the social environment in ways that may lessen the likelihood of violent conflicts for everyone.

The question, then, is how to proceed with prevention in these high-risk contexts. If the larger social context endorses and rewards violent interpersonal behavior, then systematic effort must be made to alter that context. One suggestion we would propose is to use the power of deviant peer groups to reverse the prevailing value orientation of that peer world. This is a time for testing the prevailing theories of social influence (Cialdini, 1985) and resocialization of social identity (Costanzo, 1992). One way to approach this task is to focus on the attitudes and behaviors of opinion leaders themselves. Rather than allowing the authority of deviant peer group leaders to reside solely in their ability to defy conventional authority and violate the rules of adult society, we must provide them with access to a more compelling basis for authority. Concretely, this could mean providing them with opportunities to associate with attractive youth culture idols, but to do so publicly in circumstances where they endorse nonviolent and non-risk-taking behavior. This shift in endorsed values must be supported by ongoing opportunities for personal success if these newly acquired and counter-deviant attitudes are to be sustained. In turn, this requires access to the social and economic resources of the community, in the form of jobs and training opportunities that fit the interests and skills of these peer leaders. It also requires resources that can be extended to other deviant peer group members by these peer leaders, so that peer leaders can take an active resocialization role in the lives of their friends. Ultimately, the goal must be to provide inner-city youth with nondelinquent alternatives to personal success and autonomy so that the peer culture of middle schools and high schools is not dominated by violent and life-threatening values. This is a substantial undertaking and goes beyond the usual small sample trials that characterize much of the current prevention effort for CD.

Our analysis of the implications of social context for CD prevention also extends to the level of neighborhood. The broad-based approach to prevention that we are proposing demands that we recognize the larger social context in which youth violence occurs. To be sure, marked economic and social disparities among Americans contribute to the etiology of violence in fundamental ways. Poverty as well as associated factors such as large, low-income families, poor housing, and living in high-crime areas have all been empirically identified as antecedents of aggressive childhood behavior (Farrington, Ohlin, & Wilson, 1986; Robins, 1978) as well as high rates of teen pregnancy, school failure, and violent crime (Schorr, 1988). These same risk factors have been linked to a more general sense of frustration, low self-esteem, and hopelessness about the future (Ramey & Ramey, 1990). Thus, without changing the economic and social structure of inner-city populations, there may be serious limits to what parent training and child skill-building programs can accomplish for those at risk in this middle school period.

Ironically, the contestation efforts spurred on by the growing violence and crime problem in high-risk communities have generated just the kind of community concern and motivation that is sorely needed however, traditional contestation approaches (e.g., keeping children indoors after school, sending them outside the community for social contacts, segregating them from the surrounding neighborhood) are too often isolating and defensive in orientation. The best many of these parents feel they can do is treat their home like a fortress. Prevention programs that can capitalize on these parents' concern and motivation for change while molding their energy into the promotion of a more positive and supportive neighborhood climate could go a long way toward ultimately decreasing violence and crime community-wide. One way to accomplish this goal is to begin by identifying and enlisting the aid of contestors. Linking together isolated families who share a degree of concern for their children and motivation to change their community can create a natural power source within troubled areas. The most highly motivated families can then combine their strengths and extend their umbrella of influence and protection to the other children in high-risk neighborhoods whose parents, while amenable to constructive change, are unable or unwilling to play a centrally active role themselves. By extending their influence into ever-widening circles, the most interested and involved families can foster a sense of pride and identity that ultimately permeates the entire community.

In addition to grass-roots efforts to revitalize a sense of community identity, it is clear that a more overarching course of action is necessary, as well. In certain fundamental ways, American society continues to tolerate and sometimes even condone problematic behaviors. As long as our cultural values allow aggressive tactics to achieve their instrumental ends, isolated prevention programs are likely to fail.

Ideally, prevention programs need to work on a national scale. Media portrayals should be revamped and reflect greater positive emphasis on other forms of conflict resolution. Violence should not be a tolerable option. Surrounded by a set of norms and expectations that bolster the sorts of lessons being taught by traditional prevention programs rather than competing against them, high-risk kids are far more likely to start moving in the right direction.

Conclusion

We have emphasized the importance of widening the scope of preventive efforts to include not only the individual child at risk for CD, but also the broader social, cultural, and economic context that surrounds children and their families. Individuals will differ in their vulnerability to more violent social contexts. We need to understand the potential interactions between child and family vulnerability and social context in order to plan more effective prevention programs. Naturally, the broader the proposed aims of a given program, the more difficult it is to implement. How can prevention programs be expected to have an impact on social context in such far-reaching ways? In the case of CD and juvenile delinquency, it seems clear that the only way to transform high-minded prevention strategies into concrete realities is by breaking down some of the arbitrary boundaries between academic, political, and bureaucratic professions. Educators, health professionals, child-welfare workers, and government administrators at all levels must each take some ownership of the problem and be willing to join forces in order to combat it. Ultimately, a successful prevention program will see children in the context of the family and the family in the context of its surroundings. It will offer a broad spectrum of services that collectively create a context in which high-risk children can carve out alternative paths to success.

References

Beasley, R. W., & Antunes, G. (1974). The etiology of urban crime: An ecological analysis. *Criminology, 11,* 439–461.

Bronfenbrenner, V. (1977). Toward an experimental ecology of human development. *American Psychologist, 32,* 513–531.

Cairns, R. B., Cairns, B. D., & Neckerman, H. J. (1989). Early school dropout: Configurations and determinants. *Child Development, 60,* 1437–1452.

Cialdini, R. B. (1985). *Influence: Science and practice.* Glenview, IL: Scott, Foresman & Co.

Coie, J. D., Dodge, K. A., & Kupersmidt, J. B. (1990). Peer group behavior and social status. In S. R. Asher & J. D. Coie (Eds.), *Peer rejection in childhood* (pp. 17–59). New York: Cambridge University Press.

Coie, J. D., Dodge, K. A., Terry, R., & Wright, V. (1991). The role of aggression in peer relations: An analysis of aggression episodes in boy's play groups. *Child Development, 62,* 812–826.

Coie, J. D., Terry, R., & Zakriski, A. (1992). *Early adolescent social influences on delinquent behavior.* Paper presented at the Society for Life History Research, Philadelphia.

Costanzo, P. R. (1992). External socialization and the development of adaptive individuation and social connection. In D. Ruble, P. Costanzo, & M. Oliveri (Eds.). *The social psychology of mental health.* New York: Guilford Press.

Dishion, T. J., Patterson, G. R., Stoolmiller, M., & Skinner, M. L. (1991). Family, school, and behavioral antecedents to early adolescent involvement with antisocial peers. *Developmental Psychology, 27,* 172–180.

Dodge, K. A. (1980). Social cognition and children's aggressive behavior. *Child Development, 51,* 162–170.

Dodge, K. A., & Coie, J. D. (1987). Social-information processing factors in reactive and proactive aggression in children's peer groups. *Journal of Personality and Social Psychology, 53,* 1146–1158.

Donovan, J. E., & Jessor, R. (1985). Structure of problem behavior in adolescence and young adulthood. *Journal of Consulting and Clinical Psychology, 53*(6), 890–904.

Elliot, D. S., Huizinga, D., & Ageton, S. S. (1985). *Explaining delinquency and drug use.* Beverly Hills, CA: Sage.

Farrington, D. P., Ohlin, L. E., & Wilson, J. Q. (1986). *Understanding and controlling crime: Toward a new research strategy.* New York: Springer-Verlag.

Fingerhut, L. A., & Kleinman, J. C. (1989). Firearm mortality among children and youth. *Advance data: From vital health statistics of the National Center for Health Statistics.* Publication No. 178.

Furstenberg, F. F., Jr. (1990). How families manage risk and opportunity in dangerous neighborhoods. Unpublished manuscript.

Garbarino, J., & Sherman, D. (1980). High-risk neighborhoods and high-risk families: The ecology of child maltreatment. *Child Development, 51,* 188–198.

Hawkins, J. D., & Weiss, J. G. (1985). The social development model: An integrated approach to delinquent prevention. *Journal of Primary Prevention, 6,* 73–97.

Heath, L., Bresdin, L. B., & Rinaldi, R. C. (1989). Effects of media violence on children: A review of the literature. *Archives of General Psychiatry, 46,* 376–379.

Hirschi, T. (1969). *Causes of delinquency.* Berkeley: University of California Press.

Huesmann, L., & Malamuth, N. M. (1986). Media violence and antisocial behavior: An overview. *Journal of Social Issues, 42*(3), 1–6.

Kazdin, A. E. (1987). *Conduct disorders in childhood and adolescence.* Newbury Park, CA: Sage.

Loeber, R., Wung, P., Keenan, K., Giroux, B., Stouthamer-Loeber, M., Van Kammen, W. B., & Maughan, B. (1993). Developmental pathways in disruptive child behavior. *Development and Psychopathology, 5,* 103–134.

Lynn, L. E., Jr., & McGeary, M. G. H. (Eds.). (1990). *Inner-city poverty in the U.S.* Washington, DC: National Academy Press.

Malson, M. (1992). Contesting context: Black single mothers achieving against the odds. Unpublished manuscript, Duke University, Durham, NC.

Mishel, W. (1974). Processes in delay of gratification. In L. Berkowitz (Ed.), *Advances in experimental social psychology* (Vol. 7). New York: Academic Press.

Mischel, W. (1981). Objective and subjective rules for delay of gratification. In W. Lens (Ed.), *Cognitions in human motivation and learning.* Hillsdale, NJ: Erlbaum.

Mlandenka, K., & Hill, K. (1976). A reexamination of the etiology of urban crime. *Criminology, 13,* 491–506.

Owens, D. J., & Straus, M. A. (1975). The social structure of violence in children and approval of violence as an adult. *Aggressive Behavior, 1*, 193–211.

Parkhurst, J. T., & Asher, S. R. (1992). Peer rejection in middle school: Subgroup differences in behavior, loneliness, and interpersonal concerns. *Developmental Psychology, 28*, 231–241.

Patterson, C. J., Kupersmidt, J. B., & Griesler, P. C. (1990). Children's perceptions of self and of relationships with others as a function of sociometric status. *Child Development, 61*, 1335–1349.

Patterson, G. R. (1982). *Coercive family process.* Eugene, OR: Castalia.

Patterson, G. R., Littman, R. A., & Bricker, W. (1967). Assertive behavior in children: A step toward a theory of aggression. *Monographs of the Society for Research in Child Development, 32*(5, Serial No. 113).

Perry, D. G., Perry, L. C., & Rasmussen, P. (1986). Cognitive social learning mediators of aggression. *Child Development, 57*, 700–711.

Rabiner, D. L., Keane, S. P., & Mackinnon, C. (in press). Children's beliefs about familiar and unfamiliar peers in relation to their sociometric status. *Child Development.*

Ramey, C. T., & Ramey S. L. (1990). Intensive educational intervention for children of poverty. *Intelligence, 14*(1), 1–9.

Reid, John (1993). Prevention of conduct disorder before and after school entry: Relating interventions to developmental findings. *Development and Psychopathology, 5*, 243–262.

Robins, L. N. (1978). Sturdy childhood predictors of adult antisocial behavior: Replications from longitudinal studies. *Psychological Medicine, 8*, 611–622.

Rutter, M., Maughan, B., Mortimore, P., Ouston, J., & Smith, A. (1979). *Fifteen-thousand hours: Secondary schools and their effects on children.* Cambridge: Harvard University Press.

Sampson, R. J. (1993). The community context of violent crime. In W. J. Wilson (Ed.), *Sociology and the public agenda.* Newbury Park, CA: Sage.

Schorr, L. B. (1988). *Within our reach: Breaking the cycle of disadvantage.* New York: Anchor Books.

Shakoor, B., & Chalmers, D. (1991). Co-victimization of African American children who witness violence: Effects on cognitive, emotion, and behavioral development. *Journal of the National Medical Association, 83*(3), 233–237.

Singer, J. L., Singer, D. G., & Rapaczynski, W. S. (1984). Family patterns and television viewing as predictors of children's beliefs and aggression. *Journal of Communication, 34*, 73–89.

Slaby, R. G., & Quaforth, G. R. (1980). Effects of television on the developing child. In B. W. Camp (Ed.), *Advances in behavioral pediatrics* (Vol. 1). Greenwich, CT: JAI.

Strain, P. S., Lambert, D. L., Kerr, M. M., Stagg, V., & Lenkner, D. A. (1983). Naturalistic assessment of children's compliance to teachers' requests and consequences for compliance. *Journal of Applied Behavior Analysis*, *16*, 243–249.

Toufexis, A. (1989). Our violent kids. *Time*, June 12.

Werthamer-Larsson, L., Kellam, S. G., & Wheeler, L. (1991). Effect of first grade classroom environment on shy behavior, aggressive behavior, and concentration problems. *American Journal of Community Psychology*, *19*, 585–602.

West, D. J. (1982). *Delinquency: Its roots, careers, and prospects*. Cambridge, MA: Harvard University Press.

Wilson, W. J. (1987). *The truly disadvantaged: The inner city, the underclass and public policy*. Chicago: University of Chicago Press.

Index